Design Methods in Architecture

Architectural Association
Paper Number 4

Published
by Lund Humphries
for the
Architectural Association
London

Design Methods in Architecture

Edited by Geoffrey Broadbent and
Anthony Ward

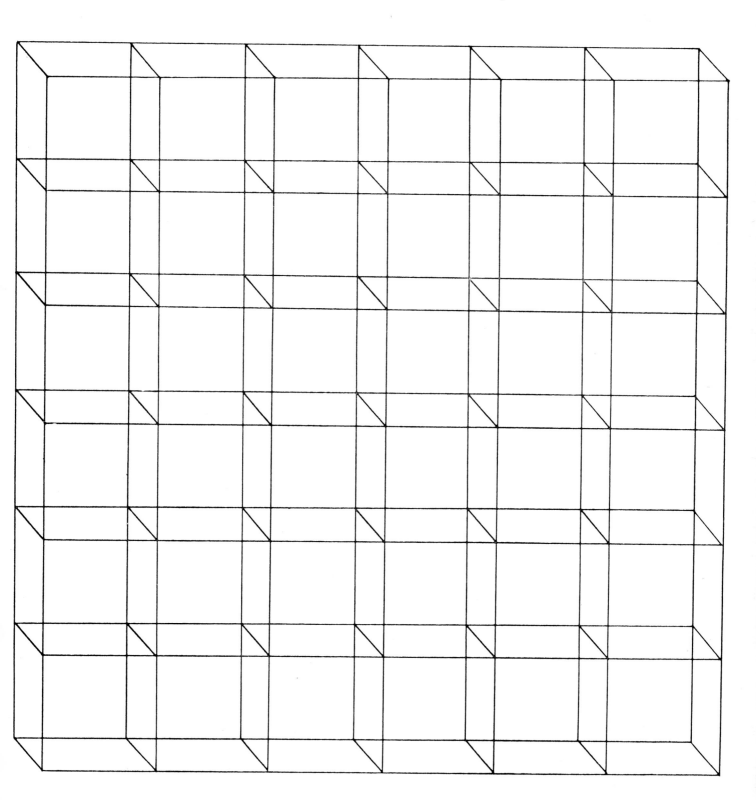

First edition 1969

Published by Lund Humphries Publishers Limited
12 Bedford Square London WC1

Casebound edition SBN 85331 244 3
Paperback edition SBN 85331 252 4

Designed by Graham Johnson and James Shurmer

Made and printed in Great Britain by Lund Humphries,
Bradford and London

Acknowledgements

The editors and publishers wish to thank the
following for permission to reproduce illustrations
appearing on the pages indicated from the sources
mentioned:

Gordon Coster, Chicago: *Scientific American*, Sept.
1965 (p.171)

Penguin Books Ltd, Harmondsworth: *New Horizons
in Psychology*, ed. by B. M. Foss (1966) (p.119);
Penguin Science Survey 1965, ed. by S. A. Barnett
and A. McLaren (1965) (p.125, Fig.14)

Methuen & Co. Ltd, London: *The Biology of Art*
by Desmond Morris (1966) (p.121, Fig.2)

Routledge & Kegan Paul Ltd, London and Human-
ities Press Inc., New York: *The Psychology of
Children's Drawings* by Helga Eng (1931) (p.121,
Fig.3; p.123, Fig.8) and *The Child's Conception of
Space* by Jean Piaget and Bärbel Inhelder (1956)
(p.123, Fig.9; p.125, Fig.12)

Tavistock Publications, London: *Discussions on
child development*, Vol.3, ed. by J. M. Tanner and
B. Inhelder (1958) (p.122, Figs.5a and 5b)

Spastics Society and William Heineman Ltd, London: *Perceptual and visuomotor disorders in cerebral
palsy* by M. L. J. Abercrombie (1964) (p.122,
Fig.6a; p.123, Fig.6b; p.125, Fig.13)

A. R. Luria, E. N. Pravdina-Vinarskaya, A. L.
Yarbus: 'Disorders of ocular movement in a case
of simultanagnosia' in *Brain*, 86, 219–28 (1963)
(p.123, Fig.7)

A. V. Zaporozhets: 'The development of perception
in the pre-school child' in *European Research in
Cognitive Development*, 30, No.2, 82–101, ed. by
P. H. Mussen (1965) (p.124)

'Design method in architecture' by Geoffrey Broadbent which appears on pp. 15–21 was originally
published in *Arena*, February 1968

Contents

Contributors

Dr M. L. J. Abercrombie

Reader in Architectural Education, Bartlett School of Architecture and Director of the Architectural Education Research Group. Trained as a biologist. Became interested in the difficulties students had in learning to be scientific and after ten years' research on the selection and training of medical students published *The Anatomy of Judgement* in 1960. Joined the Bartlett School of Architecture in 1963 to work on the selection and education of architectural students, focusing attention on human relations and the perception and manipulation of space. Has lectured extensively throughout Britain, North America and Australia.

L. Bruce Archer

Reader in Design Method at the Royal College of Art and Head of Department of Industrial Design (Engineering) Research Unit since 1962. Trained as an engineering designer and practised as a tool and production machinery designer. Started research in design method in 1957, lectured at the Hochschule für Gestaltung at Ulm in 1960/1. Won the Kaufmann International Design Award in 1964. Many published papers, including *Systematic Method for Designers*. Practises and lectures extensively in Britain, on the Continent and in the U.S.A.

Gordon Best

Graduated B. Arch. at Rhode Island School of Design in 1964. M.Sc. in Design Technology at Manchester Institute of Science and Technology (1966–9). At the time of the Symposium, was a lecturer at the Bartlett School of Architecture, and is currently doing a Ph.D. in Architecture at London University. Has published several articles in this country and abroad.

Geoffrey Broadbent

Head of the Portsmouth School of Architecture since October 1967. Graduated from Manchester University and later a lecturer in architecture there. Joined the University of York in 1961 as Secretary to the Institute of Advanced Architectural Studies and moved to Sheffield University as a lecturer in architecture in 1963. Has published several papers on Design Methods in Architecture and lectured extensively in Britain, Europe and South America. Book on 'Design in Architecture' in preparation.

Janet Daley

Graduated in philosophy at the University of California in Berkeley. Currently reading for an M.Phil. at London University. Her research is concerned with the psychological function of morality in the personality. Lectures in Social Philosophy at Kingston School, and the Bartlett School of Architecture.

S. A. Gregory

Senior Lecturer in Chemical Engineering, Department of Chemical Engineering, the University of Aston in Birmingham. Convenor of the Design and Invention Group in Birmingham. Chairman of the 1965 conference on design methods and editor of the conference papers published as *The Design Method*. Member of Council, Design Research Society.

Guido Guerra

Professor of Architecture in the Faculty of Engineering, at the University of Naples. Has contributed extensively to American Design Method publications. Is currently applying his structural matrix analysis to building design problems.

Keith Hanson

Graduated B.Arch. from Cambridge University after an initial year in Mathematics. Prepared the Housing Study which he presented at the Symposium as part of his undergraduate work at Cambridge and spent a year of professional practice doing user requirements studies in the Offices Development Group in the M.P.B.W.

J. Christopher Jones

Senior Lecturer in Industrial Design Technology, Department of Building, University of Manchester, Institute of Science and Technology. Formerly with the Council of Industrial Design and A.E.I. Manchester. Vice Chairman of the Design Research Society. Has lectured a great deal on design topics in Britain, Europe, the United States and Japan. Also published many papers and his book on design methods is to be published in 1969.

Neville Longbone

Graduated in architecture at Kingston School of Architecture in 1967. Thesis work on Alexander's Relational Theory, into *The Physical Organization of Sheltered Workshops for the Blind*. Currently working as a Research Architect with the Directorate of Development, M.P.B.W., in the Offices Development Group.

John Luckman

Graduated in statistics from University College, London. Joined the Management Services Group at Courtaulds Ltd. Worked as an Operational Research Consultant and joined the Institute for Operational Research in 1964. Worked on the research project 'Independence and Uncertainty in the Building Industry'.

Thomas A. Markus

Professor of Building Science, University of Strathclyde. Graduated from Manchester University School of Architecture, and Director of the Building Performance Research Unit. Undertook historical research into the design of prisons. In 1956 joined Pilkington Bros. Ltd, as Manager of the Product Applications Department, then in 1964 accepted a Readership in Architecture at the Welsh School of Architecture, Cardiff. Has published a number of papers on environmental matters, chiefly concerned with appraisal. Lectures extensively in Britain and the United States. Completed his Master's Degree at M.I.T. in 1955.

Ian Moore

Graduated in architecture at Liverpool University in 1947. Prepared the Whitehall Redevelopment brief with Sir Leslie Martin, and is now leader of the Offices Development Group, M.P.B.W. Developed the Ministry's *Activity Data Method* with Barry Poyner, and catalyzed *The Atoms of Environmental Structure* by Alexander and Poyner.

Barry Poyner

Qualified at the Birmingham School of Architecture. Worked from 1960 to 1963 in the War Office Development Group on his requirement studies. Transferred to the directorate at the M.P.B.W., working with Christopher Alexander on *The Atoms of Environmental Structure*. Returned to Birmingham in 1967 as Research Fellow in the School of Architecture. Has since joined the Environmental Programming Division of Scientific Control Systems, London.

Amos Rapoport

Graduated in architecture at Melbourne, and took a second degree in Urban Design at Berkeley, California. Has travelled extensively in Australia, the United States and Europe, studying primitive and vernacular buildings. Has worked on Low Cost Housing in Developing Countries, the design of prototype Low Cost Housing in California. Has published several articles and reports, and is author of the book *Housing and House Form*. Taught for two years as a lecturer at the Bartlett School of Architecture, and has recently accepted a lectureship in the Department of Architecture at the University of Sydney, Australia.

Raymond G. Studer

Graduated from Harvard University and taught for a while at Arizona State University, Columbia University, and the Rhode Island School of Design. Was Professor and Head of Planning Analysis Project at Brown University, and has recently taken a chair as Professor of Environmental Design at The College of Human Development, Pennsylvania State University, U.S.A.

Anthony Ward

Graduated in architecture from Birmingham in 1965 after five years in practice. Thesis work involved the use of a cube-root matrix computer programme to organize the activities in a design for an Electrical Engineering Faculty for Birmingham University. Joined Christopher Alexander and Barry Poyner at M.P.B.W., has done research into user requirements in prisons, mental hospitals, blind workshops and offices. Joined Ian Moore's Offices Development Group, then taught at Kingston School of Architecture. Left to accept a Research Fellowship at the Portsmouth School of Architecture in 1967. Convenor and Organizer of the Portsmouth Symposium. Currently moving to Berkeley to take up a Professorship at the University of California. Has lectured extensively in this country and the United States.

Foreword

by Geoffrey Broadbent

When Tony Ward suggested to me, on the day he took up his appointment as Research Fellow at the Portsmouth School of Architecture, that we put on a Symposium on Design Method, it seemed to me a good idea. There had been changes in the School recently, which gave us an opportunity for re-orientation, and it seemed to me appropriate that we state our intentions publicly. The School had moved from the College of Art to the College of Technology, a dynamic and expanding institution, which was determined to support us with vastly enhanced resources, in terms of staff, equipment, materials, and a new building.

We are not 'committed' to design method, in the sense that individuals are in certain other schools. Design method has, or has had, a particular connotation. It means, or has meant, the translation of techniques from Operational Research (OR) into design often to the detriment of what the designer was actually trying to do. This OR approach was first stated, consistently, at the 1962 Conference on Design Method, held in London, at Imperial College.[1] And the Birmingham Symposium of 1965 confirmed this view.[2] We felt, however, that although design in architecture has a great deal to learn from this approach – and has a lot to offer to it – it is also different in kind from many other kinds of design, because it is so complex and, above all, because it deals in environmental matters. So the Portsmouth Symposium was intended to mark the beginning of a new phase of thinking in architectural design method and, on the whole, I think this was achieved.

In many ways, our expectations were vastly exceeded. Although we had only two months, from first inception of the idea to the event itself, the Symposium snowballed on us. Four hundred people turned up, including over fifty delegates from overseas, and as our requirements for accommodation escalated, the only auditorium we could find to satisfy our needs proved to be on the South Parade Pier in Southsea, a romantic, cast iron and timber structure which, on the fact of it, was a most unlikely setting for discussions on systematic design method. But it served our purposes admirably and contributed significantly to the unique flavour of the Symposium. It has been our aim, in editing the proceedings, to retain as much as possible of this unique flavour, including the informality and something of the heat. Since the Symposium, interest in these proceedings has been world wide and now that they are in print, we hope that others too will share the stimulus and excitement which those of us felt who were there.

REFERENCES

[1] C. JONES and D. THORNLEY (Eds.). *Conference on Design Methods*. Pergamon (Oxford 1963).
[2] S. GREGORY (Ed.). *The Design Method*. Butterworth (London 1966).

Introduction

In October 1967 I accepted a position as Research Fellow in Design Method at the Portsmouth School of Architecture, under the Headship of Geoffrey Broadbent, himself recently appointed. His interest in Design Method was already firmly established, and it was, therefore, inevitable that this area of study should be seen as the basis of a new approach to architectural education at the Portsmouth School. Design Method is already incorporated as a subject into the curricula of several schools of architecture, but its application to the total teaching method was something quite new.

It was, therefore, with considerable apprehension that I approached this new appointment, particularly since the field of Design Method seemed too broad and unco-ordinated. One of my first problems was to bring the unrelated factions to Portsmouth, in order to clarify my own conception of the problem. The result was the Design Methods in Architecture Symposium, held on 4, 5, and 6 December 1967, at the South Parade Pier, Southsea, which attracted more than 400 delegates from all over the world with contributions from several countries.

My own interest in Design Method began during my final year at the Birmingham School of Architecture, where, with five colleagues, I became involved in the development of a particular kind of computer optimization programme for locating inter-related activities in 3-dimensional space.[1] This work was to sow the seeds of discontent which I felt on my return to practice in the North of England. After a brief stay, I left to join Christopher Alexander and Barry Poyner, during their work on 'The Atoms of Environmental Structure' at the Ministry of Public Building and Works.[2]

It was while I was there that I was to meet most of the people who were later to give papers at this Symposium. I worked for a while under Ian Moore, who, with Barry Poyner, had developed 'Activity Data Method'. Keith Hanson was a member of our group, doing his 'year-out' from Cambridge School of Architecture. Gordon Best I met through Barry Poyner, and Amos Rapoport, Jane Abercrombie and (in writing) Ray Studer through Gordon Best. Neville Longbone was one of my students at the Kingston School of Architecture. I had little previous contact with Christopher Jones, Sydney Gregory, and Bruce Archer, but decided to ask them to participate on the understanding that they would concentrate upon architectural design problems. They held the common belief (which was one of my own growing doubts) that *all* kinds of design problems are fundamentally similar. In this respect, John Luckman and Professor Markus were asked to provide a necessary link between the architects and the non-architects, and it is interesting to note that Christopher Jones chose John Luckman's work to illustrate a criticism of Alexander's analysis technique.

At the time of my Portsmouth appointment, the views held by each of the speakers were central to inconsistencies which I was beginning to feel in my own work. This is why my own paper touches upon the work of so many of the speakers. My (continuing) aim was to try to reconcile the differences I felt into a coherent personal philosophy. All of the speakers were invited to say things that I wanted to hear, and the audience was in a way incidental. It may consequently be that the result is of very limited interest to other people, although subsequent correspondence seems to indicate that this is not so.

It is often said that the hall-mark of the truly creative person is his ability to tolerate and synthesize opposing polemic attitudes, and, with this in mind, and from a subsequently obvious ill-founded conceit, we staged a series of polemic situations, in the hope of arriving at some conclusive solution. We didn't find a solution but the debate is still in process, for both myself and my colleagues at the Portsmouth School of Architecture.

At the Symposium, we staged not just one polarity, as has been reported in the Press,[3] but several – each with a very specific intention. There were also several intermediate hues, so to speak, so that the final product looks more like a spectrum than a series of silhouettes in black-and-white.

There were Subjective–Objective, Abstract–Real, Value–Fact, Process–Product, and Determinist–Existential polarities which were each discussed at the levels both of philosophy and application.

Perhaps the most stimulating confrontation was that between the Americans; Janet Daley, a philosopher, and Ray Studer, an architect interested in the application of behavioural psychology to design problems. But it is a mark of the very diffuse nature of Design Method at all that two such people could make any significant contribution to a symposium of this kind. It is also symptomatic of the scale of developments in Architectural Design since the first conference on Design Methods in 1962.

All previous conferences on Design Method[4] have laid great emphasis upon the essential independence of means and ends, and although architects have made contributions at these gatherings, their presentations have never had very far-reaching influences upon their own profession. Perhaps the one significant exception is Christopher Alexander whose contribution to the Imperial College Conference of a complete Design Method has had a broad if misguided effect in many schools of architecture.

At the Portsmouth Conference, four delegates had had direct experience of his developed method – myself, Neville Longbone, Keith Hanson, and Barry Poyner, who was co-author of what is probably Alexander's most significant work to date.[5] Hanson and Longbone both completed their studies during their academic education, and their papers give a useful insight into the benefits of this kind of approach for students. Perhaps because Alexander is the only architect to have had such an influence in his own field, much of the symposium was devoted to a philosophical and operational analysis of his work.

However, his early application of set-theory to design problems was paralleled by systems analysis, a much broader influence from Operational Research. Later more specialized applications from those fields were presented by John Luckman, an O.R. man from the Institute of Operational Research, whose AIDA (Analysis of Interaction of Decision Areas) programme eliminated in the works of J. C. Jones, 'some of the limitations inherent in Alexander's earlier work'. Luckman's paper was concerned primarily with the process, rather than the content (user requirements, constructional limitations, etc.), of the design problem. His use of Zwicky's Morphological Method was also taken up by S. A. Gregory, a chemical engineer at Aston University, Birmingham, and author and editor of the 1965 Conference on Design Method.[4] He was very much concerned with the strategic options available to the designer in his decision making. It is a fundamental tenet of his attitude that the process can be separated from the product, and in this he was accompanied by L. Bruce Archer, Research

Fellow at the Royal College of Art, and well-known contributor to several major conferences in this field. His philosophy, shortly to be published in a forthcoming book on Design Method, is best described in his own words, since they sum up the very basis of all interdisciplinary co-operation in the field of Design Method:

'No attempt is made here to distinguish between Architectural, Engineering and Industrial Design. Indeed, it is an essential element in the philosophy underlying this thesis that the logical nature of the act of designing is largely independent of the character of the thing designed.'

His use of Operational Research, systems analysis and statistics are to be seen in the light of this presupposition and lies at the root of the difficulty many architects have experienced in coming to terms with Design Method.

As a profession we seem to have been over-influenced by the influx of so many new techniques. Certainly, we have lacked any discrimination and have accepted anything we were presented with – set-theory, O.R. techniques, information theory, or psychological models of human existence. One of the pleasing aspects of the Symposium seemed to be the emergence of a very solid awareness of the contribution that architects can make to the field of Design Method. This point was very effectively demonstrated by the contingent from the Bartlett School of Architecture, University College, London, Jane Abercrombie, Gordon Best, and Amos Rapoport, in three of the most stimulating papers of the symposium.

Best's demonstration of the methods employed by three different architectural designers, and Rapoport's analysis of the role of subjective values, demonstrated this very effectively. Mrs Abercrombie, on the other hand, spoke of the differences between the real world and the world as perceived by our senses. At first sight, this had very little of direct applicational use, but by inference she summed up the essence of the Studer–Daley confrontation. Her emphasis on the subjective interpretation of perceived 'objective' phenomena pointed the ultimate validity of 'values' as opposed to 'facts', and for this reason it was probably the most important paper of the Symposium.

This brings me to perhaps the most esoteric part of the proceedings: Daley v. Studer.

It is to Ray Studer's credit that he withstood the onslaught with good grace. Both he and Barry Poyner were subjected to the severest of philosophical criticisms about their work and their symposium contributions. Attacking the 'naïve determinism' of behavioural psychology, Daley raised the objections, which many people felt but few could express with such eloquence, to a rigid view of human existence which attempts to separate the realms of value and fact. She criticized the 'objectification' of human existence which such ideologies imply, and with reference to the work of a psychiatrist, R. D. Laing, she left us to infer the repugnant consequences which may result.

Enjoyable though this dialogue was, its finer points were, I feel, beyond the immediate interest of today's practising architect. To many researchers, myself included, it was invaluable.

However, the structure of architectural practice is not static. Already the schools and the research and development organizations are beginning to assume leading roles in the production of design information for the architect. Both were represented at the Symposium. Ian Moore, an architect at M.P.B.W., and Professor T. Markus, a building scientist at Strathclyde University, Glasgow, set forth yet two more papers which I subsequently heard referred to as polemic. Moore, deeply involved with user-requirements, illustrated what he called a 'Scale of Human Misery', and, strange to tell, at a Design Method Symposium, he showed illustrations of actual buildings. He was very concerned with ends first, and means only as a way of achieving these ends.

Markus, on the other hand was very much concerned with Means. His use of the RIBA plan of work was set forth as an attempt to define the role of appraisal in design. He concluded that what is normally called 'feed-back' in the design process should really be called 'feed-forward' to the next project. He described the analysis of a comprehensive system of education in Scotland using cost as a criterion of objective evaluation, and in this he too came under the Daley fusillade.

The late introduction of Professor Guerra, of Naples University School of Architecture, provided a similar kind of analysis, in which the criterion of evaluation is that of structural form. His work is less well known here than in Naples where he has published numerous papers.

The Symposium was effectively concluded by J. C. Jones, whose models of 'black-box' and 'glass-box' designers seemed to have us all accurately classified. His paper will be found to be both as illuminating and amusing as we have come to expect. The high standard set by Jones and Archer did much to raise the Symposium above the average level of this kind of event.

Geoffrey Broadbent's summary deals far more effectively with the actual content of the Symposium so I will leave that task to him. My own subjective feelings left me in mind of Joseph Esherick's paper at the 1962 conference. I do not believe that means

can be separated from ends. When we choose which ends are desirable, we find we have already limited the number of means available to us. One of the problems facing architects now, is the decision about what kind of ends they desire. The means will follow naturally.

Nothing that I have seen since the Symposium has led me to believe that this problem is being faced in Design Research. In June 1968, on the day before Robert Kennedy's assassination, I gave a paper at the First International Conference of the Design Methods Group at M.I.T. McArthy buttons were to be seen everywhere, and I was later to be reminded of my own feelings about the Conference when I read Norman Mailer's description of the McArthy supporters: 'Their common denominator seemed to be found in some blank area of the soul, a species of disinfected idealism which gave one the impression when among them of living in a lobotomised ward of Upper Utopia'.[5] Of the 20-odd speakers at the Conference none seemed remotely interested in the real world of the people they were supposed to be designing for, one of whom might well have been the little fat immigration officer who vetted me at Montreal Airport. His reaction I found far more amusing.

Him: 'Wher're ya goin' in the States, Mr Ward?'
Me: 'Boston!'
Him: 'What're ya doin' in Boston?'
Me: 'Giving a paper at M.I.T!'
Him: 'Whadda ya do?'
Me: 'I'm an Architect!'
Him: 'Architect? Paper?'
Me: (embarrassed) 'Yes, you see I do Research.'
Him: (amazed) 'Jesus! They doin' Research in that as well now? Christ, does nobody work any longer?'

My 'American experience' to some extent explains the reason for what has been called my 'irrelevant Existential bias'. It lies in this hypothetical independence between *process* and *product* which I have described.

The root of all inter-disciplinary co-operation and specialization is manifest explicitly in Archer's words. His premise that 'the *logical* nature of the act of designing is largely independent of the character of the thing designed' (my italics) is not open to empirical analysis. It is an act of faith, neither more nor less valid than any other. Yet what if it were incorrect? What if the way you go about designing something does affect the quality of the thing you are designing? It is my own contention that the *logical* act of designing an environment for another human being is qualitatively different from the *logical* act of designing a machine part, because it involves an element of 'reciprocating choice' between the designer and the Other. There is at present no language available for describing this relationship, so it has never been studied, and cannot be said to be identical to the designer's relationship to the inanimate world. Indeed, the work of Ronald Laing in psychiatry seems to indicate that it is fundamentally different.

Interestingly, Professor Studer and I seem agreed that the physical environment can be seen as a 'learning system'. However, our very agreement only underlines the metaphysical nature of the problem. Our interpretations of *what constitutes* a learning system are mutually exclusive. My conception of the human condition has no place for the behaviourist's passive stimulus-response model of human existence. It is only at this level of analysis that the true metaphysical structure upon which the whole edifice of Design Method has been built is revealed. If we are to contribute significantly to the development of Design Method, we have no alternative but to make explicit the philosophical premises upon which we base our conclusions. Otherwise the logical nature of our task will remain impenetrable.

Some of the problems which I had before the event have subsequently found their resolution in my own attitudes and work. It is very unlikely that they are representative of a general feeling, so I will not use this Introduction as a means of writing yet another biased paper. The reader must use this material to find his own answers to his own problems. There is enough material to last him for a very long time.

In closing I would like to express my very sincere thanks to all the delegates. They willingly submitted themselves to what had all the symptoms of a very bewildering experience; to BASA and David Dunster for publicity at very short notice. To my friends Keith Elvin and Colin Cave, who helped in the synthesis of the idea, and Christopher Alexander in his absence, who provided the core of the discussion. I extend my thanks, and the thanks of the staff and students of Portsmouth School of Architecture, where the effect continues to be felt.

Anthony Ward, August 1968

REFERENCES

[1] A. WARD, E. ELLIS, A. BERG, M. LIGALI, P. WOON FAT, R. BELLINGHAM. 3M Design. Unpublished thesis (Birmingham School of Architecture 1965).

[2] C. ALEXANDER and I. B. POYNER. *The Atoms of Environmental Structure*. R. & D. Publication, M.P.B.W. (London 1967).

[3] *Architect's Journal*. 10.1.68, letter; 14.2.68, letter; 10.1.68, Both Facts and Fancy, pages 51–2 (editorial); 10.1.68, COLIN CAVE. Design Methods – not only how but why. Keith Elvin, page 53; 10.1.68, Basa Report by Roger Bloomfield, pages 66–7.

[4] J. C. JONES and D. C. THORNLEY (Eds.). *Conference on Design Methods*. Pergamon (Oxford 1963). S. A. GREGORY (Ed.). *The Design Method*. Butterworth (London 1966). ULM GROUP 4. *Papers and Programmes from the Conference on Design Methods in Architecture*. Ulm 1966; published from Waltham Technical College.

[5] N. MAILER. *Miami and the Siege of Chicago*. Weidenfeld and Nicolson (London 1968), page 84.

Design method in architecture

by Geoffrey Broadbent

Chris. Jones, in the last formal paper of the Symposium, presented a useful basis on which the others could be classified. He indicated six fields of design research: the 'black box' approach, the 'glass box' approach, control, observation, problem structure, and design in evolution as the basis for his analysis. The 'black box' approach is for those who believe that design is a mystery, something which happens in the brain, susceptible to manipulation, but not to analysis. It is concerned with 'creativity', which may be promoted by techniques such as Brainstorming and Synectics.[1]

As Chris. Jones pointed out, no one actually spoke about this approach to the Symposium, but we had plenty of 'glass-boxers' who believe that design can be systematized and analysed – pinned out, I always think, like a frog on a dissecting table. Bruce Archer and Professor Markus were 'glass-boxers' in this sense, they took a Systems Analysis, Operational Research view on the business of designing. As an assemblage of OR techniques, Bruce Archer's 'Logical Model of the Design Process' was enormously sophisticated. He used Critical Path Method to plan the 'design programme' itself, and he plotted the various 'properties' of an object – cost, brightness, roughness, and so on – against 'degrees of satisfaction' using a simple correlation technique from statistics. He had a graphical method for expressing the 'degrees of satisfaction' for different properties of the *same* object, which he then translated into Set Theory. He had a method for placing entire objects, such as chairs, into order of, say comfort, against the scales for psychological measurement set up by S. S. Stevens, and a way of negotiating with developers, local authorities and such, from Theory of Games. He had a detailed 'map of the design programme' based on Systems Analysis, and a method of 'decomposition' from Graph Theory, similar to Alexander's (see below). There was, however, a difference between Archer/Alexander for he (Archer) insisted that his 'decomposition' was simply a 'map' of design territory, whereas Alexander's was a 'problem-solving' device. Archer's other techniques too should only be taken as 'maps', or navigational aids: given these devices for explor-ing unfamiliar territory, one still had to 'damn well go'. And like any other wise explorer, the designer should keep his eyes open so as to observe the territory for himself, making individual decisions as to what to do next on the basis of his observations.

Professor Markus used the RIBA *Plan of Work* as his 'map' of design territory. We had some difficulties in terminology here; Professor Markus opted for Asimow's definitions[2] in which the entire sequence of events, from first inception to final completion of the building (Archer's 'design programme'), is called the design 'morphology', while the individual 'loops' of briefing, analysis, synthesis, evaluation, and implementation are called the design 'process'. But other designers use 'morphology' in a different sense (see below) and the Symposium as a whole agreed to the following definitions:
1. The Design Process is the entire sequence of events which leads from the first inception of a project to its final completion.
2. An individual 'loop' within this, of briefing, analysis, synthesis and so on, is a Decision Sequence, which brings us into line with Operational Research, Management and other fields.

Professor Markus has a particular interest in building appraisal, and the Plan of Work allows for this in its final phase, which is called 'feedback'. He suggested that this be renamed 'feed-forward' because although it couldn't help much to improve the quality of what had just been completed, it might help the designer to avoid mistakes on future projects.

His own appraisal techniques were described under four headings: Identification, Relationships, Model Building, and Optimization. The first two of these were elaborated in some detail; *Identification* is a matter of finding out what the designer's original intentions were, and then of testing his building against these intentions. *Relationships* form a valuable classification of the various 'systems' which come together to *form* a building, relating human needs to inanimate objects. The first of these, the *building* system is concerned with structure and construction; the second, the *environmental* system is self-explanatory; the third, the *activity* system is concerned with human behaviour in general, and the fourth, the *organizational* system, with the 'objectives' which prompted the client to build in the first place.

These 'map makers', who work out abstract patterns for the design process itself, came in for a good deal of criticism during the Symposium, notably from Professor Nelson, of the École des Beaux-Arts in Marseilles, who worried about their apparent lack of concern for *actual* buildings. But at this stage in the development of the art, they serve an extremely useful purpose and we should remember, after all, that Sir Francis Chichester himself is a 'map maker' by profession. It may be, however, that we have enough maps now; some of them are very elegant, but perhaps we ought to call a moratorium on the design of new ones.

Jones's next two categories, *Control* and *Observation*, were hardly represented at the Symposium. Control is a matter of self monitoring, of observing, oneself, what one does in design. A good teacher will enable a student designer to exercise control in this way – Jones cited Matchett of Bristol as someone who could do this, but OR-based design processes may inhibit the development of such control. Most of them start with a massive 'briefing' exercise, in which *all* the information, which in any way *might* be useful to the designer, is collected at the beginning of the job. This 'information explosion', as Jones described it, can be fairly traumatic for the designer. He abandons his good intentions and lapses into traditional methods. The design team too may suffer from lack of control. If one simply assembles a group of people, representing different interests, their efforts may well be abortive unless each additional brain, bringing with it extra intelligence and extra creativity, also brings with it extra control.

Observation, by Jones's definition, is a matter of watching the designer at work, to see what he does. Little has been done in this direction since Levin's brilliant analysis of a planning team at work.[3] But in contrast to these last two, the *problem structure* approach was very well represented at the Symposium. Morphological analysis, by definition, is concerned with problem structure; John Luckman and Sydney Gregory described variations of the technique which was originally given this name by Fritz Zwicky. As Gregory said, it has to do with 'pattern and shape'; in Zwicky's version, it is refreshingly simple. He takes the *requirements* of a system, calling them 'significant parameters'. For a jet engine, for instance, some of these might include thrust generation, jet, propellant state, and so on. These are listed, and opposite each parameter on his list he plots a number of ways in which it can be achieved. The solution is then assembled by taking one solution for each parameter – one entry from each line.

Luckman's technique, which he calls AIDA – analysis of inter-connected decision areas – improves on this by 'mapping' the ways in which solutions to the various parameters can be assembled to form a whole. He defines each factor in the design. Some factors can only be satisfied in one way, but others may be satisfied in a number of ways. Yet a particular solution to one factor may be quite incompatible with certain solutions to another factor. In a rationalized-traditional house, for instance, the walls may all be load-bearing, or it may be built of load-bearing cross walls with infilling panels for the end walls. In the first case, the floor joists could span in either direction but in the second case, they could only span between cross-walls. And in the same house, other factors are interconnected in similar ways. Given foundations, walls, partitions, ceilings, floors, and so on, each with say two solutions, it may appear, at first, that there are 2^{12} ways of designing the house – 4096 in all. But once certain major incompatibilities have been noted, this will be reduced quickly to 2^5 or 32, and before long, it will be apparent that there are only 2^3 or eight possible solutions. These eight could then be tested against cost, and other relevant criteria so that the most reasonable solution would quickly be detected.

Gregory drew certain analogies between chemical engineering and architecture. In designing a large chemical plant, for instance, the simple, familiar diagrams of Systems Analysis enable a very rapid check on costs to be obtained. Each step in the process is counted, to give the Functional Unit Number (FUN) and the designer's task, therefore, is to reduce the FUN as far as possible. Not only that, but in costing such a system, one assumes that each functional unit, however complex, costs exactly the same as the others, and that the overall envelope or enclosure will cost at least as much as the plant it contains. This led to certain analogies with architecture and urban design. He suggested, for instance, that Chermayeff and Alexander[4] only hinted at the morphology of enclosures – courtyards and other specialized areas. Process design offered a much richer method of analysis, which could be used not only in criticism, but in designing traffic, circulation, pipework, and other flow systems with very firm cost-control. And the idea of overall enclosure, of course, led to Fuller-type domes as the answer to environmental control.

The other analysis of problem-structure, which came in for inordinate attention during the symposium, was Christopher Alexander's method of 'decomposing' the problem into 'fit' and 'misfit' variable. In this technique, which is based on Graph Theory, the problem is broken into its tiniest, constituent components (the 'misfit variables'). Each of these is then checked for its 'connexion' with the others, and eventually, 'groups' of 'misfit variables' are built up. The problem presented by each group is then resolved by means of a 'diagram' which sums up geometrically its essential characteristics. These diagrams are then assembled, combined, and modified into each other, to achieve a total solution to the problem.[5] Alexander developed this technique, in certain directions, when he was with Ian Moore's research team at the Ministry of Public Building and Works, and several of his colleagues from that period reported this work to the symposium.

Ian Moore set the scene – he gave the first paper of the symposium – by describing the work of his team (now the Offices Development Group) in general terms. He spoke of the difficulties of finding out what people *really* want in their buildings, and of ensuring that major decisions to build – anything, whether it be an army depot, a hospital, or a housing estate – are made in full knowledge of the overall context. Context, in this case would be everything relevant which is there, now, physically on the ground, its present state and its users' future needs; all seen against a background of the national economy. I liked particularly his definition of one scale against which priorities should be plotted – that of 'human misery'. This intensely human approach permeated everything that the Ministry team had to say; it applied at all levels. Ian Moore, for instance, also mentioned the 'other half' of design which most of us pretend isn't there. However well we have taken the brief, and analysed it, however good the solution, it still has to be implemented. And that depends on *persuading* people – politicians and others who finally will make the decision to build – or not, as the case may be. If one's design process has been exceptionally thorough, it is highly likely that the solution will be so different in kind from the conventional, or what the clients expected, that its implementation will be exceptionally difficult.

As for Alexander's technique, there were four descriptions of this, and its developments, during the course of the symposium. Barry Poyner, Keith Hanson, Tony Ward, and Neville Longbone each had variations on it. It is tempting to call them the Alexander quartet, but that would be unfair, because there were considerable variations in the ways in which they had developed from the original. Keith Hanson came nearest in describing the method from Alexander's book (1964), which is not surprising, because his example was worked out as a student scheme at Cambridge University. He was concerned with a housing design, and threw some light on the difficulties of finding a meaningful diagram for each group of variables. In some cases, he said, the diagram was misleading. In other cases, it was impossible to draw one; there is considerable doubt, therefore, that a solution built up by combining diagrams of this kind can have much validity. Hanson himself was quite honest about this. Having gone through the Alexander process once, he said he would never do it again.

Barry Poyner described the research which he and

Alexander had completed at the Ministry on 'Relational Theory'.[7] This starts from the premise that in relation to particular human activities, the environment can be 'right' or 'wrong'. The impact of one on the other can be expressed in terms of 'tendencies', 'conflicts', and 'relations'. If somebody, given the opportunity, wants to do a certain thing, they call this a 'tendency'; a typical tendency might read: 'People . . . try to get a view from their offices'. That, they say, is more than an expression of 'need' – it is a testable hypothesis. At first sight, the designer ought to *satisfy* these tendencies, but according to Alexander and Poyner he ought to do something more subtle, which is to design the environment in such a way that people are encouraged to satisfy these tendencies for themselves. But tendencies conflict. You have a tendency to park your car in your garage. Your guests have a tendency to park in your drive. If they satisfy *their* tendency, yours is frustrated, you can't get out. So that the designer should plan your garage and drive in such a way that the conflict is resolved; this planning is simply a matter of *geometry*. The diagrams of Alexander's theories are expressions of this geometry; a diagram of your garage and drive would illustrate the *relations* between them.

Poyner illustrated the theory with reference to examples from a study of office entrances; Tony Ward and Neville Longbone were concerned, respectively, with prison workshops, and workshops for the blind. They each had rather harrowing series of photographs, harrowing, that is, to the designer, which showed what people do with buildings which fail to 'fit' their tendencies. They modify them, of course, they add things, take short cuts, leave things lying around. If these indications of 'misfit' could be recorded in ways which could be used directly by the designer, then the theory would have a great deal to offer. But as Keith Hanson indicated, Alexander-type diagrams can be gravely misleading and it was interesting to note that in one practical, worked example which Ian Moore described – the design of office layouts for an office building, actual mock-up furniture was built, and tested by real people in the working situation.

Professor Guerra, of Naples, also had a practical way of handling Alexander's technique. His method starts with the collection of data on the client's demands, in terms of social need, costs, and so on. He then investigates the site, under two headings: the actual, physical site and the available 'site', as defined by town planning and other statutory requirements. Finally, he looks at generalized human needs, in terms of physiology, ergonomics, and similar data. Once this material has been analysed, Professor Guerra allows the site itself to determine the choice of actual building form, by preparing diagrams of the available structural types, and 'crossing' these diagrams in an interaction chart. These structural possibilities are tested against the economic use of space, and throughout he develops two distinct kinds of information in parallel:

1. All functional matters, other than those concerned directly with structure.
2. The structural possibilities.

At the appropriate time, he collates these two streams of information, and the building finally amounts to a synthesis between them.

Alexander's Method is based essentially on the observation of human behaviour, and the drawing of conclusions from this observation. As might be expected, it draws heavily on Behaviourist psychology, and the whole Behaviourist case came in for devastating attack from Janet Daley, who simply poured scorn on the presumptions on which it is built. She questioned, first of all, the validity of the Behaviourist's belief that he can be objective in the observation of human affairs. He claims complete objectivity for his tests and measurements, but they depend entirely on his definition of 'normal' behaviour. The belief that there can be such a thing as 'normal' behaviour is itself a moral judgement, and, what is more, anyone who fails to conform to the Behaviourist's notion of normality is considered odd, eccentric, or sick, and given 'treatment' to make him 'normal' again. So Behaviourism is a 'muddle-headed' movement; it claims, by its 'objectivity', to transcend philosophy, but in fact it is based on an over-simplified, deterministic philosophy, hangover from a nineteenth-century mechanical view of the world.

Relational Theory's 'rightness' and 'wrongness' in the physical environment is equally naïve. Alexander argues that one cannot judge the environment in terms of one's own 'goals, or policies, or values'[7] but this itself is a *moral* attitude, as 'muddle-headed' as the Behaviourist's. He dismisses such judgements as 'arbitrary', thereby confusing the word 'arbitrary' with 'non-factual'. Yet the designer must make judgements on matters which are 'non-factual' – in the sense that they cannot be measured in simple, physical terms. But such judgements need not be 'arbitrary'. Janet Daley herself suggested that if she said of a house: 'I like it', that was an arbitrary statement, and of no particular interest to anyone else. But if she added: 'because it is conducive to good human contact', then that was no longer arbitrary. As a statement, it could be defended, even though there is no way of measuring 'goodness of contact' in physical terms.

Lastly, Janet Daley castigated Alexander and his colleagues (not to mention several other people in the Symposium) for inventing 'private languages'. People who use ordinary words in special ways are obviously unsure of their ground. It is impossible to *test* what they are trying to say, because if one challenges what they *appear* to have said, they can always shift their ground, and change the special meanings of their words. Words like 'tendency',

'conflict', and 'relation' are understood by most people in their simple, ordinary meanings. It can only fog the issue if these same words are used with special meanings as parts of a private language. Nor should it be necessary to use jargon. We have some fairly complex things to say, in discussing problems of environmental design, but it should be possible to say them all by means of good, honest, simple words, used with the meanings by which most people understand them.

She is right, of course, but perhaps she underestimates the power of 'in-groups' in the architectural scene, and of the desperate need that many environmental designers have to be recognized as 'respectable' by science. And it is easy to acquire a tolerant imitation of respectability by expressing simple thoughts in complex jargon. Certainly it is my experience that many architects don't *want* to be told the simple truth about what they do. And if one tells them, then they respond immediately with: 'But that is what we have always done'.

Professor Studer expressed some simple, elegant thoughts, but Janet Daley found his language in particular far too complex, and yet his avowed aim was to *find* a language in which the structure of environmental problems could be expressed. The chief difficulty, he said, in building for human needs, is that the *needs* themselves cannot be observed. We *can* see people's behaviour, which he defined as 'a system of operationally defined needs ... within a given environment'. In other words, what we *see* them do is an expression, presumably, of what they *want* to do, in a given set of circumstances. We can describe the environment – physical, social, cultural, political, and educational – and we can observe people's behaviour, but we have no language in which we can express the nature of the 'interface' between the two. The Behaviourists have such a language, or the beginnings of one, but it is not yet suitable for our purposes because it is too simple. They isolate individual phenomena, subject them to experimental test, under controlled conditions, with very few variables. Their view, consequently, is fragmented and analytical. But designers have a much more complex task. We are concerned with wholes rather than with parts, with the simultaneous interactions of a vast number of variables, with elaborate patterns of human behaviour and with synthesis in addition to analysis. So, every day, we make decisions of a complexity which is quite beyond the Behaviourist's experience. Yet his language, and especially in terms of 'operant behavioural analysis', can give us a lead, because it is a mathematical language. It is highly likely that the language we need, to describe the interface between behaviour and environment, will also be a mathematical one.

Amos Rapoport, another American, also presented a complex argument. It was decidedly non-linear, in the McLuhan sense, but it was profoundly concerned with the humanness of human affairs. He rejected entirely the validity of OR-based design methods, and of Alexander's method too; he had grave doubts, anyway, about the place of scientific method in design. The prime danger, as he saw it, was that because certain factors – such as proximity, lighting standards, and so on – are measurable in the physical sense, computable and otherwise supported by 'objective' evidence, some designers tend to emphasize them and think them all-important. But other factors, not so measurable, are equally important. They might be matters of emotion, judgement, and values; whether we like it or not, they *do* get built into buildings. He cited the example of court-houses; it would be possible to infer from the plan and sections of a court house almost everything that one needs to know about the administration of justice in a country. The physical planning, the three-dimensional relationships of chairs, tables, and other furniture, expresses a hierarchy of human relationships which is built into the actual 'form' of the building. And furthermore, any attempt to 'rationalize' the plan of a court house, to computerize proximities and make the circulation more economical *might* result, eventually, in the miscarriage of justice. For 'wasted' spaces in corridors and other circulation areas might be just those places where counsel choose to meet, informally, 'by accident', to settle things out of court.

Alexander's 'relations' are attempts to resolve the 'conflicts' between human 'tendencies' by means of clear, simple, geometrical statements. But they presuppose that everyone is going to adapt to the environment in the same way. They process and package people, but each of us adapts to the environment in different, personal ways. So instead of looking for geometrical clarity, we should encourage complexity and ambiguity – these will allow people to 'choose' how they are going to adapt, instead of forcing them into some standard pattern.

Gordon Best compared various ways of designing – Alexander's (naturally), Aalto's, as representing 'traditional' ways of designing, and a Bartlett student's, who worked according to typical, OR-based design methods. Best thought that in each case the total design process could be 'mapped' against a simple communications channel in five stages: input, encoding, processing, decoding, and output. The designers also started with a common aim, which was to reduce the vast complex of information with which they started into simple, manipulable form, a process which he called 'homomorphic reduction'. Where they differed, enormously, was in the process of 'encoding' – Alexander used Graph Theory for this purpose, 'processed' his information by means of diagrams, and 'decoded' these to form his design solution. Aalto's 'input' consisted of a conventional brief, amplified by a walk across the site. He 'encoded' his information by producing a preliminary sketch of what the building was going to

be 'like' and to do this he drew on his vast experience as a designer. The design itself, when it was 'decoded', looked remarkably like his first sketch. The Bartlett student, having no such experience to draw on, relied on the paraphernalia of OR-based design method – interaction charts, bubble diagrams and so on, for his 'encoding'. And most significantly, the final design in each case was *determined* by the system of encoding. In Alexander's case, there was a tendency to convert the lines of his diagrams into the actual lines of plans; in Aalto's, the first sketch determined the 'form' of the building, and the student's plan *looked* remarkably like his final analytical diagram.

I have described this phenomenon, which seems to me fundamental in design, as 'analogue take-over'. It occurs whenever a design problem is translated into some medium other than the actual materials themselves, manipulated to full size on the site. Drawings, models, written descriptions, and even the computer programme, all 'take over' from the designer and impose their own characteristics on what he is designing. This need not surprise anyone who listened to Jane Abercrombie at the symposium. She was concerned with two aspects of design: the ways in which we *receive* information, under the general heading of 'perception', and the ways in which we put ideas together, which she called 'construction'.

She demonstrated the fundamentals of perception, with devastating economy, by using her Ames window (a rotating window constructed in 'perspective' which affords some impressive optical illusions). And on this basis she explained that the taking in of information is a transaction, between what is 'there', physically, in the 'real' world, and what we *want* to see on the basis of schemata we have built up from what we are used to seeing. However 'rational' we may try to be, say in observing people's 'tendencies', we shall always bend the 'facts' to fit our personal predilections. Elsewhere (Avercrombie, 1965) she has cited the case of a scientist who in taking 'objective' thermometer readings was unaware of moving his head, ever so slightly, until the mercury lined up with the mark he *wanted* to read.

Dr Abercrombie had a great deal to say about the difficulty of learning *anything* new. When a child is learning to read, for instance, he throws his whole body into the act. His eyes move, and the whole of his head, not to mention his body, arms, legs, and even his toes. In trying to build up the abstract, mental concepts which reading requires, he cannot help relating them, fundamentally, to bodily feelings and emotions. We all do this, whether we like it or not, especially when we have to attempt something difficult; and if we *try* to separate mental functions from bodily ones, we find ourselves in difficulties. She cited a simple problem – cutting a plank into two parts, in a certain proportional relationship –

which people tried to split in this way. Some of them translated it directly into abstract, algebraic terms, and failed to spot an inherent ambiguity in the problem. Others saw simple, visual images, and they had difficulties too. The most efficient problem-solvers were those who could alternate these two ways of looking at things. There is a profound message here for the design methodologist. He needs to see the problem in both ways too. We know that the 'traditional' designer, who tends to work only in visual images, is prone to significant error, but the 'map-maker' too, who tries to deal *only* in mathematical abstraction, is equally prone to make mistakes, where the evidence of common sense is submerged in a welter of intellectual processes.

She talked about two levels of designing:
1. Putting real things together, which we perceive with our senses, and manipulate in three-dimensional space.
2. Designing in the abstract, which is a matter of visualization.
We tend to sneer at the first. It seems too direct and simple. Yet it seems to me that, sooner or later, our buildings are going to be experienced by other people, by means of their senses. Why, then, should we be afraid to *manipulate* design in this way? The answer, of course, is that Plato told us to beware of using *real*, material objects in the solving of problems. He castigated Archytus, a mathematician, for using models to work out solutions in geometry. And ever since, we have believed him that mental processes, somehow, are 'better' than physical ones. Yet if the two are intimately related, as Jane Abercrombie said, there is nothing inherently 'better' in one *or* the other. And if 'analogue take-over' is the insidious device I believe it to be, then the wise designer will *always* deal with real materials, to full size, wherever this is possible.

Designing in the abstract is certainly very difficult. As Dr Abercrombie showed, to do it at all, one has to learn a 'code' – the 'code', in this case, of three-dimensional visual representation. It is a difficult code to learn – analogous to learning a language. It is always easier to *decipher* a language, once one has started to learn it, than it is to *manipulate* the language oneself. One can understand other people speaking the language long before one feels confident enough to speak it. Manipulation, eventually, can only be learned by *doing*; this is true of three-dimensional manipulation as it is of learning any other code. But recently, in schools of architecture, it has become fashionable to avoid the *doing* of three-dimensional manipulation. The interaction chart has taken the place of the drawing as the object for final presentation, and while no one would wish to reinstate the presentation drawing as an end in itself, which it used to be, it is becoming increasingly clear that students are failing to *learn* the three-dimensional code, which is their stock-in-trade as architects.

Dr Abercrombie illustrated some difficulties in learning to draw with reference to experiments with spastic and otherwise handicapped children. Some of them showed marked lack of co-ordination between hand and eye, and even the 'normal' child, up to the age of 7 or so, found it difficult to draw diagonals. Even more revealing was a series of models, made from assorted building shapes, by 'normal' boys and girls. The boys tended to make forts and other outward-pointing devices, whereas the girls made hollow, protective, domestic-seeming spaces. In each case, she said, the child was simply externalizing obvious, personal bodily feelings. When design method can take account of these things too, it might begin to call itself truly 'systematic'.

Our conclusions? That design method *is* moving into a new field of enquiry. It is no longer adequate to take techniques straight from OR, or even from Graph Theory, and to foist them onto the designer. They may inhibit him, or they may be quite irrelevant to his purposes. The new approach will be based on a passionate concern for people's needs. It will draw on the resources of philosophy and the psychology of perception to help define these needs (sociology has shown itself almost impotent to deal with this problem, based, as it must be, on the analysis of people's *past* experience). There is much work to be done, at a personal level too, on the designer himself, what he does, and how he gets his results. It is likely that the new design methods will *look* remarkably like what the designer thinks he does already, but there will be a difference. They will *draw* on all the techniques available from OR, Systems Analysis, Computing and the New Maths. But they will not be dominated by these techniques. The process itself will determine *which* techniques might seem to be relevant. Such processes are available, and can be described now. But we are not ready for them yet – we have to convince ourselves, by the use of jargon and private languages – that there is a substantial discipline in what we are doing. It makes us *feel* good to talk of parameters, behaviour-contingent systems, and relations. We are not ready to make, *or* to receive, the simple statements that Janet Daley asked of us. We like to think we can be objective in our observations of the physical world; we refuse to *believe* the evidence of Jane Abercrombie's window that, inevitably, we cannot. But there are enough people now, in the field, who obviously *care* about satisfying people's needs to ensure that in the long run there could be a philosophical shift which would make this desirable aim a fashionable one. And design method then could begin to serve its purpose.

REFERENCES

[1] G. H. BROADBENT. 'Creativity' in S. A. Gregory (Ed.). *The Design Method*. Butterworth (London 1966).

[2] *Architect's Journal*. 20:12:67.

[3] M. ASIMOW. *Introduction to Design*. Prentice Hall (Englewood Cliffs, N.J., 1962).

[4] P. H. LEVIN. *Decision Making in Urban Design*. B.R.S. Current Papers 49.

[5] S. CHERMAYEFF and C. ALEXANDER. *Community and Privacy*. Penguin (Harmondsworth, 1967).

[6] C. ALEXANDER. *Notes on the Synthesis of Form*. Harvard University Press (Cambridge, Mass., 1964).

[7] C. ALEXANDER and I. B. POYNER. *The Atoms of Environmental Structure*. M.P.B.W. (London, 1967).

Design methods and development programming

by Ian Moore

Our social structure results from a system of rules. These do not exist in written form alone, as in the case of statutes and agreements, but also unwritten rules such as those pertaining to habit, prejudice, political attitude, ambition, ownership, etc. and they exert as much pressure and influence as the former.

Architecture and the form it takes are directly influenced by these rules. At this particular point in time society is confounded by a mass of rules that are barely comprehended and whose existence may not even be acknowledged. This is largely due to the rapid rate of invention in the field of technology and the massive changes in the social structure.

Previously the forms of architecture had evolved by a perceptive process of trial and error against a reasonably confined system of rules, and over a static social background of a fairly lengthy period of years. This is no longer the case. Architecture is faced with a range of unknown needs and unknown possibilities coupled with a vast demand for buildings. Architects are therefore committed to finding ways of speeding up this evolutionary process (for they cannot avoid it), in order to bring some confidence to the situation. Inevitably there is a search for ways and means. The purpose of this symposium is to examine and consider design methods that attempt to improve this situation. Let me hasten to add that if there is anyone who thinks that as a result of reading the papers he will be equipped to meet the needs of the situation, he is doomed to disappointment, because work in the field of design methodology is recent. Most of our efforts post-war have been concentrated on technology in an effort to speed up the production of buildings. Thus, by and large, the bottleneck of design has been ignored.

It is pertinent at this juncture to enquire whether there is any need for such an effort to match that called forth by technological ends. In my mind there is no doubt. The current practice of designing tall blocks of flats to house families which gives rise to the plight of the children recently brought to the surface by research, and the fully glazed slab blocks of offices that cause acute discomfort to office workers for eight

Fig.1

Fig.2

hours a day surely provide sufficient evidence and an indictment of our current priorities.

If we are to remedy this deficiency we must discuss our present efforts very frankly. If we are not seen to be doing this very actively we shall not create any confidence in the service the profession is constructed to give.

I would like to describe to you three experiences of my own. Each of these experiences has taught me that any design method not only demands a discipline from the architect who practises it, but also necessitates some considerable effort by the client. By this I mean that it almost inevitably makes the client play his full part in the proceedings, demanding his decision and agreement. (This of course is not always acceptable to some clients who prefer to retain a position from which later they can apportion blame.) I mention this now because it necessitates the architect educating his client and user; this demands time which is an expensive commodity. It can, and does, also lead to a considerable strain on personal relationships between the user, client and designer unless properly handled. My three experiences in these matters are first with a building programme; second with an individual building project; third with a building complex, i.e. a large concept consisting of many buildings over a large area.

The actual narrative concerning the development work associated with building programmes has been published by H.M.S.O. under the title of 'Preparing a Building Programme'. It is sufficient to say that it

activity	number
Repairing electrical equipment	R 68

description

The working day of a vehicle electrician (7.45am–5.15pm) is spent repairing electrical components (starter motors, dynamos, etc) at a bench, or in a vehicle bay, rewiring or repairing the electrics of a vehicle. In both instances machines are used when required during repair.

The chargehand inspects all work requiring repair. During repair he guides the work, issues tools, materials and components necessary for effecting the repair. On completion he examines and tests the repaired component, or vehicle. In addition he checks all time documents, completes other *pro forma*, and holds all stores required for the work in hand.

q people
- Chargehand
- Vehicle electrician
- Electrician

q things
- Bench
- Equipment bench
- Vehicle bay
- Inspection bench
- Desk
- Vehicle bay
- Security cabinet
- Bins/racks 1
-     ,,   ,,   2
-     ,,   ,,   3
- Containers (2ft × 2ft × 3in)
- Tank (portable, 2ft × 2ft 6in × 4ft high)
- Pillar drill
- Twin grinder
- Drying oven
- Octopus tester

layout notes

The activity centres about the benches and the vehicle bay/s. The location of the storage components and the chargehand's desk should allow easy access from and to the repair areas and the main workshop circulation, since the latter receives and issues all electrical work.

clear height   16ft

regulations and notes

Due to the possibility of fatal accidents on this work, notices about first aid action after receipt of an electric shock must be clearly displayed.

space components

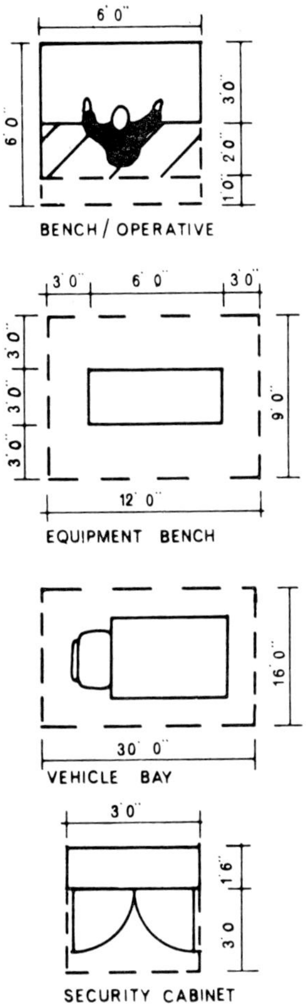

BENCH / OPERATIVE

EQUIPMENT BENCH

VEHICLE BAY

SECURITY CABINET

AIR CONDITIONS

temp °F	70	65	~~60~~	55	50	no heat
temp var	±1	±2°	~~±3°~~	±4°	±5°	
heat sources	soldering bench					
humid %	80	70	60	50	40	
humid s						
sm & fumes	flux from soldering bench					
dust free	essential	~~desirable~~	unneces			
dust sources	buffing/grinding machine					
infection						
hygiene	essential	desirable	~~unneces~~			

VISUAL CONDITIONS

lum/sq ft	50	30	~~20~~	15	7	
daylight	10	6	~~✕~~	3	1·4	unneces
glare ind	10	16	19	22	25	28
sunlight	excluded	~~undesirable~~	desirable			
view out	essential	desirable	~~undesirable~~			
privacy	essential	desirable	~~undesirable~~			
blackout	essential	~~unnecessary~~				
special						

SOUND CONDITIONS

accept n	15	20	30	35	40	60
noises	machines					
RT secs	0·75–1·0		0·75–1·5		1·0–1·5	
privacy	essential	desirable	~~unneces~~			

SAFETY CONDITIONS

human	from electrical sources
security	
fire risk	fire due to shorting of electrical circuits

DIRECT SERVICES

disposal	paper, metal swarf, cases
hot water	
cold water	
drainage	
gas	
comp a	150 lb
steam	
elect points	two sockets per bench
telephone	
other com	

DIRECT DEMANDS ON FABRIC

loading			
spillage			
foot traffic	light		
wheel traffic	light		
impacts	electrical components		
abrasion			
easy climb	essential	~~desirable~~	unneces
vib free	essential	desirable	~~unneces~~
vibration			

Fig.3
Typical 'Activity Data Sheet' used to log the spatial and environmental requirements of different human activities in a building design problem.

gave me the opportunity to question the validity of the structure of a building programme. After all, programmes are meant to be consolidation of demand which is the main spring of the design effort. In my work I have found that the building programme as it exists is really a device for listing the proposed expenditure on individual projects, and not an active piece of programming material. This then throws the problem of getting project data back on to the individual architect with all the problems of maintaining a programme timetable against an unknown objective. The programme we examined was an industrial programme and initially the first thoughts about its size were guesses that ranged from £2m – £10m, all proffered as an attempt to be helpful in order to give definition to an unknown problem. These guesses were given by a committee.

In my view a committee is a useless structure to give size and shape to any problem. All it can really achieve is to state an intended objective, outline what is known and delegate the work to achieve the objective to a small task force. At the time when we were asked to participate in this exercise there was a considerable reluctance to involve us at all. Each member of the committee had a particular vested interest which he was determined to maintain. These ranged from loyalty to various cap badges, to the conception that the whole problem was one of providing no more than lots of cheap shedding. The latter was a 'Crie de coeur' by a civil engineer who certainly did not want an architect on the scene.

The only hope in this situation was to create a body of data, shown to be the result of methodical analysis and synthesis on which it would be difficult to foster vested interests, and which would allow the evolution of impartial discussion. 'Activity Data Method' (again H.M.S.O. have published this as an R & D bulletin under that title) was developed specifically for this programme. Briefly, this method accepted the Activity as a basic unit of design. This fragmented the current unit i.f.s. or aggregate amounts of space and forced the client to consider his objectives, what he wished to do in order to attain them and consequently it became possible to talk about things without adhering to existing concepts. Gradually of course new solutions emerged. Not only did it help to give size and dimension to the problem accurately, but the programme now consisted of costed projects backed by sufficient user data for the preparation of project briefs, together with an operational system for the management of project briefing and the updating of programme material.

None of this would have been possible *or acceptable* to the client if it had not been methodically done, and *seen* to be using everybody's expertise. It gave the client and user a stake in the process along with the designer. The committee disappeared.

My second experience followed from the first. We were asked to design and build a prototype for the programme. This too involved working closely with the client and user because new arrangements for work were being tested. It became clear, however, that each successive step demonstrated the undesirability of using the particular site. Its location was not only incorrect but the restricted access actively worked against the organization. As a designer my efforts came to nought, because the situation forced a confrontation with one of those unwritten rules that quite *arbitrarily* influence a situation out of all proportion to its priority. The case for moving the site was almost unassailable, but the decision to go against such advice was dictated by a political decision that agreed to keep the site in its present location in order to prevent redundancy and hardship to workers. Because our arguments were sufficiently strong the project was abandoned by the client. However, after a period of two years when all the political personalities had changed it was seen fit to accept the recommendation to change the site and the concept of the unit. In my view, this need never have happened, and only goes to show that it is not only the client that requires educating. Although the final result may be satisfactory to me personally, I would make the point that I am an architect in an official

department, and can afford to wait. The private practitioner, on the other hand, is not in such a happy position. Money must make him act otherwise, because as a profession we are largely parasitical, and expendable, being unable to either institute the demand or produce the product.

My third and more recent experience is concerned with the preparation of a brief for the first stage of rebuilding in Whitehall. Here a concept had been established by Sir Leslie Martin. He had found during his research that precious little information was available about office design that was usable. In addition what information had been made available, in the form of Square Foot allowances per head, was inhibiting to the development of the site and the built form. It is not profitable to describe here all the information we discovered that supported this view and the means we accepted. It is relevant however to make two points. First, the gap between the well established practices of the user, the client and *the designer* and the form actually attained was enormous. So much so, that the subsequent dialogue between us *had to be supported* by the creation of a mock-up.

Essentially this mock-up was of an office floor constructed in nylon, plywood, paint and surfaced as necessary. It demonstrated essential points and left a series of messages about which the client had to think. The visual impact was sufficient to allow office users to stretch their imaginations and visualise how they would feel and act in such a different environment. It left a series of messages that said about the mock-up as a whole 'this mock-up is not an exhibition, nor does it contain things that are in the form of a final product. Typical roles found in any Central Government Office were used as a basis for the design, and it touches on points producing conflicts both inside and outside the building. There is a reason for almost every relationship.'

1 *About Entrances*
People are approaching these buildings in a car, walking or in a bus looking for the entrance to the building where the people they wish to see work. They are looking for N.E.D.C., Ministry of Technology, Electricity Council, Home Office, Welsh Office, or the Foreign Office. They have difficulty finding these things.

2 *About Reception and Enquiries*
(1) Two problems combine at the entrance of a building, one is the maintenance of security with the present pass system, the other is the direction of visitors singly or in groups – with or without appointments.
(2) Few entrances are designed that allow the doorkeeper to intercept and control people entering the building. To exercise this control the doorkeeper must be able to see the entrance, be sure that people entering will pass him, and be seen directly by people who enter.

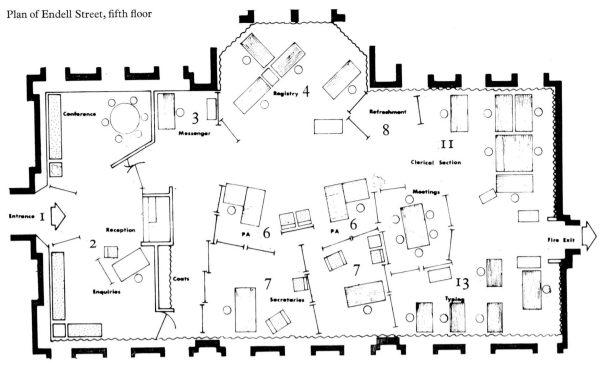

Fig.4

Plan of a mock-up office which was built to educate the client into producing more detailed briefing specifications of his organizational requirements.

(3) Once the intention of the caller has been established further assistance or direction may be necessary. This is the function of enquiries.

(4) Manpower for security checks, which is in short supply at all times, must be supplemented by mechanical means, such as closed circuit television, and code systems.

3 *About the Messenger*

The traditional Messenger is difficult to recruit. All movement of files and paper depend on him. This approach to Office layout uses his services more efficiently by reducing the distance he has to travel and the number of calling points.

4 *About Registries*

The registry and its store of paper is decentralized in order to minimize the delay in providing the papers used. This whole concept is challenged by the developments in micro-filming techniques.

5 *About Services*

(1) The telephone, lighting and power supplies for such organizations need to be evenly distributed over the whole area to minimize the inconvenience. In the nonworking model they were provided as flush floor sockets on a 6' 0" grid.

(2) In this kind of organization there is a need for a constant adaption of the layout.

6 *About the Personal Assistant*

A concentrated waiting space needs to be provided for the personal assistant but must be so arranged that the important function of control can be carried out effectively.

7 *About the Senior Administrator*

The waiting space allowed oral and visual privacy, but makes no attempt to differentiate between the grades of secretary thus challenging status as conceived now. The space occupied by the small conference table was used more effectively elsewhere.

8 *About Refreshments*

Cups of tea or coffee are obtained from a trolley service, a cafeteria, tea clubs, or made individually. Apart from the cafeteria service they are generally drunk at the working position and are taken as a refreshment and break in routine. The tea and coffee is made by individuals or clubs because it is cheaper and it can be timed to suit the staff concerned. The trolley service is officially considered to be the most effective way of providing refreshment but it is used reluctantly and, in addition, manning the trolley imposes a strain on the canteen staff already in short supply.

Some decisions need to be made on the means of providing refreshment in the new buildings. For example: 1. Is provision to be made that allows for the *service* of beverages and in the same building facilities given for individuals to make their own. 2. At present a great deal of time is spent washing up, often in inappropriate conditions. Should consideration be given to the provision of disposable cups? 3. Would vending machines provide an acceptable and economical alternative to any of the present practices? If so, how are they to be located in relationship to the working area?

9 *About Signposting*

The layout demands a reconsideration of signposting inside the building, which as at present relies on small signs attached to doors and walls.

10 *About the Working Position*

A model was evolved from a detailed consideration of the many tasks carried out at the working position.

As will be seen by comparison with the standard furniture, the total provision at the working surface has changed. It included a range of units, which could be combined to suit individual needs, designed to cater for the temporary storage of papers in current use, and the delivery of papers in priority.

11 *About the Clerical Section*

There was a need to consider the individual within large groups of people. There is evidence that on occasions, some means of providing partial separation is necessary, while at the same time allowing supervision.

The desk provides a 'barrier' with acoustic properties.

12 *About Storage*

(1) This layout does not include any storage cupboards. Currently, these are provided 'as required', and are used in a number of ways to store a large assortment of items. Originally designed to replace

allied storage

Fig.5

Work station, standard issue

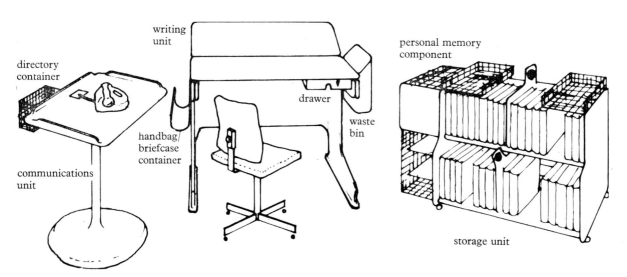

Fig.6

Work station, experimental furniture

the 'stationery store' they were used in conjunction with the stationery store. The reason for this double use, is the supply system of the stationery office, which encourages bulk orders and stock-piling at all levels.

(2) The layout envisages the use of either a regular trolley supply system, or a counter-service for individuals from a central store.

(3) Current stationery is held in the desk and the typist's desk has been designed on this basis.

13 *The Typist*

Is difficult to recruit, and once trained leaves for jobs offering better pay and conditions. All the typing and reproduction of letters and documents depends on them. The amount is increasing. Consideration was given to use of equipment that would increase their output and spread the work load. To this we added that there was need to re-examine the approach and the design of all these items. We wished to point out that adaptation was the key to understanding the real needs of the office worker.

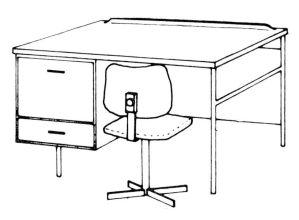

Fig.7
Typing, standard issue

The message that other concepts about many facets of the physical organization were desirable, almost essential and attainable technologically was attained, within the set time-schedule.

This brings us back to an earlier remark concerning the problems facing the architect. The enormity of the change envisaged as a result of our user studies predetermined that it was impossible to put them into effect on a large scale immediately. For instance, parts of our proposal consisted of accommodating groups of people in such a manner that the gross and net usable office areas became much closer than the usual 60% efficiency factor of the cellular plan. Since many thousands of people would be affected by such a proposal it became essential to gain some first hand experience to pass on. It is a very difficult task to take people from a known position to a totally unknown position since their only yardstick for new situations is to match them against previous experience.

Thus we were forced to build an office floor as a test bed brought to a standard of finish that enabled normal experience to progress by being able to carry out day to day tasks. Again this particular project is being published in bulletin form, but it is sufficient to note here that we have been able to accelerate acceptance of new concepts in a remarkably short time. Further we have been able to build something that tests out a known number of hypotheses, a relatively unusual, but nonetheless badly needed, practice in architecture today.

The project sought to establish principles of big room planning as a precedent for further projects. In essence the solution is a complete antithesis of the situation found in cellular offices.

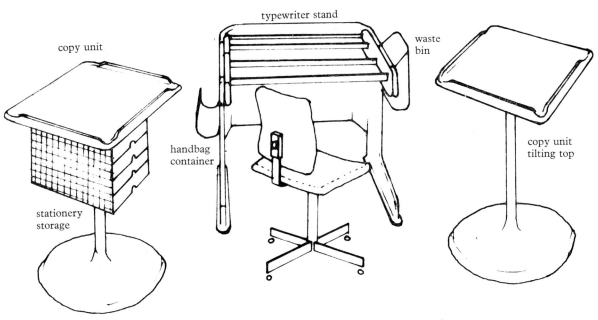

copy unit

typewriter stand

waste bin

handbag container

stationery storage

copy unit tilting top

Fig.8

Typing, experimental furniture

The basic problems of noise and vision were recognized as being of high priority. External noises were reduced by double glazing and the required sound levels to overcome the customary office sounds of talking, telephone, movement of people and furniture, typing, etc. were obtained by the extensive use of absorbants and sound barriers on walls and ceiling, and carpets on the floor. The visual problems are as important, but less is really known about them, other than that people's attention must not be disturbed by undue movement.

Colour and visual appearance however become very real subjects since everything can be *seen* and consequently must relate and be interesting.

The general layout and form of individual working positions was determined by studying the work of the staff grouped in great detail. The design of the furniture was based on the objectives of the worker and the observations of the ways in which they had adapted their current situations.

Fig.9   Furniture for meetings, standard issue

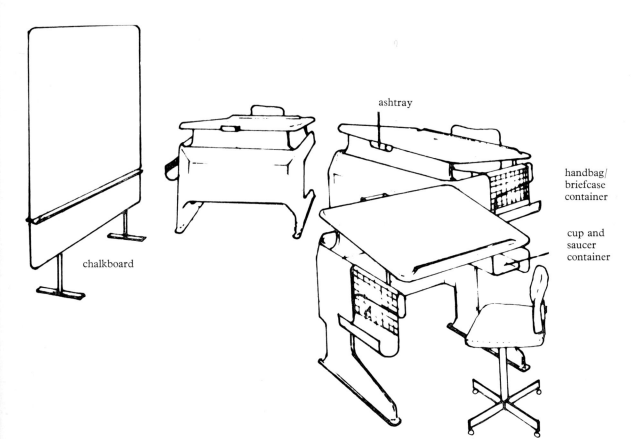

Fig.10   Furniture for meetings, experimental furniture

28

The furniture in Prince Consort House is experimental, and is a step in determining the future forms of Civil Service furniture, concentrating upon the functional aspects and on devising equipment for the working positions, i.e. typing registry units, conference tables, clothes storage, screens and plant containers. Chairs and stationery and security cupboards are adaptions of existing furniture.

Three units – the writing desk, communications unit and storage unit – have been designed to accommodate the principal activities of office staff. Ancillary components can be attached to the main units in positions convenient to those using them.

The writing space measures 850 mm × 710 mm, with a position 305 mm wide that can be tilted to facilitate reading. Both the desk top and chair can be varied in height.

Research indicated that the desk should be designed to discourage the use of working space for storage, and hence the working surface is sufficient to accommodate only the amount of material it was thought could conveniently be dealt with at one time.

The communications unit was designed for telephones, small office machines, note pads, and directories, all of which it was thought should be kept on a separate surface. This unit can be used to extend the writing unit for spreading large documents.

The desk storage unit, which is on castors and measures 850 mm × 445 mm × 710 mm high, is for storing files, which stand endwise, and are inserted from one end in order to remain in correct sequence.

The accommodation has been in use since October 1967. Its operational effectiveness has been continuously checked by the Offices Development Group in association with the Treasury Management Services Division and a report on the final appraisal is scheduled for the end of this year. From initial observations the open type plan seems to offer significant managerial, economic and social advantages.

This appraisal has produced further information for additional research and development work.

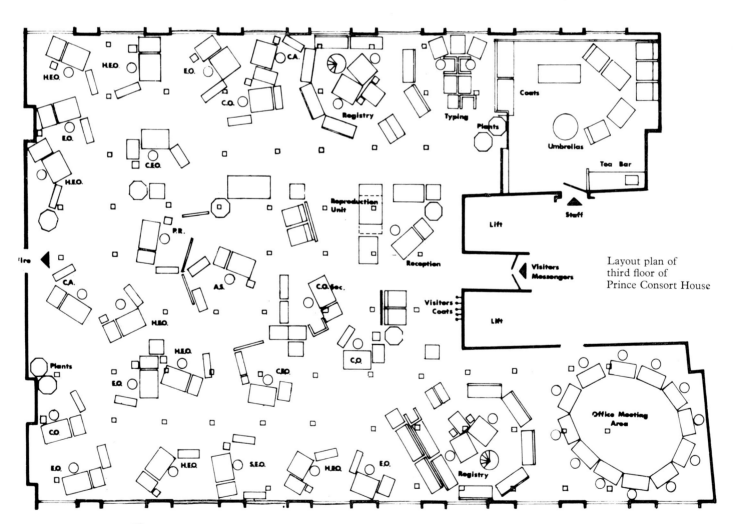

Fig. 11
Plan layout of a working prototype office floor. The furniture developed earlier was used under normal working conditions and feedback from the earlier mock-up, Fig.4, was integrated into the solution for this organization.

29

A final observation. In my view all design methods try to achieve the following situation.

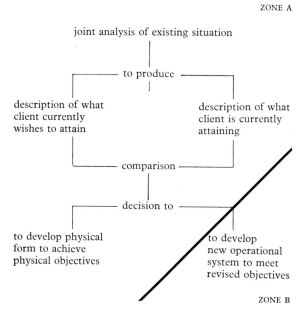

ZONE A

joint analysis of existing situation

to produce

description of what client currently wishes to attain

description of what client is currently attaining

comparison

decision to

to develop physical form to achieve physical objectives

to develop new operational system to meet revised objectives

ZONE B

Fig.16

The point for the architect to consider is whether he wishes to restrict himself to Zone A or whether he wishes to become an active practitioner in Zone B as well? If he does then it will affect the structure of the profession, the fee scale and the services we offer. In addition it will radically alter the curricula of the schools of architecture, their methods of training and examination of student ability.

Third Floor, Prince Consort House; **Fig.12** showing executive areas; **Fig.13** showing the P.A.'s position and secretary; **Fig.14** typing and secretary; **Fig.15** north east corner.

The evolution of environmental structures

by Barry Poyner

My paper has three parts. In the first, I introduce the idea of *Environmental Structure*. I try to show that there is an underlying physical organization or structure in any part of the built environment.

I then outline some of the ideas contained in the paper 'The Atoms of Environmental Structure'.[1] The 'Atoms' paper is the result of my work with Alexander at the Ministry of Public Building and Works in 1966. It describes a theory for deriving the basic pieces of environmental structure. In the paper we call these basic pieces, *Relations*.

The final part of my paper suggests a way of determining strategies for the gradual reorganization or evolution of existing environmental structures. The idea behind these strategies is quite simple: they attempt to determine which new relations should be developed and in what order.

1 Environmental structure

Let us take a simple system in our environment – the motorway. If we look at a motorway, we can see that it has a basic structure or pattern common to all motorways. This structure is a system of physical relationships; a system of physical relationships which prescribes the essential form of any motorway.

What are these physical relationships like? Let me give some examples:

The motorway has two carriageways roughly parallel and set well apart, so that traffic can move in opposite directions with little risk of head-on collision.

Each carriageway is divided into two or more lanes, to allow vehicles to move freely at their own speed.

Gradients are strictly limited.

Only gradual bends are allowed and they are slightly banked to increase vehicle stability.

All other roads cross over or under the motorway.

Access points are limited in number and spaced at intervals of several miles.

The list is far from complete, but I hope it is sufficient to show that the form of the motorway is determined by a number of these physical relationships. A complete list of relationships would define the basic structure of all motorways.

It is this basic structure or pattern which the highway engineer attempts to push through the landscape when he designs a motorway. I believe all designers use such a pattern of physical relationships whenever they design a building, or a group of buildings, or even part of a city.

I call such a pattern of physical relationships an *Environmental Structure*, and I call the physical relationships, which make up an environmental structure, *Relations*.

2 The atoms of environmental structure

The paper 'The Atoms of Environmental Structure' sets out an operational framework for the definition of relations. There is little point in reproducing the paper here, but I would like to outline some of the ideas it contains. I propose to give a very simple example of a relation, and explain it in terms of relational theory.

The relation I will give must be present in a two-car garage, if it is to function properly. The relation is: *A two-car garage must be wide enough to take two cars side by side.* We could say more precisely how wide, but this is not the central part of the relation. The central part of the relation is that the car spaces are to be *side by side* not one in front of the other or at right angles to each other or in any other relation.

Now such a relation must exist for very good reasons. Relational theory gives a very precise reason. In this example of the two-car garage, we must consider two things which people try to do at the same time. They are as follows:

[1] C. ALEXANDER and I. B. POYNER. *The Atoms of Environmental Structure*. R. & D. Paper, Directorate of Development, Ministry of Public Building and Works (London, 1967).

(a) People try to keep their cars under cover.

(b) People try to park their cars so that they can drive them away without having to move any other cars.

If the garage contains the relation, that is, if the two cars can be parked side by side as in Figure 1a, both things which people are trying to do can operate freely. People can park their cars under cover without the risk of having to move another car when they want to get their own car out again. There is no difficulty, the garage functions smoothly. In the 'Atoms' paper, we call the things which people are trying to do, *tendencies*.

Now let us look at a two-car garage which doesn't contain this relation. A garage in which the car spaces are one in front of the other, as in Figure 1b. What happens to the two tendencies now? One of them must give way to the other. If both cars go under cover, it will not be possible to drive one of them away without moving the other. If we must be able to drive away either car without moving the other, then one of the cars has to be left in the open. In this sense the tendencies are in *conflict*. Both tendencies cannot operate freely at the same time. When one tendency operates, it blocks the other.

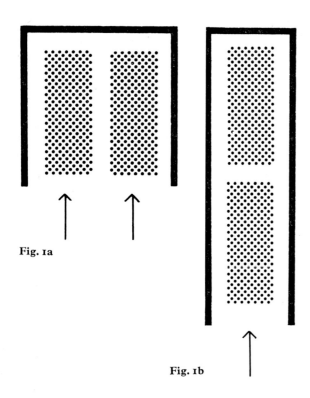

Fig. 1a

Fig. 1b

The idea of conflict is central to the theory. We claim that it is the basis from which any relation is derived. The relation for the two-car garage is well established and widely accepted, and in practice we do not have to justify it. But, if we wish to introduce a new relation, we claim that it can only be justified if the new relation prevents a conflict; a conflict between two or more tendencies.

Why tendencies? Why say 'People *try* to keep their cars under cover?' Why not simply say 'People *need* covered car parking'? Indeed, this is the more usual kind of statement used in design today. We usually talk about needs. What, then, is wrong with the concept of 'need'?

One of the main intentions of this work was to provide a more objective framework for design. We wanted to be able to make scientific statements. Statements which could either be true or false. Statements which could be tested. Statements having the same property as any good scientific hypothesis.

If we accept the traditional concept of need, we have no way of telling if a need is true or false. How can we validate a statement like 'People *need* covered car parking'? It is not good enough simply to ask people if they need it. We may get some interesting answers; but we know that people are notoriously unable to assess their own needs. We may set up a costing exercise to show that the protection given by a garage makes the car last longer, but such an exercise would not prove the need, and in any case there are so many other possibilities. People may want their cars under cover to keep them cleaner, or to make them easier to start in winter. Whatever we try we are in difficulty, because we cannot test a need.

We don't have this difficulty with a tendency. A tendency is a statement of what people are actively trying to do. It is a statement which is either true or false. Either people *are* trying to do it or they *are not*. It is a statement which can be tested. If the statement is true, then we would expect people to do it whenever they get the chance. If we can show that they don't do it when given the chance, then, the statement is false. It must be discarded or at least modified. In this sense a tendency is like any other scientific hypothesis.

How are relations derived from conflicts? The key fact is that tendencies are not inherently in conflict. There are some arrangements of the environment in which tendencies *do* conflict, and other arrangements in which they *do not*. The task in deriving a relation is to examine all the arrangements where the conflicting tendencies occur together, and determine which arrangements *cause* the conflict and which *prevent* it.

This process will define two classes of arrangement. A class of arrangements which cause the conflict and a class of arrangements which prevent it. The two classes are mutually exclusive. We must then abstract the property common to all those arrangements which prevent the conflict, in such a way that it specifically excludes all those arrangements which cause it. This abstracted property is the essential relation which prevents the conflict.

Let me illustrate this with an example taken from the original paper. It is a relation for an office entrance opening directly onto the pavement of a busy street. It prevents a conflict between people going in and out through the entrance doors, and people who hang back in the entrance in bad weather. The relation states that there should be *space immediately inside the entrance, close to the doors and clear of all entry and exit paths, with a direct view of the street.*

Clearly, such a relation includes many different arrangements. Many different entrances will contain this relation. Some may have space both sides of the entrance doors, some may have it on one side only, it might be to the left or to the right as you go in, or it might be placed between two sets of doors.

The relation also excludes many arrangements. For example, it excludes entrances which have no space close to the doors clear of entry and exit paths, and entrances where there is space at the side of the doors, but from which it is impossible to see the street.

Now, let me illustrate the idea of relations further. Figure 2 is taken from 'Relations for an Office Entrance', the second of two examples given in the original 'Atoms' paper. It is not intended as a plan for an office entrance, but it is a diagram which contains all the relations given in the example. In general, the relations deal with the arrangement of the pavement, entrance doors, lifts, and reception desk.

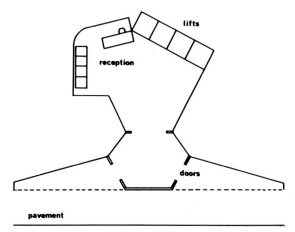

Fig.2

Here are four of the relations contained by the diagram:

(1) *The parts of the building on the ground floor, on each side of the entrance, set back to allow the entrance to project.*
Without this relation the following tendencies conflict:

(a) People tend to approach the entrance along the pavement, at an acute angle.

(b) On a busy pavement, people try to work out their path some distance ahead, to pre-position themselves to take the shortest path through the entrance.

(2) *Covered space between entrance doors and pavement, of which about 100 square feet is not immediately in front of the doors.*
Without this relation the following tendencies conflict:

(a) People stop to collapse their umbrellas before going through entrance doors.

(b) People try to get under cover before collapsing their umbrellas.

(c) People try to find a place to collapse their umbrellas, away from the stream of passers-by on the pavement, and clear of the entrance doors.

(3) *All entrance doors into the lobby grouped together in front of the reception desk, with no obstructions between the doors and reception desk.*
Without this relation the following tendencies conflict:

(a) The receptionist tries to see everyone entering the lobby.

(b) People entering the building, tend to use the door on the shortest path into the lobby.

(4) *The shortest path from outside the entrance doors to the reception desk, not less than 40 feet.*
Without this relation the following tendencies conflict:

(a) Visitors try to move directly, without hesitation, from the entrance doors to the reception desk.

(b) Visitors tend to seek time and space in which to reorient their thoughts, between leaving the busy pavement and arriving at the reception desk.

Each of these relations applies only under certain conditions. They only apply where there is a reception on the ground floor, and where the entrance opens directly onto the street. If the entrance is set back from the street, or there is no reception on the ground floor, then these relations will be redundant.

For this reason the form of every relation statement must be: *If* such and such conditions are present, *then* such and such relation is required. For example, *if* an office entrance opens directly onto a busy street, *then* the parts of the building on the ground floor, on each side of the entrance, must be set back to allow the entrance to project.

3 The evolution of environmental structures

Now, having given this brief outline of relational theory, I want to say something about my present work.

So far, work on relations has been purely speculative. I know of no project that has attempted rigorously to test a relation. Relations have been based, at best, on intelligent observations. There has been no critical experimental work. If such work were to be carried out on the examples of relations given in this paper, I expect most of them would have to be revised, and perhaps some would have to be abandoned altogether.

In future work, relations must be subjected to serious testing. But this will take time and resources. It will, therefore, become essential to decide which relations should be developed and in what order. How can this be done?

Let us look at a practical situation – the office building. If we take a close look at a typical office building, we can see that it has an environmental structure in the same sense as the motorway. For example, the linear type of multi-storey office block has the following relations:

It is strip-like, with windows along the two long sides, so that no office space is more than about 20 feet from a window.

Access to office space is by means of a corridor down the centre, so as not to block out light, and to avoid using well lit space for non-clerical activity.

The access corridor creates two parallel strips of office space, which allow almost infinite sub-division into individual or group offices.

There are two enclosed staircases at opposite ends of the building, to provide alternative means of escape in case of fire.

There is usually only one entrance, which is placed near to one of these staircases, so that the entrance is at one end of the building.

Lifts to all floors are grouped together, to form a bank of lifts, rising from the entrance lobby.

Of course, there is much more to it than that. There are many more relations commonly accepted by designers, even if they are not fully conscious of using them.

If we examine office buildings which contain this structure, do we find that they work perfectly well? They may work fairly well. For example, this linear type of office building is very easy to sub-divide into very small tenancies. However, many *problems* do arise.

Here is a typical problem. Office buildings of this kind are usually designed to be naturally ventilated. But fire regulations specify that the central corridor must be protected and have a half-hour fire resistance. This means that there can be no grills or vents into the corridor. The result is a lack of cross ventilation. As one might expect, if you go to one of these buildings on a warm day you will find people complaining bitterly about the lack of ventilation. You will find strenuous efforts to do something about it. Extract fans are put into windows, often in defiance of a lease. Doors are propped open onto the corridor, and even the self-closing doors to protected staircases are wedged open, much to the concern of the fire brigade.

At the root of any problem like this is one or more conflicts of the kind I described earlier in my paper. If we examine a number of modern office buildings, it is not difficult to find a hundred such problems. Potentially, each of the conflicts behind these problems can yield new relations.

If we want to improve an existing environmental structure we must seek out the problems it contains, define the underlying conflicts behind these problems, and from each conflict derive a new relation. These new relations can then be introduced into the existing structure, which is modified accordingly.

Figure 3 shows, graphically, what this process is like. An existing environmental structure ES is examined, and one or more problems are identified. From these problems new relations are derived and fed back into the structure, to form a new, revised structure ES_1. The process is continually repeated to produce $ES_2 \ldots ES_3 \ldots$ etc.

There will be no end to this process, because the world around us is constantly changing. There will be political, cultural, social, and economic changes. Each change can create new conflicts within a part of the environment and, therefore, new modifications to its structure. The process is one of continual evolution. As a structure evolves it gradually becomes so changed that it will eventually appear to be a quite new structure, just as the modern motorway is so different from its ancestor, the conventional main road. It is because the process is continuous, that I call it the *Evolution of Environmental Structure*.

At present, the great weakness of environmental evolution is that the modifications to structures are random. The selection of problems is not co-ordinated. Designers and research workers tend to pick on problems they think can be answered easily or spectacularly. They also tend to choose problems which lie wholly within their own discipline, like lighting physics, mechanical engineering, or ergonomics.

The effect of such a random approach is clear. It slows up the process of evolution. It diverts effort to

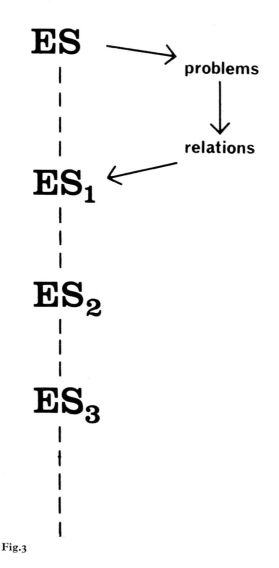

Fig.3

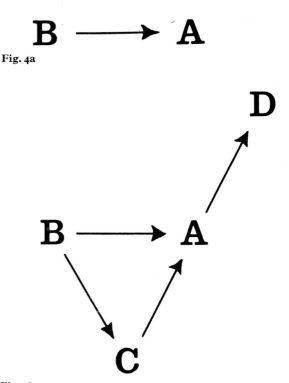

Fig. 4a

Fig. 4b

less fundamental problems. When we look at several problems at once, we find that some problems are more fundamental than others. For example, an investigation into the problem of opening lights fouling venetian blinds is interesting, but relatively trivial. It isn't likely to lead to a fundamental re-organization of the office structure. Indeed, such an investigation would turn out to be unnecessary if we find later that air-conditioning is the only answer to other problems.

My present work is aimed at reducing the random-ness of the evolutionary process. I want to create a mapping of problems so that the process is not random, but moves quickly and directly to the most fundamental problems.

One of the relations given earlier in this paper specifies that 'all entrance doors should be grouped to-gether in front of the reception desk'. This relation de-pends on the condition that the receptionist is in the entrance lobby. The condition is, in fact, another re-lation. If the receptionist is not in the entrance lobby, the first relation is redundant. We can say that the first relation *depends* on the existence of the second.

You will remember the general form of the relation statement. *If* such and such conditions exist, *then* such and such relation is necessary. If a relation A forms part of the conditions for relation B, we can say that relation B depends on relation A. We can write this as in Figure 4a.

It is possible to map out the pattern of dependence for all the relations in an environmental structure. For example, Figure 4b shows that:
B depends on A
A depends on D
C depends on A
B depends on C
etc.

In a similar way it is possible to map out the depend-ence of problems. We can make a statement of a problem in the If . . ., then . . . form. We can say that *if* such and such conditions exist, *then* such and such relation is in question.

For example, a receptionist may complain that she cannot see everyone who comes into the lobby. We can restate the problem in the following way: *If* there is a receptionist in the entrance lobby, *then* the rela-tion between reception desk and entrance doors must be critically examined.

With problem statements like this, we can map out the dependence of a large number of problems in any environmental structure. Figure 5 shows part of such a map taken from my current work. Each arrow indicates the direction of dependence. For example, the map shows that problem 002 should be solved before problem 122, but 122 cannot be satisfactorily solved until 003, 123, and 001 have been dealt with.

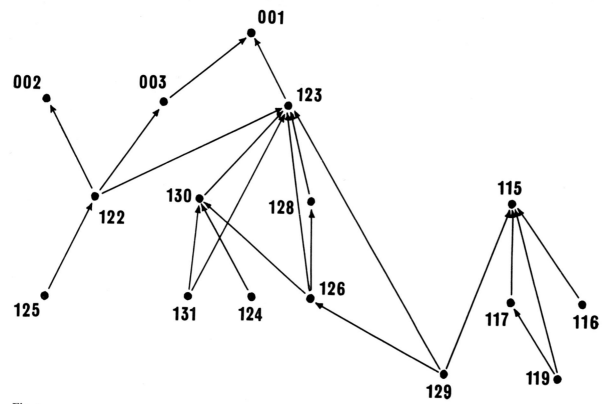

Fig. 5

How can we use this map? Firstly, we can see that problems 002, 001 and 115 are *independent problems*. They can be solved efficiently without reference to any of the other problems. Secondly, we can see that some problems are *key problems* – they open the way to many other problems. Problem 123 is a key problem. Eight of the sixteen problems shown on the map depend on it. A good strategy here, would be to solve problem 001 first, and then problem 123. This would open the way to solving all those problems in the centre of the map.

Figure 5 seems too good to be true. It is so simple. I am sure that when we make a map for many times the number of problems, many difficulties will arise. However, I hope that by using maps of this kind it will be possible to determine which relations to examine, and in what order. In this way, I believe that the evolution of environmental structures can progress more quickly and more efficiently than it does at present.

Design from linked requirements in a housing problem

by Keith Hanson

The following project was undertaken by myself and a fellow student, Stephen Brown, during the third year course at Cambridge University School of Architecture. The whole study was under the direct influence of Christopher Alexander's book *Notes on the Synthesis of Form* which had been published in this country for about a year at the time.

We can only grasp design problems fragmentedly. That is, there are practical limits to the number of notions that can be thought of simultaneously when trying to solve complex problems. The way that we overcome this inherent difficulty is to break a complex situation down into smaller parts, dealing with these parts separately, and then bringing these new ideas together to understand the situation. The ideas expressed by Alexander in 'Notes' were nearly all dealing with the way we break down large design problems to be able to cope with them and then build these smaller parts up again to get a final solution.

When the problems of the physical environment are broken down into concepts like 'services', 'heating', 'community', 'structure', 'safety', etc. and ideas about how these needs or properties are best dealt with are formed, it is highly probable that any particular way in which they function together will be forgotten. This breakdown of usefully interrelated thought, (which, of course, is not encountered in small problems or by particularly gifted designers), suggests that some other way of finding the component parts of the environment may be useful, and preferably parts that are dependent on as many of the physical properties of the environment as are necessary.

Except in very rare circumstances we do not design a new object to satisfy environmental needs from scratch. In the case of a house, library, town or piece of furniture, for example, we have the knowledge of what is happening in the use of these objects or complexes at the moment. The concept of the failure of a specific piece of the environment to work with the rest of the environment is well known. A simple case involves doors with pull handles which can only be opened by pushing. A more serious example is

when a window which must be opened to achieve adequate room ventilation overlooks a noisy street. Both of these examples illustrate functional connections between different parts of the environment, in the first case between door handles and door hinges or stops, and in the second between ventilation and noise sources. Both are situations which are outside the range of normal human adaptation, but in the second case there is *no simple way at all* for both parts to be compatible. (This assumes the principle of 'structural economy', that is, if a change in the geometric relationships between existing elements can give an additional desirable property then this is better than adding a new element. In the example of ventilation and noise it is perfectly possible to introduce a long acoustically absorbent ventilation duct, but clearly the problem is one of separating rooms that need quiet and heavily trafficked roads.) Buildings close to noisy streets cannot be ventilated by opening windows without also letting in disturbing noise. The way in which the physical environment fails at the moment is taken as the pointer to a basic requirement.

A requirement is a situation that must be present otherwise an observable human or social need would go unsatisfied. Most requirements are dependent in their solutions on other requirements. Any two requirements that would either help or hinder one another in solution therefore interact and need to be thought of together if a satisfactory solution is to be found for both. For example the requirements that visitors need to be able to park near their destination and residents need to be able to control the noise that enters their dwelling will not both be fulfilled by simple organisation if thought of in isolation, as in the standard suburban street, where next door's visitors awaken a neighbour by car doors or engine noise outside a bedroom wall.

A collection of requirements and interactions (or 'links') in pairs of this form have inherent in them a structure, which if understood makes it very much more probable that a solution will be found. The problem of finding this inherent structure in a set of pair-linked requirements is purely mathematical once it is accepted that any requirement is a requirement and that any link is a link. That is, there either is a requirement or there is not, and similarly for links (i.e. either it would be useful to think of the two requirements together or it would not). This seems to be a concept that is hard to accept, but after spending a large amount of time trying to find what is *actually* a requirement it is pointless then to go on and say it is less important or more important than others, and again similarly with links.

There are several beautiful analogies to the mathematics for finding the inherent structure of a requirement/link graph, but diagrams explain better what the resulting structure is like. Requirements are thought of as points and links as lines between them. The mathematical technique finds those groups of points that are most interlinked with one another, whilst being least linked to points outside the group. That this process can only be handled by electronic computer when there are more than say a score of requirements becomes clear if one attempts to do a similar process graphically.

Once these groups of heavily interlinked requirements have been found we have the necessary size of problem, without it being limited to a single recognisable conceptual classification. It should be possible therefore to design a schematic solution to this group of requirements. A diagram is the most useful description of the solution and memory aid at this stage. When all groups of requirements have been solved conceptually they can then be combined together, according to the groups that are most interlinked and a new, higher, set of schematic diagrams formed, involving the principles of the groups that have already been resolved. And so on until either one final organisational diagram is produced or a small set of completely disjoint diagrams. This diagram or these diagrams are then used as the basic organisation of a concrete scheme.

The method involves finding a set of requirements and their natural links, which together define an abstract structure, analysing the set, that is finding the abstract structure, and synthesising diagrams, which is to build on the abstract structure.

Use in the Housing Project
The particular project on which the method was used was a medium high density housing scheme, for families and some research students, of 120 dwellings on a 4 acre site, bounded on two sides by roads, to be carried out in three phases; the site was some way from Cambridge city centre. The time available for the whole scheme was just over a term (about 3 months). The first problem was to find what part of the total environmental organisation we were going to work on as thoroughly as possible. The particular part that interested us most at the time was the problem of site organisation, or anything that was mainly concerned with the boundary between an individual dwelling and the rest of the site. We were not concerned in the method study with the layout of the spaces or rooms within an individual dwelling, or with any particular type of construction.

Deciding what was a basic requirement for this particular housing scheme was the most searching task. The first attempts at writing down possible 'human or social needs that would otherwise go unsatisfied' were unbelievably naïve (copying some of Alexander's Indian village requirements like 'drinking water to be pure and fresh') until it was realised that we were putting down requirements that would certainly be satisfied in this situation by building regulations or just normal design procedures. Thus all the requirements that we would have to write would be extracted from situations that we had observed to be going wrong on existing housing 'estates' of a similar kind, and within the existing socio-economic context.

By observation of housing, looking back through slides, our own experience, reading and discussion, in that order, we arrived at the following list of requirements:

1 People should be able to dispose of refuse without having to store it in their dwelling and without having to leave their dwelling.
2 Refuse which is capable of being disposed directly into a soil system should not have to be collected.
3 All stored refuse should have barriers to prevent germs and smells polluting the surrounding air.
4 Refuse for collection should be stored in such a way as to facilitate ease of transfer to a disposal unit.
5 For a heating system to be efficient there should be minimum heat loss from the dwelling.
6 For a ventilation system to be efficient there should be provision for a through flow of air in the dwelling.
7 All dwellings should have some sunlight in day living areas.
8 The people in each dwelling should have access to a sunlit space which is visually private.
9 People should be able to leave a baby in a pram in the open air where they know it will be safe.
10 Delivery men need well defined routes for delivery which do not involve unnecessary retracing of steps.
11 Delivery men should be able to leave their deliveries in a secure place, those in receipt of goods should feel that their goods are secure.
12 People should be able to collect deliveries (milk, bread, etc.) protected from the weather.
13 Visitors should be able to park their cars near their destination.
14 Visitors should be able to find an address they want easily.
15 A parked car should be able to move off the site without the necessity of moving other vehicles or interfering with the flow of traffic.
16 Pedestrians should feel that they are entirely safe from traffic.
17 People should feel that their car is part of their possessions and that their parking space is their own.

18 Each person should be able to maintain (e.g. wash) his car without causing annoyance to other people.

19 Children need supervision when away from the dwelling.

20 Children should be discouraged from playing in places where they might come to harm (near refuse, etc.).

21 Children should be discouraged from playing in places where they might cause a nuisance (access ways, etc.).

22 People should feel secure against intruders into their dwellings.

23 People should not be able to see directly into any other dwellings.

24 People need an arrival point to their dwelling which is protected from the weather.

25 People should have off site noise reduced to a minimum level below that of discomfort.

26 People should be able to control the noise that enters their dwelling.

27 People should be able to control the noise between spaces within their dwelling.

28 People should be able to stop too much dirt coming into their dwelling.

29 People should be able to get large objects (pianos, prams, etc.) in and out of their dwelling easily.

30 People should feel that their dwelling is not forcing them into a state of loneliness or isolation.

31 People need the opportunity to meet their neighbours without feeling committed to their company.

32 People should feel that their dwelling is uniquely identifiable as their own.

33 People should be able to get to the shops and the city centre easily.

34 People should be able to get to a point of safety from any part of the site without having to go through any part which might be on fire.

35 There should be a control on the spread of fire should it arise on any part of the site.

36 Water for fire fighting should be available so that a hose can reach any part of the site should a fire break out there.

37 People should not have to climb more than three flights of stairs to reach their dwelling.

38 People of any one social group should not feel that they are in any way differentiated from any other social group (e.g. research students).

39 Children and animals should be prevented from interfering with or scattering refuse.

40 Each family needs a storage space related to its dwelling for bicycles, canoes, etc.

41 People should not be inconvenienced by the noise and dirt of subsequent building operations after they have taken up residence in their dwelling.

42 Invalids should be able to reach their dwelling without physical help from anyone else.

43 People should be able to bring large objects (prams, pianos, etc.) to their dwelling.

44 Service maintenance men should not have to enter dwellings to carry out their work unless absolutely necessary (i.e. to read meters, etc.).

The requirements above are only numbered for later reference; they are in no particular order. Some are straightforward physical failures like visual privacy in outdoor spaces, some are physical failures that lead to communal breakdown and some are physical failures to give the right feelings within the community, and all are concerned with site organisation (except 27 which was subsequently omitted) and all pointed to some specific kind of organisation that must be present. Requirement writing took about 3 weeks once we had decided what kind we wanted.

The definition of interactions between any pair of requirements was by discussion between the two of us, or, rather, heated argument. It was often possible to find a distant isolated case where the possible solutions to two requirements might conceivably affect one another. We had to rule out far fetched ideas. Deciding upon interactions took about a week. The diagram shows pairs of requirements that we considered interacted. The numbers refer to the requirement numbers and a blob on the matrix to an interaction. So, '14, visitors should be able to find an address they want easily' interacts with '32, people should feel that their dwelling is uniquely identifiable as their own' since both deal with the distinction between dwellings, the size of groupings of

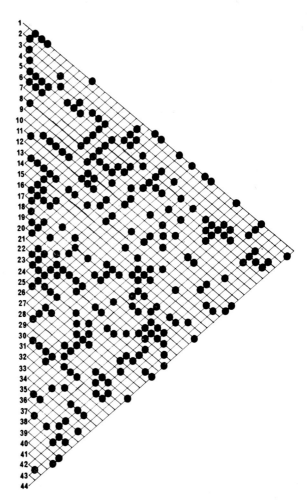

interaction matrix

dwellings and how far apart they are; and does not interact at all with '9, people should be able to leave a baby in a pram in the open air where they know it will be safe' which needs a small private space adjacent to and overlooked by each dwelling.

A computer program was then needed to break up the whole set of linked requirements into relatively disjoint subsets. It was at first thought that the programs written in America would be able to work easily in England. Such is the state of the computer world, however, that after several attempts, with letters back and forth across the Atlantic following each one, it was decided it would be quicker to write a new (and, incidentally, far less efficient) program from scratch than sort out the differences between the two computer installations.

The first problem is to find a measure of just how 'good' any particular groupings of requirements are in terms of most links inside groups and least links between groups. This measure can then be used to compare any divisions of the whole set until the best one is found. The mathematics to derive such a measure is complex and demands that all requirements have an equal probability of solution, but also shows that it makes no difference in terms of the probability of finding a total solution whether links are positive (i.e. the two requirements help one another in solution) or negative (i.e. they hinder one another). The complete mathematical derivation of this measure is given in the appendix in 'Notes' but only the result is needed. The measure for any given division into subsets is a formula $((bx - ay)/ /(y(b - y)))$ dependent on two constants (the total number of links, a and the number of spaces to which links might be assigned, b.) and two variables for the division (the number of links between requirements in different groups in the division, x, and the number of possible links there could be between requirements in different groups, y.)

In theory, then, it is known when the best division into groups of the whole set has been found. But in practice the problem of calculating this measure for all possible groupings is insurmountable. Even a small set of requirements has an astronomical number of possible groupings. In the case of 50 requirements, for example, there are 2^{50} or about 1,000,000,000,000,000 different groupings possible. This problem is overcome by a 'hill climbing' procedure. In this particular case the procedure used was to compare all possible groupings of just two requirements together with all the rest left as groups of just a single requirement. When the best pair had been found it was called a single unit and then the best pair again found of this new set. And so on until no further combination of a pair of units (i.e. either a group of requirements or a single requirement) produces a better division into groups. In this way the groups of heavily interlinked requirements were 'built up' from the set of single requirements.

We wrote a programme for the 'Titan' computer in Cambridge to perform all these operations and from the matrix of links it gave the following groups. Again the numbers are the numbers of requirements.

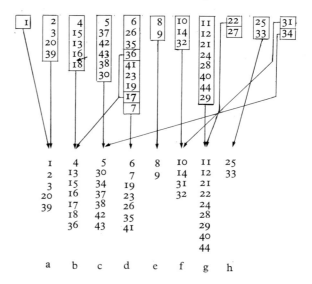

The 11 groups that the computer found were not treated as absolute. A group of one or two requirements is not very useful, especially if it had a considerable number of links in the first place. One of the reasons why the single and pair groups was produced was the particular process of computing and the fact that we only tried the process once, due to time and cost. In 'real life' hill-climbing programmes it is necessary to repeat the procedure a number of times (with, say, the requirements in a different order) since in the initial stages of the process any pair is as good as any other. The more sophisticated programmes have in practice, however, been found to give essentially similar results for even low number of tries.

So there was no reason why the small groups should not be dealt with in the best way that we could think of at the time, but now with a great deal more knowledge about which part of the problem they were most likely to fit with. These changes, with one requirement rejected, brought the number of groups down to eight, most of which were dealing with a recognisable scale of problem. The final groups are shown in the diagram.

A schematic diagram for each of the groups was then produced as the result of further discussion of what we originally intended by the requirements. It was also possible to state the basic idea behind each diagram, which necessarily left out the details.

A fixed enclosed space for collectable refuse from more than one dwelling

Group A

1 People should be able to dispose of refuse without having to store it in their dwelling and without having to leave their dwelling.

2 Refuse which is capable of being disposed directly into a soil system should not have to be collected.

3 All stored refuse should have barriers to prevent germs and smells polluting the surrounding air.

20 Children should be discouraged from playing in places where they might come to harm (near refuse, etc.).

39 Children and animals should be prevented from interfering with or scattering refuse.

3, 20 and 39 call for a fixed enclosed space for refuse (but accessible for collection), 1 calls for a direct connection between each dwelling and this space, and 2 limits this to refuse that will not go down a sink disposal unit, allowing several dwellings to be connected to the same space because of the decreased load.

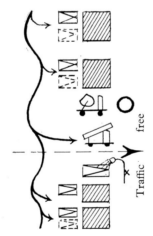

A one to one relationship car to dwelling with emergency vehicle access to an identifiable traffic free area.

Group B

4 Refuse for collection should be stored in such a way so as to facilitate ease of transfer to a disposal unit.

13 Visitors should be able to park their cars near their destination.

15 A parked car should be able to move off the site without the necessity of moving other vehicles or interfering with the flow of traffic.

16 Pedestrians should feel that they are entirely safe from traffic.

17 People should feel that their car is part of their possessions and that their parking space is their own.

18 Each person should be able to maintain (e.g. wash) his car without causing annoyance to other people.

36 Water for fire fighting should be available so that a hose can reach any part of the site should a fire break out there.

16 shows the need for an identifiable traffic free area which gives pedestrian access to the dwellings, whereas 13 and 17 call for vehicular access to the dwelling; this is resolved by a road on one side of the dwelling only with speed controlled traffic. 4, 18 and 36 call for a space where cars are not usually parked but may be brought for washing etc., and where dust carts and fire engines may stop. These spaces provide convenient points for pedestrians to cross into traffic free area, and provide an emergency vehicular access. 15 calls for any parking to be off a through road.

Group C

5 For a heating system to be efficient there should be a minimum heat loss from the dwelling.

30 People should feel that their dwelling is not forcing them into a state of loneliness or isolation.

34 People should be able to get to a point of safety from any part of the site without having to go through any part which might be on fire.

37 People should not have to climb more than three flights of stairs to reach their dwelling.

38 People of any one social group should not feel that they are in any way differentiated from any other social group (e.g. research students).

42 Invalids should be able to reach their dwellings without physical help from anyone else.

43 People should be able to bring large objects (prams, pianos, etc.) to their dwellings.

We were unable to evolve a schematic diagram for group C. The requirements have a large dissimilarity of scale, some dealing with details and others with vague concepts which we could not start to understand. This meant that a great deal more thought was necessary about the requirements themselves, which was not possible within the given time.

Group D

6 For a ventilation system to be efficient there should be provision for a through flow of air in the dwelling.

7 All dwellings should have some sunlight in day living areas.

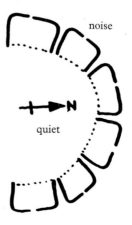

Two 'sides' to dwellings with no overlooking on the 'open' side.

19 Children need supervision when away from the dwelling.

23 People should not be able to see directly into any dwellings.

26 People should be able to control the noise that enters their dwelling.

35 There should be a control on the spread of fire should it arise on any part of the site.

41 People should not be inconvenienced by the noise and dirt of subsequent building operations after they have taken up residence in their dwelling.

As far as possible noise can be limited to one side of a dwelling, and sunlight and fresh air to the other, giving a noise barrier on one side, the closed side, for 26 and 41, and an 'open' side on the other for 7. This organisation needs to be adapted to accommodate 6 and 19 allowing for through ventilation and for watching over children; so there must be at least one window and vent on the 'closed' side. 26 and 35 show that dwellings should be separated by a noise and fire barrier. The scarcity on windows on the 'closed' side of the dwelling prevents overlooking in one direction and relative positioning in the other satisfying 23.

A safe private space in the open air to each dwelling.

Group E

8 The people in each dwelling should have access to a sunlit space which is visually private.

9 People should be able to leave a baby in a pram in the open air where they know it will be safe.

Identifiable groups of dwellings

Group F

10 Delivery men need well defined routes for delivery which do not involve unnecessary retracing of steps.

14 Visitors should be able to find an address they want easily.

31 People need the opportunity to meet their neighbours without feeling committed to their company.

32 People should feel that their dwelling is uniquely identifiable as their own.

32 requires a hierarchy such that the individual dwellings belong to a group and the groups belong to a set of groups and so on, each class of this hierarchy being recognisable. 10 and 14 clearly fit this system. The structure must have 'nodes' or corners suitable for the resolution of 31.

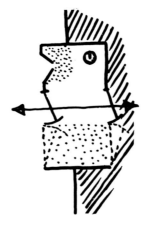

An entry 'lock' to each dwelling.

Group G

11 Delivery men should be able to leave their deliveries in a secure place, those in receipt of goods should feel that their goods are secure.

12 People should be able to collect deliveries (milk, bread etc.) protected from the weather.

21 Children should be discouraged from playing in places where they might cause a nuisance (access ways, etc.).

22 People should feel secure against intruders into their dwellings.

24 People need an arrival point to their dwelling which is protected from the weather.

28 People should be able to stop too much dirt coming into their dwelling.

29 People should be able to get large objects (prams, pianos, etc.) in and out of their dwelling easily.

40 Each family needs a storage space related to its dwelling for bicycles, etc.)

44 Service maintenance men should not have to enter dwellings to carry out their work unless absolutely necessary (i.e. to read meters, etc.)

All requirements (21 excepted) show the need for a zone between the interior and the exterior of the dwelling for weather protection, security of deliveries, stopping dirt, storage, meters, etc. This zone must be lockable for 22 and divided into subspaces for fairly long term storage, a delivery valve, and a larger space for prams and things in common use, which can easily be cleared to bring in a piano, for example. 21 appears to be insoluble in any circumstances.

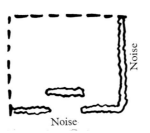

A barrier to off-site noise as complete as possible.

Group H

25 People should have off site noise reduced to a minimum level below that of discomfort.

33 People should be able to get to shops and the city centre easily.

The diagram shows a way for a pedestrian exit, where there may, for example, be a bus stop, whilst maintaining sound insulation as far as possible.

After resolutions to the separate groups had been considered they were then brought together to get one final diagrammatic resolution to the requirements. In this project it was thought unnecessary to combine the groups in stages since there were now only seven separate ideas to be considered in the final layout. This diagram was made considering the actual site that would have to accommodate the scheme; existing roads, noise sources, phasing etc. (as was group H above).

The final diagram, with the remembered details from the other diagrams was then used as a basis for designing housing for the given site. The site plans for the two different schemes are shown on page 44 (the site is about 400′ square).

It is fair to say that by going through the method, even with the short time we gave to each part, we learned more about what we wanted to do in housing than we would have done otherwise. We could not expect to resolve all the difficulties (e.g. the problems of group C, which were fundamental (to us) and not simply graphical) in the time, and would not in any case expect to get an 'ideal' solution to housing. It is, however, certain that the final site plans of the schemes closely resemble the diagram (although they did *not* have quite all the properties we would have liked them to have) because we went through the method before considering house plans.

For housing, given a similar problem, I would not go all through the process again. We learned enough about our own ideas to know what we wanted to do and what we would need to study in a future scheme. In the context of a new problem I am convinced that the approach of breaking the problem down to individual requirements and then building up again to a total solution is a necessary self-disciplining procedure.

Phase 1   Phase 2   Phase 3

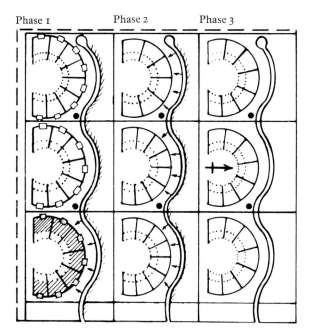

Final Diagram

The Value of the Method in Retrospect

The description of how we used the method deliberately passed quickly from the set of diagrams to the final diagram to the site plan, but these two steps took by no means the same amount of time. The final diagram came almost automatically from the separate diagrams, but the site plan came only after going all the way through from house plans, details, sections etc; in fact all the normal design procedures. The big difference was that we knew what each house had to do in relation to the site and other houses which gave sufficient limitations to make this task very much easier, and as we did not set out to organise individual house types this was expected to take a reasonable time.

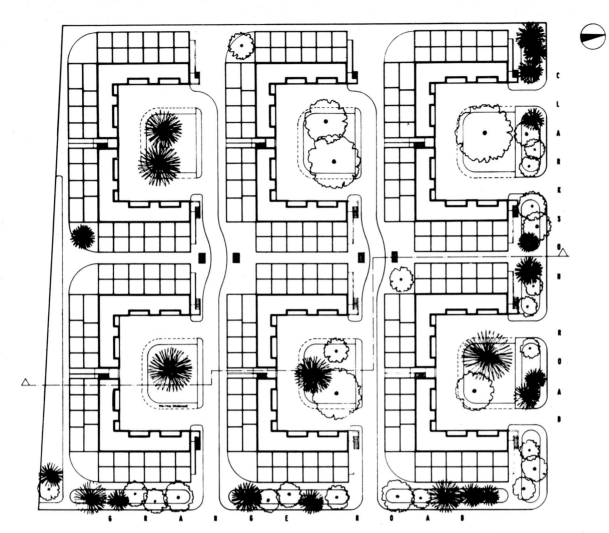

First site plan

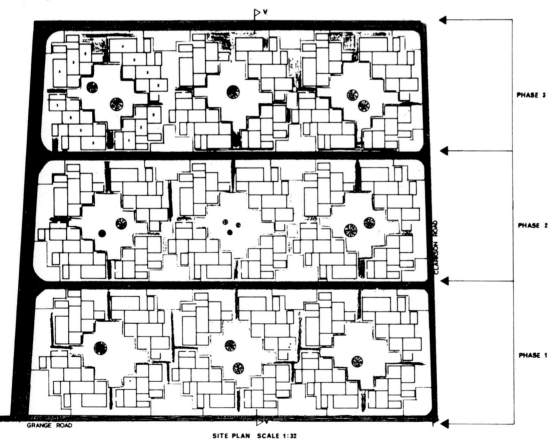

Second site plan

A geometrical method of systematic design in architecture

by G. Guerra

1 Summary of previous papers

In other papers[1] of a more philosophical than technical nature the author has studied:

(i) A doctrine of Architectural Theory (AT), as a control intended to ensure that architectural forms and types of construction can be defined empirically without losing any aspect of the objective reality *and* with enough precision to allow the comparison of the definitions themselves with the ideal types within which Engineering Sciences (ES) operate. Hence a series of correspondences has been defined, which shall be called (AT–ES).

(ii) A special systematics, which has been called Edilistics (Ed) including systemized Architectural Theory and associated aspects of Technical Sciences: from Engineering Sciences (ES) to Econometry, and to Ergonomy, etc. By this means a series of correspondences has been defined which shall be called (Ed–ES).

(iii) A complete and general correspondence between Edilistics and Systematic Design (Ed–SD). Since it has been shown that the logic system of (Ed) substantially is a geometric construction, it has been possible to show that this correspondence (Ed–ES) is reciprocal.

It is, in fact, the reciprocity which forms the philosophical basis of the method proposed in this paper.

2 Dual nature of the 'system' of Systematic Design

The objection is raised to every 'Systematic Design' of a scientific character that it does not take into account the 'human' or 'personal' factors which are always present in the creative process. The statement as to the formal identity (Ed–ES), together

with the correspondences (Ed–ES), seems to give, at first sight, substantial weight to this objection. Apparently it takes into account only one of the three vertices of the creative triangle:

Art
(Creative Instinct)

Craftsmanship   *Technical Sciences*
(ability or know-how)

At the same time, however, the above quoted duality (Ed–SD) is an identity of structure and not of function: in that (Ed) is a *System-structure* and (SD) is a *Mechanism-structure*: of a sort therefore to transform the *project data* into the *finished project*. Into this mechanism, Art and Craftsmanship can be inserted, the first as a short-cut within the creative process, the second as a complex of information to be inserted in the *control system*.

In fact, Systematic Design is defined not only by the *System-structure* which it has in common with Edilistics but also a *Procedural-structure* (which is really the way in which the *Mechanism-structure* is used).

The study of the *Procedural-structure* has always been the aim of every methodology (including empirical ones), while the study of the *System-structure* is implicit in every theory of architecture. What has remained obscure, until the most recent

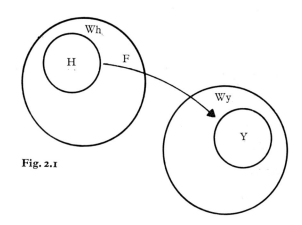

Fig. 2.1

[1] 'Considerations on the art of designing '(1958).
'Abstraction procedures of technical sciences and the interpretation of Architecture' (1965).
'Structuralistics and Theory of Architecture' (1967).

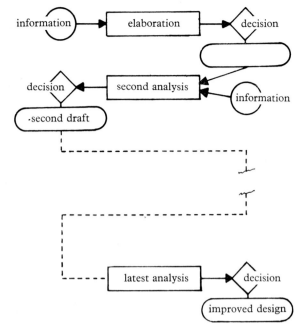

Fig. 2.2a

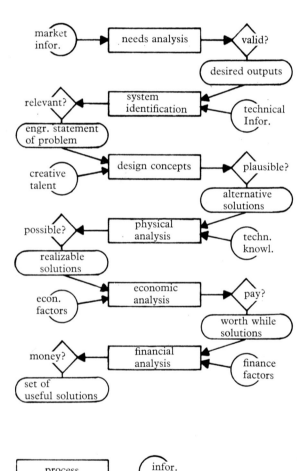

preliminary design, from Asimow

Fig. 2.2b

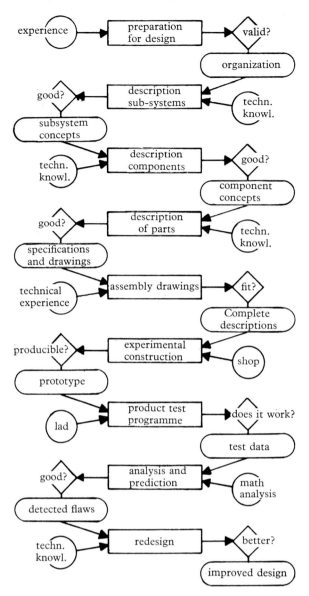

detailed design, from Asimow

Fig. 2.2c

research, is the nature of the relationship between procedure and system. The structure of procedure (which is that of the function F in Fig. 2.1b) has been expressed in cybernetic form or as flow-graph, by Asimow (Fig. 2.2a, b, c).

This representation, however, seems artificial when we compare it with the other, more classical, approach (Fig. 2.3): this shows certain essential distinctions which are ignored by the flow-chart, such as different sources of the information, and that of the necessary disciplines by which they are related. We now see that two completely different kinds of criteria are necessary in the structure of the procedure, criteria which for the sake of simplicity we have shown in two separate tables: (Fig. 2.2, 2.3) (these however make up a single scheme). But the structure of the procedure must be developed in the ambit of the *System-structure* so that every decision or choice (that is to say, each of the steps represented by a decision box in the flow-chart and by a tree in

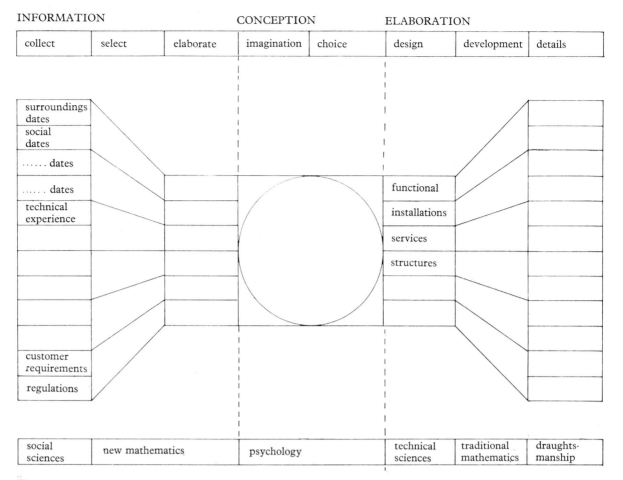

INFORMATION			CONCEPTION		ELABORATION		
collect	select	elaborate	imagination	choice	design	development	details

social sciences	new mathematics	psychology	technical sciences	traditional mathematics	draughts-manship

Fig. 2.3

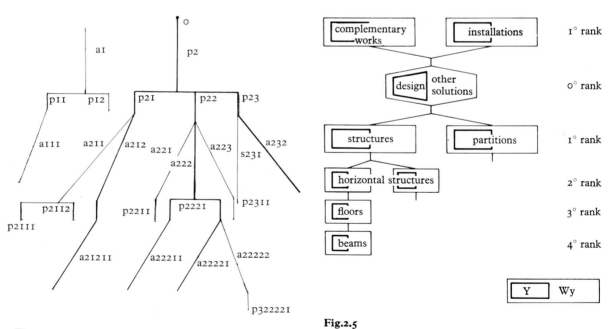

Fig.2.4

o: point of problem formulation
— solution accepted
— solution rejected
a: proposed solution, an alternative
p: a sub problem arising from any alternative
Note the sequence of the decimal indexes of a and p (from Marples)

Fig.2.5

Fig.2.4) must be repeated at every level of the *Structure-system*, Fig.2.5.[2]

For this reason, we shall differentiate between *Procedure-structure* and *System-structure*, in the following pages, as we describe the salient points of a new methodology of building design.

3 First description of the method

In the course of his work the designer receives a great deal of information from his client, from authorities, and from his own knowledge of the subject. Such information can be put together in well characterized sets, in such a way that each element can belong to only one such set. These sets, in a first approximation, are as follows:

(a)   *Technical standards.*

(1b)   *Data* reflecting the requirements of the client.

(2b)   *Environmental characteristics*, i.e. ecological and infrastructural factors.

(3b)   *Requirements* which the building must satisfy (e.g. allowable thermal range).

Such standards can arise from scientific, techno-logical, economic, or aesthetic motives (using the word 'aesthetic' in a sense which we shall clarify later), or they can be *imposed*, more or less correctly, by the relevant authorities.

If we exclude this last case (which has no place in an academic study and which serves only to simplify the procedure and render it less rational) we can proceed to a coherent classification of the data inherent in the science and art of building.

A general classification, which is valid for every type of building, was presented by the author in 1958, in a long monograph to which the research referred.[3] We shall present a simplified scheme later, sufficient for the design of an ordinary multi-floor building. In order to draw up that scheme (which we shall later propose as the fundamental instrument of design activity) we must follow certain procedures in part common to the methods proposed by Christopher Jones[4] and by Christopher Alexander[5] even if the philosophy on which my method is based turns it into a completely different and, I hope, simpler instrument.

While the technical standards, for intrinsic order within each work of architecture, must be capable of presentation in the compact and/or orderly form to which we have referred, the same cannot be said *a priori* for *data* provided by the client, for the *requirements* of quality, and for the environmental *characteristics*. The Design Method proposed will be able, in my opinion, to be used in any case: however, its practicality and elegance will be revealed when it

can make use of a suitable classification of data, characteristics, and requirements. We shall define later the various phases of the method and we shall compare them with those of the well-known design methods referred to above.

4 Bases for elaboration of a matrix of the various standards

The first operation, if a proper matrix of standards is not yet ready ('proper' means containing solutions fit to satisfy data, characteristics, and requirements), is to make a *rough* (that is to say not classified) *list* of all the characteristics which the building should possess. I note incidentally that this list, if drawn up by a master hand, can be of itself an efficacious and conclusive instrument of design. In a previous paper I have described two such lists from the many examples in the history of architecture; one from Brunelleschi[6] and another more recent, in which Torroja justifies one of his famous projects.[7] But normally we shall have to substitute – for the sovereign order existing in the mind of the architect of genius (and which is the secret of his creativity) – another, artificial order, laid out on a piece of paper. Just as in the mind of the fine artist it is the profound sense of building which generates the 'creative order', so the natural constraints to which building must conform allow us to realize this.

The criterion to which I have referred, in my first study on Systematic Design, is the classical distinction between Utilitas (U), Firmitas (F), and Venustas (V). With regard to the last, the progress achieved after some years study in the field of Systematic Design, and in particular the emergence of Environmental Design, have brought me recently to reflect on the possibility of formulating an aesthetic theory to which I shall refer later; here we divide the *rough list* into two: constructional standards and functional standards. It has been shown[8] that, contrary to the usage established in most schools of architecture, especially those in Italy, it is convenient to use the constructional necessities as the basis of the classification system.

The predominance of constructional over functional factors has been obvious to every designer, from the beginning of the art of building until halfway through

---

[2] It is clear also that we should search for the techniques of any *procedure* within the ambit of the mathematical theories, such as Dynamical Programming (DP). The fact that decisions with several variables deal with vectors is a further confirmation that the logic of Edilistics is a branch of Geometry.

[3] 'Considerations on the art of designing' (1958).

[4] J. C. JONES. A method of Systematic Design (1962).

[5] C. A. ALEXANDER. Notes on the synthesis of form (1964).

[6] cf. VASARI. *Vite dei più famosi . . .*

[7] See: *Razon y ser de los tipos estructurales.*

[8] *Abstraction procedures of technical sciences and the interpretation of engineering sciences and the theory of systematic design* (1965).

the nineteenth century: the technical capacities of the human species evolved over thousands of years which rendered them difficult to satisfy, and more recently (when man was no longer tied to the need for choosing only the solutions already guaranteed by his experience) by the stylistic persistence of architectural forms elaborated during centuries of laborious effort.

The explosion of the new technologies on the one hand, and the elaboration of the theory of structures with the consequent transformation of the schools of engineering on the other, the birth of completely new aesthetic approaches and the consequent transformation of the schools of architecture, have brought us to repudiate absolutely (and all excesses are unhealthy) the idea that works of architecture should be classified by constructional types: and this led to the research for a new rationalism based initially on functional criteria. This attempt, over several decades, has not led to any significant result in the field of systematics: on the contrary, problems posed in purely functional terms have shown themselves to be almost always unsolvable. But taking into account all the possibilities of a technology in continual evolution and the self-classifying nature of the mechanical bases of most of the modern constructional systems (which can help, if suitably used to interpret the traditional solutions), attempts to return to a constructional classification have proved particularly fruitful.[9] And what is more, the work of integrating the functional needs in a constructional classification has proved easy (and without ambiguities).

The basic reason for this is that functional needs are usually expressed by topological relationships (which can be represented by ordinary graphs) while constructional needs, and especially static needs, require quantitative representation (they can be indicated, to a maximum of abstraction, by flow-graphs) and hence are by their nature nearer to traditional graphic representations of architecture.

A constructional classification takes the same natural shape as the formal description of the building, and can also be built up by successive approximations,

introducing successively the following categories: Typology, Enumeration, Ratios, and Measurements. On the other hand a similar procedure can be carried out at all levels or ranks of complexity (groups of buildings, a single building, a floor, etc.), thus arriving at the drawing up of the classification itself according to a double entry matrix (Fig.4.1).

5 Complete form of the standards matrix

A simple example will help us to realize the meaning of a classification in this form. Let us consider the first couple of columns in Fig.4.1: these refer to elementary typological factors and combinatorial factors, in other words to such determining factors as are not quantified. The second couple of columns on the other hand, refer to quantified factors (i.e. investigations of relationships, proportions, etc.; and the effective definition of measures and quantities). Since the third line of the table refers to problems concerned with designing floor by floor, we shall have to classify completely all the problems relating to the choice of the load-bearing structure in the divisions III 1a, III 1b, III 2a.

In order to be really rational, a choice of this kind demands a knowledge of all constructional types; which is possible only if a complete classification of the types themselves is available. Fortunately, as we have seen, there are the 'internal constraints' (i.e. the nature of the constructional forms) which allow the setting up of such a classification.

Having distinguished the quantified factors from the non-quantified ones enables us first to set up, on the basis of the latter, a classification into a finite number of categories, and then to consider the other factors as determinants of possible variants within the general classification.

As for locating elements on plan (considered for the moment only from the formal point of view) we choose the building form (e.g. rectangular) and with it the possibility of representing various combina-

[9] Cp. also SIEGEL. *Strukturformen* (1960).

	not quantified		quantified		
	1a tipology	1b combinations	2a proportions	2b measurements	
I					environment
II					building
III					floor

Fig.4.1

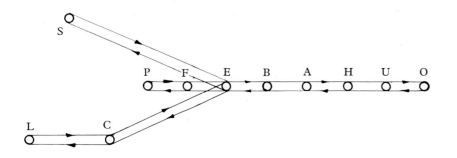

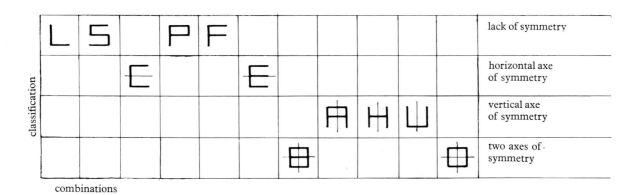

classification										
L	S		P	F						lack of symmetry
		E			E					horizontal axe of symmetry
						A	H	U		vertical axe of symmetry
					⊟				⊡	two axes of symmetry

combinations

Fig.5.1

direction of the sheets	mother form	variants	notes	design	detailed design
parallel		. . . .	. . . .		
radial		. . . .	. . . .		
combined		. . . .	. . . .		. . . .
. . . .		. . . .	. . . .	. . . .	. . . .

Fig.5.2

tions by the addition or subtraction of elements (horizontal co-ordinate in Fig.5.1) and of classifying them into various categories of symmetry (vertical co-ordinate, same figure). The topological relationships measured on the same table indicate the degree to which the various forms themselves relate to each other. Graph theory, however, not to mention the theory of symmetry groups, allows us to ensure that all possible combinations have been examined.

Lastly in the typology of structure we should consider the possibility of variations, which may occur either during the combinatorial phase (considering pseudo-symmetries, that is to say those corresponding to an irregular grid) or while choosing the elementary types.

A system of cataloguing the possible variants of each basic form, as indicated in line II of Fig.4.1, has been proposed by H. Hottinger[10] for buildings with hanging roofs and has been applied by the writer to air structures[11] (see Fig.5.2). We can then complete this classification by comparing constructional forms (which are basically 'building types') with the mechanical characteristics.[12]

Constructional standards, therefore, can be divided into:

(i) Standards dictated by statistics.

(ii) Standards dictated by the technology of non-load-bearing walls and other complementary works.

(iii) Standards dictated by servicing installations (heating, air-conditioning, etc.).

(iv) Standards dictated by other technical matters.

These standards will be represented in the squares of plane α Fig.5.3. We can imagine each square subdivided as Fig.4.1 and hence the constructional standards can be catalogued in their respective boxes. The operation can be carried out analogously on plane β for the functional norms: locating them down in their respective boxes according to whether they refer to: (I) a group of buildings; (II) a whole single building; (III) a single floor of a certain building, etc. Plane β also will have several squares, whose number will vary, naturally, according to the type of building complex which may also be different from the number of squares of plane α (the constructional standards plane). Within the squares of plane β (functional standards) we shall be able to pick out, as necessary in each project, those which refer to:

(i) Functional characteristics (e.g. concerned with town infrastructures, form and placing of the various parts of the buildings, etc.).

(ii) Possibilities of natural lighting (the orientation of the building, the size of the windows, etc.).

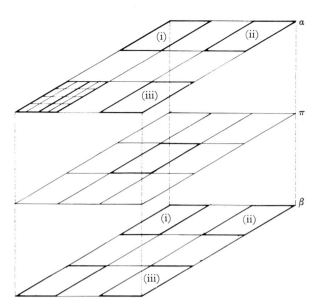

Fig.5.3

(iii) Climate control (e.g. the amount of thermal insulation in the external walls).

(iv) Other characteristics.

It will be necessary, when fixing the number of boxes in each square, to distinguish between perimetral and internal rooms (each class is particularly suitable for certain purposes); to define – for the external rooms – the relationship between the size of the windows, the floor surface, the room volume, etc.

Roughly speaking the standards written on the plane α come within the province of the structural engineer, while those written on the plane β, especially those to be noted in square (iii) and those following, require the services of other consultants.

6 Reduction of the matrix Fig.5.3

The correlation between standards belonging to different boxes are very tenuous and often non-existent: and the closest relationships are to be found between boxes stacked in the same box of different planes (e.g. III 2b of square (i) of Plane α and III 2b of square (i) of Plane β). This suggests that we ought to study the relationships described above 'in the abstract', apart from any specific project. In this way, we shall achieve a first selection of 'possible combinations' between the various factors which will then help to determine the practical selection for a particular case. A study of this type is certainly important: and we believe that some

[10] In: *Möglichkeiten der Gestaltung von Bauwerken mit Spannseilbinder systemen.*
[11] In: *Systematic design of pneumatic structures* (1967).
[12] In my *Statistics and constructional technique of ancient and modern domes* (1958) I demonstrated how, in order to understand the effective static behaviour of a construction with traditional masonry vaults, it is necessary to use different static schemes at the same time, according to an *ad hoc* methodology.

institute ought to undertake this type of research. If they were specifically equipped for it they would certainly obtain useful results.

The techniques for realizing a study of this kind can obviously be reduced to two categories:

(a) Research into the hierarchy of relationships,[13] starting with a simple written classification of planes α, β. The need for computerization undoubtedly would be very much as in Alexander's method.

(b) Comparison between 'blocks' of standards which could be achieved by comparing the 'structures' relating standards belonging to homonymous boxes (i.e. those stacked vertically above each other in planes α and β).

Certainly (β) at the moment would be too complex for the digital computers. The author believes, however, that certain techniques in mathematics are adequate for solving problems of this kind; it is not impossible, therefore, to think of setting up a sort of 'analogical calculus'.

We should remember that in each box the standards are already classified according to criteria which can be considered as dictated by geometry (cp. Fig.5.1) which means that we are facing problems of the following types: (A) a study of group transformations: (B) a study of correlations between configurations.

By this means we can supply all the standards that Architectural Science provides, in order to define the field of feasible solutions, no longer in the form of a rough list, but in the form of relationships which are susceptible to mathematical expression.

7 Data, characteristics and requirements of design

Passing to the study of a single project; given the mass of *specific information* (information of a general character has been called 'technical standards' and has been discussed in 3–5), it is necessary to distinguish the following classes:

(1) *Data* relating to the client's demands.

(2) *Ecological characteristics* (or of the natural surroundings).

(3) *Infrastructural characteristics* (or of the artificial surroundings).

(4) *Requirements* which the building complex (or part of it) must satisfy.

The designer must work upon each of the above classes of data, using suitable technical knowledge – to be precise:

(1) The client's needs must be studied and transformed into project *data*, bearing in mind that any building (even a house) is part of the fixed investment of some economic enterprises (for a house, the unit will be of the simplest possible kind, i.e. the single family). The project data must be determined, therefore, not with the aim of reducing the cost of the construction to a minimum, but as a means of optimizing (if necessary *only* from the economic point of view) the programme of the group which will use the building itself. Hence, in the case of a building to be used by a single group it will be necessary to carry out *econometric research*. The question can be generalized even further if we think of a developer concerned with a particular complex of buildings. We must bear in mind that the developer intends to recuperate over a given period his capital, interest, and profit. It will be necessary to investigate the economic status of potential buyers of each flat. Information must be inserted into *market research* to decide the size and characteristics of the enterprise. The question becomes even more general when the programme is of public concern, in that we pass from marketing to the *theory of investments* and, if the programme is large, we must think of possible feed-back from possible *sociological* effects of the project.

(2) *Ecological characteristics* (orientation, the amount of sun, maximum range of variation of climatic factors) must be studied with the help of a series of specific sciences which are not always found in the technical equipment of the architect: but, if these *ad hoc* elaborations are missing, an historical-statistical enquiry into vernacular solutions used in the area can be useful.

(3) *Infrastructural characteristics* are generally rough data, imposed by circumstances or by the authorities.

(4) The *requirements* to be satisfied are extremely varied: for example, as we have already said in 3, the maximum thermal range permissible in each room, or the maximum range (according to season) of light intensity in each zone of each room, etc.

Generally physiological considerations will decide these requirements: either drawn from sensory psychology or, if related to the size of the room, from ergonomics. It is useful, for example, to distinguish between the need for adequate fresh air (which can be defined directly in terms of quantity) and satisfied by an air-conditioning plant as an alternative to openings in the external envelope and the need for a view, which influences the psychological behaviour of the user but may be difficult to satisfy artificially. This list of requirements could continue to a point of banality: from sound-proofing to various safety precautions – in particular those against fire.

[13] C.A. ALEXANDER. *Hidecs 2* . . . (1962).

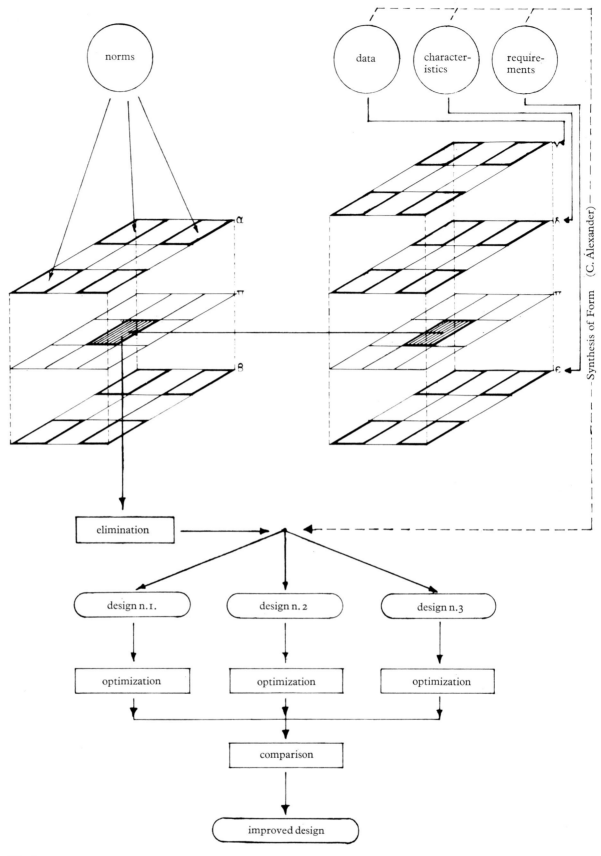

Fig.8.1

The data, characteristics, and requirements can refer to the entire building complex or to parts of it (e.g. differing orientation according to the ways in which various wings of the building are placed and the direction in which the single elevations face). Hence it is possible to put these various classes of information into boxes, in tables of type 4.1. It may be possible to catalogue all the information relating to a specific project according to a scheme not unlike that in Fig.5.3 – a scheme which we shall call: bundle of planes ($\gamma, \delta, \varepsilon$).

53

8 Structure of design procedure

The scheme of Fig.8.1 indicates the proposed procedure. It consists of the following steps:

(1A) List all functional and constructional standards according to the various solution types which are possible for the project in question.

(2A) List specific data, characteristics, and requirements of the project.

(1B) Compilation (and reduction) of the bundle of hyperplanes (α, β).

(2B) Compilation (and reduction) of the bundle of hyperplanes $(\gamma, \delta, \varepsilon)$.

(3) Elimination, in the bundle (α, β) of the solutions which do not match information from the bundle $(\gamma, \delta, \varepsilon)$.

This elimination will generally be made between homonymous boxes (but taking into account certain cross-interference). We shall thus be able to determine – e.g. starting from ecological and sometimes from infra-structural characteristics – certain simple ratios which will serve to direct formal choices: e.g. the most advisable (perimeter/area) ratio will lead us to choose between simple geometrical figures (circle, hexagon, square, rectangle of differing lengths) or complex figures (star, swastika, etc.). Having made a preliminary sketch (this is by no means indispensable but it is useful) we shall be able, at this point, to calculate how the (useful area/net area) ratio changes in relation to the (perimeter/area) ratio of the various solutions.

Moving to greater detail, we shall note, for example, that vertical availation areas can be distinguished from aerial rooms because they usually have a different structure. In fact, as Professor Cavallari-Murat has suggested, it is useful from the start of the design process, to distinguish between volumes with such different structures from other spaces in the building. So given several solutions which are functionally possible we shall be able to establish an overall preference by comparing elements of the bundle $(\gamma, \delta, \varepsilon)$. They will have to be chosen within units dictated by possible solutions with reference to structure and servicing systems (squares ii, iii of plane α) and will have to be checked with the constraints imposed by the structural frame (square i of plane α).

This is a simple explanation; it will be expanded in a future paper which will present a concrete application.

(4) At this point, we have reduced considerably the number of possible types and we can now draw up a feasibility study of the project (or rather of as many projects as we still retain as types). In these studies, for instance, the dimensions will be fluid, often expressed in terms of ratios without precise measurements.

(5) This step is followed by optimization procedures in two categories:

(a) *Mathematical procedures*: e.g. studying the plan of a certain building, using the following symbols for the particular areas:

A_u = useful area
A'_u = useful area in optimal conditions of natural lighting
A_p = internal circulation
A_c = common circulation
A_v = vertical circulation
A_z = area of the load-bearing structure
A_t = area of complementary structure (e.g. partitions)
A_i = area of services

We shall thus establish, according to the project type, one or more relationships (r) for optimization.

Of these A_z is subject to static conditions, A'_u is subject to lighting conditions, etc.; and we can use linear programming as the basis for mathematical optimization.

(b) *Experimental optimization*. This is a very popular area of study at the present time in my laboratory, for example, we have built models of varying dimensions (the external wall is so built that we can move it backwards and forwards) and by testing them on a heliodon we can determine suitable economic values (r) for given standards of lighting. We can insert these procedures into a complex programme of optimization to obtain what I have defined as correct morphological methods.

(6) By comparing optimization curves for single solutions we obtain all the elements necessary for a complete and final optimization of the project.

9 Remarks on Technical Aesthetics

It has been said, *en passant*, that some problems (e.g. the advantages which would be obtained from a beautiful view) might be solved by artificial means. It is the author's opinion (which he hopes to demonstrate in a future work) that a collation of the many studies now available on the laws of human behaviour, in the light of physiology and, if necessary, of psychology, could serve to define a form of 'Technical Aesthetics'. Its purpose as a study of architectural aesthetics would be to solve otherwise unsolvable functional problems.

When this happens the Vitruvian doctrine of Architecture will have been transformed and we shall be able to express it symbolically (F=Firmitas, U=Utilitas, V=Venustas).

The dynamics of behaviour-contingent physical systems[1]

by Raymond G. Studer

In his analysis of scientific revolutions, Thomas Kuhn (1962) identifies characteristics of scientific development which may have relevance for the environmental design community. He argues that what gives continuity to disparate research activities in a particular or scientific area is the pervasive recognition of a *paradigm*. Historically the process of arriving at a firm research consensus is extremely arduous. Once acquired, however, the shared paradigm permits the more esoteric type of research which is characteristic of mature scientific status. The developmental pattern of a mature science, Kuhn points out, is the successive transition from one paradigm to another via revolution. The design community cannot be said to have experienced a revolution in this sense, but it has seen the need to identify a research consensus. Collectively we seek a paradigm.

The following remarks are intended to suggest the basis for a paradigm of sorts. As such, they are necessarily and frankly quite broad and somewhat theoretical. Hopefully something of the real world comes through, for there may be useful implications for environmental design and research. Whatever else might be gained, the search for a paradigm almost immediately makes explicit and conspicuous the nature of our ignorance, a fact which will be made abundantly clear many times throughout this presentation. In this regard one can take heart in Karl Popper's suggestion that 'It might be well for all of us to remember that while differing widely in the various little bits we know, in our infinite ignorance we are all about equal' (Popper, 1959). The underlying objective in these formulations is the accommodation, or integration, of two generally emerging, but hitherto tenuously connected ideas: a more lucid epistemology of the man-made environment, and more effective design methods. This is obviously a period of great attitudinal change within the design community, and the Zeitgeist embodies an impressive array of concepts which are both highly innovative and disparate. In such a *milieu* it is often difficult to know where one's own ideas begin and another's end. The intention here is both to build upon, and refute, certain aspects of recent work in design method (e.g. C. Alexander, 1964). If this is the case, so much the better, for it suggests that the design disciplines may at last be moving toward a research consensus, one whereby knowledge – not of products but processes – becomes cumulative.

The move to externalize, evaluate and model more viable design procedures is having a trenchant effect. The potential success and/or failure of these various efforts has led this researcher to become less concerned with the methods of formal synthesis *per se*, and more concerned with the precepts which guide problem formulation. The reasons for this concern are quite obvious. Our understanding of and mode of conceptualizing the problem space have a profound effect upon internal procedures, not to mention the resultant product. To put it another way, there is the distinct possibility that a designer, or method, may operate quite effectively while solving the *wrong problem*!

These arguments are based upon the proposition that what is critically needed in environmental design is a unit of analysis with dimensions which are both relevant and empirically accessible. 'Relevance' has meant many things for designers, but in terms of this historical situation an acceptable unit must have relevance in terms of the *participating organism(s)*.

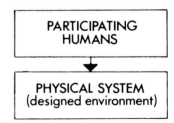

Fig.1

The most commonly accepted unit for design purposes is 'human need'. Such a concept has relevance perhaps; what it lacks is empirical substance. That

[1] Aspects of this research and preparation of this manuscript were partially supported by Contract CST-408, U.S. Bureau of Standards, Institute for Applied Technology.

is, we cannot observe need, but can only infer its existence through observation of its empirical counterpart, *behaviour*. Human behaviour appears to be the more correct unit of analysis; it has characteristics which are relevant, empirically verifiable, and they are operationally definable. Assuming behaviour as the class of independent variables – an index of biological and non-biological need – what are the implications for environmental design?

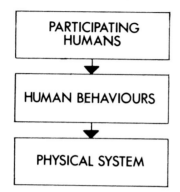

Fig.2

A behaviour-contingent paradigm challenges not only the concept of 'need', but conventional problem space descriptions and boundaries generally. 'Building', 'urban core', 'house', 'city', 'school', 'room', and so forth, are conceptual entities which may have little relevance in the description of appropriate problem spaces. These historically preconditioned terms obviously bias and inhibit both the logical and behavioural aspects of problem-solving; but more important, they describe the *wrong class* of variables. That is, physical characteristics are defined (in intension[2] as it were) in a manner which begs the very (design) question which a viable design process is intended to answer. The 'building type' mentality thus assures that the problem space is arbitrarily described, prematurely closed, and the behavioural goals of the inhabitants constrained without ever having been analysed. A new taxonomy of problem formulation is in order, one which objectifies with greater fidelity the implicit continuum of highly differentiated events – the ordered variety – which characterizes human life in a particular context.

A behaviour-contingent approach then rejects the stereotyped 'list of physical requirements' in favour of a more basic and relevant taxonomy. The detection, isolation, and structure of environmental problems grows out of an analysis of human behaviour systems. It is only through an analysis of this class of variables that quantities, qualities, and relationships of elements in the *designed environment* (Studer, 1966) can be properly determined. A designed environment is essentially a system of energy-matter elements which are interposed between a collection of human participants and ambivalent forces in the general, impinging *milieu*, i.e. the designed environment complement. When properly configured, these energy-matter elements produce and support the

[2] See B. Russell on intensional and extensional definitions (1956).

56

various activities required to meet the goals of the human participants under analysis. That is, the designed environment can be analysed as a *prosthetic* phenomenon. It functions prosthetically in two distinct, but interrelated modes: (1) it is *physiologically* prosthetic in that it supports behavioural goals through maintenance of required (behaviourally correlated) physiological states; and (2) it is *behaviourally* prosthetic (Lindsley, 1964) in that it intentionally configures specific behavioural topographies.

We need no particular label for such physical systems, and it adds nothing to our understanding of the substance of the problem, or its solution, to assign them. Indeed it is in response to the linguistic amorphism which abounds within the design community that generic concepts are used throughout this presentation. When the terms 'designed environment' or 'physical system' are used, for example, this should not be construed as a self-conscious attempt to promote a more esoteric jargon. It is rather a straightforward recognition that terms such as 'architecture' and 'buildings' are too restrictive and dissimilar in conventional meaning adequately to characterize the intended phenomena.

The systems which must be accommodated in a behaviour-contingent approach are rather easily identified, at least in general terms. They are, however, very difficult to realize. The conceptual and technical issues which must eventually be dealt with involve the following operations, each of which will be briefly discussed:

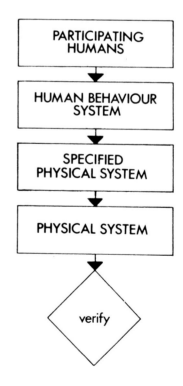

Fig.3

(1) Defining the requisite behaviour system.

(2) Specifying the requisite physical system.

(3) Realizing the requisite physical system.

(4) Verifying the resultant environment-behaviour system.

Aspects of a behaviour contingent approach

Defining the requisite behaviours to be accommodated in a particular problem situation has not traditionally been an aspect of concern in design method. It is an essential aspect, however, and the implicit operations must come to be better understood. One quite naturally seeks an approach with empirical substance. Careful observation and extensive interviews with the potential users would therefore seem to yield the kind of behavioural data required. Naturalistic observations of, and verbal reports from, the human participants (or class of them) to be re-accommodated are obviously important and necessary to gain insight into a problem situation. Such information alone, however, will not produce the requisite behaviours, because what is being observed (and responded to) is a physical setting which is ostensibly in a state of malfunction. If this were not the case no problem situation would exist. The task of identifying behaviours for environmental design is not fundamentally empirical, but *normative*. Like the economist, the environmental designer 'does not try to prescribe *what* people ought to want – he is not normative in that sense – but he does try to prescribe *how* they should go about getting what they want' (G. A. Miller, 1964). Objectifying and identifying the values and purpose of a particular sub-culture can sometimes be a difficult and delicate procedure. Without such information, however, no environmental problem can be conceptualized. In other words, it might be said that a collection of humans with no identifiable purpose can have no identifiable problems. Indeed every interacting collection of humans, whether large, small, formal, or informal, evolves and maintains itself in response to some explicit or implicit purpose. James G. Miller defines purpose as follows:

'By the information input of its charter, or genetic input, or by changes in behaviour brought about by rewards and punishments from its suprasystem, a system develops a preferential hierarchy of values that ... determine its preference for one internal steady state value rather than another. This is its purpose.' (Miller, 1965.)

A human organization's purpose in turn delimits its goals and the kinds of behaviours required to accommodate them. Beyond the difficult questions involved in identifying values and purpose, the task of extensionally, or operationally, defining a human organization's goals in terms of a behavioural network is a complex proposition, with highly technical ramifications. Because no inductive procedure seems

possible (see comments above), defining the requisite behaviour system in a particular problem situation is essentially a problem of *design*. It is a problem of (behavioural) design in the sense that no deterministic procedures exist for delineating a behaviour system for a given set of goals.

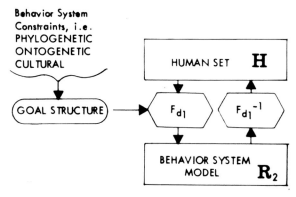

H: set of all participating humans.
F_{d1}: set of operations to define a requisite behaviour system for a given goal structure.
F_{d1}^{-1}: set of operations required to specify a requisite set of humans for a given behaviour system.

Fig.4
Dynamics of behaviour

This behaviour system design is constrained by the physiological and psychological characteristics of the population under analysis. It is also constrained by the cultural suprasystem within which the population, or participating humans, must operate. Fortunately, some powerful analytic tools are becoming available which can assist the conceptualization of behaviour systems for environmental design. These include, for example, the interrelated resources of: behaviour-orientated organization theory (March and Simon, 1958), information network theory (J. Rothstein, 1954) and simulation of human groups (Guetzkow, 1962). Indeed any heuristic or algorithm which facilitates the solution of multiple outcome problems has relevance for this kind of design task. The result could be called the *behaviour system model* (see R_2 in Fig.5).

It is only after a behaviour system has been conceptualized – in response to the organization's purpose(s), goals and subgoals – that the very existence of a physical problem can be determined. Without a proper behavioural analysis we are not only likely to mis-structure physical problems, but may also misclassify them as well. That is, we often see a problem as physical when it is another aspect of the environment which is causing behavioural dissonance. A physical problem exists if and only if there is disequilibrium between requisite behaviours and the designed environment.

The tests (see Fig.5, 'Test 1') which must be applied to determine physical dissonance include: (1) systematically comparing the conceptualized requisite behaviour system (R_2) to the extant system (R_1) in

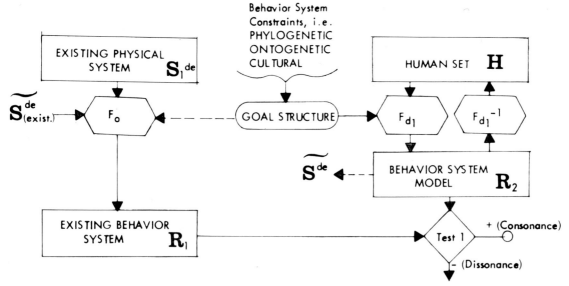

F_o: set of organismic functions which produce particular system of behaviours given a particular environmental state.

S^{de}: other related classes of environmental elements, e.g. social, economic.

Test I–I: Compare requisite behaviour system (R_2) with existing behaviour system; 2) identify dysfunctions due to S_1^{de}.

Fig.5

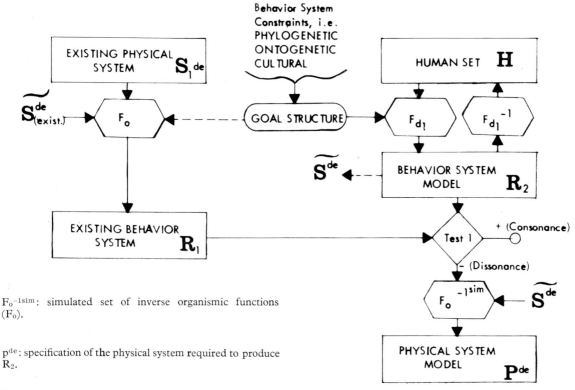

F_o^{-1sim}: simulated set of inverse organismic functions (F_o).

p^{de}: specification of the physical system required to produce R_2.

Fig.6

order to detect disparities (according to certain tolerance thresholds); and (2) determining whether or not these disparities are attributable to elements in the physical system (S_1^{de}). Dysfunction may, in fact, be attributable to some other aspect of the environment (S^{de}),[3] e.g. social, economic, educational, etc. (Ostensibly tests for evaluating dissonance in other stimulus domains would proceed similarly.) If such tests indicate the existence of a physical dysfunction, an alternative environment (P^{de}) must be conceptualized.

Specifying the requisite physical system consists of systematically correlating conceptual elements of an environmental system (P^{de}) with conceptual elements of a behavioural system (R_2). What must be

[3] The mis-classification of environmental problems is not in the least uncommon. An industrial firm may construct additional quantities of space, when the actual conflicts result from inventory and/or sales policies. Insufficient space quantities are often identified as the source of dysfunction in educational environments, when the real problem may grow out of an inappropriate and ineffective teaching system.

described is a specific (designed) environment-behaviour interface. Describing such an interface in a comprehensive integrated and functional sense assumes the resources of a comprehensive, integrated and functional science of behaviour. No such science exists. We all understand this, and are presumably attempting, in one way or another, to do something about it. What is required is empirical evidence and a language for describing functional mappings between elements in these two systems. These kinds of mappings are difficult to come by, which is probably what leads psychologist Robert Sommer to conclude that 'the entire art of design rests on empirical underpinnings so weak that no consensus exists about what arrangements are efficient, beautiful, or even relevant to a given activity'.

The phenomena to be described (in P^{de}) are quantities, qualities, and relationships in the spatial environment. Specification of these physical requirements is in essence a model of the system of physical contingencies which will produce the requisite state of behavioural affairs. If such a proposition seems obscure it is because we have yet to develop a functional language for describing such systems – for mapping the interface – at the appropriate levels of precision. Like all abstract language systems, it must facilitate descriptions which are sufficiently explicit and unambiguous, while admitting many concrete (real world) interpretations.

The nature of this interface model will ultimately depend not only upon a great deal of incomplete empirical evidence, but also upon the system, theory, or paradigm found to be, or believed to be, most viable in explaining the etiology of human behaviour (Marx and Hillix, 1963). There must be a commitment to those resources in the behavioural sciences which one considers most adequate and reliable. It is well known that there are controversies, and that there are several competing paradigms in the behavioural sciences. Designers, if they are genuinely and technically interested in accommodating human requirements, must be drawn into these controversies. They must become knowledgeable of the issues and, of course, familiar with those techniques which have been found successful.

Why are resources in the behavioural sciences so difficult to assimilate for our purposes? Beyond the fact that the data are simply not in, the behavioural scientist has a mission (and a language) quite unlike the designer's. In the laboratory he usually deals with the isolation and control of a few variables, with small and fragmented samples of behaviour. Even when investigating larger samples he usually examines stimulus domains other than the designed environment, e.g. interpersonal relations, and he isolates only those aspects which he chooses to examine. With but few exceptions, he deals with analysis. The designer, on the other hand, must deal

with environment-behaviour complexes as they come. He must understand wholes, large and complex behavioural continuums; he deals with synthesis. The environmental designer daily attempts to accommodate a level of behavioural complexity which no scientific analysis has ever approached in a unitary and functional sense (or in a mode required for environmental design). In selecting phenomena to study, the behavioural scientist generally has two choices. He can investigate a multivariate situation which reflects somewhat the complexities of real life. The price usually paid for such a choice is, of course, imprecise control of variables and ambiguity regarding the functional relations between environmental and behavioural events.

'Real life with its multiplicity of variables may present interactions not readily observed in simpler laboratory experiments ... (but) the ultimate scientific test of theoretical principles is an experimental one, and real-life models should serve as guides rather than criteria or objectives.' (Marx and Hillix, 1963.)

The most scientifically prestigious data are produced in experimental situations which are artificially impoverished in order to observe the effects on behaviour of single (environmental) variable manipulation. The resulting data are reliable, replicable, and predictable, but they are highly limited. In terms of real-world application this is the behavioural scientist's dilemma – but it is also our dilemma.

Before we have the capability to control, predict and explain human behaviour at the levels required for environmental design we must come to understand a greater breadth of phenomena along what Brunswik identifies as the environment – environment continuum (Brunswik, 1952) (see Fig. 7). Brunswik was somewhat unsuccessful in making a sound scientific case for his 'probabilistic functionalism', but he did identify the level of understanding which seems necessary in applications to environmental design. The behavioural sciences cannot yet deliver reliable resources at this level, and designers must operate with a great deal less. Like many others attempting to apply resources in the behavioural sciences, this researcher's own views of this complexity of means are not entirely resolved. At this juncture, they are generally as follows.[4]

Behavioural science, like any science, seeks not 'truth', but a useful way of organizing experience.

[4] It is extremely important to note here that these particular views on the nature of the (designed) environment-behaviour interface neither validate nor invalidate the arguments for a behaviour-contingent paradigm. There are obviously several competing systems or theories within which one could interpret the operations denoted in Fig.6 (F_0^{-1sim}).

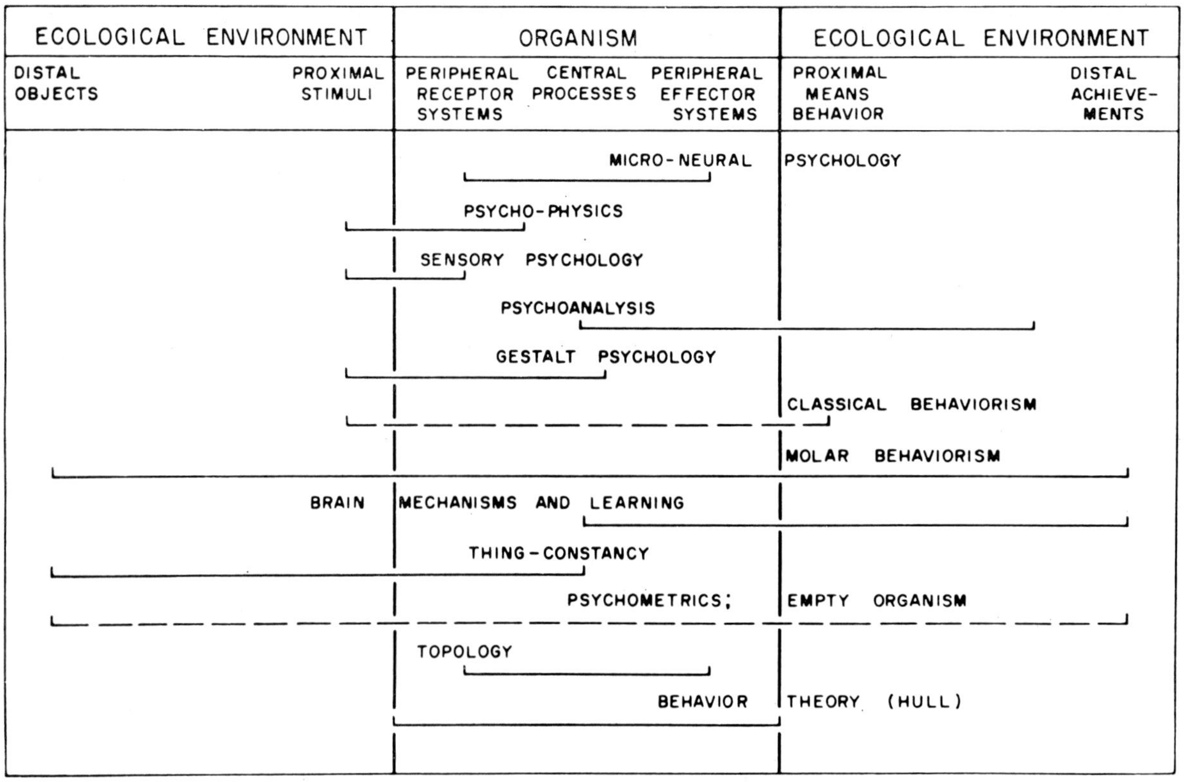

Fig. 7

ECOLOGICAL ENVIRONMENT		ORGANISM			ECOLOGICAL ENVIRONMENT	
DISTAL OBJECTS	PROXIMAL STIMULI	PERIPHERAL RECEPTOR SYSTEMS	CENTRAL PROCESSES	PERIPHERAL EFFECTOR SYSTEMS	PROXIMAL MEANS BEHAVIOR	DISTAL ACHIEVEMENTS

MICRO-NEURAL PSYCHOLOGY

PSYCHO-PHYSICS

SENSORY PSYCHOLOGY

PSYCHOANALYSIS

GESTALT PSYCHOLOGY

CLASSICAL BEHAVIORISM

MOLAR BEHAVIORISM

BRAIN MECHANISMS AND LEARNING

THING-CONSTANCY

PSYCHOMETRICS; EMPTY ORGANISM

TOPOLOGY

BEHAVIOR THEORY (HULL)

The place of representative schools and problems of psychology on the basic psychological unit. Defined by Brunswik.
(from R. Barker, 1960).

Designers are primarily interested in resources describing orderly relations within which human behavioural events (as affected by elements in the designed environment) can be explained, predicted, and controlled. When attempting to apply what behavioural science has to offer, designers are justified in selecting those resources which are (technically) most relevant to an environmental design context. Questions regarding a behavioural theory's comprehensiveness – its 'aesthetic' qualities – is something to be worked out at another level, e.g. within the behavioural science community.

It is generally held by those who study such matters that a person's behaviour is caused by three interdependent classes of phenomena: genetic endowment, history of interaction with the environment, and the existing environment. A skilled surgeon or a biogeneticist can exert effective control over the first; a comprehensive account of the second would also yield a high level of control. Designers, however, exert influence only upon the existing environment. The existing environment, needless to say, is composed of many sub-systems, e.g. social, economic – and the designed environment (i.e. those limited energy-matter variables under the direct control of the environmental designer). This sub-system includes some fairly significant behaviour-controlling variables,[5] but little in the way of a scientifically based understanding has developed.

Designers are essentially interested in the fact, beyond any theory which explains it, that particular physical states will produce discrete and predictable behavioural states. For environmental design purposes, our interest in intervening organismic variables is quite limited. This is true *provided* we have resources by which behaviour can be effectively predicted and controlled via manipulation of variables within the effective domain of the designer. In order to specify the characteristics of an appropriate physical system we must obviously understand the psychophysical limits of processing incoming stimuli (Dember, 1963). Beyond this, however, the exclusive interest on the part of some designers in perception as a basic resource is in many ways misdirected[6] (Studer, forthcoming).

Let us look at the nature of the interface problem. A desired behavioural state (R_2) has been specified. The participants have not been previously emitting this particular system of behaviours but another

[5] That designers control human behaviour is an indisputable empirical fact. The issue is not whether they *ought* to control but whether this control is to be exerted via accidental contingencies or upon understood techniques.

[6] That is, unless the behavioural consequences of such investigations are examined, it is difficult to see their relevance for environmental organization. Two common errors occur when designers turn to perceptual investigations, when: (1) they confuse conceptual and perceptual phenomena; and (2) they (quite selectively) seek 'scientific' support for their aesthetic beliefs and dogmas.

(R_1) (otherwise no environmental problem would exist). It is desired that they will. They have quite diverse, generally unspecified behavioural histories, and the problem is one of specifying an environmental configuration which will produce, with the highest probability, the specified state of behavioural events. What this clearly describes is a *learning* situation, i.e. the acquisition of, or modification toward, a new system of behaviours.

There is a branch of psychology which has developed resources which seem particularly relevant to this kind of problem. An *operant* behavioural analysis (Skinner, 1953) deals exclusively with events and elements in the environment, i.e., temporal and spatial relations between behaviour and its *consequences*. Extensive and highly controlled laboratory experiments have isolated and defined orderly relations among three classes of variables in the environment which have relevance in controlling and predicting human behaviour. These are: (1) the situation, or *stimuli* (2) the behaviour, or *response;* and (3) the consequence, or *reinforcer*. Predictable response probability comes about when reinforcing consequences are made *contingent* upon a particular behaviour in a particular situation. The manipulation of these *contingencies of reinforcement* brings about a change in the organism that we call learning. The designed environment can be viewed, and programmed, as a *learning system* (Studer, forthcoming), a system in which energy-matter variables are arranged to bring about the requisite state of behavioural affairs.

Some behavioural scientists contend that humans appear to behave *as though* influenced not only by contingencies in the extant environment, but also by a structured hypothesis concerning future environmental-behavioural states (Miller, Galanter, and Pribram, 1960). This hypothesis is constantly revised in response to events as they occur in the real world. Such *planning* behaviour is probably explicable for the most part in terms of a history of interaction with the environment. The environment appears to reinforce this planning behaviour in that survival apparently favours the organism which anticipates future events. If this interpretation is correct, no additional constructs seem to be required beyond extensive refinement of the operant framework mentioned above. In any event this is a phenomenon to be better understood if response probability is to be more accurately predicted. Some researchers explain anticipatory behaviour as a phenomenon whereby a human constructs a model of the environment, runs the model faster than the environment, and predicts that the environment will behave as the model does (Galanter and Gerstenhaber, 1956). If this is the case, prior knowledge of the participant's 'environmental model'[7] would give

the designer important data regarding probable response patterns. In order to make such information available to a design analysis it must obviously be somehow *externalized*, and this can be a rather formidable task.

Finally, it would seem that formal models which correlate environmental and behavioural variables are an eventual necessity in the behaviour-contingent approach. The ability to describe precisely and manipulate variables in order to delineate the (designed) environment-behaviour interface is fundamental to a clear and precise understanding of physical requirements at the appropriate levels (see above comments on a descriptive language). Reliable mathematical models, as they are developed and generalized to describe a greater breadth of behavioural phenomena, can hopefully be utilized to express the functional mappings required (to describe P^{de}).

Realizing the physical system in the real world is, of course, that aspect which has been most extensively investigated, and a more sophisticated understanding of these processes is emerging. At this level in the process new complications arise as the requisite physical states (P^{de}) come under the influence of another class of variables. These impinge when the system is analysed in a particular spatial-temporal (geographic) context. Such variables might be classified as 'external' constraints (see Fig.8). A solution has been adequately realized when matter and energy have been ordered so as to accommodate these 'external' constraints, as well as the previously conceptualized quantitative, qualitative, and relational requirements.

Sophisticated investigations of both the normative (logical) and behavioural (empirical) aspects of environment problem-solving have and will produce tools which greatly increase our capacity to deal with the complexities of physical synthesis. For purposes of this explication one need not go too deeply into this aspect of the process, except to note that the procedure seems to be one of successive approximations toward a specific real-world system via the following states:

(1) An abstract description of the requisite environment-behaviour interface (P^{de}).

(2) A description of the same interface, but made more specific as a result of accommodating the 'external' constraints related to a particular spatial-temporal context.

(3) A series of analogues or simulations of the real-world system at greater and greater levels of specificity, each iteration terminating in a test for consonance with respect to the requisite behaviour system.

(4) Final realization of the physical system (S_2^{de}).

[7] This term seems tentatively preferable to that of 'image' which has been used to connote all manner of metaphysical things.

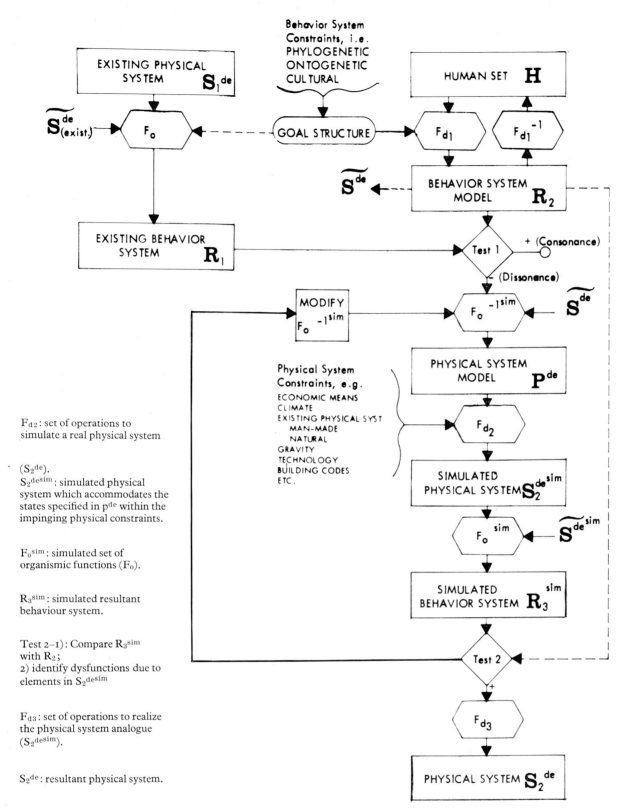

Fig.8

F_{d2}: set of operations to simulate a real physical system

(S_2^{de}).
$S_2^{de\,sim}$: simulated physical system which accommodates the states specified in p^{de} within the impinging physical constraints.

F_o^{sim}: simulated set of organismic functions (F_o).

R_3^{sim}: simulated resultant behaviour system.

Test 2–1): Compare R_3^{sim} with R_2;
2) identify dysfunctions due to elements in $S_2^{de\,sim}$

F_{d3}: set of operations to realize the physical system analogue $(S_2^{de\,sim})$.

S_2^{de}: resultant physical system.

One of the generally agreed upon characteristics of creative problem-solving is that it occurs with the discovery, or invention, of entirely new patterns of relationships, and avoidance of preconceived contexts. The behaviour-contingent approach may help both the normative and behavioural aspects of problem-solving in at least three ways: (1) the taxonomy of independent variables, i.e. units of behaviour, tend to minimize preconception in terms of known physical configurations; (2) this class of variables

suggests a systematic 'linking' procedure (Studer, 1966); and (3) behavioural variables can be defined in very small (single class) units, thus increasing the probability that new conflict-free patterns of relationships can be more easily generated.

Verification of the physical system in the real world has never been demanded of, or by, the design community. One consequence of this is a conspicuous lack of cumulative knowledge regarding

humans. For purposes of design the human participant is customarily considered to exhibit steady-state response probabilities in the presence of a given physical setting. Findings in the behavioural sciences do not justify this assumption. Indeed they do not, as a rule, furnish directives for producing physical settings which are either optimal, *or* time-independent. Rather they deal with relationships, i.e. dependencies among relevant variables. Such dependencies are not static or absolute, as many design strategies assume, but are subject to changing probabilities along a continuum. Variability in the human participants, brought about by the interdependent effects of adaptation, deprivation states, and particularly learning, have a significant and inevitable impact upon the environment-behaviour interface. These changes in the participants in turn affect equilibrium in the ensemble.

Behaviour is greatly modified as a person *adapts* to an environment which is, for example, visually, sonically, or socially noisy. In experimental situations, the effects of environmental manipulations cannot be properly assessed until stable behavioural *baselines* have been established; that is, until the organism adapts to the experimental situation. Behaviour before and after adaptation differs greatly. It is also well known that response probability varies when a stimulus situation (either conditioned or unconditioned) becomes satiating, i.e. when environmental elements lose their effect on behaviour with sustained contact. Constant overexposure of participants to an impressive external (or internal) vista provides an interesting example. When such reinforcing events are indiscriminately and/or grossly introduced, their effect is diminished with time.

A more remote possibility or organismic variability is that of gross physiological[8] change. When persons grow older or become disabled we observe a number of prosthetic devices appearing in the environment, e.g. hearing aids, wheelchairs, ramps, special lifts, and so forth. Unforeseen changes in human metabolic, perceptual, or skeletal-musculature systems demand new behaviour and/or physical *configuration* if the goals of the organization remain constant.

The above organismic changes are possible and frequently occur, but the most interesting and important source of variability is brought about by *learning*. One is likely to satiate in undifferentiated, low-information environments. Highly complex settings can, on the other hand, produce disorientated and ineffective behaviour; that is, until one learns – comes under the influence of – its ordering principles. Laboratory experiments (and common sense) indicate that response probability and the requisite stimulus configuration change with time and context. Modifying behaviour toward a viable or specified state, that is, effective stimulus control,[9] and the acquisition of appropriate (and behaviour influencing) *stimulus discriminations*[10] involve mul-

tiple, varying presentations. Programmed instruction provides an interesting and relevant example. The new technology of teaching (Holland, 1960) is based upon a principle whereby extant behavioural capacities are modified through a series of modest steps of increasing difficulty. Appropriate responses to complex, high-information environments generally come about as an organism acquires increasingly complex repertories. An environment which reinforces these acquisitions is one which is constantly modified.

The reality of day-to-day events produces still further complications for the environment designer. Superimposed upon the basic learning functions above are effects brought about when social and other classes of contingencies modify a participant's perception of, and response to, aspects of the designed environment. A positively reinforcing series of social encounters which are related in a particular way to aspects of the designed environment will greatly modify response probabilities within it. Aversive social events will modify this in yet another way.[11] Indeed the participants' varying histories of environmental interaction add a complicated dimension generally. It is because of such histories, on the other hand, that effective behaviour in most designed environments is possible at all.

These phenomena of organismic variability are basic and well known. One need go no further into the complexities of them to realize that the requisite system of physical elements is, in effect, *highly variable* if behavioural equilibrium is to be maintained.

To recapitulate, the sources of variability in the ensemble include the interdependent effects of: (1) changes in the organization's goal structure; (2) changes in the external physical constraints; (3) changes in other (internal) stimulus domains; and (4) changes in the participating humans. These sources of conflict and variability remind us that human systems are above all *dynamic*. The precise characteristics of this dynamism are, within the context of present knowledge, extremely unpredictable. The paradox encountered by designers as they attempt to accommodate the dynamic human problem with a static formal solution, i.e. 'architecture', is a familiar one. What must be decided is

[8] All the organismic changes mentioned herein produce physiological changes. What is intended here is a situation in which the physiology is so altered that it becomes an overriding consideration.

[9] When a behaviour is reinforced in the presence of certain stimuli there is a higher probability that this particular behaviour will occur in their presence in the future. Response to these similar stimulus conditions is called stimulus control (Terrace, 1966).

[10] A situation in which an organism, having been reinforced in the presence of particular stimuli, comes to discriminate these (and respond to them in a somewhat consistent way).

[11] A way which is not 'equal and opposite', but one which requires a more complex analysis.

whether or not increasingly complex, technologically sophisticated cultures really tolerate the resulting conflicts indefinitely. The 'crisis' mentality[12] within the design community is generally overstated, and has produced little more than platitudes. It must be conceded, on the other hand, that highly complex ecological systems can go out of equilibrium with little advance warning.

The adaptation interface

The arguments for well-fitting designed environments are dismissed as pedantic by some on the grounds that the human organism is, in fact, highly adaptive. He will prevail, it is insisted, regardless of our design decisions. There is a great deal of truth in this. The human is endowed with a marvellously adaptive physiology, and he does emit highly adaptive behaviour in designed environments. Species whose behaviour was excessively stereotyped, i.e. failed to respond differentially to varying environmental conditions, are obviously no longer with us (Sidman, 1960). A continuously changing *milieu* ensures a high level of adaptive behaviour in humans, forcing as it does the emission of a wide variety of behaviour in our repertories.

In general, however, the simplistic notion (held by many designers unfortunately) that man is 'infinitely adaptable' is critically erroneous. Both common sense and excellent laboratory data indicate that there are limits to adaptability. We already know that certain modes and intensities of environmental dissonance can produce physiological and behavioural disintegration long before an organism can adapt to them (Solomon *et al.*, 1961). There is obviously a great deal more to be learned about the more subtle side effects brought about by environments which are biologically and extrabiologically dissonant. Long-term ethological studies of lower organisms in stressful environments (Calhoun, 1966), for example, command serious attention. One question which could be asked is what adaptive states have the greatest utility. A conflicting environment may be overcome via adaptation, but the new organismic state could be found undesirable in terms of long-range demands (Dubos, 1965). For example, a person continuously subjected to very loud sounds may adapt, but become less sensitive to lesser sounds. The resulting adaptive state, i.e. deafness to certain intensities, could be critically dysfunctional in other environmental contexts.

The real issue here is that the human participant may, in fact, and usually does, survive both physiologically and psychologically in dysfunctioning environments. He may, however, fail to attain his defined goals. It must be remembered that it is not survival alone which defines environmental requirements, but the human *goal structure*, and this includes a great deal more.

A second and more sophisticated argument against well-fitting physical systems says that a certain level of conflict with the environment is essential to the survival and well-being of an organism, human or otherwise. Evolution appears to favour the organism which survives stress and hardship. Taken to an extreme, such an argument would, on a medical front, ostensibly legislate against immunization altogether, on the grounds that a new disease could annihilate future generations made vulnerable by not having survived smallpox. The argument does have merit, however, and if a certain level of conflict has utility for human well-being, then it requires careful attention. It must be systematically included as an important aspect of the problem space, since we could hardly leave such a fundamental requirement to chance. There are several questions involved here. How much and what kind of stress is desirable? Also, how much energy should a human expend simply overcoming conflict in the designed environment – what are the risks? There is obviously a rather delicate balance between well-fitting and inordinately stressful environments. We might call this the *adaptation interface*. It is not a phenomenon which can be understood in ethical or speculative terms. It is rather another of the many areas requiring the attention of a scientific analysis.

Maintenance of environment-behaviour systems

These comments outlining the complexities of behavioural accommodation – the many ways that environment-behaviour systems can go out of equilibrium – are not intended as nihilistic. Neither do they suggest that we should abandon the behaviour-contingent paradigm. They do suggest that designers and design methods have not been altogether realistic in dealing with the human dynamic, i.e. changing requirement states.

Variability of the several interdependent systems – the sources of dissonance – presents an extremely complex problem if we are to realize well-fitting systems. Beyond this, our knowledge of human behavioural phenomena is generally impoverished. As a consequence of these two kinds of difficulties, our ability to conceptualize, order, specify and realize appropriate physical settings is highly problematic. This is true regardless of how effective our design method *per se*. Clearly the designer is committed to a problem-solving situation of great uncertainty.[13] Uncertainty obviously does not preclude

[12] By this is meant the persistent warning from designers that humanity is most certainly doomed unless man takes drastic action to improve his 'visual' surroundings. John Beshers (1962) has labelled this simplistic notion as 'architectural determinism'.

[13] That is, his efforts are constrained by a limited knowledge of behavioural causes, by what he can predict concerning future requirements and by limited methodological tools generally.

action, but have we really faced this uncertainty in our formulations, that is, beyond the simplistic demand for 'flexibility'?

The behavioural sciences are developing resources which move beyond folk wisdom. As we come to understand the technical basis for the vast uncertainty facing designers, we must also come to question generally the *solution-orientated* precepts held by most conscientious designers and methodologists. In spite of my obvious enthusiasm for the behaviour-contingent approach, it must be conceded that our ability to respond incisively within the bounds of present knowledge is critically limited. We haven't the conceptual tools, nor do we have an adequate empirical understanding precisely to correlate environmental and behavioural variables. But more important is the undeniable fact that the human problem changes in most instances, before a physical solution to it can be realized. In short, the goals implicit in seeking 'the solution' should be *abandoned*. The quest for this elusive entity has too often led to physical settings based either upon information-rich but steady-state requirement systems, or information-poor generalizations. Our design goals should be redirected so as to respond more directly and realistically to the dynamics of human systems. We must address the problems of unpredictable response configurations, the adaptation interface, and the general maintenance of the environment-behaviour ensemble – on a *continuing* basis. An environmental solution, considering the uncertainties involved, should not be viewed as a solution at all, but a complex *hypothesis*. No matter how refined, a (behaviour-contingent) physical system can be nothing more than a hypothesis, which can be verified only when placed in its real-world setting. Furthermore, it must be reformulated each time relevant constraints vary. Designed environments, then, should be viewed as *experiments* in which relevant variables – either behavioural or environmental – are manipulated (either by the participants or others) to move the system toward a state of consonance with respect to the goal structure in effect. Figure 10 denotes the hypothetical characteristics of an environment-behaviour system moving toward a state of equilibrium. This process is assumed and denoted as a generalized learning configuration. In such a situation the environment, the participants, and the decision-makers produce a complex information-decision system, one which constantly responds to dissonances with respect to a specified goal structure and requisite behaviours. It should be noted that under such circumstances the characteristics of the ensemble change as it becomes asymptotic to an equilibrium state. If such systems do in fact behave this way, it is clear that pre-asymptotic and post-asymptotic aspects require physical systems with significantly different levels of adaptability. In Fig.11 we see such a hypothetical ensemble, perhaps on a greater time scale, in which the organization's goal structure is periodically modified.

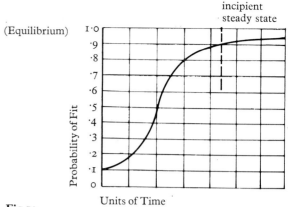

Fig.10
Hypothetical R-S^{de} accommodation with constant goal structure.

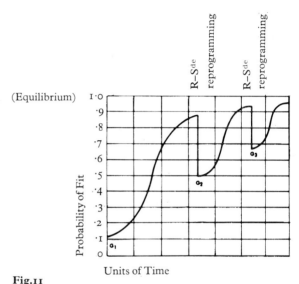

Fig.11
Hypothetical R-S^{de} accommodation with variable goal structure.

The suggestion that we abandon 'solutions' in favour of experimental contexts may seem subversive to traditional views of design, and a somewhat austere response to the designer's dilemma. In light of the realities of human processes, however, the commitment to finite-state design objectives is not justified. Indeed we will no doubt come to understand that the experiment *is* the solution. A design effort committed to human well-being is one which seeks an environmental setting which is systematically linked and responsible to human variability. It is one which is constantly refined, constantly adapting to (quantitative and qualitative) dissonance – constantly moving toward a state of equilibrium.

The above argues for a more appropriate response to the human dynamic; beyond this, however, we obviously need a much better understanding of environment-behaviour relationships generally. Competent, laboratory-trained psychologists are beginning to examine larger behavioural samples in larger, more complex environments. They seek further to verify and extrapolate from successful laboratory situations. Naturalistic observations in real environments have led to interesting and important insights (Barker, 1960; Sommer, 1966). These must, however, be supplemented with the rigorous kind of data which can only be obtained in an experimental analysis. In the near future millions will be spent to create expanded laboratory settings, and billions will be spent for environments which don't work behaviourally. It would appear that these two efforts can be consolidated for the good of all. The designer and behavioural scientist have complementary goals, and in many instances designed environments could and should become experimental in a more rigorous and systematic sense. Manipulations required to bring an ensemble into equilibrium also yield invaluable data concerning the environment-behaviour interface generally. Such data should, therefore, be carefully recorded, stored, and analysed. Designer-behavioural scientist collaboration has not been particularly successful. In a properly conceptualized environment-behaviour setting these two can interact in a meaningful and productive context.

Conclusions

To summarize the points presented, there is a great need within the design community for a paradigm, a framework to facilitate more viable designed environments, to implement findings in other disciplines, and to assess developments in design research. In order to evolve such a framework, the basis for formulating design problems should be re-examined. Fundamental to this is the identification of a viable unit of analysis. The generally accepted unit human 'need' lacks the required dimensions, and it is suggested that units of behaviour describe a more fundamental taxonomy of problem formulation. The practice of formulating problems in terms of 'buildings' and other preconceived concepts should be abandoned in favour of more relevant problem spaces which are detected, isolated, structured, and realized through an analysis of human behavioural systems. Requisite behaviour systems cannot be defined empirically, but must be essentially designed in response to the participants' physiological and psychological capacities, and to their goals. Given a requisite system of behaviours, the problem of specifying a correlated system of physical contingencies is one of describing a particular environment-behaviour interface – a formidable undertaking considering the limited conceptual and empirical resources available. Realization of the appropriate physical system depends not only upon the problem-solving repertoires of an individual designer, but also upon methodological tools which are now being developed and refined. Before environmental design can become a truly viable enterprise, it is essential that the physical product be verified. Because units of behaviour can be well defined and empirically observed they form a reliable basis for verifying the physical results. Our capacity to conceptualize and solve environmental problems is generally limited by our problem-solving tools and knowledge of behavioural processes. Beyond this, however, are the intrinsic limitations of predicting future sources of environment-behaviour dysfunction, i.e. changing goals, external physical constraints, other stimulus domains and participating organisms. Because of our empirical and conceptual limitations, and because the human problem changes almost before its solution can be actualized, long-term, well-fitting environments are within present tools and knowledge, unrealizable. Under the circumstances we should abandon the finite state problem-solving commitment in favour of realizing experimental settings which respond to disequilibrium on a continuing basis. This shift in design objectives will not only ensure more integral and appropriate physical settings, but provide an effective context for acquiring critically needed information concerning environment-behaviour relations generally.

Designed environments, then, should be both conceptualized and realized as dynamic systems capable of moving toward more appropriate states. They should be viewed as experiments to test hypotheses and record relevant aspects. The conceptual schema presented earlier (see Fig.9) embodies the general characteristics required, and with one minor adjustment (see Fig.12) physical systems can be conceptualized as dynamic. That is, the resultant behaviour system (R_3) becomes (at the completion of all tests and manipulations to realize a physical state) the 'existing' behavioural system (R_1). The entire process is thus analysable as an iterative one. An integral component of such systems would be an information and control system which would have the capability to perform or assist the following operations:

(1) Identifying and testing the consequences of the organization's goal structure.

(2) Reprogramming requisite behaviours in response to changes in the goal structure.

(3) Reprogramming contingent physical configurations.

(4) Monitoring behavioural and physical configurations.

(5) Testing for dissonance within the ensemble.

(6) Improving predictions (short, intermediate, and long-range) by simulating future behavioural and environmental aspects. (These simulations would be based upon past histories of the ensemble and/or hypotheses concerning future configurations.)

(7) Analysing data obtained from particular isolated experiments to: (a) upgrade the ensemble and/or (b) gain general knowledge concerning the environment-behaviour interface.

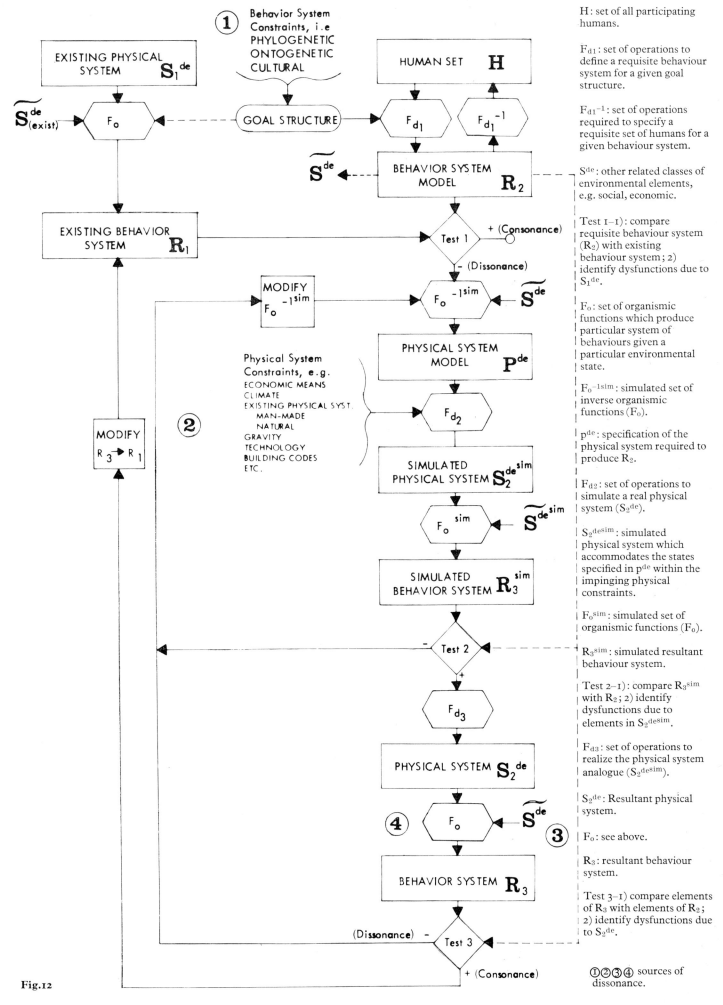

Fig.12

(8) Interfacing with, and communicating these phenomena to human decision-makers at the appropriate stages.

Such an information and control system assumes an on-line, digital computation capability – hardware and software – of some sophistication. Such tools are, however, realizable within existing or soon to be developed technology.

While quite outside the scope of this presentation, it should be noted that a behaviour-contingent approach implies new modes of physical technology. It suggests sub-systems open-ended and highly adaptive along a continuum. There has never been any serious question regarding our ability to produce physical systems of great technical sophistication. The limitations have not really been so much technological as conceptual. A culturally conditioned predilection for 'permanence' in our artifacts, for example, may have low utility in accommodating environmental requirements for highly dynamic, technologically sophisticated cultures. Innovative attempts to accommodate well-fitting environment-behaviour systems at the levels suggested herein, may provide the necessary link to our latent technology, and to the greater physical design freedom implicit in highly developed mass production capabilities.

REFERENCES

C. ALEXANDER. *Notes on the Synthesis of Form*. Harvard University Press (Cambridge 1964).

R. G. BARKER. Ecology and Motivation. *Nebraska Symposium on Motivation*. Nebraska University Press (1960).

J. M. BESHERS. *Urban Social Structure*. Free Press (Glencoe 1962).

E. BRUNSWIK. *The Conceptual Framework of Psychology*. U. of Chicago Press (Chicago 1952).

J. CALHOUN. The Role of Space in Animal Sociology. *Journal of Social Issues, 4* (1966).

R. DUBOS. *Man Adapting*. Yale U. Press (New Haven 1965).

W. DEMBER. *The Psychology of Perception*. Holt, Rinehart and Winston (N.Y. 1963).

J. M. FITCH. The Aesthetics of Function. *New York Academy of Sciences Journal, 128* (1965).

E. GALANTER and M. GERSLENHABER. On Thought: The Extrinsic Theory. *Psychological Review, 63* (1956).

H. GUETZKOW (Ed.). *Simulation in Social Science*. Prentice-Hall (Englewood Cliffs, N.J., 1962).

E. T. HALL. *The Hidden Dimension*. Doubleday (Garden City 1966).

J. G. HOLLAND. Teaching Machines: An Application of Principles from the Laboratory. *Journal of the Experimental Analysis of Behaviour, 30* (1960), pages 275-87.

T. KUHN. *The Structure of Scientific Revolutions*. U. of Chicago Press (Chicago 1962).

O. R. LINDSLEY. Geriatric Behavioural Prosthesis. In R. KASTENBAUM (Ed.), *New Thought on Old Age*. Springer (New York 1964), pages 41-60.

J. MARCH and H. SIMON. *Organisations*. John Wiley (N.Y. 1958).

M. H. MARX and W. HILLIX. *Systems and Theories in Psychology*. McGraw-Hill (N.Y. 1963).

G. A. MILLER. *Mathematics and Psychology*. Wiley (N.Y. 1964).

G. A. MILLER, E. GALANTER, and K. PRIBRAM. *Plans and the Structure of Behaviour*. Holt, Rinehart and Winston (N.Y. 1960).

J. G. MILLER. Living Systems: Basic Concepts. *Behavioural Science, 10* (1965), pages 193-237.

K. POPPER. *The Logic of Scientific Discovery*. Basic Books (N.Y. 1959).

J. ROTHSTEIN. Information, Organisation and Systems. *IRE Transactions on Information Theory* (1954), pages 64-6.

B. RUSSELL. Definition of Number. In J. R. NEWMAN (Ed.): *The World of Mathematics*. Simon and Schuster (N.Y. 1956), pages 537-43.

M. SIDMAN. *Tactics of Scientific Research*. Basic Books (N.Y. 1960).

B. F. SKINNER. *Science and Human Behaviour*. Macmillan (N.Y. 1953).

R. SOMMER. Man's Proximate Environment. *Journal of Social Issues, 22* (1966).

P. SOLOMON *et al. Sensory Deprivation: A Symposium Held at the Harvard Medical School*. Harvard U. Press (Cambridge 1961).

R. G. STUDER. Alexander's Notes on the Synthesis of Form. *Architectural Association Journal, 80* (1965).

R. G. STUDER. On Environmental Programming. *Architectural Association Journal, 81* (1966), pages 290-6.

R. G. STUDER. Experimental Analysis of the Programmed Instruction Environment. Programmed Instruction Project. Harvard University (Sept. 1962).

R. G. STUDER. Behaviour Manipulation in Designed Environments. *Connection*, publication of the Graduate School of Design, Harvard University, *5* (1967).

R. G. STUDER and D. STEA. Environmental Programming and Human Behaviour. *Journal of Social Issues, 22* (1966).

H. S. TERRACE. Stimulus Control. In W. HONIG (Ed.): *Operant Behaviour: Areas of Research and Application*. Appleton-Century-Crofts (N.Y. 1966), pages 271-344.

R. ULRICH, T. STACHNIK, and J. MABRY. *Control of Human Behaviour*. Scott, Foresman and Co. (Glenview 1966).

A philosophical critique of behaviourism in architectural design

by Janet Daley

Whither Behaviourism?

I have long been of the opinion that behavioural psychology and its various ideological tributaries (behaviouristic sociology, statistical psychology, etc.) were suffering from a regrettable paucity of sensitivity and imagination but it is only recently that I have become aware of the insidiousness of the disciplines: they are not simply fatuous, but, in fact, seem to be verging on a new intellectual fascism which could have most frightening results. All this megalomaniac social influence attaching to what seems to me a fundamentally incoherent and ideologically muddle-headed movement, strikes me as cause for serious alarm. I have already transgressed, of course, a number of the self-devised boundaries of the disciplines in my description of them, *viz.* behaviourism is specifically labelled by its adherents as *non-ideological* and certainly not a 'movement' in any ordinary sense of the word. It is, I am told, simply a set of *methods* of experimentation and practice with which one can achieve specific empirical results: no cosmic abstractions here, no high-flown unrealistic theories – just a given set of tools for achieving practical ends. And it is precisely at this claim that I want to aim my most vituperative abuse: at the naïve notion that because behaviourists operate in a conceptual vacuum it follows that their practices (not to speak of their ends) do not *inherently* contain theoretical presuppositions and even (!) ethical assumptions. Their insistent claims that they have no commitments to theory attempt to depict a bevy of hard-headed, down to earth social engineers who have no truck with abstraction but simply ply their pragmatic methods in the most antiseptically objective of atmospheres: the technicians of human behaviour. When we fill out this industrial metaphor, however, we encounter some interesting breakdowns in the technocratic analogy: engineering could not be done (or have evolved) without physics – there are (and can be) no technicians without a theoretical grounding the factors of which can be manipulated, and within whose boundaries coherent experimentation can be performed. Without a conceptual framework, without theory-laden points of reference and self-assumed ideological limitations, no system of random technical devices and methods could even get off the ground, let alone be intelligible in full flight. What I want to claim, of course, is that behaviourists not only do operate from within the bounds of a rigid and systematic theory but that it is precisely their refusal to recognize and acknowledge the theory-laden quality of their endeavour which is most disturbing: one cannot examine a theory in a socially and intellectually responsible way if one refuses to admit its existence; an ideological position cannot be combed for contradictions if it is so entrenched as to be invisible. It is precisely the conceptual presuppositions of behaviourism which I would like to examine, for it seems to me that they rest on a naïve philosophical position compounded of the crudest forms of eighteenth-century empiricism and Newtonian mechanization. The central theoretical tenet involves seeing all mental events as *kinds of* actions: identifiable (and theoretically isolatable) mechanistic processes. Behaviour is seen as composed of a series of traceable mental movements analogous to Newtonian motion with a principle of cause and effect as primitive as Hume's example of billiard balls knocking against one another. Thinking is defined as one sort of activity: a set of behavioural patterns. In the cases where mental phenomena do not readily lend themselves to being depicted in this way (e.g. beliefs, attitudes, etc.) the behaviourists claim, rather coyly, that these are simply examples of more subtle, hidden behaviour.

In Robert Thomson's behaviourist tract *The Psychology of Thinking*, he states:
'All such (reasoning, cogitating) thinking is motivated towards a particular goal, and *is determined by previous learning and experience.*' (My italics.) So one must have assimilated experience and *learned* before one can reason and *think* (as such). How intelligible is this? Presumably Thomson would want to claim that *judgement* was a feature of that later more sophisticated process of *reasoning* and not of the more primitive *learning* phase, for surely if he were to grant that judging went on at the earliest stage, he could not avoid the admission that reasoning did as well and *that* he must avoid to keep his argument

intact. Hence, that earliest level of learning and experiencing upon which the possibility of reasoning rests must be devoid of faculties of judgement: no order must be imposed *on* experience by innate mental capacities. Thus, sensations and perceptions (in the very primitive state in which behavioural discussion must depict them) are just accumulated in an empty receptacle of a mind, in the chaotic and unrelated way we would assume they impinge on the infant's consciousness, and *somehow* result in an ordered backlog or reference file. I would claim that no amount of sense experience (*on the basis of which* one is later to be capable of judging and reasoning) would result, in and of itself, in an ordered set of back references providing the emerging consciousness with the rudiments of *knowledge* about the world. Learning must, to remain intelligible and hence useful as a notion, involve primary processes of judgement: the *ordering* of sensations and perceptions is inherent in the having of them, and in the using of them as coherent experiential patterns. Judgement (and hence, reasoning) is not a separable 'process' from *learning, perceiving,* and *reacting* (as these terms are used by behaviourists) and it can by no means be intelligibly seen as resting in an *a posteriori* relation to them. The suspiciously all-encompassing notion of 'learning' used to explain all behaviour leads to similar conceptual confusions: in attempting to describe the development of consciousness and the personality, within the limitations of this concept, behaviourists are compelled to say some very strange things indeed. Most psychological theories have attempted to come to grips with the problem of how the infant consciousness learns its conceptual way about the world. How, for example, it makes the distinctions necessary for effective action: those between wish fulfilment fantasy and reality; between 'inner' sensations and 'outer'- stimulated perceptions of the actual world. The behavioural interpretation is roughly this: the infant *observes* (and hence, *learns*) that certain of his sensations and impulses do not result in actual consequences in the world, while others do, and on that basis sorts out the internal-phantasy-sensations from the outer-world-related perceptions. What sense can we make of such a categorical dualism as inner phantasy-outer reality, simply evolving out of increased sense experience? Could any number of *actual-outer-stimulated-perceptions* and *phantasied-inner-wish-fulfilment-hallucinations* provide the fledgling consciousness with criteria for distinguishing between them? Or even the conceivability of such a dichotomy? Such a claim could only result from the most naïve sort of empiricist assumptions. The predisposition to function in terms of such categories must be somehow prior to the experiences to be evaluated in these terms and the *judgement* involved in so functioning must be inherent in the experiencing. How would the infant, with no *a priori* criteria, determine which *consequences* were *actual* as opposed to those which were *hallucinatory*? The determining of what constitutes *actual* consequences seems to rest on the same distinction between *real* and *not real* as the dichotomy for which we are attempting to account, so any explanation in terms of perceiving *actuality* would seem doomed to hopeless circularity. The whole concept of reality-testing seems to me to rest entirely on a faculty for judgement, for the notion of 'testing' (let alone of 'reality') – evaluating, comparing – is unintelligible without criteria.

The behaviourist view of concept formation, as based on learning, seems to me to end in a maze of hopeless contradiction. A concept is defined as a sequence of learned responses which are utilized for the organization and interpretation of sense experience; in this way, it is claimed, the residue of past experiences (learned concepts) can be applied to the ordering of present experience. As Thomson says, 'Using concepts is simply applying past learning to a present situation.' On this model, we could never get started at all. If concepts are necessary for the organization and ordering of sense experience, from whence did the individual's first (original) concepts arise? From something other than sense experience? (Surely not – good empiricists, as the behaviourists are, would never admit to the existence of innate ideas.) From early sense experience in its raw and 'unordered' state? Hardly, as the notion of unordered (and hence, unintelligible) sense perceptions producing (in and of themselves) systematic concepts, is simply a logical absurdity. One is beginning to sense the presence of tail-chasing here: of definitions being established which require consent to other definitions which, in turn, refer to the first definitions. That is, concept formation depends on learning and learning is impossible without concepts. In Bruner's theory of how we perform conceptual classification, it is explained that the way we learn a (classificatory) concept is by sorting out and recognizing what distinguishing attributes items must possess in order to belong to the given class. But this is a tautology, not an explanation: to have learned what distinguishing characteristics constitute membership of a given class *is to have learned the concept* of that class. To assume that the recognition of the attributes is an activity or process which *goes on* (in the way that breathing *goes on*) and which *culminates* in my arriving at the concept, is just nonsense. This characterization of concept formation which *presupposes* (instead of explaining) the ability to establish and discern criteria can end in nothing but an infinite regress: it would be necessary, on this framework, to learn how to learn.

A final point against the internal contradictions of behaviourism: one of the proudest claims of this school of thought is that their every proposal and hypothesis is susceptible of straightforward empirical proof or disproof. While the 'metaphysical' claims of Freudian and Jungian theorists require the acceptance of a dogma, behaviourism is purely objective with each of its proposals subject to experimental evidence. If it works – achieves the desired result – it is acceptable, otherwise, not: a true science of human behaviour. What we must question here is what counts for 'working' in the behavioural context and whether anything within the terms of the behaviourists' frame of reference, could ever falsify *the system itself*. This must be the crux of the matter: the behaviourists' complaint about Freudianism is that it interprets all data in its own terms and as such is never susceptible of disproof *as a system*. I would claim that this is equally the case with behaviourism: that while individual proposals can be tested for truth or falsity within the narrow experimental limits devised, no experiment or test ever approaches the *presuppositions within which* experimentation is carried out. One tests the stimulus-reaction patterns of rats, the problem-solving time ratios of children; one does not question – let alone *test* – the applicability of one's notion of 'learning' to human development. The system – the set of presuppositions involving minds as complex machines, all human mental phenomena as based on a model of internalized action – is accepted with every bit as great a leap of faith as is involved in the commitment of the Freudians. And if it is the case that no number of unsuccessful behavioural experiments can disprove the theory, then it follows that no number of successful experiments can prove its validity. The experiments are only successful or unsuccessful *in the terms* of the theory, which, of course, begs the question. Dr R. D. Laing, about whom I will have more to say later, cites an incident of a psychotic patient who consistently regarded his wife as a thing and often referred to her as 'it' (from *The Divided Self*): 'He would, for instance, tell her (it) an ordinary funny joke and when she (it) laughed this indicated her (its) entirely "conditioned", robot-like nature, which he saw indeed in much the same terms as certain psychiatric theories would use to account for all human actions.'

Within the context of this patient's delusion, the fact that his wife laughed at a funny joke counted as 'evidence' that she was of a thoroughly conditioned nature. What he chose to consider as applicable evidence was determined by his presuppositions: such behaviour on the part of the wife could be used as 'evidence' for a number of diverse conclusions, depending on the preconceptions of the observer; most of us would allow it as evidence for the fact that she (1) was conscious, (2) understood the language in which the joke was told, (3) understood the joke, (4) was normally intelligent, (5) considered the joke funny. Only with some sort of exceptional criteria (requiring additional explanation) could it be seen as indicating what the psychotic claimed it indicated and, even then, it could not count as *evidence* precisely because there is no way of falsifying such a story: it is logically impossible for us to disprove or rule out the psychotic's interpretation – it is a way of looking at things, which creates its own terms of reference and criteria for evidence. I think that behaviourism can be characterized in exactly this way: that it is a way of looking at things whose presuppositions are incapable of disproof (or proof). One cannot invalidate the notion that men are machines to a behaviourist because he will allow nothing to count as disproof: all data are read from within the context of the system of beliefs; just as one cannot *invalidate* the notion of the 'unconscious' to a Freudian. Behaviourism seems to me to involve a grotesquely over-simplified view of human experience, and of its own procedures.

I mentioned at the outset that in addition to containing inherent theoretical presuppositions, behaviourism was also riddled with implicit ethical connotations. 'Connotations' might be an unfortunate word: behaviourism does not involve simply ethical *implications* as do many sciences (nuclear physics, for example) by virtue of their possible *consequences*. It is *based on* a particular and readily identifiable kind of moral position: that of the most monolithic sort of utilitarianism. There is no point in my reiterating here what has been said so brilliantly and sensitively by Dr Laing on the subject of psychiatric treatment which reifies and alienates the patient. (See *The Divided Self*, *The Self and Others*, etc.) Thus, I will confine myself to the wider ethical argument that behaviourism in practice (practices including aversion therapy, the exclusive use of drug and electric shock treatment) implicitly and unavoidably regards the *utility* and *conformity* of the human being as a societal unit, as the ultimate and all-embracing value. Evaluating the worth of the demands of a given society *on* individuals is *practically* and *morally* beside the point: it is the individual who must be made to fit, made to be socially viable – a 'useful citizen' in the most harrowing and relentless sense. Behaviourists cannot be permitted to get away with the insistence that they are scientifically 'amoral' (hardly an honourable claim anyway, for those who literally manipulate human behaviour); by the very practice of their techniques they are acting on and carrying out an ethical conviction: society and its internal coherence must be preserved; non-functioning units of the communal organism must be 're-conditioned' (an insidious term if ever I heard one) and slotted back into the system. One summons up macabre visions of misanthropic individuals being conditioned with aversion therapy and turned out as, say, well-adjusted SS officers, and what *must* be considered is that the insane or the neurotic are different and perhaps more complex kinds of *dissenters*: society's drop-outs who could not, or would not play the game, *perhaps with good reason*. One has an absolute moral obligation in the treating and affecting of human behaviour to decide just what sort of games it is permissible to force (or condition) people to play. What if the world were really intolerable? Would it do to 're-condition' all those sensitive enough to find it so?

73

Relational theory

In his paper, 'The Atoms of Environmental Structures', Christopher Alexander sets out a preamble of philosophical justification and/or explanation for his design theory. This discussion attempts to establish a conceptual framework within which the principles of design method are to be viewed. To a professional philosopher much of his presentation seems grotesquely, and rather dangerously, naïve and confused. I realize, of course, that Alexander is not a philosopher and that it would not be just to hold him responsible for knowledge of the more sophisticated subtleties of a discipline which is not his own. He does, however, make himself susceptible to this sort of attack (that is, the philosophical one I am about to give) by venturing into the realms of moral discourse and theory of language. If he is to make pronouncements in these fields, he establishes himself as a fair candidate for abuse by the specialists. He also must be held responsible, of course, as must anyone who attempts to sustain an argument in virtually any field for being *incoherent* and it is in this capacity that a dose of philosophical criticism can be most relevant and useful.

Firstly, Alexander dismisses in a paragraph an issue which has consumed generations of moral philosophers and which still constitutes the most momentous controversy in philosophical discussion of ethics: that of the empirical or non-empirical status of value judgements. With breathtaking arrogance he states that the view which he describes thusly, is simply wrong: 'the rightness or wrongness of a programme is not a question of fact, but a question of value. These people argue in the same way about the physical environment itself. They say the environment cannot be right or wrong in any objective sense, but that it can only be judged according to criteria, or goals, or policies, or values, which have themselves been arbitrarily chosen.' He does not slow his pace long enough to investigate the difficulties in dismissing such a view; he does not even examine why it is that people in varying disciplines have been so inclined to take this kind of position: that is, what it is about the grammar and the conceptual implications of value statements (e.g. notions of 'rightness' and 'wrongness') which makes regarding them as straightforward factual issues so counter-intuitive. Much of the confusion in his statements can be traced to the fact that he clearly confounds the notions of 'non-factual' and 'arbitrary'. He wants to re-classify statements about 'rightness' and 'wrongness' in the environment as being factual rather than moral because he assumes that to be non-factual in the way it would seem that moral statements are, is to be (by definition) arbitrary. He does not seem to be aware of the fundamental distinction between empirical and analytic statements, for example, in which analytically true statements such as 'There are no round squares' are clearly non-empirical (or non-factual in Alexander's terms) but are not, therefore,

arbitrary. The proposition that there are no round squares is not empirical because it is not about the *world* as such: we do not perform laboratory experiments to determine whether or not it is true. It is a statement about how we use the language; it states that within the set of definitions involved in the conceptual system of geometry, there can be no such figure as a round square because such a thing would be *a contradiction in terms*. But the statement 'There are no round squares' is anything but *arbitrary*. It states a coherent and essential aspect of a system of concepts; it has a clear and necessary function in the language. There are, I want to make it clear, many ways of being non-empirical without being arbitrary. In the case of value statements – and propositions about 'rightness' and 'wrongness' are, *by definition*, value statements no matter how much Alexander would like to rework the linguistic categories to re-define them – there are overwhelming difficulties in regarding them as empirical because we simply would not know what it meant to treat them in the same way as we do straightforward empirical propositions. How, for example, do we *test* them, measure them against objective standards to determine their truth or falsity? 'It is raining outside' is a non-problematic empirical proposition. I check its accuracy by looking out the window. What equivalent checks are there for statements like 'This building programme is wrong' or 'This structural form is right'? Just what objective state of affairs is it to which I look to see if such statements correspond, in the way I look at the world to verify the statement 'It is raining outside'?

At the same time, value statements need not be *arbitrary* (although they *might be*, in the way that any statement *might* be arbitrary). We know perfectly well, in fact, how to distinguish arbitrary value statements from non-arbitrary ones. If someone says 'This building plan is right' and when asked why, says simply 'Oh, I don't know. I just like it. That's the way I think building plans ought to be. It seems right to me.' I am justified in calling his value judgement arbitrary. If, however, he backs up his statement about the rightness of the building plan, with a coherent and logically consistent set of principles and criteria of value (e.g. that it is conducive to good community relations and human contact) then there is nothing *arbitrary* about his value statement (although it is still decidedly non-empirical).

Having thus condemned value judgements as hopelessly arbitrary, Alexander then goes on to make a value judgement so dazzlingly arbitrary as to approach whimsy. He decides to regard all human tendencies (a term which he never bothers to define adequately) as *worthy* of being fulfilled, having value in and of themselves; and he goes on to state that what counts as being 'right' in a design programme are those forms and structural relations which allow for the maximum fulfilment of human tendencies. The philosophical and practical moral problems here are myriad: surely there are all sorts of *undesirable* human tendencies (genuine tendencies none the less) which, any reasonable man would grant, are anti-social, destructive, etc. One must be prepared to come to grips philosophically with this sort of case. The mere fact that we can make sense of the idea of *undesirable tendencies* means that tendencies in themselves are not sensible candidates for absolute standards of value. Issues of what constitutes value cannot be settled by edict. To attempt to do so, is simply to make nonsense of the language and to dismantle the framework within which it is possible to talk sense.

Alexander betrays a quite primitive and unfortunate theory of language. He seems to confuse, for example, 'intelligibility' with 'utility'. He says at one point that a certain statement about 'needs' has 'so many ways of interpreting it, that the statement is almost useless'. He then implies that the statement is thus *meaningless* ('We don't know what it really says'). What he means by 'useless' is, apparently, 'not capable of immediate application to the given problem'. To condemn all statements which have no immediate *utility* as being unintelligible is almost incredibly philistine and insensitive. Statements are not tools or engineering implements. This kind of view represents a gross misconception of what language is about.

There seems to be a real necessity for sorting out presuppositions from conclusions in Alexander's theory. While he assumes that he is spotting conflicts in the environment, *as such:* that he is observing conflicts which exist in and of themselves and are only being *brought on by* inadequate forms, he often, in fact, seems to be defining conflict in terms of his own preconceived ideas about what constitutes bad form. This is even more the case with his discussion of 'tendencies'. This notion ('tendency') needs a great deal of philosophical work before it can be made intelligible. Is it meant to include only what might be called 'natural' tendencies: those which would exist in any or no architectural environment? Or does it also encompass tendencies induced by environment? It is, as it stands, an almost totally amorphous and inapplicable concept. And, of course, he makes no allowance for ambivalent or self-contradictory tendencies, e.g. a single individual having mutually contradictory tendencies or desires. (The tendency towards monogamy which coexists with the tendency towards infidelity in most of us.) On this point Alexander would, I should think, be plunged into the sort of moral dilemma he so ardently wishes to avoid: he would have to decide *which* of the tendencies was worthy of fulfilment or facilitation by the environment, and *that* sort of decision, which would surely crop up repeatedly in any realistic assessment of human conditions, requires an appeal to values beyond Alexander's simplistic fiat that the sole criterion of 'rightness' in environment is the fulfilling of human tendencies.

I think it is appropriate here to recall, in regard both to behavioural theories generally and Alexander's statements, a warning traditional in English philosophy: beware of jargon; disciplines which encourage, thrive on, or revel in, incestuous private languages should always arouse suspicion. Coherence and clarity are not simply aesthetic attributes: they are the most reliable and consistent indicators of the integrity and intelligibility of a discipline.

The structure of the design process

by L. Bruce Archer

1 Introduction

This paper attempts to set up a framework within which the set of skills, sensibilities, and intellectual disciplines that, taken together, constitute the art of designing might be logically related so as to form the basis of a science of design. No attempt is made here to distinguish between architectural, engineering, and industrial design. Indeed, it is an essential element in the philosophy underlying this thesis that the logical nature of the act of designing is largely independent of the character of the thing designed. By the same token, no attempt is made here to define 'good design'. The argument presented is concerned with the theory of navigating towards a chosen destination rather than with the identity or merit of the destination itself.

A logical model of the design process is developed, and a terminology and notation is adopted, which is intended to be compatible with the neighbouring disciplines of management science and operational research. Many of the concepts and techniques presented are, indeed, derived from these disciplines. A primary purpose of this work is to provide a conceptual framework and an operational notation within which designers might work and upon which case study analyses might be based.

The range of techniques and disciplines which might be employed at various stages in the conduct of a design project are referred to only in general terms. Different design problems, and different classes of design activity, will call for different techniques and different emphases of various stages. There is no suggestion here that all design should be conducted according to a given formula – only that the logic of any design problem may be better perceived against the background of a common framework.

In certain instances, the general form of the laws which are thought to connect certain phenomena common to most design problems is indicated. It is hoped that the logical model, terminology, and notation presented will facilitate the accumulation of the case study data, and the derivation of the more precise general laws, upon which an emergent science of design must be based.

2 The nature of the act of designing

2.1 Man sets different values[1] on different conditions. Those values may vary from person to person and from time to time. When a man discerns that there is a discrepancy between a condition as it is and the condition as he would like it to be, he experiences discontent. Should the feeling of discontent be sufficiently strong, the man takes action calculated to change the condition so that it more nearly approximates to the condition he desires. The condition giving rise to desire is here described as a property (of the environment), the attainment of a state of satisfaction in response to that property is described as the goal, and the action calculated to achieve it is described as a goal-directed action.

2.2 When the action appropriate to the correction of a particular unsatisfactory condition is not apparent, a problem is said to exist. The problem may be concerned with the correct identification of the nature of the improvement required, or with the identification of the means for achieving it, or both.

2.3 The presence of the unsolved problem, acting as a barrier to the achievement of the goal, is itself an undesirable condition, requiring action to remove it. The problem-solving activity is thus itself a goal-directed activity.[2]

2.4 The activity of resolving the problem therefore precedes the activity of correcting the condition. For the purposes of this argument, the aims of a condition-correcting activity (implementation) will

---

[1] The unavoidability of reference to a value system in defining objectives is well argued on p.29 of I. D. J. BROSS's *Design for decision*, Macmillan, 1953. The terms used in the present paper also owe a great deal to those used in HORST RITTEL's *The universe of design*, University of California, Berkeley 1966.

[2] See also *Executive decisions and operations research* by DAVID W. MILLER and MARTIN K. STARR, Prentice Hall, 1960.

be referred to as goals, and the aims of a problem-solving activity (planning) will be referred to as objectives. Many of the objectives of a problem-solving activity will be simply the re-expression of the goals of the condition-correcting activity to which the problem refers. Thus a goal in constructing a house might be to provide the property of durability. If the form of construction which will give maximum durability is not immediately apparent, then a problem exists. The relevant objective in the problem of deciding how to construct the house simply re-expresses the goal of providing the property of maximum durability in the construction. In addition, the activity of deciding has its own goals, such as to come to a conclusion as quickly as possible.

2.5 The term 'design' has been previously defined by the author as 'to conceive the idea for and prepare a description of a proposed system, artifact or aggregation of artifacts'. The condition in which the designer would like to be is that in which he can offer an adequate description of the proposed system or artifact. The activity of getting into this condition is a goal-directed activity as described in paragraph 2.1. Where (as is usual) the nature of the design idea and its development is not immediately apparent, then a problem exists as described in paragraph 2.2.
The activity of designing is thus a goal-directed activity and normally a goal-directed problem-solving activity.[3] The properties which are required to be exhibited by the proposed artifact are defined by the objectives of the problem. The details of the design are the designer's conclusions as to the means by which those properties may be provided.

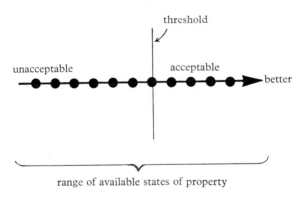

Fig.2.1
An objective nominates a property, indicates the direction in which changes would be for the better, and identifies a threshold between acceptable and unacceptable states.

2.6 In a goal-directed, problem-solving activity, all the properties required to be present in the end result may be thought of as having existed, in varying degrees, in the prior, unsatisfactory situation. Some of the desired properties may have been present and satisfactory already, others may have been absent (that is to say, present in zero degree) and others may have been present, but to an unsatisfactory degree. The objectives of the activity are thus ambitions, not merely to cause those properties to be present, but to cause them to be present to a satisfactory degree

or to as high a degree as possible. Each objective thus nominates a property, indicates the direction in which changes would be for the good and identifies a threshold between 'good enough' and 'not good enough' (Fig.2.1).

2.7 Since the properties referred to may be of many different kinds, and since they may be subject to different scales and units of measurement, it is convenient to introduce a convention or form of notation by which they may be more uniformly expressed:[4]

O signifies an objective or goal
P signifies a property or condition
O(y) signifies a particular degree of fulfilment of an objective
P(x) signifies a particular state of a property or condition
P(u) signifies the ideal state of P in respect of a given objective
P(l) signifies a minimum acceptable state of P
P(m) signifies a maximum acceptable state of P
P(v) signifies a state of P which represents total lack of fulfilment of an objective

It is clear from the definition elaborated upon in paragraph 2.6 that the degree (y) or fulfilment of an objective O is a dependent variable, controlled by the state (x) of the property P exhibited in the solution, that is:

$O(y) = f P(x)$ (where f signifies 'some function of')[5]

2.8 P(x) is expressed according to whatever scale is most appropriate to the property concerned (that is to say, dimensions are expressed in inches or centimetres, weight expressed in pounds or kilograms, time expressed in seconds, minutes, and hours, etc.). According to the conventions adopted here, O(y) is always expressed on the scale:

$O(y) = 0$ (zero) when there is total lack of fulfilment of the objective
$O(y) = 0.5$ when the related property is at the threshold between fulfilling and not fulfilling the objective
$O(y) = 1$ (unity) when there is total fulfilment of the objective

---

[3] RUSSELL L. ACKOFF, in *Scientific method: optimising applied research decisions,* Wiley, 1962, p.73, describes design problems as falling into the general class of developmental problems, which he defines similarly.
[4] Somewhat similar definitions and notation are used in separate chapters by RUSSELL L. ACKOFF and C. WEST CHURCHMAN in *Progress in operations research, volume I,* Wiley, 1961 (Ed. Russell L. Ackoff). See also *Games and decisions,* by R. DUNCAN LUCE and HOWARD RAIFFA, Wiley, 1957, considered by some to be the best work on value theory.
[5] Non-mathematicians are often greatly put off by para-mathematical notation. Any reader who shares this feeling is invited to try the trick of reading out in the mind's ear the full verbal equivalent of each cipher, thus: 'The degree (y) of satisfaction of objective O is some function of the state (x) of property P'.

Moreover, according to this convention, the key states of a property P defined in paragraph 2.7 are always related to the key values of degree of fulfilment of its related objective O in the following way (Fig.2.2):

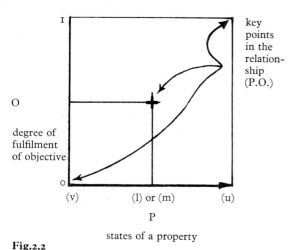

key points in the relationship (P.O.)

states of a property

Fig.2.2
The degree of fulfilment of objective is a dependent variable, governed by the state of its associated property.

when $P(x)=P(u)$ then $O(y)=1$
when $P(x)=P(m)$
or $P(x)=P(l)$ $\Big\}$ then $O(y)=0.5$
when $P(x)=P(v)$ then $O(y)=0$[6]

Paragraphs 2.9 to 2.19 below examine this relationship more closely. Paragraph 2.20 takes up the thread of the main argument.

2.9 Where the states of a property P can vary along some continuous scale, such as a scale of centimetres or kilograms, then the relationship between the degree (y) of fulfilment of objective O and the state (x) of its associated property P may be expressed in the form of a curve.
Sometimes the relationship between O(y) and P(x) is a linear one (Fig.2.3). For example, a design might be required to entail minimum wastage of the raw material (say, steel sections) from which it is made, the maximum acceptable wastage P(m) being 50%

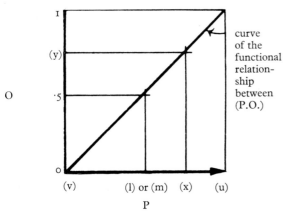

curve of the functional relationship between (P.O.)

Fig.2.3
Example of a relationship between an objective and a property taking the form:

$$O(y)=1+\frac{P(x)-P(u)}{2(P(u)-P(l))}$$

and the ideal wastage P(u) being 0%. The states of property P may be expressed in terms of some convenient ratio scale for weight or volume, say pounds or cubic feet. In such cases the relationship between O(y) and P(x) may take the form:

$$O(y)=1+\frac{P(x)-P(u)}{2(P(u)-P(l))} \qquad 7$$

Thus, if the relevant values of P are known or can be predicted, an index of degree of fulfilment (y) of the objective O can be calculated.

2.10 In other cases, the ideal state P(u) of a property may be indeterminate or indeterminable. For example, a product may be required to be as profitable as possible, with a low limit of profitability, but no high limit (Fig.2.4). In these cases the relationship between O(y) and P(x) may take the form:

$$O(y)=1-\frac{P(l)}{2P(x)} \qquad 8$$

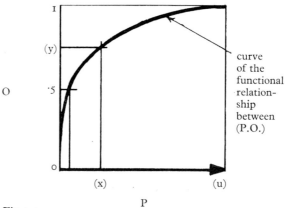

curve of the functional relationship between (P.O.)

Fig.2.4
Example of a relationship between an objective and a property taking the form:

$$O(y)=1-\frac{P(l)}{2P(x)}$$

2.11 In some circumstances, both the ideal state P(u) of the property (i.e. that which totally fulfils the objective) and the zero state P(v) (i.e. that which totally fails to fulfil the objective) may be indeterminate (Fig.2.5). For example, a surface might be required to be smooth, with an expressible threshold between acceptable smoothness and unacceptable smoothness, but with no determinable states of P to

[6] Often, the nature of a property is such that the concept 'total lack of fulfilment of the objective' is unreal. In any case, the decision maker is not normally very interested in the precise evaluation of degrees of fulfilment of objective much below the threshold of acceptability (that is, where O(y) is much below 0.5). In practice, therefore, the identification of a real world value for, or state of, P (v) can usually be dispensed with.
[7] This is simply the expression for a straight line graph passing through P(l) and P(u). P(l) and P(m) are interchangeable in this formulation, and either term may be employed, to suit the context of the problem.
[8] This, and the following rather unwieldy formulations, describe typical property/satisfaction curves. In practice, it is usually easier simply to draw the curve most appropriate to the circumstances, and to read off, rather than to calculate, the merit indices associated with given values of P.

represent total success or total failure in fulfilling the objective. In these cases, the relationship between O(y) and P(x) may take the form:

$$O(y) = \tfrac{1}{2} + \frac{\arctan\,(P(x) - P(l))}{180}\,[9]$$

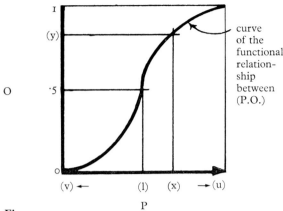

Fig.2.5
Example of a relationship between an objective and a property taking the form:

$$O(y) = \tfrac{1}{2} + \arctan \frac{(P(x) - P(l))}{180}$$

2.12 Again, there may be both a maximum P(m) and a minimum P(l) state which represent the thresholds of acceptability in a property, with the ideal state P(u) lying somewhere in between (Fig.2.6). For example, the brightness of illumination of an instrument (say, a speedometer) might be required to lie between two limits of dimness and glare, with the ideal brightness at a given level in between. In these cases the relationship between O(y) and P(x) may take the form:

$$O(y) = 1 - \frac{(P(x) - P(u))^2}{2(P(u) - P(l))^2}\,[10]$$

or

$$O(y) = 1 - \frac{(P(x) - P(u))^2}{2(P(m) - P(u))^2}$$

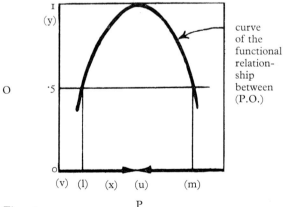

Fig.2.6
Example of a relationship between an objective and a property taking the form:

$$O(y) = 1 - \frac{(P(x) - P(u)^2}{2(P(u) - P(l)^2}$$

2.13 Sometimes, as in the example described in paragraph 2.12 above, the values P(x) of the property concerned should relate, not just to the requirements of one particular user in one set of circumstances, but to a given range of people or circumstances. The relationship between O(y) and P(x) might therefore be subject to statistical conditions or range and frequency distribution, so that a given state P(x) of the property would be interpreted as providing a certain probability of fulfilling the objective O to the indicated degree O(y) for a certain range of users (Fig.2.7).

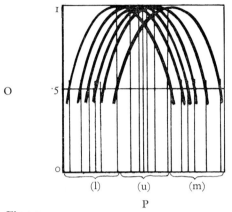

Fig.2.7
Example of a property with statistically distributed optimum and limiting values.

2.14 All the examples above have been related to properties whose states may vary continuously along scales based on some agreed unit or interval.[11] Such scales are known as ratio scales or interval scales. Not all properties can be expressed on interval scales. Beauty, convenience, and importance are examples. This is because there are no units of beauty, units of convenience or units of importance with which ratio scales could be constructed.[12] However, in such cases, it is usually possible to compare designs (or whatever it is that is under discussion) and to list them in descending order of merit, according to the

[9] 'Arctan' means 'the angle whose tangent is . . .'. To evaluate O(y) the value for [P(x)–P(l)] must be calculated from the given states P(x) and P(l) and this value looked up in a table of tangents of angles. From this table the equivalent degrees of angle must be identified and this number inserted in the numerator of the formula in place of the expression 'arctan [P(x)–(Pl)]'. Of course the concept of an angle in the geometrical sense is irrelevant here, the arctan occurring simply as a convenient device for providing the right pattern of values.
[10] Either formulation may be used, according to which side of P(u) the state P(x) happens to lie in the case in question.
[11] S. S. STEVENS, in 'On the theory of scales of measurement', *Science* 1946, 103, pp.677–80, recognizes ratio scales (having a non-arbitrary zero and a constant unit of measurement), interval scales (having an arbitrary origin and a unit *assumed* to be constant), ordinal scales (having an order but no unit of measurement) and nominal scales (having identities by neither order nor measurement). See also CLYDE H. COOMBS in 'Psychological scaling without a unit of measurement', *Psychological Review*, 57, May 1950, 3, pp.145–58.
[12] The rankable, rather than the quantifiable, basis of perceptual and aesthetic criteria is argued by E. H. GOMBRICH in his book *Art and Illusion*, Phaidon, 1956, and by MARTIN K. STARR in *Product design and decision theory*, Prentice-Hall, 1963.

property concerned. This rank ordered list constitutes what is known as an ordinal scale, and the act of constructing the list is called 'ranking'.[13]

2.15 Sometimes, in setting up an objective for an ordinal property in a design, it is possible to select as an example another design L which can be taken as a criterion or threshold of acceptability which the new design must beat. In other words, this example represents P(l) on a specially constructed ordinal scale. It might also be possible to select a number of exemplars W, Y and Z (such as competitors' designs) which could be ranked in respect of property P, to fill out an ordinal scale (Fig.2.8). The proposed new design X could be compared with the exemplars and assigned a place in the scale. The item (say, exemplar W) which is judged best in respect of property P is represented by the point P(u) on the scale and the rank of the proposed design X is represented by the point P(x). The degree of fulfilment O(y) of the objective may then be determined by the formula (see paragraph 2.9) for linear relationships between O and P, thus:

$$O(y) = 1 + \frac{P(x) - P(u)}{2(P(u) - P(l))}$$

where
P(l) signifies the rank of the criterion or threshold design L
P(u) signifies the rank of the exemplar judged best in respect of P (that is, rank 1)
P(x) signifies the rank of the proposed design X

The problems of value judgement in connexion with ordinal properties such as beauty and convenience and the techniques for ranking are dealt with further in my forthcoming book.

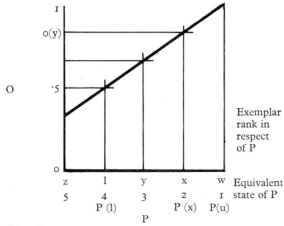

Fig.2.8
Properties whose states cannot be expressed in terms of interval scales may be expressed in terms of exemplars on an ordinal scale.

2.16 One of the difficulties sometimes encountered in ranking is that although the steps between ranks are theoretically equal, the person or group of people performing the ranking may regard them as being unequal in the real-life situation. The person or group will be referred to here as 'an arbiter'. Thus,

an arbiter might decide that chair X is more comfortable than chair Y, and chair Y more comfortable than chair Z. However, he might consider that the difference in comfort between chairs X and Y is a great deal less than the difference between chairs Y and Z. He may feel that, had he been given 100 chairs to rank, he might well have ranked chair X first, chair Y second, and chair Z seventy-fifth. This concept can be more conveniently expressed as a rating scale, where the arbiter assigns chair X 100 points, chair Y 99 points, and chair Z 25 points (Fig.2.9). Under suitable controlled conditions, human subjects can assign merit ratings of this kind to non-measurable properties in a reasonably consistent and repeatable way. For most arbiters, a scale of 1–100 seems to be about the most easily handled.[14] This technique is equivalent to using human beings as indicating-instruments in those circumstances where no physical indicator is available. Within the context of a given design problem, rating scales can be perfectly adequate substitutes for ratio scales, providing that the arbiters are correctly chosen and the conditions for judgement are adequately controlled.

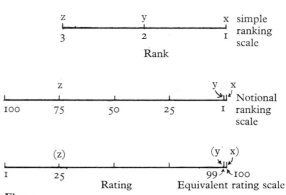

Fig.2.9
Where, in the real-world situation, the steps between rankings are felt to be unequal, the items may be ranked as if they were in a much larger collection. This may be conceived as a rating scale, where each item is assigned 'merit points' or 'an importance rating'.

2.17 There are some properties, such as the property of identity, which are not even susceptible to being ranked in order of merit or importance. For example, the use of certain listed colours for electrical wiring or pipework may be required or forbidden by statutory regulations. The items in such a list may be described as being on a nominal scale (Fig.2.10),

[13] Techniques for ranking and testing the validity of rankings are well described in M. J. MORONEY's *Facts from figures*, Penguin, 1951.
[14] A study of the validity of subjective scaling, carried out by Dr Samuel J. Messick at the University of Illinois, is referred to by OSGOOD, TANNENBAUM and SUCI on p.146 of their *The measurement of meaning*, University of Illinois Press, 1957. In another paper (E. ADAMS and S. MESSICK, 'An axiomatic formulation and generalisation of successive intervals scaling', *Psychometrika*, 1958, 23, pp.355–68) many ordinal scale models and validity tests are listed, and a technique presented for the testing of the consequences of assumptions about successive ordinal scales. C. H. COOMBS, in 'Psychological scaling without a unit of measurement', *Psychological Review*, Vol.57, May 1950, No.3, introduces an 'ordered metric scale' derived from the relationship between a subjective scale and an associated physical scale.

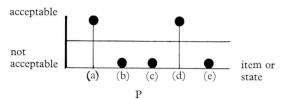

Fig.2.10
There are some properties whose various states cannot be set out on either ratio scales or ordinal scales, but merely identified. The objective may still nominate one or more states as 'acceptable'.

that is to say, a scale giving identities to various possible states of the property, but neither rank nor a unit of measurement, apart from the distinction 'acceptable' or 'not acceptable'.

2.18 In a sense, according to the conventions adopted, nominal scales are merely rating scales with only two ratings – above the limit and below the limit. Similarly, ratio scales are merely rating scales where the interval between ratings is fixed at the smallest available interval of the unit measurement. For convenience, however, the scales of all the properties of a design can be regarded as falling into three classes; ratio scales for measurable properties, ordinal scales for merit-rateable properties, and nominal scales for 'acceptable/not acceptable' properties.

2.19 In all cases, having assigned limits of acceptability (u) and (l) in a property P, the degree (y) of fulfilment of the objective O emerges as a value on the scale 0–1 (Fig.2.11), on calculation by one or other of the general formulae set out in paragraphs 2.9, 2.10, 2.11, 2.12 or 2.15 or by whatever other law might connect the amount of property present with degree of fulfilment of objective.

2.20 Returning to the thread of the main argument set out in paragraph 2.7, it must be noted that few problems are concerned only with the fulfilment of a single objective. Any solution will fulfil the various objectives in varying degrees. In order to find some way of illustrating the interdependence of the degrees to which a given design will fulfil two or more co-existing objectives, some further notation must be introduced:

O_n signifies a given objective ⎫ where n is an iden-
P_n signifies a given property ⎬ tifying number or
                             ⎭ letter

i signifies a given design
j signifies an alternative design.
P(w) signifies a particular state of a property (alternative to (x))
O(z) signifies a particular degree of fulfilment of objective (alternative to (y))

Thus a given design i will exhibit state (x) of property P_1 and state (w) of property P_2, fulfilling objective O_1 to degree (y) and objective O_2 to degree (z). This can be illustrated according to the convention of co-ordinates (Fig.2.12).

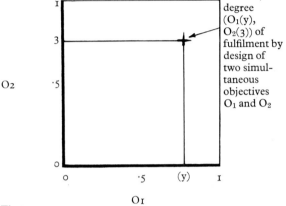

degree $(O_1(y), O_2(3))$ of fulfilment by design of two simultaneous objectives O_1 and O_2

Fig.2.12
A given design may fulfil two simultaneous objectives to the same or differing degrees.

2.21 Similarly, the performance of two or more designs in respect of two co-existing objectives may be indicated by co-ordinates (Fig.2.13).

O(p) ⎫ signify particular degrees of fulfilment of
O(q) ⎬ objective (alternatives to (y) or (z))

2.22 Two objectives co-existing in a problem may be referring (albeit in different ways) to the same property in the desired end result. For example, the bed of a machine tool may be required to be extremely stiff not only to maintain the alignment of slides and spindles, but also to prevent the transfer of working loads on to weak structural members. The property of stiffness serves two objectives. In this

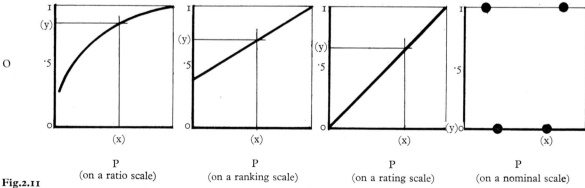

Fig.2.11
The alternative states of all the types of properties may be assigned relationships with degrees of fulfilment of objective,

and any particular state of the property will be associated with a value for O(y) lying between xero and unity.

81

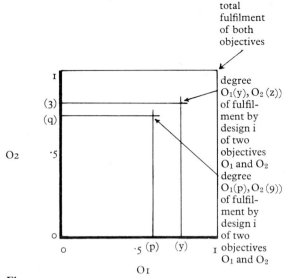

Fig.2.13
The degrees to which two alternative designs fulfil two simultaneous objectives can be compared with the ideal degree of fulfilment.

case the better states of the property lie in the same direction – greater stiffness. These two objectives may be described as co-operating objectives (Fig. 2.14). On the other hand, two co-existing objectives may refer to the same property but seek opposite ideal states. For example, a piece of equipment might need to be as light as possible in order to be portable but as heavy as possible in order to be stable in use. Such objectives may be referred to as opposing objectives. Or again, two objectives may refer to different properties in the end product (say, durability and cost), but these properties may themselves be interdependent, so that the fulfilment of the objectives, too, becomes effectively interdependent. Some objectives may, of course, be only distantly connected.

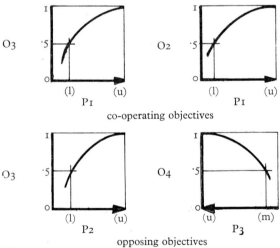

Fig.2.14
Two objectives referring to the same (or interdependent) properties and pointing to the same ideal states may be referred to as co-operating objectives. Two objectives referring to the same (or interdependent) properties and pointing to opposite ideal states may be described as opposing objectives.

2.23 It has been seen in paragraph 2.20 that the two coincidental values of degree of fulfilment by a design of two co-existing objectives can be shown according to the convention of co-ordinates. Where objectives are dependent the locus of the points of coincidental states of a property or properties will mark out a curve of feasible mutual states (Fig.2.15).

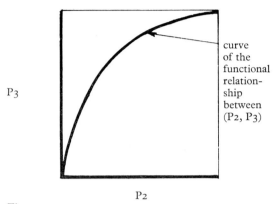

Fig.2.15
Where two properties are interdependent the locus of the points of coincidental states of the properties marks out a curve of feasible mutual states.

2.24 The limiting states of the properties concerned may be similarly set out according to the conventions of co-ordinates (Fig.2.16). The spaces marked off by these limits indicate the field of mutually acceptable degrees of fulfilment of the co-existing objectives. Any solution whose mutual states of the associated properties lie within this field is an acceptable solution.

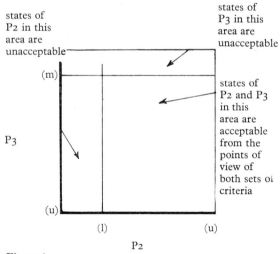

Fig.2.16
The spaces marked off by the limiting states of the properties indicate the field of mutually acceptable states.

2.25 Where objectives are dependent, the curve of feasible mutual states may be superimposed on the fields of limiting states[15] (Fig.2.17). In some cases a

[15] This invokes the technique of linear programming. See S. VAJDA's *An introduction to linear programming and the theory of games*, Methuen, 1960, and/or G. B. DANTZIG's *Linear programming and extensions*, Princeton University Press, 1963. See also the AIDA technique (analysis of interconnected decision areas), referred to on p.27 of *Interdependence and uncertainty*, Tavistock Publications, 1966.

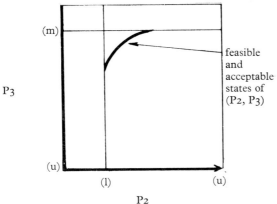

Fig.2.17
The superimposition of the fields of acceptable states of a property upon curves of feasible states marks out the range of feasible and acceptable states.

section of the curve of feasible mutual states of the properties concerned will lie within the field of mutually acceptable degrees of fulfilment of the objectives. In these cases, feasible *and* acceptable solutions are available. In other cases there might be no solution which is both feasible and acceptable. The only escape from such a situation is *either* to move one or both of the limits of acceptability *or* to introduce some inventive step to change the inter-relationship of the objectives. The former course of action constitutes a change in the performance requirements of a design[16] (that is, in solution by negotiation), while the latter constitutes an act of invention (that is, solution by innovation).

2.26 Where, as in most problems, there are more than two objectives, these can be taken pair by pair and expressed in the terms described above. In aggregate the interaction of fields of acceptability will constitute an n-dimensional domain of accept-ability. This domain may be discontinuous, that is to say, there may be more than one acceptability-space, each bounded by limiting states for various proper-ties, implying that there is more than one distinctive class of acceptable solutions.

2.27 Similarly, the interdependence of the curves of feasible mutual states will constitute an n-dimen-sional hypersurface of realm of feasibility. An im-portant prerequisite for an ultimate solution is that at least a portion of the realm of feasibility should intersect the domain of acceptability, producing an arena within which a solution must be found (Fig.2.18).

2.28 Thus the act of designing consists in:

1. Agreeing objectives
2. Identifying the properties or conditions required by the objectives to be exhibited in the end result
3. Determining the relationships between varying states of the properties and the varying degrees of fulfilment of their respective objectives

[16] Most designers tend to regard the solution of a problem by an act of invention as being more 'respectable' than solution by an act of negotiation.

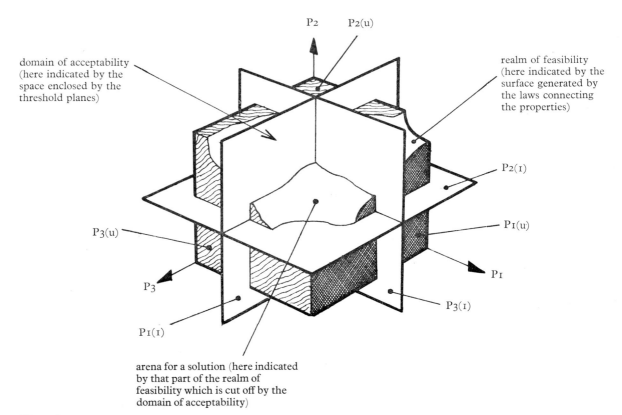

Fig.2.18
The interdependence of the states of the properties consti-tutes an n-dimensional hypersurface on realm of feasibility. The product of the erection of limiting states of the properties is an n-dimensional space or domain of acceptability. The superimposition of the domain of acceptability on the realm of feasibility marks out the arena within which a solution is to be selected.

4. Establishing the limiting and ideal states of the properties, and hence the domain of acceptability implied by the objectives
5. Identifying the laws controlling the interdependence (if any) of the properties
6. Ensuring that the interdependence of the properties constitutes a realm of feasibility and that this lies at least in part in the domain of acceptability
7. Selecting an optimum solution within the arena thus delineated.

2.29 In most design activities more than one person is involved. The people concerned may include the financial backer, the constructor, and the salesman, as well as the designer.[17] Any one of these may be an individual or a group. Certain individuals or groups, whether or not participating in the resolution of the problem itself, are entitled to nominate objectives or limits of acceptability – for example, the user and regulatory bodies such as health and safety authorities. People, bodies of people or impersonal forces who do or who are entitled to define objectives or limits of acceptability will be referred to here as the arbiters in a problem.[18] The set of objectives in a problem arise from the union of the sets of goals of the arbiters involved.

During the course of the problem-solving activity new objectives may tend to form and reform. At any one stage the situation may indicate that the total set of objectives will prove to have been fulfilled in varying degrees, so that individual arbiters will be satisfied with the apparent outcome in varying degrees. The then prevailing discontents may give rise to new problems, or result in shifts of emphasis in the pursuit of objectives or load to the assignment of new limits of acceptability.

3 The systematic model

3.1 Where two phenomena are causally related, that is to say where one phenomenon is caused to occur or to change its state by the introduction or change of state of another phenomenon, these two are said to form a system[19]. A spring balance, for example, is such a system, since adding a load to the pan causes the spring to compress an appropriate amount (Fig.3.1).

3.2 In systems terminology, the causal phenomenon is described as the input and the resulting effect is termed the output (Fig.3.2).

3.3 Where information about, or energy produced by, the output of a system is used to adjust the input (for the purpose of controlling the output), this cycle is called 'feedback'.[20] For example, in the case of the spring balance referred to previously, if the user watches the indicator and controls the amount of (say) sugar poured into the pan until the indicator reaches a desired point, this watch-and-control activity is an example of feedback. Feedback can be

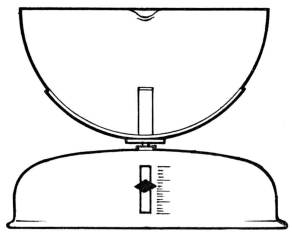

Fig.3.1
A spring balance is a system where the addition of a load causes a spring to extend or compress.

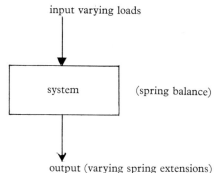

Fig.3.2
Spring balance described in systems terms.

exercised through human perception and control, or it can be automated. Thermostats in heating systems and speed governors in engines are examples of automatic feedback (Fig.3.3).

3.4 In many cases, systems are influenced by more than one input and may have more than one output. For example, an electric motor is a system in which the input of electrical energy at a certain voltage and a certain amperage will produce mechanical energy with a particular speed and power. Varying either or both the inputs will result in a variation in either or both the outputs (unless the input variations are self-compensating). A factor which could or does

[17] LUDWIG VON BERTALANFFY, in his paper 'General systems theory' (*Human Biology*, 1951) argued that all human societies, or segments of it, are essentially goal-seeking open systems. See also paper on 'Individual motives and group goals' in *Group dynamics – research and theory* by Cartwright and Zander, Row Petersen and Co., 1962.
[18] This is well demonstrated in DAVID W. MILLER and MARTIN K. STARR, *Executive decisions and operations research*, Prentice Hall, 1960.
[19] For an admirably clear statement of the systems idea, see W. ROSS ASHBY, *Introduction to Cybernetics*, Chapman and Hall, 1957. See also K. E. BOULDING 'General systems theory: Skeleton of a science', *Management Science*, April 1956, and GORDON PASK, *An approach to Cybernetics*, Hutchinson, 1961.
[20] Norbert Weiner's exposition in *Cybernetics*, Wiley, 1948 of the concept of 'feedback' as a principle of control, common to machines, animals and human beings, formed the basis of modern systems theory.

84

take up one or more of a variety of states is called a variable. This name will be applied to all the inputs and outputs in a system even where they happen to take, or have always taken, a fixed state (Fig.3.4).

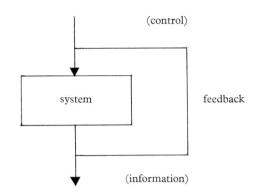

Fig.3.3
The feedback concept in systems theory.

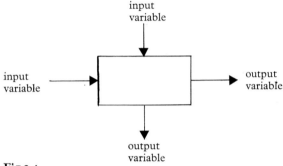

Fig.3.4
Systems may have more than one input and more than one output.

3.5 Often, certain of the inputs are under the control of an operator or decision maker (for example, a designer may be able to choose the depth of a beam to be incorporated in a structure), while others are governed by circumstances outside the operator's control (for example, the designer will have no control over the tensile strength of the beam material). The former are described as decision variables and the latter as context variables (Fig.3.5).[21]

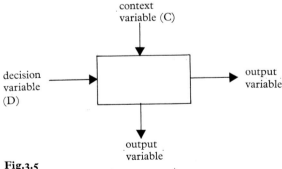

Fig.3.5
Some variables (C) may be outside the control of the decision maker and some variables (D) may be within his control.

[21] RUSSELL L. ACKOFF and C. WEST CHURCHMAN, in separate chapters of *Progress in operations research:* Vol.1, (Ed.) Russell L. Ackoff, Wiley, 1961, use similar definitions and notation.

C signifies a context variable
C_n signifies a particular context variable (where n is an identifying number or letter)
$C_n(k)$ signifies a particular state k of context variable C_n (where k is an identifying letter or a value according to some scale)
D signifies a decision variable
D_n signifies a particular decision variable (where n is an identifying number or letter)
$D_n(i)$ signifies a particular state i of decision variable D_n (where i is an identifying letter or a value according to some scale).

3.6 Similarly, outputs may consist of those which the decision maker wishes to control (for example, a designer may wish to ensure that a structural beam is capable of bearing a given load) and those to which he is indifferent (for example, the volume of metal in the beam). The former are here described as relevant outputs and the latter as incidental outputs (Fig.3.6).

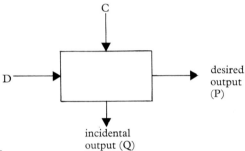

Fig.3.6
Some output variables (P) will be those which the decision maker wishes to control and others (Q) may be merely incidental.

P signifies a relevant output (this is the same notation as for a property. See paragraph 3.9)
Q signifies an incidental output
Q_n signifies a particular incidental output (where n is an identifying number or letter)
$Q_n(s)$ signifies a particular state s of incidental output Q_n (where s is an identifying letter or a value according to some scale)

3.7 The incidental output of one system, however, might be the context variable of another (Fig.3.7). For example, the volume of metal which was only an incidental output from the structural system referred to in paragraph 3.6 might be a context variable in another system, say costing or building operations. Where two systems are being handled simultaneously, these two systems can be said to form a larger, or complex, system.

3.8 Where one system in a complex of systems produces outputs which affect another in the same complex, it is convenient to regard the decision variable in the first as being also a decision variable in the second (Fig.3.8).

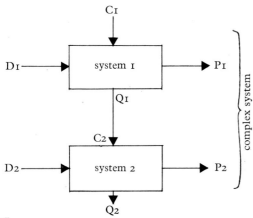

Fig.3.7
An incidental output from one system may be a context variable in another.

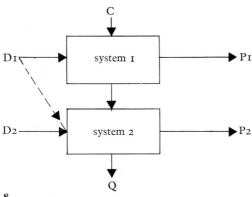

Fig.3.8
A decision variable in a system which partly controls another system may be regarded as being a decision variable in the second system also.

3.9 A design problem, or any other sort of problem can be expressed in systems terms.[22] In Section 2, problem-solving activities were described as being directed towards the provision of certain properties, or certain states of certain properties, in the end result. The problem is thus a system, with the decision variable(s) as input and the property(ies) as output (Fig.3.9). The set of laws determining the ways in which given properties vary under the influence of different decisions constitute the external or general disciplines within which a problem must be solved.

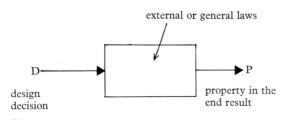

Fig.3.9
A design problem may be expressed in systems terms.

3.10 The way in which varying states of a property relate to varying degrees of fulfilment of a goal also constitutes a system, with the property as input and the degree of fulfilment of goal as output. The laws connecting states of properties with degrees of fulfilment of objectives constitute the internal or

specific disciplines of a problem. A complete goal-decision system is therefore a linked pair of systems, where the decision variable(s) controls a property and the property controls an objective (Fig.3.10). In a complex of goal-decision systems, where a decision variable may directly or indirectly control a number of properties, there may be some ambiguity as to how the goal-decision systems should be conceived. For the purposes of this argument, a goal-decision system is constructed so that it contains one and only one objective, so that the system can be identified with, and named after, the objective it contains.

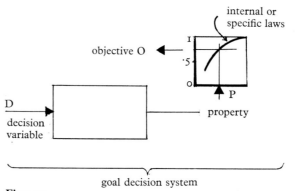

Fig.3.10
Where a decision variable controls a property and the property controls a degree of fulfilment of objective, the whole is said to form a goal-decision system.

3.11 In a complex of goal-decision systems, the aim is to select a set of states for the decision variables, such that the resulting set of states of the properties satisfy their respective objectives, allowing for the indirect, as well as the direct, effects of the decision variables (Fig.3.11).

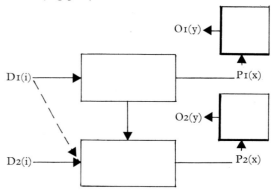

Fig.3.11
The aim is to select a set of states for the decision variables, such that the degree of fulfilment of objectives is optimized.

3.12 In real-world circumstances, the decision variables themselves may be subject to limiting values or states (Fig.3.12). For example, the machinery

---

[22] This is demonstrated for general problems by RUSSELL L. ACKOFF in *Scientific method: optimizing applied research decisions*, Wiley, 1962, and by MILLER and STARR in *Executive decisions and operations research*, Prentice Hall, 1960. For design problems it is demonstrated by HUGH M. BOWEN in a series of articles on 'Rational design' in seven successive issues of *Industrial Design*, commencing February 1964.

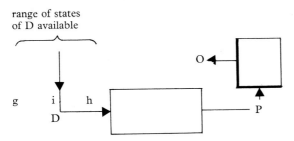

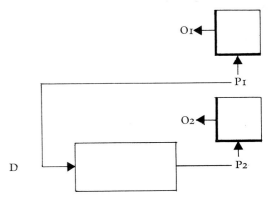

Fig.3.12
The decision variables may be subject to limitations.

Fig.3.13
A decision variable, as well as controlling a property, may itself be a property, having more meritorious and less meritorious states in itself.

in a factory which is to manufacture a product under design might only be capable of handling metal sheet within certain limits of thickness and width. The state i selected for a decision variable D_n must therefore lie within the permitted range, thus:

$$D_n(i) \subset \{D_n(g) \ldots D_n(h)\}$$

where

$D_n(g)$ signifies a limiting stage g of decision variable D_n (where g is an identifying letter or number, or a value according to some scale)

$D_n(h)$ signifies another limiting state h of decision variable D_n (where h is an identifying letter or number, or a value according to some scale)

$\subset$ signifies 'is contained within the set of possible states'

The set of decision variables available to the decision maker, and their limiting conditions, will be referred to as 'the design resource' (or in the case of non-design problems, the 'decision resource').[23]

3.13 In some circumstances, certain states of the decision variables may be regarded as more desirable than others, not because of their good and bad effects upon the properties they control, but because of some merits or demerits attached to the states of the decision variables themselves. For example, in the case of the factory referred to in paragraph 3.12, it might be organizationally or economically more useful to employ certain machines or certain thicknesses of metal rather than others. The fact that different merits are attached to different states of a variable means that the variable is a property within the terms of the definition in paragraph 2.1, and the relationship of different states of the decision variable with different degrees of fulfilment of objective is determined by some arbiter, as described in paragraph 2.29. Thus a decision variable, as well as controlling a property, may itself be a property (Fig.3.13).

3.14 The distinctions as to whether an input variable is a decision variable or a context variable, whether or not certain states of a decision variable are accessible to the decision maker, and whether or not a decision variable is also a property, are all part of the definition of the problem rather than part of the problem to be handled. The persons or bodies of people, or the impersonal forces making these distinctions will also be referred to as arbiters in the problem, as suggested in paragraph 2.29. When an

arbiter is beyond reach of any persuasion or modification, he may be regarded, or referred to, as 'nature'.

3.15 A set of states selected for the decision variables in a particular case constitutes 'a proposal'. In the case of design problems, this may be referred to as 'a design proposal' or 'a design'. If the proposal were to be implemented, the consequence would be a set of states of the properties which might be called 'the outcome'. In the case of design problems, the outcome may be variously described as 'the design' or 'the product' or as 'the properties of the product'. Strictly speaking, the product, as a piece of hardware, does not appear until it has been embodied by the set of goal-directed activities to which the problem-solving activities relate (see paragraph

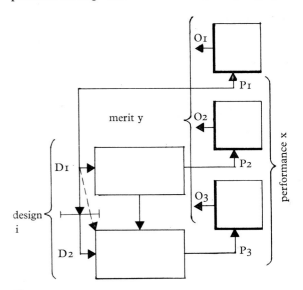

Fig.3.14
A set of states i for the decision variables constitutes a design.

A set of states x for the properties constitutes a performance.

A set of states y for the degrees of fulfilment of objectives constitutes the merit of a performance.

[23] A similar reference to the concept of the decision resource occurs on p.43 *et seq.* of *Interdependence and uncertainty: digest of a report from the Tavistock Institute*, Tavistock Publications, 1966.

2.4).[24] However, since the problem-solving activities are conducted with the end product in mind, these distinctions are difficult to make. For the purposes of this argument, the set of states of the decision variables selected by the decision maker will be referred to as 'the design'[25] (or, in the case of non-design problems, 'the proposal') and the set of states of the properties arising from a proposal will be referred to as 'its performance'. The set of degrees of fulfilment of the objectives appropriate to a particular performance will be referred to as 'the merit' of this performance (Fig.3.14). This may be expressed in notation as follows:

Design i→Performance x→Merit y (where→signifies 'leads to').

Design i $= \{D_1(i), D_2(i) \ldots D_n(i)\}$
Performance x $= \{P_1(x), P_2(x) \ldots P_n(x)\}$
Merit y $= \{O_1(y), O_2(y) \ldots O_n(y)\}$

$\{D_1(i), D_2(i) \ldots D_n(i)\}$ signifies a set of states i for a set of decision variables $D_1, D_2 \ldots D_n$.

$\{P_1(x), P_2(x) \ldots P_n(x)\}$ signifies a set of states x for a set of properties $P_1, P_2 \ldots P_n$.

$\{O_1(y), O_2(y) \ldots O_n(y)\}$ signifies a set of states y for a set of objectives $O_1, O_2 \ldots O_n$.

3.16 Similarly, the set of states of the context variables which apply in a given case constitutes the context of the problem (Fig.3.15). It is the combined effects of the proposal and the context which determine the outcome, or performance.

Context k ↘
 Design i ↗ Performance x→Merit y
(where → signifies 'leads to').

Context k $= \{C_1(k), C_2(k) \ldots C_n(k)\}$

$\{C_1(k), C_2(k) \ldots C_n(k)\}$ signifies a set of states k for a set of context variables $C_1, C_2 \ldots C_n$.

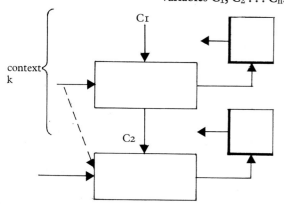

Fig.3.15
A set of states k for the context variables constitutes the context.

[24] This distinction between the situation in the real world and the problem solver's mental concept of what might be done in that real world is studied on p.37 of RUSSELL L. ACKOFF's *Scientific method: optimising applied research decisions*, Wiley, 1962.

3.17 The set of criteria against which performance is measured is described here as 'the performance specification'.[26] A performance specification will lay down the properties which the outcome is required to constitute, and will indicate the way in which various states of these properties will be regarded as being more or less satisfactory. In other words, it lists the properties and defines the goal/property relationships (Fig.3.16).

$\{(O_1=fP_1), (O_2=fP_2) \ldots O_n=fP_n)\}$ signifies a performance specification relating to properties $P_1, P_2 \ldots P_n$.

For example, the performance specification for a chair may lay down that it must accommodate people of a prescribed range of statures and build, withstand certain structural tests, sell at less than a certain price, and earn a profit at a certain rate on investment. The design resource will be the set of materials, processes, shapes, finishes, and so on, which the designer has at his discretion. The context will be the characteristics of materials, prices of commodities, and other imponderables which will affect the result, but over which the designer has no control. The design will be the set of decisions (materials, processes, shapes, finishes, etc.) that he actually chose. The performance of the design would be the range of statures and build of people that the chair (if embodied) would actually accommodate, the tests it would meet, the price at which it would sell, and the profit it would earn. The merit of this performance would be the degree to which it approached the ideals indicated in the performance specification.

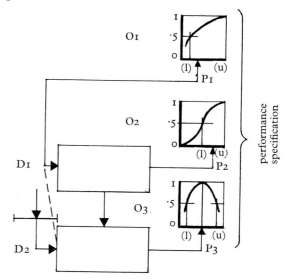

Fig.3.16
A performance specification lists the properties required and defines the relationships between states of the properties and degrees of fulfilment of objective.

[25] The term 'set', as used here, and the notation which follows are in accordance with the conventions of the theory of sets. See IRVING ADLER's *The NEW mathematics*, John Day, 1958.

[26] The term 'performance specification' (or P-spec) is used in a similar sense by J. CHRISTOPHER JONES. See 'A method of systematic design' in *Conference on design methods*, (Ed.) J. Christopher Jones, Pergamon, 1963.

3.18 It has been pointed out in Section 2 that the co-existence of a number of objectives in a problem defines a certain domain of acceptability. The limiting states of the properties and the laws governing their interrelations were said to define a certain realm of feasibility. The superimposition of the domain of acceptability and the realm of feasibility were described as defining the arena in which an adequate performance must be developed. In a similar way the ranges of limiting values and the laws governing the interrelationships of the decision variables define what may be termed 'the scope' of the design (or decision) resource.

3.19 The description of the nature of the act of designing which was set out in paragraph 2.28 can now be expanded to take in the concept of the goal-decision system:

1. agreeing objectives
2. identifying the properties or conditions required to be exhibited in the end result
3. determining the relationships between varying states of the properties and the varying degrees of fulfilment of their respective objectives
4. establishing the limiting and ideal states of the properties, and hence the domain of acceptability implied by the objectives
5. identifying the decision variables available to the designer, and the scope of the resources as defined by their limiting states and interrelationships
6. formulating a model of the goal-decision systems present, linking the decision variables with the properties, and the properties with the objectives
7. ensuring that the interdependence of the properties constitutes a realm of feasibility and that this lies at least in part in the domain of acceptability
8. proposing one or more sets of states for the decision variables, within the scope of the resources; establishing the predicted performance(s), that is to say, the resulting sets of states of the properties; and ensuring that at least one performance lies within the arena defined by step 7 above
9. selecting the optimum proposal

3.20 In a particular design problem it may be possible to produce several feasible and acceptable designs. Although it is quite possible for two different designs to exhibit an identical performance, it is more usual for alternative designs to fulfil the given objectives in differing degrees (Fig.3.17).

Design j→Performance w→Merit z
Design (or proposal) j = $\{D_1(j), D_2(j) \ldots D_n(j)\}$
Performance w = $\{P_1(w), P_2(w) \ldots P_n(w)\}$
Merit z = $\{O_1(z), O_2(z) \ldots O_n(z)\}$
where $D_n(j)$ signifies an alternative state j of decision variable D_n (state j being an alternative to state i)

3.21 It is also likely that attainment of a satisfactory performance in respect of some objectives will be regarded as more important than the attainment of a

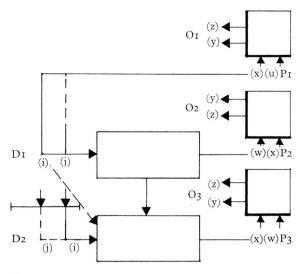

Fig.3.17
Design i might give rise to performance x of merit y.
Design j might give rise to performance w of merit z.

satisfactory performance in respect of others. That is to say, the objectives themselves have an order of importance.
In a diagram of performance, the relative merit of alternative designs may be more readily discerned if the objective fulfilment scales are arranged in order of importance and the merits of the individual performances are indicated on them (Fig.3.18).

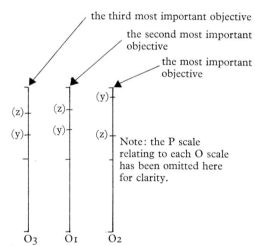

Fig.3.18
To assist in discerning relative overall merits the objective fulfilment scales may be represented arranged in order of importance.

3.22 It is likely that in the case of any two competing designs each will score well in a different set of objectives. In general, a solution which scores well in high ranking objectives is to be preferred over one which scores well only in low ranking objectives.
On the diagram comparison is simplified if the points indicating merit for a particular performance are joined (Fig.3.19). Overall merit can be evaluated by comparing the resulting curves.

3.23 In two merit curves, a tendency to lie above is better than a tendency to lie below, since according to the conventions adopted the direction called good always points upwards (Fig.3.20).

89

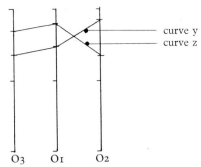

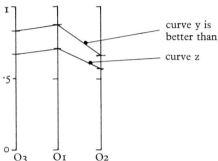

Fig.3.19
Comparison is simplified if the points representing the degrees of fulfilment of objective relating to each performance are joined.

curve y
curve z

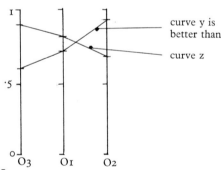

Fig.3.20
A tendency for a merit curve to lie above its fellow is better than a tendency to lie below.

curve y is better than
curve z

Similarly, a tendency to a positive slope (north-east to south-west) is better than a tendency to a negative slope (north-west to south-east), since the higher scores should be in the higher ranking objectives (Fig.3.21).

Again, a convex curve (intermediate values tending upwards) is better than a concave curve (intermediate values tending downwards) since the intermediate values score better in the convex curve (Fig.3.22).

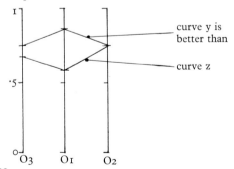

Fig.3.21
A tendency to a positive slope is better than a tendency to a negative slope.

curve y is better than
curve z

Fig.3.22
A tendency to a convex curve is better than a tendency to a concave curve.

curve y is better than
curve z

3.24 However, the analysis of these curves is hampered by the fact that in real-world design problems the notional difference in importance between (say) the objective ranked first and the objective ranked second may be regarded by the arbiters as very much greater (or less) than the difference in importance between (say) the objective ranked second and the objective ranked third. Hence a rating scale, such as that employed for the rating of merit in respect of non-quantifiable properties (paragraph 2.16), may also be employed for the rating of importance.

3.25 It is convenient to begin by rating the importance of objectives on a scale of 0–100 (Fig.3.23).[27] Thus, in a project with say, forty objectives, that objective which is regarded as overwhelmingly the most important might be rated at 100. The next most important at 75 and most of the others between 60 and 50. A very minor objective might be rated at 5. Two or more objectives may take the same rating, where necessary, and the scale may be extended or modified as convenient.

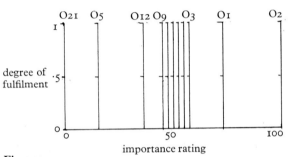

Fig.3.23
As a further assistance in discerning overall merits of alternative performances, the objective fulfilment scales may be represented arranged according to a scale of importance.

3.26 The comparative evaluation of merit curves, as sought in paragraph 3.22 then becomes simpler. Each curve is fully described by the location of the points on it, using the convention of co-ordinates. The importance scale becomes the horizontal axis and the merit scale becomes the vertical axis (Fig.3.24).

r signifies an importance rating (where r is any factor appropriate)
r_{0n} signifies the importance rating of objective O_n
$\{(r_{01}, O_1(y)), (r_{02}, O_2(y)) \dots (r_{0n}, O_n(y))\}$
signifies the merit curve y for a set of objectives $O_1, O_2 \dots O_n$

3.27 An ideal overall performance (Fig.3.25) would be one in which each objective is completely fulfilled – that is to say, where $O_1(y)=1$, $O_2(y)=1 \dots O_n(y)=1$. Hence:

curve of ideal performance =
$\{(r_{01}, 1), (r_{02}, 1) \dots (r_{0n}, 1)\}$

3.28 The relative merits of the performance of two or more designs may be expressed in terms of their

---

[27] But see also certain qualifications set out in para. 3.29.

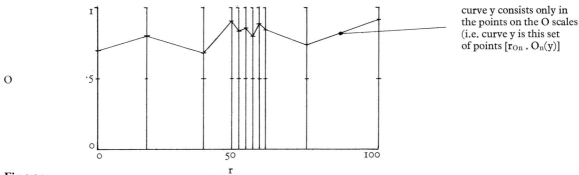

curve y consists only in
the points on the O scales
(i.e. curve y is this set
of points $[r_{On} . O_n(y)]$

Fig.3.24
A merit curve consists in the points defined by the degrees of
fulfilment of objective and the importance rating of each
objective.

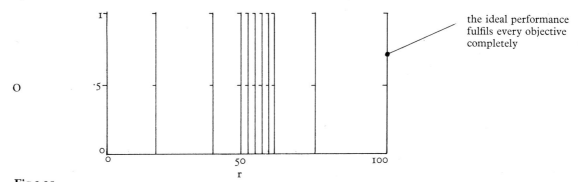

the ideal performance
fulfils every objective
completely

Fig.3.25
The merit curve of an ideal performance consists in the set
of points defined by the 'totally fulfilled' end of the objective
fulfilment scales.

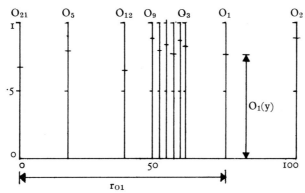

Fig.3.26
The index of merit is calculated by:

$$\text{index of merit} = \frac{[r_{O1} . O_1(y)] + [r_{O2} . O_2(y)]\ldots + [r_{On} . O_n(y)]}{r_{O1} + r_{O2}\ldots + r_{On}}$$

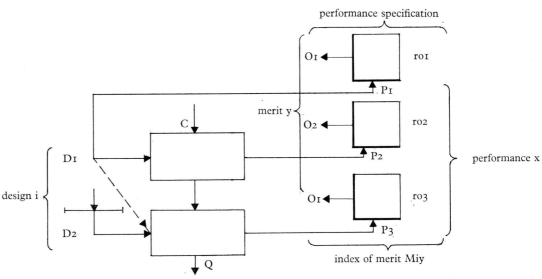

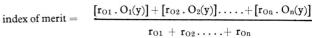

Fig.3.27
Diagrammatic form of systematic model of a design problem.

departure from the ideal performance. All the criteria for merit comparison set out in paragraph 3.23 are satisfied when the overall merit of a design is calculated as the ratio of the sum of the degrees of fulfilment of the individual objectives, each weighted by its importance rating, to the sum of the ideal degree of fulfilment of objectives, weighted by their importance weighting (Fig.3.26):

$$M_{iy}(t) = \frac{\Sigma(r_{o_n} . O_n(y))}{\Sigma r_{o_n}}$$

where

M signifies an index of merit

M_{iy} signifies an index of merit M relating to a performance y arising from a proposal i (where i and y are identifying letters or numbers for particular proposals and performances respectively)

$M_{iy}(t)$ signifies a particular value t for an index of merit M_{iy} (where t is a number lying between zero and unity)

In this formulation, overall merit in respect of any given number of objectives is rated on the scale zero-to-unity in exactly the same way as degree of fulfilment of a goal is measured. That is to say, when the index is 1, the performance is ideal; when the index is 0.5, the merit of the performance is at the threshold between acceptability and unacceptability. The technique of employing this index of merit for the evaluation of performance will be described here as the 'rated-objective merit-index' technique (ro-mi).

3.29 Clearly, the validity of the rated-objective merit-index hangs upon the validity of the importance ratings by which the degrees of fulfilment of individual objectives are weighted. Equally clearly, the importance ratings assigned to objectives are human judgements and prey to all the fallibilities of human judgement.[28] However, the presence of human values in a problem is inherent in the concept of problem solving as a goal-directed activity as here defined (see paragraphs 2.1–2.6). The mechanism by which value judgements are made, and by which importance ratings are assigned, are dealt with in greater detail in my forthcoming book.

3.30 However, the occurrence of an incorrect assignment of an importance rating at the commencement of a project need not be a disastrous event. It is open to the arbiter or arbiters in a problem to manipulate the importance ratings in any way they wish, and to revise their ratings at any stage they

wish, so as to represent their true aims and interests as the consequences of their decisions emerge, or fresh information becomes available.

3.31 Where it is desired that good fulfilment of a lower ranking objective should be capable of outweighing a less good fulfilment of a higher ranking objective, then small intervals may be chosen between their respective ratings. For example:

Where the rank of O_1 is greater than the rank of O_2 but where $r_{o2} . O_2(y)$ is to be permitted to exceed r_{o1}, $O_1(y)$
then r_{o1} might be assigned 100
and r_{o2} might be assigned 99
Thus, when $O_1(y) = 0.5$
and $O_2(y)$ $= 0.6$
then $r_{o1} . O_1(y)$ $= 50$
and $r_{o2} . O_2(y)$ $= 59.4$

3.32 Alternatively, where it is desired that even the maximum fulfilment of a lower ranking objective should never be capable of outweighing even the most marginal fulfilment of a higher ranking objective, then large intervals between ratings may be chosen.
For example:

Where the rank of O_1 is greater than the rank of O_2 and where $r_{o2} . O_2(y)$ must not exceed the threshold value of $r_{o1} . O_1(y)$
then r_{o1} might be assigned 100
and r_{o2} might be assigned 50
Thus, when $O_1(y) = 0.5$
and $O_2(y)$ $= 1$
then $r_{o1} . O_1(y)$ $= 50$
and $r_{o2} . O_2(y)$ $= 50$

3.33 In addition to selecting appropriate importance ratings for the objectives in a project, arbiters must also ensure that the correct values are chosen for[29] the key values of the properties P identified by the objectives, particularly in respect of the limits of acceptability P(l) or P(m). According to the conventions adopted in the ro-mi technique, a design is totally unacceptable if it falls below the limit of acceptability in respect of *any* objective. If, in order to obtain a solution at all, arbiters are compelled to accept a design falling *below* the threshold previously adopted in respect of a certain objective, the decision to accept the design is equivalent to deciding to shift the level of acceptability in respect of that objective.

3.34 The combination (Fig.3.27) of the ro-mi technique thus defined with the systematic model described in paragraph 3.15 provides a further reformulation of the nature of the design act, thus:

[28] The point that the selection of objectives necessarily involves a more or less arbitrary decision, based upon an individual's set of values, somewhere along the line is clearly argued by DAVID W. MILLER and MARTIN K. STARR in *Executive decisions and operations research*, Prentice Hall, 1960. The repeatability of subjective measurement is demonstrated by S. S. STEVENS in 'On the theory of scales of measurement', *Science 1946*, 103, pp.677–80; by E. ADAMS and S. MESSICK in 'An axiomatic formulation and generalisation of successive intervals scaling', *Psychometrika*, 1958, 23, pp.355–68; and by CLYDE H. COOMBS, in 'Psychological scaling without a unit of measurement, *Psychological Review*, Vol.57, May 1950, pp.145–58.

[29] In order to provide room for manoeuvre in seeking an optimum solution, and indeed in order to maximise the probability of obtaining an arena for a solution at all (see para. 2.27), the low limits of acceptability must be set at that threshold below which performance would really be quite unacceptable.

1. agreeing objectives
2. rating objectives
3. identifying the properties required to be exhibited in the end result
4. determining the relationships between the varying states of the property and the varying degrees of fulfilment of their respective objectives
5. establishing the limiting states of the properties and hence the domain of acceptability implied by the objectives

} preparation of a product performance specification

6. identifying the decision variables available to the designer, and the scope of the resources as defined by their limiting states and interrelationships
7. formulating a model of the goal-decision systems present, linking the decision variables with the properties, and the properties with the objectives

} establishment of the design resources

8. ensuring that the interdependence of the properties constitutes a realm of feasibility and that this lies at least in part in the domain of acceptability
9. proposing one or more sets of states for the decision variables, within the scope of the resources; establishing the predicted performance(s) (that is to say, the resulting sets of states of the properties); and ensuring that at least one performance lies within the arena defined by step 8 above

} development of design solution(s)

10. evaluating the merit of the predicted overall performance(s)
11. selecting the optimum solution
12. communicating design description

} evaluation of design(s)

3.35 The diagrammatic form of the systematic model employed in this argument so far (for example, Fig.3.27) becomes excessively complicated when more than four or five properties are involved.[30] A more flexible model is provided when the variables are displayed in the form of a matrix (Fig.3.28). In the course of formulating a problem and developing a solution the matrix is gradually filled out, in interplay with the real-world situation and with the analogues adopted, as described in section 4. The matrix form lends itself to automatic computation and replication. In the remainder of this text, the diagrammatic form of the systematic model will be retained as a conceptual model, but the matrix form will be regarded as the effective form.

4 The operational model

4.1 The systematic model developed in Section 3[31] is an effective means for setting out the logical structure of a problem, but it does nothing in itself to establish what the solution might be. That is to say, it is not an operational model.

4.2 In any given system, the ways in which the outputs vary in response to changes in the inputs will be governed by appropriate 'laws'. The corpus of knowledge about such laws constitutes the disciplines of physics, chemistry, mechanics, electronics, economics, sociology, psychology, ethics, aesthetics, etc.[32] The main justification for the employment of

[30] For example, see Figs.6.3 to 6.6.
[31] The relationship between a real world system, a logical model of the structure of that system, and an analogue used to imitate the behaviour of the system is examined on p.372 of RUSSELL L. ACKOFF's *Scientific method: optimising applied research decisions* Wiley, 1962 (see also para 3.15).
[32] W. I. BEVERIDGE in *The art of scientific investigation*, Heinemann, 1957, draws a nice distinction between the heuristic disciplines of the manager, designer and technologist, which are directed towards getting answers which work, whether the reasons are understood or not, and the classical discipline of the scientist, which is directed towards finding proofs for hypotheses, no matter how limited or useless (in the 'pure' science sense) these may appear to be.

systematic model of a multi-objective goal-decision system

item	performance specification					decision resource							proposal	evaluation of proposal	merit so far			
O_n	$O_n = f P_n'$	r_{On}	$O_n y = f(P_n(l), P_n(u), P_n(x))$			$P_n = f(C_n, D_n)$			$C_n(k)$	$D_n(i) \subset \{D_n(g), ..D_n(h)\}$			$P_n(x) = f(C_n(k), D_n(i))$	$O_n(y) = f P_n(x)$	$M_{iy}(t) = \dfrac{\Sigma r_{On}.O_n(y))}{\Sigma r_{On}}$			
n_O	$n_P =$	$r =$	$l =$	$u =$	$f =$	$n_C =$	$n_D =$	$f =$	$k =$	$g =$	$h =$	$i =$	$x =$	$y =$	$r_{On}.O_n(y) =$	$\Sigma r_{On}.O_n(y) =$	$\Sigma r_{On} =$	$t =$
1	2	3	4	5	6	7	8	9	10	11	12	13	14	15	16	17	18	19
					1 ·5 0													
					1 ·5 0													

Fig 3.28
The variables in a systematic model of a goal-decision system may be displayed in the form of a matrix in which, in interplay between the real world and various analogues, the problem may be formulated and a solution developed.

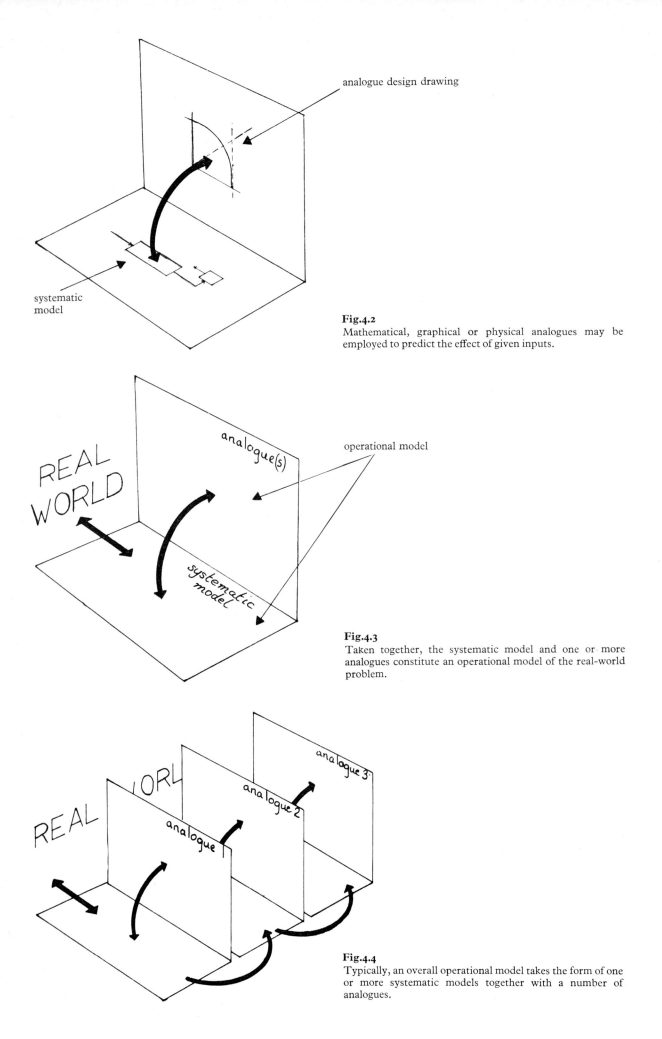

analogue design drawing

systematic
model

Fig.4.2
Mathematical, graphical or physical analogues may be
employed to predict the effect of given inputs.

analogue(s)

operational model

REAL
WORLD

systematic
model

Fig.4.3
Taken together, the systematic model and one or more
analogues constitute an operational model of the real-world
problem.

analogue 3

analogue 2

REAL   ORL

analogue

Fig.4.4
Typically, an overall operational model takes the form of one
or more systematic models together with a number of
analogues.

6. by agreement between arbiters, assign importance ratings to the objectives (col.3)

7. in consultation with the arbiters, determine the limiting states of the properties which are to be equivalent to the ideal and threshold degrees of fulfilment of their respective objectives (cols.4 and 5)

8. establish the relationships (internal or specific laws) connecting varying states of the properties with varying degrees of fulfilment of their respective objectives (col.6)

9. establish the domain of acceptability defined by the superimposition of the limiting states of the properties (if necessary, in order to gain a positive domain of acceptability, negotiate changes at 7, and repeat) (cols.4 and 5)

10. identify the relationship (external or general laws) governing any interdependence existing between the states of properties identified at 5 above (cols.4 and 5)

11. establish the realm of feasibility defined by the compatible ranges of states of the properties (if necessary, in order to obtain a positive realm of feasibility, take an inventive step creating new relationships at 10, and repeat) (cols.4 and 5)

12. establish the arena within which a performance must be found, as defined by the superimposition of the domain of acceptability and the realm of feasibility (if necessary, in order to obtain a positive arena for performance, negotiate changes at 7, and/or create new relationships at 10, and repeat) (cols.4 and 5)

13. identify the context variables which contribute to governing the goal-decision systems under examination (including those context variables which arise from sub-problems already handled) (col.7)

14. identify the decision variables governing the states of the properties (col.8)

15. erect a (or improve the existing) systematic model of the goal-decision systems connecting the decision variables with the properties, and the properties with the objectives, in the sub-problem

16. identify the laws connecting the varying states of the decision variables and context variables (inputs) with the varying states of the properties (outputs) in the goal-decision systems identified at 15 (col.9)

17. establish the ranges of states of the individual context variables which apply to the case in hand (col.10)

18. establish the context defined by the superimposition of the prevailing states of the context variables (col.10)

19. establish the ranges of states available in the individual decision variables (cols.11 and 12)

20. identify the laws governing any interdependence existing between the states of the decision variables at 14 (cols.11 and 12)

21. establish the scope of the design resource defined by the compatible ranges of states of the decision variables (if necessary, in order to obtain a positive scope of design resources, negotiate changes at 19, and repeat) (cols. 11 and 12)

22. erect one or more analogues to represent the laws identified at 10, 16 and 20

23. identify the decision maker(s) entitled to select states of the decision variables in the sub-problem

24. by agreement among the decision makers, and using the analogues erected at 22 for the laws at 20, select a self-compatible set (design i) of states for the decision variables (col.13)

25. using the analogues erected at 22 for the laws at 16, determine the resultant set (performance x) of states of the properties (col.14)

26. establish whether or not performance x lies within the arena for performance defined at 12 (if not repeat from 24). If no solution is obtainable, create new relationships between the properties at 10 (inventive step), or re-work sub-problems giving rise to context variables at 13 (reappraisal), or negotiate new limiting values for the properties at 7 (re-statement), and repeat (cols.4 and 5)

27. evaluate merit y of overall performance x in respect of all objectives handled so far (rated-objective merit-index M_{iy}) (cols.15–19)

28. repeat from 24 (alternative design j) as often as necessary or as often as time and money will permit, until the merit z of overall performance w is as high as possible (rated-objective merit-index M_{jz})

29. identify and validate any critical assumptions or approximations made during the course of the solution of the sub-problem

30. repeat from 1 until the overall problem is resolved

4.15 This formulation is quite general, however. It describes problem-solving behaviour in terms which include, but are not limited to, the needs of the activity or arriving at a configuration for a proposed artifact. The application of problem-solving behaviour to the specific class of problems called design is developed in Section 5.

5 The design programme

5.1 Although there are exceptions, the great majority of design tasks are carried out by designers on behalf of employers or clients, rather than on their own behalfs. The nomination of some, at least, of the objectives and the acceptance or non-acceptance of some, at least, of the standards of performance then lie within the discretion of the employer or client rather than, or in addition to, the discretion of the designer.

5.2 The community, represented by government and other agencies, have their own intersecting sets of objectives, some of which will impinge upon the design project, and in most circumstances they will impose certain overriding requirements and limitations on the design, mainly through laws, regulations, and standards. In the case of[39] products exposed for sale or hire, the user and the community also exercise a form of control through the machinery of the market place.

5.3 Similarly, where the thing designed is constructed, marketed, or used in a competitive situation, the actual or potential actions and objectives of competitors will influence decisions made by the designer and/or his employer or client.

5.4 Where the designer is working for an employer or client, not only the product objectives but also the objectives of the design task itself (notably the duration and cost) will be subject to the employer's, professional associations', or governmental bodies' control or veto. Here, too,[40] the laws of supply and demand may affect what the employer can ask and what the designer will concede. In any event, the objectives and the limits of acceptability in respect of the design task itself will constitute a formula agreed between the parties concerned.

5.5 A high proportion of the design tasks commissioned or committed to designers are regarded by the clients or employers as investments calculated to offer a given probability of yielding a prescribed return by way of income or capital gain. For example a developer commissioning an architect to design a building is concerned that there is a high enough probability of the architect's producing within given limits of time and cost a design with a high enough probability of being erected within given limits of construction time and cost, and with a high enough probability of commanding a profitable enough rent or sale price.[41] The person or group who controls the deployment of financial resources in a project, whether the capital is his own or supplied by a backer, will be referred to here as 'the developer'.

5.6 In general, the movement of capital through the money market[42] results in higher yields being demanded on investments to which the higher risks are attached (Fig.5.1).

5.7 Hence, where a developer has to raise capital for the conduct of a project, he has much to gain from first putting himself in the position of being able to show evidence of the degree of risk attached to, and the extent of returns expected from, the venture.

5.8 Even where the developer has adequate resources of his own, he will normally put only a given proportion of his capital at high risk, or invest a given proportion of income in new development. If, over a period of time, a developer undertakes a number of projects, he will normally expect some of them to fail. Consequently, those projects which succeed must, in the long run, offset the losses of

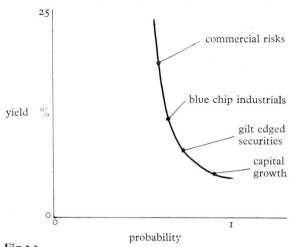

Fig.5.1
The effect of the interplay of supply and demand on the money market results in higher yields being required on investments subject to higher risks.

those which fail. It follows that the average yield on a developer's projects must reflect their actual mean risk.

5.9 In virtually all cases, therefore, a development project will go through an exploratory phase in which feasibility, cost, risk, and probable yield are estimated. Usually this exploratory phase[43] is conducted on a limited budget, rounded off with a formal report, sometimes extended to the preparation of sketch designs and/or models and almost always submitted to investment analysis before authority is given for the project to proceed to detailed design stages.

5.10 With certain exceptions, the bulk of the cost of an investment in a design development project resides in the cost of tooling and manufacture, with a lesser but still large investment in marketing. Once the design is completed, but before funds are finally committed in these directions, it is usual for a further study to be made of production and marketing prospects and costs.

5.11 The design act must therefore be seen within the context of a more extensive process which includes the realization of the design proposals as well as the formulation of them. The overall process will

[39] An interesting description of the relations between the participants in a problem-solving activity, using sociological and communications theory models, is given on pp.36, 39 of *Interdependence and uncertainty: digest of a report from the Tavistock Institute*, Tavistock Publications, 1966.
[40] The book *Economics of research and development*, edited by Richard A. Tybout, Ohio State University Press, 1965, contains a collection of histories and theoretical papers, many of which relate to these aspects of the design function.
[41] See the preface to R. SCHLAIFER's *Probability and statistics for business decisions*, McGraw Hill, 1959.
[42] Or alternatively, at any given yield, capital will tend to flow to those investments which offer the least risk. See *Investment appraisal*, National Economic Development Council, Her Majesty's Stationery Office, 1967.
[43] The presentation of business activities in this sort of problem-solving format can be seen in A. M. MCDONOUGH's *Information economics and management systems*, McGraw Hill, 1963.

be referred to here as a product development programme.

A product development programme will thus normally contain the following phases,[44] with reappraisal and the opportunity to withdraw at the end of each phase:

Phase 1   policy formulation
Phase 2   preliminary research
Phase 3   sketch designs
Phase 4   detailed design
Phase 5   prototype construction
Phase 6   marketing appraisal
Phase 7   production design
Phase 8   production planning
Phase 9   tooling
Phase 10 production and sale

5.12 In the light of such a programme the primitive concept of the design activity set out in paragraph 3.34 can be seen to be more an outline for a specific

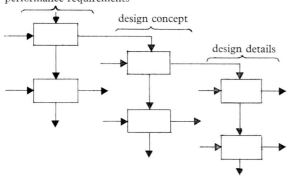

Fig.5.2
A design project will usually contain a sequence of problems, the results of one stage becoming the context for the next.

phase than a model of a complete design development project. A design project is, in fact, a sequence of design problems, each[45] aspect of the problem and each component of the product becoming a new design problem, to be resolved in the context of what has been decided so far (Fig.5.2).

5.13 Reverting to the operational model of the design process referred to in paragraph 4.7, the design programme may be thought of as co-existing with the systematic model and the analogues, but on a third plane (Fig.5.3). Thus the systematic model describes the logical relationships of the parts of the problem, and permits evaluation of predicted performance so far; the analogues, selected according to need, simulate the behaviour of systems in the problem and predict the consequences of postulated decisions; while the design programme indicates what should be done next if the information is to become available, and the decisions are to be made, in the right order.

Outside all three is the real world, in which the problem arises, against which the arbiters set their standards and in which the product will eventually be constructed and used.

5.14 The design programme (and indeed the entire product development programme) can be made even more effective as a control over the design and/or product development activity if the conventions of

[44] Numerous model product development programmes have been set out by various authors, for example L. Bruce Archer, Morris Asimow, Hugh M. Bowen, J. Christopher Jones, R. J. McCrory, E. Matchett, and Martin K. Starr.
[45] F. DE P. HANIKA in *New thinking in management*, Hutchinson, 1965, describes management problems generally as examples of programmed problem solving.

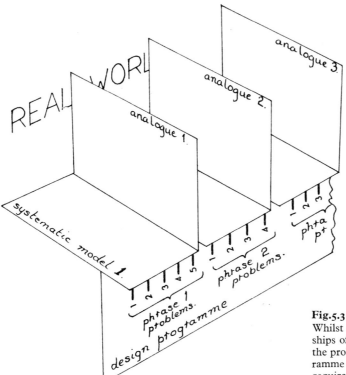

Fig.5.3
Whilst the systematic models describe the logical relationships of the parts of a problem and the analogues simulate the probable consequences of proposed solutions, the programme indicates the sequential relationships of the activities required to resolve it.

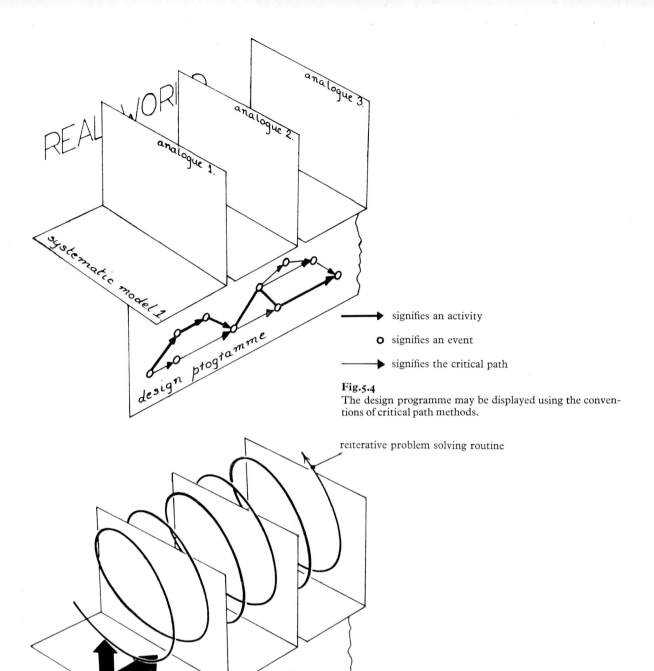

signifies an activity

o signifies an event

signifies the critical path

Fig.5.4
The design programme may be displayed using the conventions of critical path methods.

reiterative problem solving routine

branching of the
problem into its
logical parts

advance through
the programme

Fig.5.5
The design process may be thought of as having three main components: the advance through the project and through time, as indicated by the design programme; the branching of the problem into its logical parts, as indicated by the systematic model; and the cyclical problem-solving process, described by the reiterative routine.

critical path methods are adopted (Fig.5.4). According to this convention every[46] activity which must be carried out in order to implement the programme is indicated by an arrow. An activity takes place over time, and maximum and minimum time allowances for that activity can be laid down. Every event which terminates an activity (for example, the declaration 'All detail drawings are now completed!' is such an event) is indicated by a box or circle at the end of its associated arrow. An event occurs at an instant in time, and earliest and latest permissible dates for the event can be laid down. Two or more activities may

have to be completed before an event can take place (for example, all the drawings for a project may have to have been printed, and all the schedules and a covering letter may have to have been typed before the event called 'All documents now ready for despatch to contractor!' can take place). The

[46] A lucid explanation and attractive approach to critical path methods is contained in A. BATTERSBY's *Network analysis for planning and scheduling*, Macmillan, 1964. See also K. LOCKYER's *Critical path analysis*, Pitman, 1964. A model design programme in network form is given by L. BRUCE ARCHER in *Systematic method for designers*, Council of Industrial Design, 1966.

'critical path' is that set of sequential activities which, added together, determines the time span of the whole operation.

5.15 The design process may therefore be thought of as having three main components (Fig.5.5):

1 The advance through the project and through time, indicated by the design programme, and accomplished with the aid of various analogues.
2 The branching of the problem into its logical parts, independent of time, indicated by the systematic model.
3 The cyclical movement through the sub-problems, occupying man-hours but perhaps co-existing in time, connecting the real world, the systematic model, various analogues and the design programme as described by the reiterative routine set out in paragraph 4.14.

5.16 The complexity of a problem is partly a function[47] of the number of systems embraced by the problem field and partly a function of richness of inter-connection of these systems.

5.17 The boundaries of the problem field mark off both the *external* context – that is to say, the environment from which emanate uncontrollable variables such as the ruling market prices – and the *internal* context – that is to say, the elements of construction which exhibit uncontrollable variables such as the physical properties of materials. It is usually an objective to minimize the total work content of a programme (in order to cheapen or shorten it), so that the designer will normally strive to keep the problem field small. Sometimes, however, a context variable will prove to be so restrictive or so uncertain that the designer will extend the problem field in order to gain control over it, increasing the complexity but reducing the intensity of the problem.

5.18 The intensity of a problem is a function of the certainty required[48] in the solution relative to the certainty exhibited by the input variables. Clearly, it is much more difficult to produce a highly predictable result on uncertain data, than to produce a very approximate result on reliable data. It is possible, nevertheless, to develop a design which is relatively insensitive to inaccuracies in the data, or to reduce uncertainty by a carefully graduated development and test programme.

5.19 Examination of case studies[49] indicates that a characteristic programme in the consumer goods and light industrial products field is as follows:

Phase 1 – Policy formulation
1 establish objectives
2 lay down outline timetable and budget

Phase 2 – Preliminary research
1 identify problem boundaries
2 establish the existing state of the art (library research)
3 prepare outline performance specification (specification 1)
4 identify probable critical problem areas

Phase 3 – Feasibility study (sketch designs)
1 conduct information generating experiments[50]
2 resolve critical problems
3 propose outline overall solution(s) (sketch design 1)
4 estimate work content of phases 4 and 5 and probability of a successful outcome

Phase 4 – Design development
1 expand performance specification (specification 2)
2 develop detailed design (design 2)
3 prepare design documentation

Phase 5 – Prototype development
1 construct prototype (prototype 1)
2 evaluate technical performance of prototypes
3 conduct user trials

Phase 6 – Trading study
1 appraise market potential[51]
2 appraise marketing/production problem
3 revise objectives and budget
4 revise performance specification (specification 3)

Phase 7 – Production development
1 develop a production design (design 3)
2 execute production design documentation
3 construct pre-production prototypes (prototype 2)
4 conduct technical, user and market field-tests

Phase 8 – Production planning
1 prepare marketing plans
2 prepare production plans
3 design jigs and tools

Phase 9 – Tooling
1 construct jigs and tools
2 construct trial batch of products off tools (prototype 3)
3 test trial batch
4 instal marketing machinery and production control

Phase 10 – Production and sale
1 initiate marketing effort
2 commence production and sale
3 feed-back market and user information

[47] See STAFFORD BEER's *Cybernetics and management*, English Universities Press, 1959.
[48] Some aspects of the relationship between the intensity of a problem and uncertainty, mainly in connection with the design and construction of buildings, are discussed on pp.17–25 of *Interdependence and uncertainty: digest of a report from the Tavistock Institute*, Tavistock Publications, 1966.
[49] This model programme is based mainly upon examination of case studies.
[50] In order to obtain general information about probable future reactions to a product which has not yet been designed, it is often necessary to introduce one or more experimental devices, which may or may not be very like the ultimate end result. The term 'brown box' has been used to describe such a device.
[51] Marketing considerations will also have figured prominently in Phases 1 and 2, of course.

The reiterative problem-solving routine set out in para. 4.14 would be applied to each of the sub-problems comprising each of the steps in this design development programme.[52]

5.20 Taking the model *Plan of Work*[53] published by the Royal Institute of British Architects as a basis, the equivalent programme for a building would be as follows:

Stage A – Inception
1 set up client organisation for briefing
2 consider requirements
3 appoint architect

Stage B – Feasibility
1 carry out study of user requirements
2 carry out study of site conditions
3 examine planning, design and cost feasibility

Stage C – Outline proposals
1 develop brief further
2 complete study of user requirements
3 carry out study of technical problems
4 carry out study of planning, design and cost problems

Stage D – Scheme design
1 finalise brief
2 full design of project by architect
3 preliminary design by engineer
4 prepare cost plan
5 prepare full explanatory report
6 submit proposal for all approvals

Stage E – Detail design
1 complete designs for every part and component of building
2 complete cost checking of designs

Stage F – Production information
1 prepare final production drawings
2 prepare schedules
3 prepare specifications

Stage G – Bills of quantities
1 prepare bills of quantities
2 prepare tender documents

Stage H – Tender action
1 despatch tender documents
2 examine tenders and select tenderers
3 let contracts
4 notify unsuccessful tenderers

Stage J – Project planning
1 arrange effective communications system
2 agree project programme

Stage K – Operations on site
1 provide design and construction information
2 implement construction programme
3 instal and effect budgetary control
4 instal and effect quality control

Stage L – Completion
1 inspect completed construction
2 specify rectification of defects
3 make good defects
4 complete contracts and settle accounts
5 relinquish possession to owner

Stage M – Feedback
1 analyse job records
2 inspect completed building
3 study building in use

5.21 The advance permitted in a single assignment on a phased programme is generally based on the scale of the investment so far, the expected return on capital to be employed and the probability of attaining it (Fig.5.6).[54] As the work proceeds, the certainty of the result improves, the return demanded on the investment diminishes, and hence the ratio of investment to return can be increased. Indeed, the whole product development programme can be characterized as an attempt to attain greater certainty. The main function of design management is to sustain a proper balance between the mounting cost of gaining greater certainty and the diminishing return that the overall investment will yield due to these mounting costs.

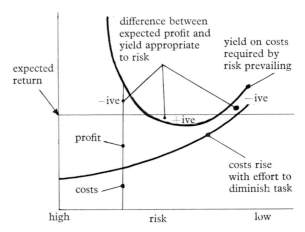

Fig.5.6
The main function of design management is to sustain a proper balance between the mounting costs of gaining greater certainty and the diminishing profit that the project will yield due to these mounting costs.

Note: This paper was the forerunner of a longer text, under almost the same title ('The structure of design processes'), soon to be published by the Royal College of Art.

[52] The checklist which formed an important part of *Systematic method for designers*, Council of Industrial Design, 1966, embodied in a single list earlier forms of both the cyclical routine and the design development programme.
[53] See *Plan of work*, reprinted from *Handbook of architectural practice and management*, Royal Institute of British Architects, 1967; *A code of procedure for selective tendering*, National Joint Consultative Committee for Architects, Quantity Surveyors and Builders, 1963.

[54] See ROBERT LEDUC's *How to launch a new product*, Crosby Lockwood, 1966, EDGAR A. PESSEMIER's *New product decisions: an analytical approach*, McGraw Hill, 1966, and R. SCHLAIFER's *Probability and statistics for business decisions*, McGraw Hill, 1959.

Morphological analysis: some simple explorations

by S. A. Gregory

Introduction

To begin I had better say something about morphological analysis itself to refresh your memories. Fritz Zwicky seems to have made the first public pronouncements under the title of 'morphological' in 1948 although it is likely that people had been using the general notion for quite a time before then.

Morphological analysis consists first in breaking down a system or activity into its essential parts. What constitutes 'essential' depends upon the level of scrutiny and, possibly, upon a value system. The level of scrutiny must be particularly respected for systems. It is important to distinguish between the necessary actions, or parts, 'in principle', and the ways of carrying them out in practice. The relationship between these parts or actions is then noted. This relationship is the pattern of the item concerned. The set of parts of actions and the relationship between them comprise the morphology.

This morphology holds for systems or activities of the same general class.

Given the morphology of existing items in a class we are then able to work out the potential composition of other items of the class yet to be discovered or invented.

Zwicky used this approach to work out possible forms of existence of agglomerates of matter in the universe and other subjects. Better known, probably, is his morphological approach to forms of space vehicle and this has been widely quoted (Fig.1).

Most of us have to deal with things which are likely to be nearer to the ground. Norris has used the morphological approach in the study of land transport. For us, whether dealing with the commonplace, or otherwise, there are interesting possibilities within morphological analysis which still appear to need working out and give prospect of valuable consequences.

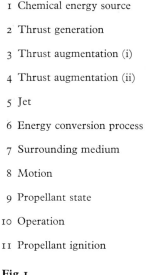
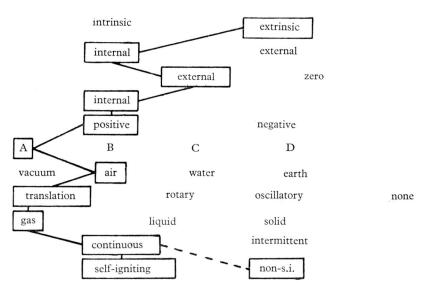

1 Chemical energy source — intrinsic / extrinsic

2 Thrust generation — internal / external

3 Thrust augmentation (i) — external / zero

4 Thrust augmentation (ii) — internal

5 Jet — positive / negative

6 Energy conversion process — A / B / C / D

7 Surrounding medium — vacuum / air / water / earth

8 Motion — translation / rotary / oscillatory / none

9 Propellant state — gas / liquid / solid

10 Operation — continuous / intermittent

11 Propellant ignition — self-igniting / non-s.i.

Fig.1
Jet engine possibilities
(line connects ramjet)

There are eleven significant parameters which define the operation of a simple jet engine. Incompatibility reduce the 36,864 theoretical possibilities to 25,344 feasible simple engines. The line linked series shows parameters involved in a ramjet powered by energy derived from the surrounding medium (excited and ionised atoms and molecules).

103

Varieties of morphology

When we begin to examine common objects and systems it is soon clear that there are differences in the kinds of patterns involved. Thus, we may find patterns in which there is no sequence, all the essential parts being simultaneous. A common example of a simultaneous morphology is in an electric kettle embodiment. All the parts have to exist together (Fig.2).

Electric kettle

Embodiment

components

vessel capacity	
vessel filling	Lid spout
Alarm	None whistle...(compatibility)
Safety device	None/ejector/self reset
Heater location	
Heater capacity	
vessel material	

Fig.2
Example of 'simultaneous' morphology
(can be heterogenous)

In others there may be a simple sequence of actions in a 'single thread'. But even here there are several kinds of possibility: the sequence may be rigid or 'tight' as in the pagination of the normal book (Fig.3);

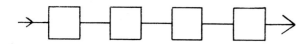

Fig.3
Single thread Rigid Morphology
e.g. a book without cross referencing

alternatively the sequence may be 'slack', as in the actions required to shape a piece of wood. Much more complex patterns may also be discovered, such as in multiple thread systems, typified by the alternative transport routes employed by members to go from London to Southsea (Fig.4); in sequential systems associated with simultaneous groups, and in sequential systems with recycles (Fig.5).

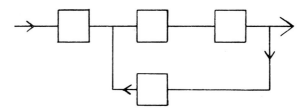

Fig.5
sequential system with recycle

The designer and morphology

For the designer the morphology provides a basis of structures for working out alternative forms. For each part of a discovered or invented pattern all available or conceivable alternatives may be tried. This is the process of generation of design possibilities by permutation.

These possibilities may be for now or for some time in the future. The morphological approach is, in fact, a key technique in technological forecasting.

With a slack morphology the range of possibilities of generation may be much greater than in a tight morphology because, in this kind of pattern, we

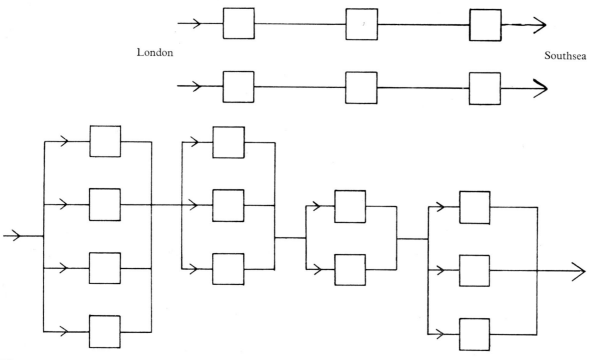

London   Southsea

Fig.4
Multiple thread morphology
include possibilities of interchange

are able to make combinations by changing the sequence of the items as well as varying by substitution as in permutation within a tight morphology.

Where some actions or functions depend upon others it is not usually possible to change their sequential relationship.

As well as time sequence relationships in complex systems there may be other necessary interactions.

Where sequence may be changed it is likely that the actions or parts involved are of the same general kind or 'homogeneous'. As already noted, a book has a tight morphology although the pages are of the same general kind. In the cutting of wood the actions employed may be all of the same type and varied according to the sequence in which they are employed. (Fig. 6) But with some shapes geometrical constraints may be imposed which cut down the slackness.

If the designer discovers or invents the necessary morphology and then carries through a methodical generation of alternatives he becomes faced with the obvious problem of making a suitable evaluation of the fitness of the alternatives available for the immediate function and the overall situation.

There is no unique method of evaluation prior to making a selection of the most suitable set of alternatives. However, the designer usually requires some approximate guide for selection which represents briefly what are believed to be the most significant criteria relevant to the proposed situation.

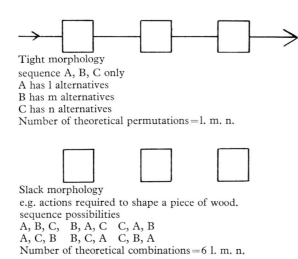

Tight morphology
sequence A, B, C only
A has l alternatives
B has m alternatives
C has n alternatives
Number of theoretical permutations = l. m. n.

Slack morphology
e.g. actions required to shape a piece of wood.
sequence possibilities
A, B, C   B, A, C   C, A, B
A, C, B   B, C, A   C, B, A
Number of theoretical combinations = 6 l. m. n.

Fig.6

Some properties of morphologies

A particular morphological pattern is not the unique characteristic of a specific system. The same pattern may represent a variety of systems, for example. Thus, a four-component linear sequence may repre-

sent a mechanical, or a hydraulic, or an electrical, or a chemical, or an information system.

It is possible, then, for patterns to display properties which are, as it were, intrinsic to the patterns and not to the systems as such. For this reason notions developed in one field may be interesting or valid in another field. This is the conjecture behind my paper.

Work study and morphology

About a decade ago work study was seen as the contemporary method of cutting down resource utilization in any undertaking. The original emphasis was upon labour saving but spread to include action saving, where the action might be provided by a machine. The present method of resource saving is value analysis, which is primarily directed at materials saving but may well include action saving.

One of the well-established group of proposals within work study directed towards action saving consists of the rules:
(a) eliminate (b) combine (c) transfer

Although one might see (a) and (b) as practical expressions of the use of the principle of Occam's Razor, i.e. that entities should not be multiplied without necessity, there has never been, as far as it is known, an empirical basis to justify such steps. People have accepted the proposals as intuitively correct. On such a basis they have been taken over and used in design.

Morphology and cost evaluation

Intuitive judgement is not sufficient where large resources are at stake and other people are involved. Some more objective basis must be found, if possible.

In the past few years I have been faced with the problem of finding process systems of low capital cost. The most important criterion, assuming that all potential candidates operate satisfactorily, is low capital cost.

In searching around for simple ways of evaluating capital cost it was noted that some American workers (Zevnik and Buchanan) had suggested that capital cost might be directly proportional to the number of process steps.

This, subject to confirmation of their proposed method of cost estimation, was particularly attractive since it gave the possibility of a direct exploitation of a morphological analysis scheme. The pattern would consist of process steps of a defined kind. Furthermore, in addition to the possibility of generating process alternatives by a simple computer program, the simple cost estimation scheme could be added to provide the means of evaluation in terms of capital cost immediately. By such means it was possible, in fact, for the computer to forget high-cost sequences once generated and print out only the interesting low cost sequences.

Fundamental to this kind of evaluation was the notion that, in conditions of low information, the hardware for each process step costs the same amount for a given process capacity. An almost invariable reaction to this notion was that it did not agree with normal practice, that obviously each piece of hardware must be different in cost. The essential feature of this approach is that low information is specified. If, in fact, we know for sure that some items cost more than others then we should use this information. However, if, as in the case where many thousands of alternatives have to be evaluated, there is no possibility of adequately specifying individual designs then we may reasonably assume minimal information. Under these conditions we are forced to operate along the lines of Bernoulli's conclusion that in a state of ignorance all possibilities are equi-probable. We must assume that each piece of hardware costs the same amount.

Practical test of such evaluation

Because of the great interest and potentialities of the proposed approach a research project was set up. For this all obvious capital cost data for process plants of all kinds published over a decade were collected (about 500) and analyzed for self-consistency. To make analysis possible all capital costs were converted to a common currency (U.S. dollars) and adjusted by the use of indices to a common date (1964). All processes of a given type were then plotted for capital cost against capacity. Those types giving a narrow spread and a smooth relationship were classed as consistent and used as the basis for further work. This involved test of capital cost against number of steps and regression analysis to find the effect of other factors.

The results of the tests showed quite categorically that capital costs for a given capacity were directly proportional to the number of process steps. The process steps were, as already noted, carefully defined in kind and identified as functional units. Their number was, of course, Functional Unit Number (FUN) and this became the primary determinant of capital cost.

If allowances were made for other factors as determined by the regression analysis it was possible to predict capital costs for a range of well-known processes to within $\pm 20\%$.

Here, then, was a striking verification of what, initially, appears to be an almost too simple approach to a complex problem. Since the detailed use of the technique was worked out the approach has been discussed with several major industrial companies and each time the response has been enthusiastic.

From this basis of success in a particular class of system we begin to conjecture that the approach may be plausible for analogous systems generated by the morphological method. But before so doing it is worth examining whether any further interesting results may be obtained with process plant.

The individual piece of process plants

Such an opportunity exists in the consideration of individual pieces of process plant. Already we have had some opportunity to discuss overall systems. These may be likened, in architectural terms, to communities. The working of the community takes place through interlinked occupancy units. Such units are the equivalent of individual pieces of process plant.

A plant unit, just like a house or a hospital, a bank or a bingo hall, consists first of an enclosure, and within the enclosure are one or more compartments inside which a range of operations may be carried out.

The unit is separate and isolated and for each one we may write out as a list the functional elements which provide for the fulfilment of all the actions needed. This list of functional elements and their interconnexions comprises the morphology of the individual unit.

This morphology is usually quite different from the overall process morphology.

Further, it is interesting to note that in our analysis of an individual unit we begin to destroy the simple assumptions employed in the evaluation of the overall process system. There, with minimum information, each unit costs the same. Now that we begin to examine individual units we expect each to have a different capital cost. But before putting a specific figure to any unit we are able to explore some generalizations.

Characteristic of the individual unit is the enclosure function. In beginning with minimum information we can say that a plant unit consists of an enclosure which surrounds everything and is rather expensive, and within the enclosure is a set of internals any one of which must obviously cost less than the enclosure. If we know little else we must suggest that each internal section has the same cost as any other. This follows from Bernoulli's conclusion cited earlier. A next simple assumption is that all the internals together cost the same as the enclosure.

If we set out to find the unit of lowest cost we must of necessity maintain the enclosure under normal circumstances, but within the enclosure we may attempt to use the work study rules: eliminate, combine, transfer.

What are the means of obtaining lowest enclosure cost? This is tackled by way of geometry and materials. Alternatively we use a second-hand shell. Whatever the means adopted, if it is low overall capital cost that we require, then we design the enclosure first as a low cost enclosure and then we fit what is necessary inside. Some give-and-take may be possible and, indeed, is preferable for optimization, but our main effort is on the enclosure. Any internals have to be adjusted to fit, and these internals should be as few as possible.

Effect of the scale of occupancy

In process plants there is a well-known economic phenomenon. This is the effect of magnitude of operation on capital cost. With the normal kinds of plants we know that, for a change in capacity from Q_A to Q_B, the original capital cost will only be increased in the ratio $(Q_B/Q_A)^{2/3}$.

There is nothing particularly magical about the exponent $\frac{2}{3}$. We may increase capital cost in the same ratio as the increase in capacity by a careful but uneconomic choice of plant design. What we attempt to do, in order to gain advantage, is to increase the volume of the equipment while only increasing the amount of material used in construction to a smaller extent. If we just multiply units in parallel to increase capacity we fail because the amount of material of construction employed goes up linearly with the increase in volume.

If we have to choose vessels which give good economy with increase in scale this is usually achieved by choosing those with the fewest internals. This follows from the geometry of the situation. Similarly, our exponent of $\frac{2}{3}$ may be deduced from the geometry. If we take a spherical vessel we are familiar with the fact that the volume is $4/3\ \pi r^3$ whereas the surface is $4\ \pi r^2$. The capacity increase is as r^2 whereas the material, and hence the cost, goes up as r^3 only.

What do these points have to do with architecture?

The three points mentioned above as of interest to the process designer are:

(a) finding the minimum cost sequence.
(b) finding the minimum cost unit.
(c) finding the cheapest design for scale-up.

In order to lay the basis for some conjectures I shall make certain assertions:

(i) Process system design is similar in kind to planning a community. This planning is initiated by a theoretical study which is followed by successive studies of possible realization.
(ii) Individual unit design is similar in kind to the design of units of kinds of occupancy. Here again there is initiation by theoretical study which is followed by realization studies.

For convenience I shall now refer to some notions which have already appeared within the literature of architecture and planning. In particular I refer to two books which deal with morphology:
S. Chermayeff and C. Alexander. *Community and Privacy*
C. Alexander. *Notes on the Synthesis of Form*

The second of these devotes particular attention to the study of the patterns of communities and to ways of developing the most inclusive morphologies. The first gives considerable care to the development of individual living units, emphasis being placed upon the many needs of the enclosure function, specialized areas within the enclosure, and general areas of 'courts'.

The preferred morphologies which are developed by the authors become 'principles' which are then used as a basis for criticism of previous designs.

It is clearly possible to go beyond criticism. This criticism is, indeed, only a criticism of pattern. It is not a criticism of a particular form of realization nor of the best use of resources.

On the basis of what has been shown possible with process plants there is clearly more which might be done within planning and architecture.

First, it should be possible to develop some simple form of capital cost estimating suitable for initial planning purposes. The value would lie in the ability to test many alternatives.

I would not care to suggest that the identical simple estimating technique utilized for process sequences should be employed. Rather, it would seem valuable to introduce one of the extra factors found to be significant by regression analysis. For buildings this would be a nominal occupancy factor. The community may be represented by a complex diagram with flows and occupancies which change throughout the day and night. The flows have to be accommodated in suitable channels; similarly the people have to be accommodated but within a wide variety of occupancy units, depending upon age and inclinations. It is worth mentioning that studies on models have confirmed earlier empirical observations that the capital cost of all other items may be related by simple factors. Thus the cost of pipework, etc., to accommodate flows at a given capacity is closely related to the cost of the units connected as a totality.

For individual units many of the proposals likely to follow from a pursuit of the principles set out for process plant units are likely to have been discovered already in practice, although not necessarily expressed formally. Minimum internals not only lead to lower costs but, in the eyes of Chermayeff, for example, some reduction in internals provides positive value in the form of 'courts' and other spaces for joint enjoyment.

To gain advantage in capital cost from increased magnitude is not so obvious at first sight in respect of human occupancy. Human beings persist in the same size and shape and their families do not vary much in average size with time. We seem, therefore, to be restricted to the use of a multiplicity of units related in number to the population.

However, since a dominant factor in the cost of a unit is the cost of the enclosure, what are the possibilities of greatly reducing the overall costs of enclosure? Looked at this way the question begins to suggest an answer. Why not replace the individual enclosures by one much greater enclosure?

We find, of course, that others have already put this question. Designs for communities of the future allow for overall enclosure of the community and reduced need for expenditure of resources on individual enclosures. In searching for this advantage other advantages have been discovered.

Conclusion

We set out with some ideas about morphological analysis. These were elaborated to assist design where the expenditure of resources was to be kept low. Within the province of process design and plant unit design some practical principles and techniques were developed. After success here it seemed interesting to test whether analogous approaches might be used in planning and architecture. This remains for you to judge.

The role of building performance measurement and appraisal in design method

by Thomas A. Markus

Summary

This note is an exploratory study of the way in which measurement and appraisal can become part of design method. It shows their relevance both as generative techniques of use during the creative stages of the design process, and as evaluative techniques of use during later, retrospective stages.

Design method is described by its two different structures – the design process, leading by phases from inception to completion, and the decision sequence, leading from analysis to communication.* Appraisal is shown to play a linking role in the first – tying separate projects into a unified series – and a decision-making role in the second.

Four main appraisal activities are discussed: identification, finding relationships, model building, and optimization. The need for quantification, and hence for measurement, is argued.

Introduction

1.1 The Building Performance Research Unit was set up in the School of Architecture at the University of Strathclyde to devise methods for measuring and appraising the performance of buildings. The aim of this research is to make available to building designers techniques for obtaining an increased amount of reliable performance data to aid design decision-making. It is postulated that the resulting improvement in design activity will result in better buildings.

1.2 Measurement and appraisal of performance is an evaluative activity consisting, as it does, of the application of various evaluative yardsticks to design solutions. These evaluations enable alternative solutions to be ranked and, possibly, to be placed in relationship to a 'best' solution arrived at by analytical means. It is widely believed that the chief role of these techniques is in the appraisal of buildings-in-use, and that obtaining data from this source is useful but peripheral and not central to design.

1.3 This paper attempts to show that appraisal is central to design for two reasons. First, because data from buildings-in-use are the means whereby what would remain a series of isolated and closed design projects becomes a single linked design activity, in which the connecting elements are a series of performance appraisals. Data can be used in subsequent designs only if they are produced in a form which fits the pattern of subsequent design activity.

Second, because the complete building-in-use is only one of many embodiments of a design concept, albeit the last, most detailed and precise. Models generated at earlier stages in the design have sufficient detail for many of the performance appraisal techniques to be applicable. Thus, while appraisal presupposes earlier design activities of a generative kind, which have produced testable solutions, it itself is part of the generative process.

1.4 Many people are interested in carrying out building appraisals, other than building designers: for instance central or local government building clients; universities, hospital boards, and industrial and commercial undertakings. It will be seen that they too, in so far as they have to create yardsticks for appraisal, participate in a kind of design process.[1]

Design activity

2.1 STRUCTURE OF DESIGN

Scientific method is a process for solving problems of research: design method is geared to solving

---

*We have altered Markus's terminology of 'design morphology' and 'design process' respectively to bring it into line with British (and the Symposium's) usage. (Eds.)
[1] As a result of past appraisal work on several major building types Peter Manning has developed a model of the design process which enables the results of such appraisals to be incorporated at various stages. (See P. Manning, *Appraisals of building performance and their use in design* in preparation for publication during 1968, probably by the Research Group, Institute of Advanced Architectural Studies, University of York.)

problems of design decision-making. Pask[2] draws attention to the similarities and analogies between the two methods and these need not be developed here.

The study of design method is recent compared to knowledge of scientific method. Knowledge about it is characterized by uncertainty and lack of universally acceptable principles. However, one agreement seems to have emerged and is embodied both in such fundamental design theories as Asimow's[3] and in such practical guides as the RIBA Handbook.[4] This is the recognition that there are two distinct structures in design – a 'vertical' one of sequential phases and a 'horizontal' one of iterative and cyclic processes.

The first is characterized by a chronological sequence advancing from the abstract and general to the concrete and particular and is here referred to as the *design process*. The second is a decision process characterized by stages which proceed from analysis through synthesis and appraisal to communication (there are as many varieties of and descriptions of this cycle as there are authors) and is referred to here as the *decision sequence*. In principle this second structure is that of a sequence, all or parts of which apply to each phase of the design process; while Asimow and the RIBA Handbook make this point, others (e.g. Archer,[5] Levin,[6] and Broadbent[7]) describe the decision sequence only. This would remain an incomplete description of design method except in the case of relatively simple problems which can be solved by one phase in the process.

Appraisals carried out on completed buildings are of interest primarily in the design process; those on earlier design models, in the decision sequence. These two are therefore considered in that sequence and context below.

2.1.1   DESIGN PROCESS

The Handbook describes the following twelve chronological phases in the processes ('Plan of work'):
1. Inception
2. Feasibility
3. Outline proposals
4. Scheme design
5. Detail design
6. Production information
7. Bills of quantities
8. Tender action
9. Project planning
10. Operation on site
11. Completion
12. Feedback

Asimow's equivalent design process (for engineering products) is:
1. Feasibility
2. Preliminary design
3. Detailed design
4. Planning for production
5. Planning for distribution
6. Planning for consumption
7. Planning for retirement.

Allowing for differences between the products, the Handbook's phases 2 to 5 correspond to Asimow's 1 to 3.

Both authors make it clear that the structure of the process is sequential and not iterative; any retracing of steps from a later phase to an earlier is seen as a design failure. In a major project, involving design teams, it would mean either collapse of the project or gross overspending of design resources. The Handbook draws attention to this danger by marking two critical stages: at the completion of phase 4 'Scheme design', after which the brief should not be modified; and at the completion of phase 5 'Detail design', after which 'any change in location, size, shape, or cost . . . will result in abortive work'.

The importance of completing each phase before starting the next is generally emphasized; upon this principle the design office is organized, including possible changes in personnel between phases.[8]

Thus each phase has an input, which is the output of the previous one. The activities which transform the input into the output within each phase are varied; but those phases concerned with design decisions (2 to 5 in the Handbook) contain all or some of the activities of the decision sequence, described in 2.1.2 below.

[2] G. PASK. The conception of a shape and the evolution of a design. *Conference on design methods* (Eds. J. C. Jones and D. G. Thornley). Pergamon Press (London 1963) (Ba4).
[3] M. ASIMOW. *Introduction to design*. Prentice-Hall (New Jersey 1962).
[4] ROYAL INSTITUTE OF BRITISH ARCHITECTS. *Handbook of architectural practice and management*. RIBA (London 1967).
[5] L. B. ARCHER. Systematic method for designers. Reprint from *Design*. Council of Industrial Design (London 1965).
[6] BUILDING RESEARCH STATION. Decision making in urban design. *Building Research Current Papers Design Series* 49. P. H. Levin (1966).
[7] G. H. BROADBENT. *Design method in architecture*. AJ, (14 September 1966), pages 679–84.

[8] It is interesting to speculate that if the process of briefing and writing a performance/product specification on the one hand becomes separated, organizationally, from product design and construction on the other, then the impossibility of retracing any steps from the second half of the process to the first will cause this principle to be even more firmly established. That this division will take place in the building industry is an open question; but already analyst design teams, working with clients, are tending to appear; and of course, product design teams, working with manufacturers and constructors, are familiar in the design of complete buildings as well as components and subassemblies.

Phase 12 'Feedback' is intended to yield data about the management of the project, the construction of the building and its performance in use. The last of these three is of most interest for performance appraisal. By the time phase 12 is reached it is too late to alter the design (except by changing the activities and/or building) and therefore the data yielded can be of use only in solving the *next* design problem. Hence, just as each phase is linked to the previous one by the latter's output, so the output of phase 12 must become the input into an early phase of a subsequent process. That this is in fact intended by the Handbook is clear since in describing the decision sequence the first stage 'Assimilation' includes as an activity 'reference to previous solutions and experience'.

If the decision sequence can, in some form, be applied to each of phases 2 to 5, how can it be used in the feedback phase (12)? Para 2.12 below shows the characteristic cycle of activities in the decision sequence, be they described as 'assimilation, general study, development and communication' (Handbook) or 'analysis, synthesis, evaluation and decision, optimization, revisions and implementation' (Asimow). These activities involve construction of testable models of design solutions, starting with the most abstract which fully expresses the concept of the design *idea* and finishing with the most concrete which can be afforded of the design *embodiment*. The models may be drawings, three-dimensional representation, mathematical analogues or simulations of various kinds. In a sense the building-in-use is the final full scale model of the design – complete in every constructional and human detail.

Phase 12 can therefore be viewed as starting with assimilation or analysis of the full scale model and finishing by communicating the performance of the building in terms which compare the predicted events in phases 2 to 5 with the observed events of phase 12. The separation in time (perhaps by several years) between phases 2 to 5 and 12 results of course from the effort and organization involved in constructing the final 'model', i.e. the building. Phases 6 to 11 are in fact those parts of the process specifically concerned with getting this model made as accurately (phase 6), cheaply (7, 8), and quickly (9, 10, 11) as possible. It might therefore be more sensible to rename phase 12 'feed forward' since its output is the link with a future project. It can be argued that the data are of no use to the client – unless he has a large, and continuing building programme – and are primarily a method enabling the designer to build up his own experiences. Against this it is often argued that similarities between projects are fewer than differences and that what is learnt from one usually has only faint relevance to the next; this belief is so strongly held by most designers that carrying out phase 12 has up to now been largely a question of lip-service. The result is that each new project is started almost *ab initio* as

if it were the first of its kind, but without the radical and thorough analysis which should precede a novel problem. While it can be accepted that similarities between complete buildings may be few – an account of large differences in site, climate, finance, and social environment – it is clear that the size of component or sub-assembly which is capable of standardization is increasing. From simple constructional elements – a screw, block, or tile – through assemblies such as sanitary suites, windows, and staircases, to functional units such as operating suites, sanitary blocks, classrooms, and hospital wards, more and larger items are being developed to meet standard environmental specifications and human needs. As new forms emerge they take on the characteristics of prototypes: these need field testing, as do prototype aircraft or cars. When proved, later examples are mass production repetitions for which production control tests are more appropriate.

Therefore the case for the designer carrying out phase 12 thoroughly is primarily to enable him to arrive at satisfactory prototypes and thus reduce his future design effort. Only in the most general sense can an individual client be expected to be altruistic enough to pay for this self-improvement; it must be covered by an adequate fee structure which accepts such work as a major professional task.

It is time now, however, to examine the decision sequence – the 'horizontal' structures of systematic design – to see what is understood by measurement and appraisal of performance, how it is carried out at the various phases of the process, and what research is needed to make it more reliable.

2.1.2 DECISION SEQUENCE

This is the decision-making method for solving problems of design. Various stages have been identified and labelled by different authorities, some of whom are referred to below. There is an underlying agreement, however, about two salient points of the sequence.

First, that the core of it is sandwiched between a preliminary stage of fact-finding, information-gathering, briefing, assimilation (Handbook), and programming; and a concluding stage in which the decisions taken are communicated or implemented. The first of these stages is merely the context within which design takes place; the other externalizes decisions in a way meaningful for further action.

Second, that the core activity consists of the following stages:

Analysis Clarification of goals; identification of problems; nature of difficulties; exploring relationships; producing order from random data.

Synthesis Creation of part-solutions; combination of part-solutions into consistent and feasible overall solutions; generation of ideas.

Development Expansion of synthesis in more detail.

Appraisal Evaluation; application of checks and tests; application of criteria, constraints and limits; selection of 'best' solution from a set; consistency testing.

Of course neither design theory nor design practice can be rigidly defined or contained within any such simple scheme; the concepts and categories are merely aids to provide a framework.

Asimow states explicitly and the Handbook implicitly that the decision sequence, in full or in part, is essential to *each* phase of the process. It accepts for analysis the output of the previous phase, and communicates a design concept or concepts in the appropriate degree of refinement for development in the next phase.

The decision sequence is characterized by its iterative and cyclic character; it has vital feedback loops and demands that the task is repeated as often as necessary within the limits of design resources available at any phase. In the Handbook version these feedback loops are shown diagrammatically (see Fig.1). In Asimow's six-stage breakdown – 1 analysis, 2 synthesis, 3 evaluation and decision, 4 optimization, 5 revision, 6 implementation – the reference back to earlier stages is formalized by 'evaluation', 'optimization' and 'revision'.

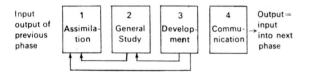

Fig.1

Levin[9] breaks the decision sequence down even further, into eleven stages, and because of the consequent greater detail for our purposes his categories are more useful.

1 *Identification of design parameters* Measures of controllable causes; the design itself.
2 *Identification of independent variables* Uncontrollable causes and effects, e.g. climate, economic state of the community.
3 *Identification of dependent variables* The designer's goals; effects the designer wishes to achieve, e.g. a given environment, a level of activity.
4 *Identification of relationships among parameters and variables* Cause-and-effect or weaker links.
5 *Prediction of value of independent variables.*
6 *Identification of constraints governing dependent variables* Upper and lower limits.

[9] P. H. LEVIN. See note 6 above.

7 *Identification of constraints governing design parameters* Limits on the means by which design may be achieved; cost limits; standards; regulations.
8 *Identification of value of design parameters* In any design each parameter will have a unique value.
9 *Identification of expected value of dependent variables* Prediction of effect of setting design parameters at chosen values.
10 *Investigation of consistency of values, relationships and constraints* Sub-solutions; consistency of these with each other; optimization.
11 *Comparison of and selection from alternative sets of design parameters* Using dependent variables as criteria, selecting best solutions.

Levin shows that the correspondence between his stages and those defined in the accepted design theories referred to above is quite close.

In this sequence, too, there are formalized feedback loops during which a solution is tested or evaluated by reference to an earlier stage. For instance, the effects of a particular design (i.e. 'expected values of dependent variables resulting from a particular set of values of design parameters') can be determined only by looking back at the relationships assumed in stage 4. Investigation of consistency can be carried out only in the light of the identification activities carried out in stages 1 to 7. Comparison and selection of solutions can be made only by reference back to stages 3 and 6 in which the criteria (the dependent variables) were identified and limits set upon them. Each time such feedback produces an unsatisfactory answer, the sequence must be started again from a certain stage.

What then is measurement and appraisal of performance in the decision sequence? It appears to take place whenever the designer pauses to evaluate what he has done. These occasions are the feedback loops, shuttle action, and other departures from linearity indicated in most models of the decision sequence. These are introspective and retrospective acts; for he looks back to earlier decisions to discover there the evaluative yardsticks – his objectives – which help him to select a solution and proceed to develop it. He is also constantly applying checking tests – Are partial solutions to sub-problems compatible? Are they within functional or cost constraints and limits? Are they feasible technically?

Does the decision sequence cycle, as expressed in the simple model such as the Handbook's, apply to the Handbook phase 12 'Feedback'? If the notion of the building-in-use as the final model is accepted there is no reason why it should not. There are difficulties however. The decision sequence, when applied to earlier phases of the process, starts with assimilation and analysis of the design as expressed in the model of the previous phase. In phase 12 it starts with the building-in-use – i.e. a model built during phases 6 to 11 on the basis of the previous model in phase 5.

Thus now the model building, because of its complexity, has been taken out of the context of a decision sequence cycle and we have two successive models in which the second has not been derived from the first by the full series of analytic, synthetic, evaluative and appraisal activities. Just for this reason this deficiency has to be made good retrospectively in phase 12.

Assimilation and analysis is therefore a full understanding of the performance of this model (the building-in-use) – of necessity including quantification and hence measurement. The synthesis and development stages are concerned now not with designing a building to obey relationships and achieve stated objectives, but discovering what relationships are obeyed and what objectives achieved in an existing design.

The appraisal now consists of comparing the relationships obeyed and objectives achieved with those set out in earlier phases of the design process. Finally the results of this appraisal are communicated for the beginning of the next design project in language meaningful to early decision-making.

Thus we have the makings of a classical inductive-deductive-inductive sequence. The conclusions drawn from a particular appraisal are used to reformulate general theory, the inductive stage. The new theory is used to derive a particular solution, the deductive stage; this in turn is appraised and by inductive reasoning the theory is reformulated.

Appraisal activities

3.1 Appraisal by evaluation and testing is poorly developed in comparison with analysis and synthesis. To carry out the appraisal four main types of activity seem to be needed:

3.2 *Identification* Descriptions of buildings deal, at least theoretically, with objects with finite characteristics, but appraisals are infinite since any objectives can be applied as evaluative yardsticks. The appraiser may be a designer or acting in a 'judicial' capacity on another designer's creation. He may use: the designer's explicit objectives (his own if his appraisal is part of his design process); implicit, underlying, objectives (if they can be discovered); objectives which could have been formulated by the designer but which he ignored or rejected; objectives which have become established through subsequent research; objectives formulated on the basis of projected future needs. The appraiser, therefore, needs to state the objectives he is seeking to attain (criteria, limits, values, constraints, priorities); activities, 1, 2, 3, 6, and 7 of Levin's list are all concerned with identifying the variables which define the objectives. This task of identification is difficult for the designer, for he must learn what to take on

trust, what to question, and what to reject. He must learn how to probe below his client's explicit objectives into 'folklore' and prejudice, and must do all this at speed. For the appraiser assessing other designers' solutions there are the additional difficulties of uncovering the reasons for decisions. Both designer-appraisers and judicial-appraisers could be helped by systematic identification routines and techniques.

3.3 *Finding relationships* Levin's activities 4 and 9 are identification of relationships among parameters and variables and prediction of expected values of dependent variables (design objectives) resulting from any design.

To do this the appraiser, be he the designer or not, must assume as proved a number of hypotheses. He must assume various complex relationships to exist between various aspects of the design; or between the design and costs or environmental consequences; or between environmental conditions and the users' activity, behaviour, or performance. In assuming these relationships the appraiser acts as a scientist who has proved, experimentally, a number of hypotheses. In fact most of building research in the past has been aimed at proving these, and where reliable research findings exist the appraiser uses them. In other cases he must make the most enlightened guess he can, at the same time drawing attention to research gaps. Some of these gaps are likely to need field experiments, i.e. buildings-in-use, especially experiments concerning users' activity and behaviour which is often impossible to simulate in the laboratory.

Each building is therefore a potential piece of apparatus capable of testing any hypotheses the appraiser wishes to set up. These may be the relationships assumed by the designer or by a judicial-appraiser. (It is important that hypotheses be formulated in a way which allows them to be proved false – only in this way can experimental evidence lead via deductive reasoning to valid general conclusions, as Popper[10] has shown.)

The BPRU has set up a conceptual model of the relationships in the building-user system. It has four main parts (see Fig.2):
1. The building system, consisting of all the sub-systems, assemblies, and components of which a building is constructed. There are three main sub-systems: constructional, services, contents.
2. The environment, spatial and physical, generated by the building system and the activity of the occupants.
3. Activity and behaviour of the occupants, which is affected by and affects the environment.

[10] K. R. POPPER. *The logic of scientific discovery.* Hutchinson (London 1959).

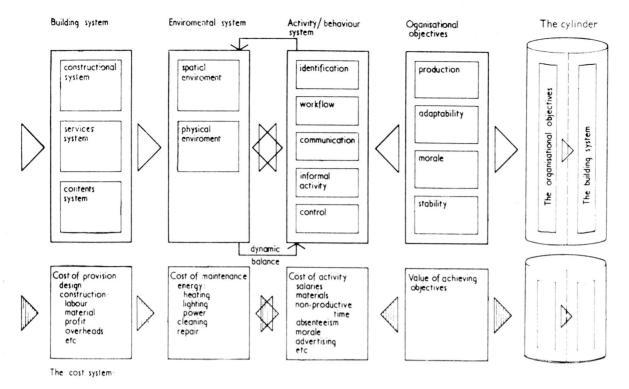

Fig.2

The building-environment-activity objectives system: a conceptual model.

4. Objectives of the organization to which the occupants belong and which has decided to put up the building.

This model is useful for research in buildings-in-use; as a framework for designers to make relationship decisions; for evaluation and classification of existing research; for identifying gaps for further research.

The most important single characteristic of such a relationship-model is that all characteristics have to be quantifiable on scales – this means abandoning rich, unique, analogue descriptions and moving towards more general quantities. Diagram 2 can be viewed as the developed surface of a cut cylinder. The four parts are linked in the following way, indicated by the arrows:

3.3.1 *Objectives and activities* An organization exists to achieve certain objectives – for instance, profit, social status, achievement of identity, social function (e.g. teaching or healing). To achieve them it needs to initiate and sustain certain activities and behaviour, for instance, production, communication, informal behaviour, perpetuation and identification activities, and so on.

Organization theory has provided many classification systems of objectives and activities and measurement techniques capable of quantifying the categories. For purposes of building research these may be too general, and in any particular type of organization it may be easier to use more specific categories. For instance in the case of a school, its

objectives may be academic attainments and social and emotional development of children; high morale among teachers; flexibility; economic use of resources; usefulness in the local community. Each of these will require a group of activities; for instance formal teaching/learning; informal activities; disciplinary behaviour; identification; communication among teachers and between teachers and parents. Measures of all these are possible, including, of course, verbal behaviour as an aspect of behaviour in general. The only objectives that should appear in the model are those sustained by activities which need a building to house them.

Thus the organization 'designs' activities which sustain it, and also briefs a design for a building which houses it – hence an arrow pointing in each direction from organizational objectives. Both activities and buildings are paid for by the organization's resources.

3.3.2 *Building system* The building system – and its three main sub-systems, the constructional, services, and contents – includes every concrete item, component, assembly, and system. A complete description gives not only all the physical characteristics of these parts but also their dimensions and dimensional relationships. The system includes all that is normally described in a set of drawings, specifications, and bill of quantities. Much of today's interest in automatic data processing and handling of these documents misses the realization that the characteristics of a building must not only be able to be described unambiguously but must also be *quantifiable* if worth-while predictive relationships are to be obtained.

Thus one will need to develop scales for, say, constructional systems, which will say that building x measures 22 on a scale of 0 to 50 of 'framed-structuredness' (perhaps the admixture of exo- and endo-skeleton elements). This value will then enable the designer to predict the cost of such a system and, for instance, its effect on spatial environment.

3.3.3 *Environmental system*

The environmental system has two main sub-systems, the spatial and the physical. The spatial sub-system refers to the dimensional and geometrical properties of single spaces, closely related to anthropometric characteristics, as well as to the pattern of overall layout and configuration. Again quantifiable measures of spatial systems (e.g. of their concentration/sprawl; repetitiveness; cellularity; flexibility, etc.) will have to be devised.

The physical sub-system refers to those characteristics of the environment which can be perceived by the senses; the visual, thermal, aural, tactile, and olfactory characteristics, of which good measures already exist.

3.3.4 *Homeostasis*

These aspects of environment are the direct outcome not only of decisions about the building-system, but also of the occupants' activity. For example, the noise level in a classroom will be a function of both construction and planning (party walls, absorption, separating distance), i.e. fixed variables, and the noise generated in adjacent classrooms, corridors and play areas, i.e. transient variables. The two-way arrows in the centre of the diagram represent the fact that the environment and activity are mutually interactive and reach a homeostasis. Thus an organization moving into a somewhat unsuitable environment alters its activities to make the best use of it, and in turn moulds the environment.

The two-way arrow spans the biggest gap of all, the interface between an inanimate and animate system (the ergonomist's 'man/machine interface'). The disciplines needed for measurement of the left-hand side are architecture, physics, engineering; for the right, the social and behavioural sciences and organization theory.

The interface would include what can be called the reaction of the building occupants to the environment. Such central notions in design and research as privacy, aesthetic reaction, attitudes, and opinion are in this area. For use in decision-making they have to be considered in terms of either side of the interface (i.e. environment or activity/behaviour consequence), where they can also be costed. Hence these all-important concepts do not appear in the model.

3.3.5 *Cost*

There is a second cylinder (indicated at the bottom of 2), that of costs. Each of the four major parts has cost consequences:
the building costs something to design and construct;
environment costs something to maintain (energy, cleaning, repair, maintenance);
activity costs something to provide (salaries, wages, non-productive time; sickness; absenteeism, turnover, recruiting, advertising, morale, materials for production); objectives have values and priorities upon which some costs can usually be founded.

Only by following this cylinder round, in relationship to the four parts above, can a rational decision on the 'best' design be made – i.e. the design that achieves the best allocation of resources by maximizing cost-benefit.

One major task facing building research workers in analysis of cost data is to discover systematic cost variation with changes in design parameters. Without this, cost analysis will remain a checking tool and real *design* with costs cannot take place.

Cost becomes, therefore, the single criterion for optimization. Without a single criterion alternative solutions for parts of the design can never be combined nor the best overall solution be found. It is meaningless to ask, 'Which is better, a good lift service or freedom from glare?' But it *is* quite meaningful to ask which of two lift designs is better or which of two lighting installations produces less glare.

3.3.6 *Specification*

One interesting aspect of this model is that it shows that the specification of a building or any part of it can be achieved at several levels. Take lighting as an example. Treated in the first of the four parts, one could specify the design of a fitting and mounting height, giving detailed drawings and specifying the lamp. This is a component specification. In the second part of the model one might specify the environmental performance of the required fitting; its lumen output, surface luminance, BZ classification (flux distribution), and life. This is an environmental performance specification. In the third part of the model one would specify the required activity or behavioural consequences of the lighting: visual performance, glare sensation (glare index), effect on judgements of pleasantness, gloom, modelling, or character, effect on faces and hence inter-personal perceptions, safety attention-focusing; and other criteria arrived at by experiments using people. This is an activity performance specification.

The first is the safest and simplest to use; this is the 'deemed-to-satisfy' approach. It leads to safe, sound, uninventive solutions; it makes innovation difficult. The second is more directly related to human needs and makes innovating design feasible; however, in this case the designer needs to know the relationship between the component and its performance and to carry out a number of calculations. The third, the most likely to lead to original and economic solutions, calls for most skill and requires research knowledge to be properly handled. Even skilled designers therefore normally stop at the environmental specification and much research is needed to make the third level of specification feasible.

Summarizing, then, the question of finding relationships, the appraiser (designer or not) will need to predict relationships *within* parts of the system – e.g. construction and services; and *between* parts – e.g. between the services system and the physical environment; or between the spatial environment and communication; and between any part and costs.

3.4 *Model building* To appraise any design concept it must be embodied in a testable model. This is nothing more than a representation of an abstract concept in more or less concrete form – symbol, mathematical relationships, schematic diagram, detailed design drawing, three-dimensional model or a network simulation system. In any of these, design variables (design parameters) can be changed and the consequences (dependent variables) can be measured.

Model building in this sense – as *representation* of a system in which the relationship of parts is fully understood – has a different purpose from the model building in which the research worker engages in order to explore relationships and formulate testable hypotheses. The scale and nature of models built for these two purposes is different and often neither purpose is adequately achieved owing to initial lack of clarity.

The increasing complexity of models built as a project advances, with the consequently increasing cost consequences of abandoning a design, makes it vital that the simplest possible model which expresses the relationships of interest should be built at any time. Also the maximum amount of information has to be squeezed out of each model.

The completed building is the most detailed model of the concept available – complete in every detail, including human activity.

In each phase of the design process the cycles of the decision sequence take place around models appropriate to the phase. Assimilation and analysis use data from the previous phase's model. The synthesis will integrate the part-solutions into a new, more detailed model, which is developed and appraised. The output of the solution is communicated as an input to the next phase.

A model of any kind must have some similarity to the object it represents. For the physicist this is easy,

as long as the relationships expressed by his equations are in dimensionally homogeneous units and he can therefore use dimensional analysis[11] to determine a number of dimensionless products which have the same definition in the model as in the real situation (e.g. Reynolds' Number or Mach's Number).

In making models of buildings the only aspects that can be modelled are those which can be quantified. Hence the importance of appraisal of performance – or measurement – which enables quantities to be assigned to aspects. Once quantification is possible, it is possible to reduce in scale (as with length and area) and to apply rules to check that scale effects do not distort the behaviour of the system. Without quantification model building is impossible.

Successful model building appears to obey the following rules:
Scale changes do not alter behaviour of the system.
Simplification by omission of variables (or 'details') must not cause a significant change in the relationship of the variables which remain.
Models of concepts should be at the simplest levels which just express them.
Models of design embodiments should be as concrete and detailed as resources allow.

The modelling technique must allow all possible solutions to be constructed and explored.

In appraising alternative solutions they should all be represented by the same type of model. Hence where the model is a real building and its performance is to be compared to that of other, non-existent hypothetical but feasible solutions, the real building will have to be represented by a simpler model.

It is possible not only to place models on an abstract-concrete scale, but also to classify them according to their prime purpose. In business management it is now customary to speak of three classes of models[12] which seem to have useful analogies for the building designer.

Descriptive models The prime function of these is to portray the relationships that are seen to exist in a situation. For instance models of circulation movement showing the relationship of corridor and lift dimensions to flow capacities; structural equations showing the relationship of shape and dimension of members to stress and deflection. Most research findings produce descriptive models of this kind.

[11] H. L. LANGHAAR. *Dimensional analysis and theory of models*. Wiley (London 1951). W. J. DUNCAN. *Physical similarity and dimensional analysis*. Edward Arnold (London 1953). D. C. IPSEN. *Units, dimensions and dimensionless numbers*. McGraw-Hill (London 1960).
[12] P. KIRCHER. *Measurements and managerial decisions in measurement – definitions and theories* (Eds. C. W. Churchman and P. Ratoosh). Wiley (London 1959).

Predictive models Given a set of relationships (descriptive models), if one variable can be predicted and the relationship holds, then the other variable(s) can be predicted. For instance for a given size and speed of lift the waiting time (under a specified arrival pattern) can be predicted. For a given shape of building the air-conditioning load can be predicted.

Decision models From a set of predictive models (alternative solutions) one must be chosen. This requires the use of a criterion. When this is done analytically, to derive an optimum, by such techniques as linear programming for instance, the optimization procedure (see para 3.5) involves building this decision model.

The use of digital computers now makes it possible to construct and operate quite complex simulation models in which not only are aspects of the building design represented but also aspects of activity or behaviour. It is likely therefore that the use of simulation will increase, especially for predictive models; but much research will have to be done before adequate models of all the major design parameters and their consequences can be constructed. In the meantime the designer is able to operate successfully on partial information – a feat beyond the computer, which needs complete information otherwise it will give inaccurate results or come to a halt.

3.5 *Optimization* This is the fourth and final appraisal activity and is closely linked to the building of decision models. It consists of selecting the 'best' design from any number of possible solutions – i.e. that being as good as or better than any other. It is the design having the optimal set of design parameters. This set can be found only by reference to the criterion of judgement; if the criterion is changed a different optimal set will be found.

Strictly an optimum can be obtained only on one criterion; for instance cost. Where different criteria exist for different aspects of the design they must either be combined into a single composite criterion in which each component is properly weighted, or be converted into constraints giving them upper and lower limits within which the design has to be optimized (one or other limit may be implied only). Many of the environmental 'criteria' in building design are of this type – e.g. temperature (62°F to 68°F); noise levels (up to 55 dBA); space (not less than 15 sq.ft per person); and so on.

The cost-benefit criterion, where realistic, is the most useful for optimization. It leaves the designer, of course, with the vast problem of evaluation of benefits. For cases where a single criterion is used there are powerful mathematical optimization techniques designed to find the low or high point in a curve; Asimow[13] outlines these. They can take into account different types of constraints on design parameters.

Mathematical optimization techniques are nevertheless far from being able to lead to overall building design optimization, chiefly through lack of data. They can, however, be most useful in sub-optimization in areas where all the variables are identifiable and can be quantified and also as design teaching and training tools.

Development of mathematical techniques for rational optimization of building design, and intuitive techniques for situations not capable of full analysis, is a major research task in itself. They are as necessary for creative design as for appraisal.

Conclusion

Appraisal is based on a varied set of techniques, each appropriate for different design activities. It is as much a generative technique as an evaluative one, since the difference is largely semantic.

In common with other aspects of design method, appraisal techniques are far from fully developed and much research and practical experience is needed for them to start playing a major, strategic part in design. Currently they are used merely as tactical tools – checking devices which ensure that there is no catastrophic failure.

Acknowledgements

My thanks are due to my colleagues in the BPRU, since it was in the attempt to fit their work into a framework which marries with the designer's aims that this paper was written. The conceptual model 2 described in section 3 was jointly developed by all of us; its shortcomings are likely to be the result of my adaptation and presentation of it.

I am also indebted to Peter Levin, Rowland Mainstone, and Christopher Jones for valuable comments, including warnings about the dangers of regarding the design process as linear.

The Symposium paper given by Professor Markus was similar to that published in the *Architect's Journal* on 20th December 1967.

[13] M. ASIMOW. Chap. 11. See note 3 above.

Perception and construction

by M. L. J. Abercrombie

What people were talking about yesterday when they talked about psychology, was concerned with watching other people's behaviour, so that they could learn how to manipulate the environment, in order that it shall manipulate other people's behaviour in predetermined ways. But there is another use of psychology, and it is one that I am particularly interested in, and that is in helping us to understand ourselves; it isn't only the other person who has a black box in his skull, it is also you and I, and the more each knows about his or her own behaviour, the more likely he or she is to behave in a reasonable way, and make their own behaviour more effective.

In talking about the processes of learning to design, one can consider design under two headings: receiving information (perception can be defined as the process of taking in information) and putting things together. It is because I am dealing with the putting together at an extremely elementary level, that I chose the word 'construction' rather than 'design' for the title of my talk. The point I want to make is that both in perceiving and in constructing, it is very important to be active and to be working actually with the material.

The rotating trapezoidal window demonstrates how much construction is involved in what seems to be straightforward perception. What most people see when they look at it is a window which swings backwards and forwards. When a rod is placed in the window it seems to swing independently of the frame; it moves at right angles to it, sometimes closely pressed against it, and at some point or other it gets to the other side of the frame. It seems to do this in various ways; some people see the rod elongate and bend and twist round the frame, some see it break through the frame, and some people hear it break through the frame! When a little red cube is stuck on a corner of the window there may be some difficulty in describing exactly what it is you see, but what most people see is that the cube moves independently of the window; it may slide up and down it, or it may leave the window and circle it like a satellite. The explanation of the things that you've seen here, is that you attribute to the piece of card-board, which is painted to look like a window, all the properties of a rectangle. We are surrounded in Western European civilization by rectangular shapes, but a rectangle is very seldom normal to the line of vision; it is much more often at an angle, so that the image it throws on the eye has a long side and a short side. When you look at this thing which is *actually* a trapezoid, you assume that it is a rectangle seen in perspective, and this could be the case only if the short side always remained at the back. The window goes round and round, but when the short side comes to the front, it seems to be at the back, i.e. the window is seen swinging backwards and forwards, and not rotating. The reason why this gives you a slightly uneasy feeling is that of course the length of the image on the retina in fact changes; when the long side is at the front, it throws a longer image on the eye than when it's at the back, but you think it's still at the front, and this gives you the impression that the window swells and shrinks in size.

The point I want to make here, is that a great deal of work is going on when you are apparently passively receiving information of this kind, and that you can't get accurate information unless you ignore your preconceptions about the nature of rectangles. It is possible to look at this window until you're blue in the face, and never see it as anything but a window going backwards and forwards; it's only when you put the rod in or the cube on, that you see that there is something really very odd about it. You could understand its nature by changing your position relative to it; you could, for instance, stand above it, and then you would see that it is in fact a piece of cardboard, going round and round.

What you do in learning to receive information is to build up a series of patterns or schemata which helps you to see the things that you're used to seeing, and which makes it impossible for you to see something which conflicts with it (see Abercrombie, 1960). This learning to see is very much a matter of learning to act; not only to receive the information, but to act on the information. The building-up of these habits is a very long and laborious process, but fortunately, when you repeat a learned action, you don't necessarily have to go through all of the stages that you used in building up the habit. Consider, for instance, the way in which a child learns to read (and, almost certainly, you will have forgotten how difficult this was). He reads with most of his body to begin with; he moves his head along the line, he often moves his finger along it picking out the words, he moves his eyes along the line, and he may grunt or twiddle his toes or screw up his whole body if the job is really difficult. But as he becomes more and more skilful at reading, he localizes these movements to the eyes only, and the eyes of a really skilful reader just go straight down the middle of the page, because he has learned to take in information over a much wider span. The other day, I was sitting opposite a woman and her son in a tube train, and you could see the difference between a child's and an adult's movements. The little boy was reading a comic with a very narrow column, and his head was going backwards and forwards, and the woman was reading a book with a wide page, and she sat with her head absolutely still.

When we are confronted with a task which is too difficult we tend to revert to the early infantile patterns of behaviour. If I'm reading a foreign language, or a difficult piece of English prose, I tend to move my head and pick out the words with my finger; I will actually mouth the words to myself, making it easier for me to focus attention on them, and to take the new information in. The development of a habit requires quite an elaborate process of bodily movement as well as of brain work. The skill may become perfected for a certain level of difficulty of task, but still not be adequate for higher levels of difficulty, and when you tackle a more difficult job you fall back on more primitive ways of coping with the situation. So it was quite interesting to hear Keith Hanson say yesterday, after his discussion of the very elaborate procedure of using Alexander's technique, that having done it once, he didn't have to do it again. Now, one might interpret this in all sorts of other ways, but the way I want to interpret it at the moment is this: that he'd gone through the motions of learning how to do this task, and could then compress them into a flash, in just the same way as in reading you no longer have to go along the line word by word, but take it in at a single glance.

I want next to talk about something that actually happens in the studio about these habits of work. The work of students in the studio ends in a series of drawings or, at the best, models (and when I use the word model, I mean model – I mean something made to look like the real thing, usually a little thing that looks like the big thing), and it doesn't end in a building which can be tested in use; as a matter of fact, precious few buildings are appraised in the way Tom Markus was talking about. Now for those people who can understand this code which the student has been using, the drawings or models

actually represent buildings, and the test of the worthiness of the student's design is whether his critics think that the building that they would visualize as potentially materializing from these drawings or models would in fact be a good or a bad building. That is to say, they look at the marks on paper, and they imagine a building, and they can judge whether the building is good or bad. So that a very important part of learning to design consists in learning to use this code, and the student must not only be able to interpret the code as the critic does, but he must manipulate the code.

There has been a tendency recently, at least in this country, in architectural education, to belittle the importance of learning to draw and to make models (and it is interesting that the models that are fashionable now are not the sort I am talking about, but mathematical models). I think that this is partly because the chief role of drawing and model-making has been seen as one of communicating; they are for the student to communicate his intentions to his teacher, or for the architect to communicate his intentions to his client. Now exquisite methods of presentation easily become an end in themselves, and they stop students doing all sorts of other intellectual things that they ought to be doing, and that the academic upgrading of the curriculum requires. There is a feeling that good presentation may conceal bad design. Another criticism is that although these exquisite drawings or models may impress the client, they may also mislead him. There are very real difficulties in communicating to lay people what it will be like to walk past a building, let alone to walk into a building, or to use it, and even the most polished sketches or the most accurate models may be very misleading in this respect. I have been present when a design team was discussing how to present its preliminary proposals to a meeting of its clients, and it was said that it would be safer to present rough sketches and talk about them, to give a general impression to the client, rather than to present him with anything more detailed in the way of a drawing, because if he didn't understand the rough sketch and the talk, at least he wouldn't be so misled by them as he might be by a detailed drawing. Nicholas Taylor, writing recently in *The Sunday Times* under the title 'Uninhabitable Cities' said: 'Those who intend to destroy our cities feed us first with lies, damned lies and artists' impressions. Look for example at the proposed re-modelling of King's Cross station, unveiled to the Press last Tuesday. The unknown watercolour painter commissioned by the British Railways Board

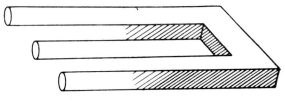

Fig.1

has created a Garden City landscape of railways-in-parkland which his employers have tried to pass off as the truth about the terminus's future appearance.' The artist's sketch was shown and alongside it a screeching Scarfe cartoon showing what the environment would really look and feel like. It certainly is easy to mislead by drawing, as Fig.1 illustrates. An 'impossible' figure can be represented in two dimensions, but it could not be made in physical reality.

Analogous with this deceptive, impossible figure is the difficulty that some people may have if they use a code too slickly. In some very interesting work on problem solving (Paige and Simon, 1966) subjects were given problems expressed verbally to make into algebraic equations, for instance, 'A board is sawn into two parts, so that one part is two-thirds of the board. The other part exceeds the first part by four feet. What is the size of the board?' People fell into roughly two classes, according to the way they handled this sort of problem. Some of them would simply translate word for word into algebraic symbols, and other people would think in terms of physical objects; they might say, 'Oh, I'd have to draw a diagram to get this straight'. The people who translated words into algebraic symbols straight away often didn't notice the incompatibility in the formulation of the problem, whereas people who thought in physical terms could more easily do so, and the people who used both methods, who could switch, would be good at detecting ambiguities. Strange though it may seem, in some cases it was not until people drew the board and cut it into two-thirds and one-third that they could see that if you take two-thirds away, the remainder could not exceed it in length. Those who did not visualize what the board would have looked like would change the sign of the terms, or would misinterpret the words and think that the second part was said to be less than the first, or would recast the statement to make it ambiguous, e.g. 'The difference between the two parts was four feet' instead of stipulating which part was the larger one.

This illustrates the importance of moving continually backwards and forwards from the code in which you are working to at least some visualisation of what the physical thing is. The main trouble I think with students, is that they have not yet learned how to visualize the building from the plans. This is where I think that practice in the appraisal of buildings by students, and in relating the appraisal to the original designs of the building, would be an extremely useful exercise.

Whether or not we agree that students should acquire the technical skills of drawing and model-making in order to communicate with their teachers and clients, we cannot doubt that they need to learn how to use them as tools of design for themselves. My colleague John Weeks has defined designing as putting things together so that they work. I'm sure he has all sorts of other definitions of design as well and would not like this one to be nailed on to him once and for all, but I'd like to use this very simple meaning because it matches up with my term 'construction'. It is clear that there are two quite different levels at which design can be carried out, defined in this way. The first is the simple, primitive and concrete one of being able just to put things together – real things together, to get a satisfactory result. This skill simply involves the ability to perceive and manipulate and appreciate spatial relationships. The second kind of skill is the much more difficult one of designing in the abstract, which involves manipulating an analogue or a code, because you simply can't manipulate the real things – they're either too big or too heavy, or too complex, or they're not there anyway in the case of a building that you are projecting. Our First Year was recently asked to make an anthropometric study of their own room and describe activity patterns in it, and then they were asked to redesign the room if it didn't match up to the optimal conditions. In redesigning the students fell into two groups, roughly: there were those who attempted to design on the basis of the elaborate tables and charts they had made, of priorities, constraints, quantified value judgements and all the rest of it, but a few simply shoved the furniture around, lived with it for a few days, and shoved it around again until they liked it or until their room-mates said they would throw them out if they didn't stop. These two quite different levels of skill of designing, working with a code, and working with the real object, can be demonstrated in some psychological tests. The subject is given some blocks which are coloured differently on different sides, some of the sides with two colours on them, and asked to copy certain patterns with them. If you make a pattern with four blocks, building it under the child's eyes, and give him the right number of the right sort of blocks, he can fairly easily copy it. A more difficult task is set if a diagram of the block pattern is given, seen from above, full size. A full-size diagram with the lines between the blocks removed is still more difficult, for the subject has to dissect it himself, and relate the parts to real blocks. A still more difficult model to copy is a diagram reduced by half, still further removed from the real thing. A child who can make a copy from the real thing may be unable to decipher the various degrees of difficulty of code. It is quite difficult to decipher a code, but it is much more difficult to manipulate the code, as you will recall, when you think how much easier it is to understand a foreign language than it is to express yourself in it. Architectural students have to learn to work in code.

Architectural design involves prediction or extrapolation, and our recognition of this fact is partly obscured by the ambiguous meanings of the term design. According to the Oxford Dictionary, it can mean a pattern, or a piece of decorative work, an artistic device, the combination of details which go to make up a work of art (as you might say, a wall-paper design by William Morris). Or it can mean, and this is the way we use it mostly in the studio, a plan or a scheme conceived in the mind of something which is to be done, the preliminary conception of an idea that is to be carried into effect by action. Now what came from William Morris's hand was a pattern of coloured shapes which would be very similar to what the client would get on his wall. Whereas, what comes from the architect's hand is something very unlike the building he is designing, and it is not only that the client has difficulty in understanding what he is going to get for his money, it's that the student has difficulty in manipulating the code himself. It may seem that I am making terribly heavy weather about this business of manipulation of code, but over and over again in the studio we see how, by manipulating lines on paper, a student is not really understanding what they could represent in terms of buildings. He can make designs that are like the impossible figure; they wouldn't work in reality. 'You just couldn't open that door' a tutor might say, and comparable things happen at all levels of teaching. In a Fourth Year Class, for instance, designing a school of management, one of the critics commented that a student had placed two spaces near to each other that ought to be near to each other, but that access was so arranged that people could not easily actually get from one to the other. This, I think, is largely because we tend to think in terms only of visual coding, and a lot of the representation should be of the movements of body through space.

This brings me to the general topic of the importance of movement in drawing and in design, and I shall go quite a long way back, to the drawings that sub-human primates make. The subject has been reviewed by Desmond Morris in his interesting book, *The Biology of Art*. Morris made detailed studies of paintings by the chimpanzee Congo, whose work made a hit when it was exhibited in London. Congo would paint with his fingers or with a brush held in a variety of ways. Photographs of him at work demonstrate the extreme intensity of his involvement in his self-appointed task (which is, of course, just like what we see in the studio). The paintings that he made are representations of bodily movements; the fan-shaped pattern represents the way the ape scratches straw from around itself to make its bed. It is not however, only the bodily movement that the animal enjoys. If you give him a stick that doesn't leave a mark instead of a brush filled with paint, he is not interested. But he is definitely interested in the marks that he makes, and when he gets involved in painting he refuses raisins and grapes and other things he might at other times think desirable. The marks that he makes are by no means random. On a clean sheet of paper he may embroider the edges or pick out the corners, and any marks already on the paper constrain the animal and reduce his area of choice. In some cases, he just

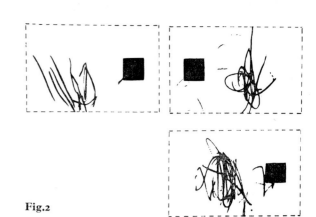

Fig.2

scribbles over the marks, and if they are far enough apart he puts his mark between them, or he tends to balance with his scribbles a mark that is off-centre (Fig.2). So that he has what you might call a sense of where things ought to be, of balance or composition, a feeling for design in the William Morris sense. But although the ape gets to some level of design or of aesthetic appreciation, the veriest child is much more like an architect. Drawings made by a chimp and by a child brought up with a chimp (some of the people who have done the most interesting studies on chimpanzees have brought them up with their own babies), show that at first they produce very much the same sort of thing; later the chimp has got better command of his pencil, but is still scribbling, while the child is drawing a human being – maybe a very specific one – if you ask a child what does that mean, he'll say something like, 'Daddy, of course'. That is to say, the child is drawing a representation of something, and he knows what it is, even if you don't. No cases have been recorded of a sub-human making any attempt to copy or represent anything.

From the earliest ages babies are more interested in the human face than in anything else. Experiments made by watching babies' eye movements show that the child looks four times as long at a diagram of a face as at a red or a yellow or a white disc (Fantz, 1961). The child chooses to look at the human face whenever it can, and it builds up schemata of the

Fig.3

human face in just the same way as we build up schemata of rectangles. These schemata are used as models for interpreting and representing the world. In a drawing of the Wolf and Red Riding Hood by a 4-year-old (Fig.3), you have to count the legs to know which is which. Next to people, children like drawing houses, and their houses resemble the human face; they tend to be symmetrical even if the house they live in is not – the mouth is the door, and a lot of children leave out the lower two windows so that the upper ones look more like eyes (Fig.4).

Fig.4

Children with behaviour disorders tend to make rather nasty houses, too long and thin, or with the windows in the corners (Kerr, 1937). It is worth noting that Itten (1964), one of the Bauhaus teachers, writing on his students' productions, commented on how one girl's paintings were lopsided and asymmetrical until he pointed out to her that they might reflect her own hip ailment which made her a bit crooked, and ever after that she drew symmetrical pictures.

What I am trying to build up is a picture of the importance of experience of the body generally, on how one sees the world. A psychiatrist (Erikson, 1958) asked children to represent an exciting scene with bricks and toys, and he thought that an exciting scene nowadays would mean something from telly or films or stories – something really exciting – but an example of what the girls turned out is shown in

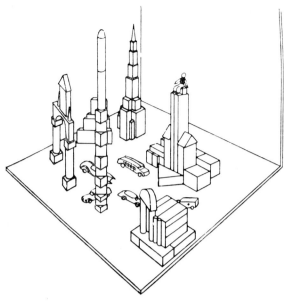

Fig. 5b

Fig.5a; peaceful, domestic interiors, very definitely indoor scenes with people quietly sitting gossiping or playing the piano. Whereas the boys constructed the outside world, high walls and turrets; there's no peace and quiet here; cars are dashing about and there's an ambulance to repair the damage (Fig.5b). Erikson thought that these different ways of perceiving the world were partly socially conditioned; obviously girls are supposed to grow up to be interested in the house, and boys are supposed to grow up and do manly things out of doors, but he believes that the constructions also represent a sort of model of the body, expressing the different experiences of the body that boys and girls have. MacKinnon (1961), in his study of creative architects, found that the more creative architects rated higher on personality scales for femininity than the less creative architects, so it's comforting to think that you're all going to be as interested in the design of insides of houses as in their outsides.

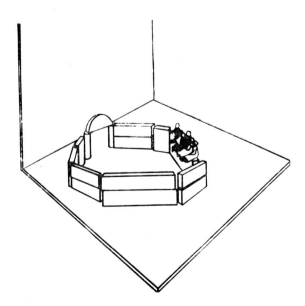

Fig. 5a

Fig. 6a

Another thing that MacKinnon found was that most of the creative architects had drawn and painted from an early age, and since you won't realize how difficult it is to learn to draw and how very difficult therefore to learn how to manipulate this code, I'd like to talk about some difficulties of drawing. Figure 6a shows a drawing by a brain-injured girl who has various disorders of movement. She was 15 years old at this time and she was verbally quite fluent, but she drew a man the way a child of $4\frac{1}{2}$ years old would draw it. By contrast, a boy in the same class, 9 years old but not brain damaged, drew Fig.6b. There is an enormous difference in their

Fig. 6b

styles of drawing, although their speech was not so very different. The girl for instance, would say: 'This is a diagonal. I can spell diagonal' and then she would spell it, but she couldn't copy a diagonal line (Abercrombie, 1964). Figure 7 shows a brain-

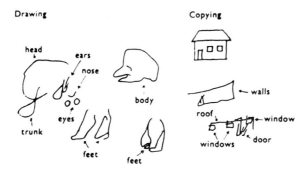

Fig.7

injured adult's attempt to draw an elephant, and to copy a house (Luria, 1963). The pictures are fragmented; there is no good spatial relationship between the parts. This difficulty seems to be related

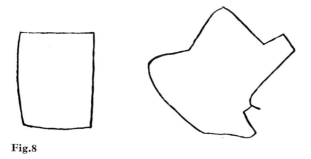

Fig.8

to a disorder of connexions in the brain between the input from the muscles and the input from the eyes. It is probably this sort of co-ordination which is extremely important for the technical skill of drawing and for the appreciation and manipulation of spatial relationships generally. Figure 8 shows the attempts of a normal child of 5 to copy a square and a diamond (Eng, 1931). A diamond is an extraordinarily difficult thing for a child this age to copy (Abercrombie, 1964b). It can do the simple job of drawing a rectangle, so there is nothing the matter with its co-ordination of the movements required for making a square, but it can't yet draw a diamond. What is it that goes on when you learn how to draw a diamond? It isn't simply a difficulty of differentiating shapes. A child certainly can distinguish between things long before it can represent the differences. Figure 9 shows the 'pure scribble' of a child

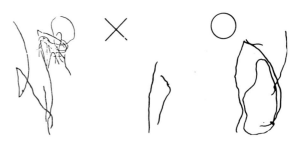

Fig.9

of say, 2 years old; a child of $3\frac{1}{2}$ makes a different sort of scribble when it is copying a cross than when it is copying a circle (Piaget and Inhelder, 1956). So that even when it can't make the differences clear to us, it tries to do so, and the differences it notices particularly are those between open figures and closed figures; almost any closed figure will be drawn as a rough circle, and any open figure tends to be drawn as a series of straight lines. This is interesting because this basic repertoire of two kinds of line permits the representation of the structure of the body, the round face and the round eyes and the straight legs. One reason why the human body is represented so often by children is that it combines these two primitive types of movement.

In Fig.10 you see what it is that helps children to learn to draw a shape. The zigzagging lines represent the eye movements of a child when it is looking at the shape. Notice that at 3 to 4 years the child fixes its eyes roughly on the middle of the shape, but that as it gets older, more and more it follows the outlines. That is to say, more and more it is representing with its eye movements, drawing with its eyes as it were, the contour of the figure. The shape of the figure becomes stored in the brain as a record of these eye movements, first of prolonged fixation on the middle, later of excursions round the edge. This ability to analyse the figure with movements is essential for the ability to recognize the figure when seen later, and ultimately to draw it.

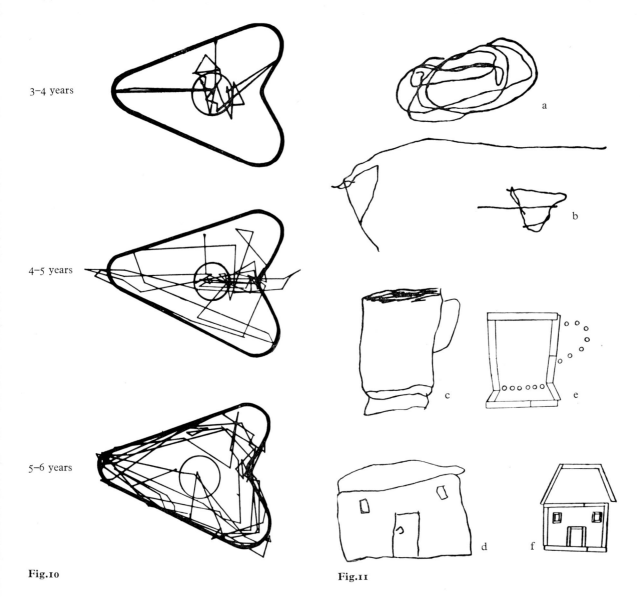

3–4 years

4–5 years

5–6 years

Fig.10

Fig.11

Not only eye movements, but hand movements and possibly movements of other parts of the body are important in learning to see and represent shapes. Figure 11 shows the results of some Russian experiments on attempting to help children to draw (Zaporozhets, 1965). Figure 11a shows the drawings made by a 3½-year-old girl when copying a cup or a shovel. The child was then taught to model a cup or to model a house with sticks that it actually manipulated physically in its own hands; it was not taught to draw, but it was taught to look at, and analyse the structure of, the cup or the house, by having to represent the outline in sticks and beads, and then, not having been trained in drawing, it was able to make very much better drawings than it could do before (Fig.11b).

There are special difficulties in perceiving and copying an oblique line; in attempting to draw one, a child has to tip its head or whole body to align with it, or trace it with a finger. Even an adult, if asked to copy an oblique line on a piece of paper which is itself askew on the table, on to another piece of paper at a different angle, when prevented from moving the body and unable to line the paper up, will get a

pain in the eyes from frustrated efforts to perceive the relationships by skewing his body into line (Vereecken, 1961). This is another example of the way we fall back on more primitive ways of behaving if the task is difficult.

Figure 12 illustrates the stages in learning to draw a diamond. At first, it is drawn as a circle with nevertheless an indication that this won't do exactly, because a corner is indicated by the little twig. Later the child draws it as more or less of a square shape illustrating that it sees that there are straight sides, and it puts ears on the square to represent the corners. Then the drawing gets more or less polygonal, and more and more diamond-shaped, until finally at the age of 7, if it is lucky, the child can draw a diamond. But it has by then learned quite a lot. It knows that the lines must be of the same length and that opposite angles must be equal, for instance.

Sometimes this sort of analysis, which, as I say, has been helped by movements of the eyes and body and by the representation within the brain of previous movements, breaks down when the job gets too

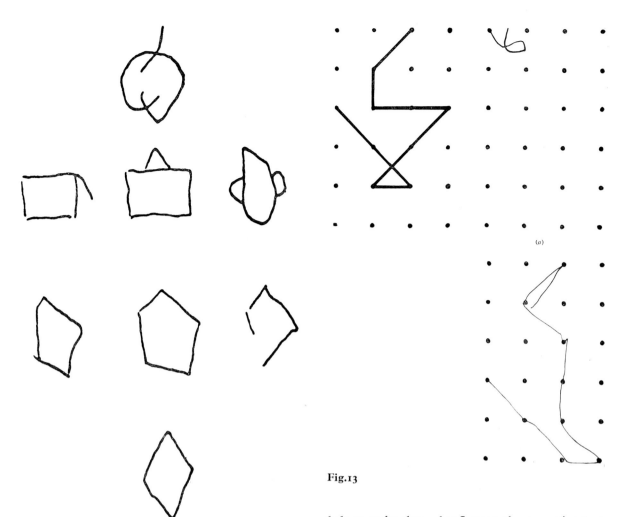

Fig.12

Fig.13

difficult. This is illustrated in Fig.13. A child is asked to copy the figure on the left on to a grid of dots. In this case the task was too difficult for the child (it can normally be done by an 8-year-old) and he suddenly said, 'Oh, it's a sort of eight' and drew a little eight at the top, not the right size nor in the right place, but he'd got the general idea of the figure, in the same way as the diamond, or the triangle or the square at an early age are represented with a general idea of the closed figure. He represented the new difficult figure with something out of his head, his store of experience. He doesn't locate it in space correctly, and instead of looking back to the model to see how well he is doing, he looks up at you, to see if this will do. This again is what the student does in the studio, indeed he can't do anything else; he can't match his attempt against reality, all he can do is just look up at his tutor. Figure 13b shows a different approach by another child who found the task too difficult, but who did look back at the model; he counted the dots and started on the right one, and drew the first oblique correctly, but then he went askew. He got much nearer the right size of the figure and its location, but he didn't get the 'idea' right. It isn't for another year that these children will be able to do this task correctly. An earlier example in the same test will

help to make clear what I mean about reaction to a task which is too difficult for the level of skill available. The test (Frostig *et al.*, 1961) consists of a series of figures that the child has to copy, and each is more difficult than the last. The first is simply a bar across the middle of three pairs of dots. A child of 3 gets the idea of a horizontal line, but doesn't much care where it goes; its actual spatial relationships, its size and exact position in space, don't really matter. A child who makes the 'It's an eight' response to the more difficult 8-year-old task may be able to do correctly all the previous ones. But the child who makes the same sort of response at an early simple stage certainly can't yet go beyond it. The more difficult the task, for that particular person, the more regressed he is in the approach he makes to its execution.

Now this business about getting the general idea is, of course, one of the things that happens in design; it's all very well for the analytical people to advise that you begin by collecting all your information, start with your analysis, but in fact many architects don't work this way. A sketch or doodle made by Gibberd when he was first thinking about Liverpool Cathedral which *The Sunday Times* published, looked unmistakably like the building that materialized. Many architects will scribble on the back of an envelope something which is recognizably the 'image' of the building which they are designing. What I think is happening here is that the general 'feel' of the problem is got intuitively and is scribbled down in the same way as the general feel of what a diamond is is scribbled down as a circle, and only much later is articulated as a straight-sided figure. This psychological process of getting a 'feel' applies not only to visual images, it applies also to other perceptions which are too difficult and complex to make full sense of. You can make ordinary people's perception of a pattern too difficult, either by flashing it on a screen so that they don't have long enough to look at it, or by reducing the illumination so that it is hardly visible. You can flash on a screen a sentence or phrase that a person won't be able to get the first time, or the second or third or the fourth, but will be able to read accurately the fifth or sixth time. In this sort of experiment, people are thrust back into an infantile state in respect of the difficulty of the task; the task is too difficult under those particular conditions. But they are not as though blind, they do perceive something, in shadowy, or embryonic, simplified form. They regress to the condition in which they get a general idea. If you flash on to a screen an expression such as 'gentle wind' in such conditions that a person can't see first time what it says, but can read it the sixth or seventh time, then what he reports each time you flash it on is some general feeling about what the words mean (Werner, 1956). A person will say, for instance, that what he sees concerns something 'soft' or 'warm' or 'balmy' – he gets some feeling of movement of air, a nice feeling. It is this global, general, unarticulated perception of too difficult a task which partly conflicts with the excessively analytical approach to it.

Having begun with the problem of working in analogues, or codes or models, I shall close with an analogue or model of what goes on in the studio. Figure 14 shows some diamonds drawn by 6-year-old children. As I said, most children cannot draw a good diamond until they are 7. A hundred 6-year-old children in ordinary schools were asked to copy a diamond, and three-quarters of the drawings were more or less like diamonds. But the rest of them were these funny-looking shapes; a quarter of the children couldn't yet manage a decent diamond. At the various levels of studio work, we are finding the equivalent of diamonds like these. Just as the too young child cannot yet copy a shape because he cannot internalize it by analysing it with his own movements and then bring it out again, so the student cannot yet analyse and internalize too complex a problem; he has not sufficiently experienced what the code he works with means or represents in reality.

What to do about it? For what it is worth, my opinion is that neither of the two current solutions to the problem of learning to design, used alone, is optimal (naturally I exaggerate the dichotomy to make my point). I refer to the practice of setting the student a graded series of concrete design tasks, each within his growing competence, from a simple cell to a

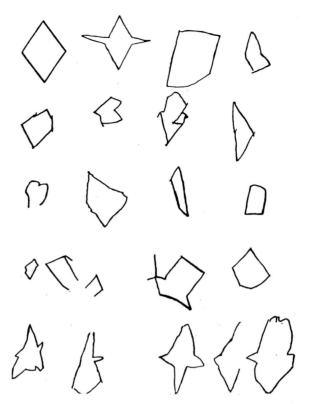

Fig.14

complex of buildings, and to the practice of postponing design until the 'fundamentals' of the necessary disciplines have been taught in theory long before they can be used in the studio. In the first case, the student does not profit from his ability to perceive complexity greatly in advance of what he can construct; in the second, he does not necessarily internalize the products of analysis which the teacher has put before him in such a way that he can bring them out in design. It seems to me necessary to make an attack on the coding problem; to give the student plenty of practice both in manipulating real spaces and constructions of manageable size, and in studying complexes of buildings and spaces. In both cases he should deliberately relate his visual, auditory and kinaesthetic perceptions to drawings and models of the realities he experiences.

REFERENCES

M. L. J. ABERCROMBIE. *The Anatomy of Judgment.* Hutchinson (London 1960).

M. L. J. ABERCROMBIE. *Perceptual and Visuomotor Disorders in Cerebral Palsy: A Survey of the Literature.* Heinemann/Spastics Society (London 1964a).

M. L. J. ABERCROMBIE. On drawing a diamond. In s. A. BARNET and A. MCLAREN (Eds.): *Penguin Science Survey 1965* (1964b), pages 36-54. Harmondsworth: Penguin Books.

H. ENG. *The Psychology of Children's Drawings.* Kegan Paul, Trench, Trubner & Co. Ltd (London 1931).

E. ERIKSON. Sex differences in play construction of 12-year-old children. In J. M. TANNER and B. INHELDER (Eds.): *Discussions on Child Development:* Proceedings of the Third Meeting of the World Health Organisation Study Group on the Psycho-biological Development of the Child, Geneva, 1955. Volume 3 (1958), pages 91-215.

R. L. FANTZ. The origin of form perception. *Scientific American,* 204 (May 1961), pages 66-72.

M. FROSTIG, D. W. LEFEVER, and J. R. B. WHITTLESEY. A developmental test of visual perception for evaluating normal and neurologically handicapped children. *Percept. mot. Skills, 12* (1961), pages 383-94.

J. ITTEN. *Design and Form*. Thames and Hudson (London 1964).

M. KERR. Children's drawings of houses. *Brit. J. Med. Psychol., 16,* (1937), pages 206-18.

A. R. LURIA, E. N. PRAVDINA-VINARSKAYA, and A. L. YARBUS. Disorders of ocular movement in a case of simultanagnosia. *Brain, 86* (1963), pages 219-28.

D. W. MACKINNON. The personality correlates of creativity: a study of American architects. Proc. XIV International Congress of Applied Psychology, Copenhagen. *Munksgaard,* 2 (1961), pages 11-39.

D. MORRIS. *The Biology of Art*. Methuen Paperbacks (London 1966).

J. M. PAIGE and H. A. SIMON. Cognitive processes in solving algebraic word problems. In B. KLEINMUNTZ (Ed.): *Problem Solving: Research, Method, and Theory,* Wiley (New York 1966).

J. PIAGET and B. INHELDER. *The Child's Conception of Space*. Routledge, Kegan Paul (London 1965).

P. VEREECKEN. *Spatial Development*. J. B. Wolters (Groningen 1961).

H. WERNER. Microgenesis and aphasia. *J. Abnorm. Social Psychol., 52* (1956), pages 347-53.

A. V. ZAPOROZHETS. The development of perception in the preschool child. In P. H. MUSSEN (Ed.): *European Research in Cognitive Development, 30* (1965), No.2, pages 82-101.

An approach to the management of design[1]

by John Luckman[2]

Abstract

This paper is offered as an operational research contribution to design methodology. The process of design is defined as a decision-making process where the total problem is divided into sub-problems or levels of the process. Within each level, the stages of analysis, synthesis and evaluation are defined. Difficulties associated with the interdependence of decisions are described with reference to attempts of others to find systematic methods for assisting designers. The author shows that interdependence between decisions can be represented by a graph (collection of nodes and arcs) and a technique known as the analysis of interconnected decision-areas (AIDA) is introduced. AIDA can be used to determine the number of solutions and their form and, if criteria of choice are available, can be used to find optimal solutions. The use of AIDA is illustrated by examples drawn from the fields of engineering and architecture. The paper concludes by indicating possible new areas where the technique may be applied.

1 Introduction

In the past decade, much has been written about design. So far Operational Research has contributed very little to design methodology and this paper is offered as a possible link between OR and design.

Our introduction to the subject was by way of a study of the process of design as seen by architects.[3] We have subsequently extended our early ideas to two other research projects concerning engineering design and city planning.

The definition of design we have used, following Fielden is, 'The use of scientific principles, technical information and imagination in the definition of a structure, machine, or system to perform pre-specified functions with the maximum economy and efficiency.' This definition is, if anything, a little more bold than others in that it includes scientific principles from the beginning.

Designing has become more difficult than it was. In a rapidly changing technological world, the number of materials, the variety of size, shape, and colour of parts or the whole, the variation in manufacturing methods, the range of qualities that are required, the refinement of tolerances that are acceptable, and the pressure on performance of the finished article have all combined to make the designer's job more complex. This has led towards an almost universal search for systematic methods to assist in unravelling the problems that these factors pose.

However, as research progresses, it becomes apparent that a study of the design process on its own is not sufficient, since the majority of pressures on the designer are external to it. To understand the limitations, constraints and objectives of the design process, it is necessary to know more of the research and development process of which design is a part. Within this larger process, design needs to be managed.

2 The process of design

The process of design is the translation of information in the form of requirements, constraints, and experience into potential solutions which are considered by the designer to meet required performance characteristics. Here we shall insist that some creativity or originality must enter into the process for it to be called design. If the alternative solutions can be written down by strict calculations, then the process that has taken place is not design.

Research workers in the field of design have not yet agreed upon a single set of axioms or even termino-

[1] A substantial part of this paper has already appeared in *Operational Research Quarterly*, Vol.18, No.4, December 1967.
[2] This paper is an individual team member's presentation of work in which a number of colleagues have taken part, notably Mr W. N. Jessop, Mr J. R. Morgan, and Mr J. Stringer.
[3] Part of the Building Communication Research Project carried out jointly by the Tavistock Institute of Human Relations and the Institute for Operational Research.

logy in their models of the design process. Some ground that is common, however, is that the design process can be described in terms of a number of stages.

In this paper we will be using three stages – other authors use three, four or six. The stages are:
(i) Analysis
The collection and classification of all relevant information relating to the design problem on hand.
(ii) Synthesis
The formulation of potential solutions to parts of the problem which are feasible when judged against the information contained in the Analysis stage.
(iii) Evaluation.
The attempt to judge by use of some criterion or criteria which of the feasible solutions is the one most satisfactorily answering the problem.

In practice for all but very small design problems, the whole process of design will consist of many levels, progressing from very general considerations at the start, through to specific details as the project nears completion. In architecture, for example, the process will start with the general problems of spatial layout, site access, amenity, etc., and progress through problems of room relationship and treatment of exterior elevations until at the level of final working drawings, the problem of floor finishes, decorations, and minor items such as door handles, lighting fitments, etc. arise.

Thus, a level is synonymous with a sub-problem within the total problem where a set of interconnected decisions must be taken, and at every level to a greater or lesser degree, the stages of Analysis, Synthesis and Evaluation are used.

For the majority of the earlier levels, the stage of Evaluation is performing the function of an indicator of satisfactory areas for development at the next level. Any decisions made become part of the input to the next level and naturally situations can arise when it is better not to single out one potential solution, but rather keep several ideas open to allow more thorough exploration of the next level. By so doing, the designer is leaving open the chance of using feedback to the earlier levels.

This broad overall model does not conflict with common sense since the majority of design problems cannot be totally comprehended without taking the logical step of trying to break them up into sub-problems which are as independent as possible. The total solution is then built up from the solutions to the sub-problems, step by step.

However, Christopher Alexander argues strongly for a careful reconsideration of the way in which sub-problems are defined. He contends that sub-problems are commonly defined using concepts that are on occasion arbitrary and unsuitable and gener-

ally without full regard to the underlying structure of the total problem. Because of this, the sub-problems themselves are highly interconnected and offer no savings or shortcuts in reaching the total design solutions. We feel this point is highly relevant and we discuss this again later.

3 One level of the decision process

What is the designer or design team doing when taking decisions within any one particular level of the design process?

Firstly, information is collected at the outset of the project. This comes from many sources, including information from previous levels resulting from earlier decisions and information from the individual designer's experience. Sometimes the information is not formally written down (and indeed sometimes cannot be written down). Our interpretation of the Analysis stage is one of collecting, classifying, and collating this information to a greater or lesser degree depending upon the designer. In this sifting and sorting activity, the designer is seeking the creative step that will take him on to the next stage, Synthesis.

The design process develops by formulating a potential solution which is a result of the creative step just taken, checking its constituent parts against the original information or possibly information freshly collected.

The designer will proceed only if his potential solution is compatible with that information. Each potential solution is taken to the stage of Evaluation where it will be tried and tested against the criteria that the designer or the process dictates. If accepted it will add to or replace some or all of any previously evaluated potential solutions. The cycle of Analysis, Synthesis, and Evaluation is repeated until the level is completed by the acceptance of one or more of the evaluated potential solutions, and this signals a move to a new level of the total problem.

Now it is clear that this concept of what is happening within a level of the design process takes longer to write down in many cases than it will take to carry out in practice. The designer does not consciously take every step laboriously, but like a good chess player can see several moves ahead and back and is often checking feasibility of an idea at one level with ideas for other levels.

4 Systematic methods

Can help be given to a designer or a design team faced with a design problem? Research work so far suggests several systematic methods that can assist designers.

It should first be made clear that being systematic does not mean that the designer is superfluous with solutions being generated by a computer. The principal area where systematic methods have been tried is in the Analysis stage. Orderly and logical presentation of basic data is a great advantage in helping the designer to make his creative step to a potential solution, expecially in complex design problems. Systematic Analysis comes into its own when the amount of basic information is large, when the consequences of coming up with a poor or wrong solution are expensive or wasteful and when the chance of coming up with a poor or wrong solution is high, i.e. when there is a lack of prior experience in the field.

Some of the simplest systematic techniques that are commonly used are in the form of 'check-lists'. These check-lists set out the information which the designer ought to have thought about, and while, of course, they do not ensure that the designer has the right thoughts, at least the particular item has not been completely forgotten. A typical method is that of J. Christopher Jones of Manchester University who advocates the recording of 'random factors' by each member of the design team who are encouraged to write down anything that occurs to them to be relevant to the problem. This 'brain-storming' extracts a great deal of information in a short time. The factors are classified into check-lists which then guide the designers in the collection of relevant data.

Whatever technique is used, however, it is at this point that the crucial problems arise. If anything, the improved information that has been collected will have widened the area for search of a solution. The drawback to the conventional design process is a lack of a model of the decisions that need to be taken. The designer tends to go on from here in the abstract and since his answer will depend on his having synthesized a large number of factors each of which has its limitations and constraints, its own set of choices and its own range of acceptable values, we feel that more could be done to help him through the maze. Because of the complexity we have just described, the practical search method is of necessity carried out by making assumptions about the factors so as to reduce the area of search to a size that is manageable by the single designer or team. Unfortunately, the factors are nearly always highly interdependent and the whittling down process that is conducted often leads to dead ends when a complete set of compatible factor choices cannot be found. Designers have tended to fall into the trap of expecting an optimum solution to a total problem to be the sum of optimum solutions to its sub-problems regardless of the fact that the sub-problems are highly interdependent.

J. C. Jones has extended his check-list ideas to cover interdependence by creating an interaction matrix showing which factors on the check-list will affect others. Interactions so found are then treated as sub-problems requiring solution. In our opinion this definition and description of interaction between factors does not go far enough and so we developed the model which is described below.

5 Coping with interdependence

For any level we defined each of the factors where there was a choice or range of acceptable answers as a *decision-area*. In the field of architecture a decision-area might be:
(i) The state of the whole or part of a building such as height, position, direction of span, or colour.
(ii) Individual components of a building such as a window, roof cladding, or type of door handle.

The definition of the decision-areas will, of course, be dependent upon the particular level under study. The majority of decision-areas will be directly linked to or related to others, meaning that the decisions can only be made with reference to one another. In fact if the total problem structure has been recognized correctly, the majority of such links should be concentrated within the levels rather than between them. If we represent a decision-area by a point and a relation or link between decision-areas by a line, then the resulting picture is a topological graph. The Analysis of Interconnected Decision-Areas (AIDA) is the technique or tool with which to try to assist the designer in his hypothesis formulation.

The graph is *not* a directed graph, with some decisions preceding others. Any ordering of the taking of decision should stem from the structure of the graph and not from preconceived ideas of the relative importance of the decisions. The taking of decisions sequentially is a common procedure and as we shall see in a later case study, this has its own pit-

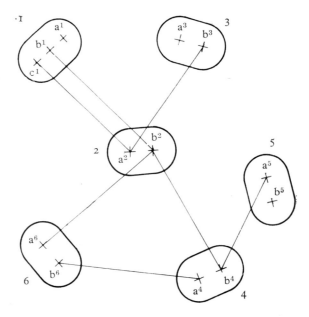

Fig.1
Option graph

falls. We wish to preserve the notion at this stage that all decisions are effectively taken simultaneously.

The next step in the process is to examine more closely each of the decision-areas. Because each represents a factor about which a decision has to be taken, each will consist of a set of choices or *options* which we will define such that one and only one option will be selected in the course of making a single decision. Each decision-area link is expanded to determine the relevant option links. We define the mapping of the decision-areas, options, and option links as an *option graph*. Figure 1 shows an example of a 6 decision-area option graph, with a, b, c, and appropriate subscripts as options within the decision areas.

The option link represents incompatibility[4] between the options in one decision area and the options in an adjacent decision-area. Thus a_1 is compatible with a_2 or b_2, whereas b_1 is not compatible with b_2, and c_1 is not compatible with a_2.

The graphical approach could be used in the assessment of critical sets of decision-areas and hence give guidance as to the deployment of the development team. For example, it may be that where a 'ring' exists in the option graph (e.g. Fig.1 – decision-areas, 2, 4, and 6) this is an indicator of a need for a co-ordinated exploratory and problem-solving subteam. It could be that the option graph for a development project breaks into a number of separated networks, where the implications, regarding deployments and control of the team, are different again.

Having defined the option graph, we can then find feasible solutions to the problem. A feasible solution must include one option chosen from each area in such a way that there is no contravention of the incompatibilities shown in the option graph. For small problems such as in Fig.2 the solution can be found by simple hand calculations. Larger problems would need to be tackled with the aid of a computer.

Referring to Fig.1, we see that a_1, a_2, a_3, b_4, b_5, a_6 is a feasible solution, while a_1, a_2, b_3, b_4, b_5, b_6 is not. There are in fact only eight feasible solutions in this case and it is interesting to note that none of them includes options c_1, b_2, or b_3.

Where there is a single quantifiable criterion of choice (cost for example) associated with each option or combination of options, it is possible to find that feasible solution which best satisfies the criterion. It is more likely, however, that compromise will

---

[4] We originally defined an option link as existing where choices in adjacent decision-areas were *compatible* but the resulting graphs tended to become heavily congested with lines and were difficult to follow. This newer definition of incompatibility is also more logical since the absence of links between two decision-areas implies that they are independent.

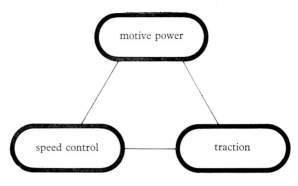

Fig.2
case study 1.
Decision graph

have to be sought between several criteria, which may not be capable of being related to a single scale of measurement.

The descriptions adopted so far have seen the design problem as being deterministic. It is clear that in real life many of the links and criterion values may only be expressible in terms of probabilities. Thus, for example, the feasible link between any two options in adjacent areas may express the facts that some expenditure on research would increase the chance that these options can be made compatible with one another. To handle decisions of this nature, it would be necessary to include statistical decision theory in the methods of choice available within the AIDA technique.

The problem of analysis of option graphs lies principally in their combinatorial nature. There do not need to be many decision areas and options before the analysis must be handled by a computer. Such analysis can be stated as the need to find sets of options, one from each decision-area given the following constraints:
(a) Certain pairs of options may be incompatible.
(b) Certain higher order combinations of options may be incompatible.
(c) Compatibility in the foregoing causes may be probabilistic rather than deterministic.

6 The design dialogue

The process of design, using AIDA, is foreseen as a dialogue in which working through the logical consequences of the current options and decision-areas poses new questions to the design team. The answers to these questions define the area of search, redefine the decision graphs, define new criteria and combinations of criteria, and make way for the next level of the design process. To facilitate such a dialogue, the following output information may be required at each level:
(i) The number and description of feasible solutions. (If too many, criteria of choice will be required; if too few, new technical options may have to be sought or the initial restrictions and requirements relaxed.)

(ii) The number of feasible solutions associated with any specified option or partial set of options.

(iii) The number of feasible solutions which meet specified additional criteria and conditions.

(iv) The criterion values for all those feasible solutions which are dominant. (A 'dominant' feasible solution is one which meets the condition that there is no other having more favourable values of *all* the criteria.)

(v) A short list of feasible solutions defined for example, as those which (a) meet specified conditions, and/or (b) head a list of solutions ranked according to one criterion, or (c) are dominant, or (d) have criterion values close to those of the dominant set.

(vi) A list of those options which do not appear in any of the feasible solutions contained in the short list.

The number of feasible solutions to a particular problem can be found by treating the decision graph as a directed graph labelled and if necessary augmented by artificial links, so as to have one source and one sink and be acyclic. The option links between each pair of options are written in matrix form with 1 or 0 in the ith row and the jth column representing compatibility or incompatibility between the ith option in the first decision-area and the jth option in the second. Artificial links are represented by a matrix of 1's.

The exact number of feasible solutions to the problem can then be calculated by using combinations of matrix multiplication and elementwise matrix multiplication. Manipulation of the matrices can also be made to yield the specification of the options in the solution and, if a single criterion is available, the value of the best solution.

For larger problems or for more exhaustive analysis of a problem a computer programme has been developed. This can provide output information of types (i), (ii), and (iii) above. Only a single criterion at a time can be dealt with at present.

Returning briefly to our earlier model of the technical content of a level of the design process, we see that AIDA is really a systematic technique for the Synthesis stage. By restructuring the data contained in the information groups into decision-areas and options together with their interdependence characteristics, a large number of feasible solutions can be found. In our view the provision of such solutions before Evaluation represents a definite improvement upon the present method of judging each potential solution as it is formulated. It has been our experience in the study of the design process that at best only a few potential solutions are ever explored (admittedly the designer will have chosen some of the better ones in his search process) while at worst, the first is often accepted because 'it fits the bill' and time is too limited to seek more than marginal improvements.

A further advantage in our approach is in the area of design team coordination and invidual participation. In the field of architecture for example, consultants brought in to advise on their specialty at an early stage have only a limited view of where their part of the design process fits into the total picture. Design work that proves abortive is often carried out because the implications of another's work are not sufficiently appreciated. If all members of the design team were to assist in the definition of option graphs, these problems of communication might to some extent be overcome. The teams choice of options at any level will give a much tighter and more clear-cut specification within which to plan their detailed design work. Individual members of the design teams are too often at different levels of the design process.

AIDA for the most part is a method for Synthesis. However, it has been found from experience in trying to apply the method that the Analysis stage often benefits from the necessity to provide coherent and orderly information as input material. Similarly, the structure imposed by the AIDA formulation, makes it possible to incorporate any available criteria in such a way as to assist in the task of choosing, thus contributing to the stage of Evaluation.

7 Case study 1

Suppose that, in the design of a locomotive, there are three main areas for decision: motive power, speed control, traction. Each of these aspects of the problem can be represented by a decision area (see Fig.2).

The links mean that, in this case, any design decisions about motive power might affect or be affected by decisions about control or traction, and decisions about control or traction may also affect one another.

We can then consider the nature of each area in more detail to see what decisions are at all possible within it. Two types of engine might be considered, there may be three methods of speed control and two ways of preventing wheel-slip. If we indicate these options as points within each area, the designer can relate them more precisely by drawing an option graph (see Fig.3).

Figure 3 shows how some of the choices of ways to control speed are not compatible with ways of providing motive power (EL-SC.1, E2-2SC.2) and how a possible design option for preventing wheel-slip is not compatible with one source of motive power (E2-T.1), while the other option in the 'traction' decision area is incompatible with the remaining option for controlling speed (T.2-SC.3).

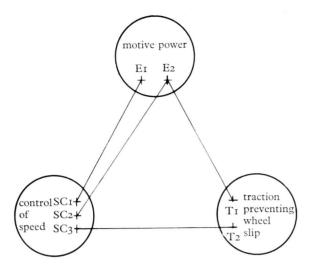

Fig.3
case study I, Option Graph

We can see that, in this case, four solutions are possible:

EI	SC2	TI
EI	SC2	T2
EI	SC3	TI
E2	SCI	T2

Each of the options, E2, SCI, and SC3 appears in only one solution. If the situation therefore is one in which development work will be necessary to establish the feasibility of the chosen options, we might select (other things being equal) the 'robust' solutions EI, SC2, T2, since it provides the greatest freedom for manoeuvre if the development work is unsuccessful for any of its constituents. Furthermore, it may be desirable to concentrate initially on the development to establish the feasibility of EI since it appears in three of the four compatible solutions and, if successful, would preserve the greatest freedom of action for later choice in the other decision areas.

8 Case study 2[5]

This case study concerns one level of the process of designing a house to be built on a large scale. We were present at many of the design meetings that were held on this project and we were able to observe the emerging design.

The design team developed their design from conceptualization to the drawing board in a very short period of time. However, in our opinion much of the design team's effort went into exploring, in the intuitive fashion, those aspects of the problem reflected in the linkage between decision-areas.

The most important point that we observed in the teams' discussions was that they were attempting

[5] This study arose as part of the Building Industry Communications Research Project carried out jointly by the Tavistock Institute of Human Relations and the Institute for Operational Research.

to make their decisions sequentially, when in fact almost every decision was affected both by those that had gone and those that were yet to come.

Subsequent to their exploration and agreement on a practical solution we drew a graph of the principal decisions and their probable dependence pattern as shown in Fig.5 which relates to the house sketched in Fig.4.

The option graph relating to the house is shown in Fig.6 where for simplicity we have omitted the peripheral decision-areas 'Roof (cladding materials)',

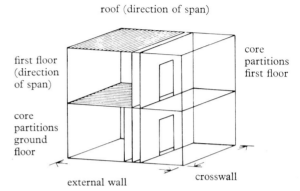

Fig.4
Sketch of House

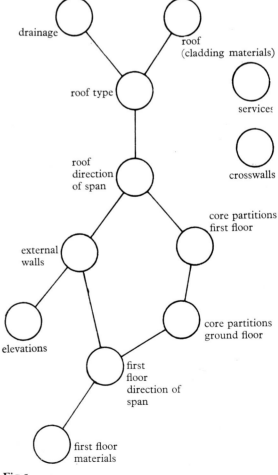

Fig.5
Decision graph for the House

'Drainage' and 'Elevation' together with the two independent decision-areas 'Services' and 'Crosswalls'.

Note that the two decision-areas in the strategy graph 'Roof (type)' and 'Roof (direction of span)' were linked under the assumption that they were interdependent, whereas the options chosen were subsequently discovered to be fully compatible with each other.

Note also that there are two options within the decision-area 'Roof (direction of span)' labelled crosswall. Although these two options perform approximately the same function, they differ both in their compatibility with options in adjacent decision-areas and in their cost and therefore must both be included (see Fig.6).

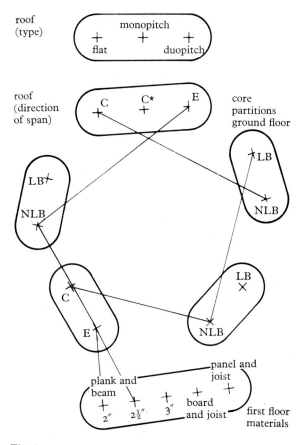

Fig.6
Decision graph for the House

KEY:
c: crosswall
e: external wall
Lb: load bearing
N.L.B: non-load bearing
*: with counter battens

The design team in their discussions (without the benefit of an option graph) had started their exploration with the decision-area 'Upper floor (direction of span)'. They made a choice from the options available, and then moved on to discuss other decision-areas which were thought to be connected, making their choices and moving on again until they felt they had reached an acceptable total solution.

The main difficulties that the team experienced were recalling their choices of options after more than about two steps, remembering what decision-areas were and whether they were dependent upon one another and finally reaching options on the opposite side of the circuit that were consistent.

To demonstrate the application of AIDA, we set out to find all the feasible solutions to the problem.

For simplicity of presentation we took up the problem at the point where a duopitch roof had been decided upon. Furthermore, the 'Crosswall (counter battens)' option in the decision-area 'Roof (direction of span)' had been ruled out on cost grounds, and the option 'Board and joist' in the decision-area 'Upper floor construction (materials)' had already been selected for reasons of cost. The option graph is now reduced to that shown in Fig.7. For ease of

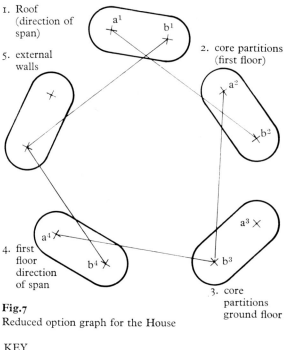

Fig.7
Reduced option graph for the House

KEY
a^1, a^2: crosswall $\qquad$ a^2, a^3, a^5: load bearing
b^1, b^2: external wall $\qquad$ b^2, b^3, b^5: non load bearing

calculations we have assigned numbers to the decision-areas and letters with subscripts to the options within the decision-areas.

It can be shown that there are eight feasible solutions to the problem, each of which satisfies all the conditions of compatibility.

The last part of the problem is to choose one of these eight solutions. To obtain a 'best' solution in this example, the design team were pleased to accept any feasible solution provided that it cost as little as possible. We costed the options within each decision-area. The cheaper option was given a cost of zero, while the more expensive option was given a cost equal to the difference in cost of the two options. We then compared the total costs of eight feasible

Decision-area	Option	Cost	Feasible combinations 1 2 3 4 5 6 7 8							
1 Roof	a$_1$ Crosswall span	27	I	I			I			
	b$_1$ External wall span	0			I	I		I	I	I
2 Core partitions First Floor	a$_2$ Load-bearing	6	I	I	I		I	I		
	b$_2$ Non-Load-bearing	0				I			I	I
3 Core partitions Ground Floor	a$_3$ Load-bearing	11	I	I	I	I	I	I	I	
	b$_3$ Non-Load-bearing	0								I
4 Upper Floor Construction	a$_4$ Crosswall span	0	I	I	I	I				
	b$_4$ External wall span	13					I	I	I	I
5 External walls	a$_5$ Load-bearing	23	I		I	I	I	I	I	I
	b$_5$ Non-Load-bearing	0		I						

Total Cost of combinations 67 44 40 34 80 53 47 36

Table 1 Feasible Solutions for the Circuit of Five Decision-Areas

solutions. The solutions and their comparative costs are given in Table 1 above.

The minimum cost solution was in fact the same solution that the design group had arrived at independently.

9 The wider view

The decision graphs and option graphs illustrated so far have been specific to each case and have concerned only part of the decision process. There is no reason in principle, however, why a comprehensive map of the total set of important decisions to be taken at all levels of a project should not be produced. The resulting picture would be an involved one and its compilation would be a formidable task. This, however, is no bar to using the *concept* of a complete AIDA network as a background against which such problems as the definition of the roles of design team members can be discussed.

Once the completed option graph has been compiled, moreover, it has relevance to all the possible members of a whole class of designs. There may be areas of decision which are special to individual cases but the same broad 'shape' of AIDA networks may well be found to apply over a range of similar projects. If this turns out to be so, then several interesting possibilities are opened up:
(i) Basic networks of wide usefulness could be prepared and made available as a design management aid. At the very least this would provide a form of 'check-list' for the designers and planners of a new project. This does *not* mean however, that all new designs must look alike. The criteria applied to evaluating possible solutions will vary widely from case to case.
(ii) The factors involved in specific designs could be recorded in a manner which would form a useful 'bank' of data and experience. This would help to minimize repetition of mistakes. It could also help to increase the speed of innovation.
(iii) Analysis of the structure of the basic network could suggest the forms of organisation and communications best suited to particular classes of design projects.

The foregoing possibilities do not only describe the design process. In particular, (iii) above includes organization and communication. By studying the interdependence of decisions that are taken within the whole or part of an organization, AIDA may help us to examine the appropriate role structure of the decision-makers.

In our current work on decision-making in local government we have been studying city planning. Our models resemble decision and option graphs, although very much more complex. The decision-makers in these models are the committees, departments and sections, etc., with certain spheres of responsibilities. The breakthrough will come if we can improve the relationship between the needs of the city and the structure of the organization that has been elected to provide for them.

REFERENCES
S. VAJDA. *Mathematical Programming*. Addison-Wesley Publishing Co. Inc. (Reading Mass. 1961), page 47.
G. B. R. FIELDEN et al. *Engineering Design*. HMSO, (1963).
J. C. JONES. Design Methods Compared. *Design* (August and September 1966).
M. ASIMOW. *Introduction to design*. Prentice-Hall Inc. (1962).
C. ALEXANDER. *Notes on the Synthesis of Form*. Harvard University Press (1964).
F. HARARY, W. N. JESSOP, J. STRINGER, and J. LUCKMAN. An Algorithm for Project Development. *Nature*, Volume 206 (3 April 1965), page 118.
D. HINKLEY, W. N. JESSOP and J. LUCKMAN. Unpublished paper, IOR/35. Institute for Operational Research (1967).

Facts and models

by Amos Rapoport

Everyone uses a method when they work, but I take it that what is meant by method at this meeting is used in a very special sense. It is used to describe certain attempts to systematize methods and to give models of the design process which help to generate design in a more systematic and 'objective' way. What I want to do is to ask a series of questions which bear on whether these attempts are the most urgent need, or what other needs there may be, as well as on some potential problem areas which should be considered in the development of any method.

I will start off by asking why there is currently a strong interest in models and design methods and suggest that there are two possibilities which are not mutually exclusive:
(1) This interest may be due to some real need to improve working methods.
(2) It could be a cultural phenomenon of some sort, reflecting certain values and goals.

After dealing with these two points and examining the role of facts in design I will consider how the designer's mind works, and the problem of buildings as opposed to diagrams.

The need for improved design methods

The interest in methods and models is due to a conviction that designers are not doing as well as they might be, that the new scale of problems and complexity of new needs are such that new methods are urgently needed. This need seems intuitively very likely but it has never really been demonstrated. When designers really do go wrong, we need to identify *why* they go wrong and what can be done about it. We need to decide if there are areas where additional information, or new ways of presenting it so as to make it more usable, may be more important than new methods for handling information.

Nor has it been demonstrated that the new methods work *better*. We need, of course, to define what we mean by 'better'. We can look at this in two ways: increased efficiency in terms of man hours, lead time

and the like; or a better product. I want to discuss it in terms of the latter, because it is by far the more difficult and interesting problem. All I say is to be seen in the light of this. In these terms a method is only better than another (whatever it may be) if it produces a better building or environment. The concept 'better' involves a value judgement – better than something else – and is related to goals and values as well as knowledge.

Most methods assume, as an implicit value, that constant innovation is the goal – that each problem is new and to be solved from first principles. This is not necessarily the case. Each solution is not a considerable departure from existing designs. Each problem is *not* new – there are the forces of history, tradition, the constant elements in man's needs, and many others. If each project were indeed started from scratch it would be impossible to build up a body of knowledge and experience which we all agree is needed. The value of traditional solutions is, I think, greatly underestimated. Such solutions may tell us much. Often when we ignore tradition we are throwing away thousands of years' experience – *facts* and very valuable ones. This experience represents many multi-variable experiments in real life situations and it needs to be stressed that there is evidence for constancy as well as change in the human condition.

One part of the total design problem, the built environment, which the models attempt to represent is, in our case, the organization of space at different scales – from the region through the city to the building, the room and so forth. When we speak of design we are therefore speaking of the organization of space in the physical environment. It is thus necessary to discuss how space is organized, who organizes it and for what reasons, and how a given organization is perceived by, and affects, people. There is very little information available on these very complex matters which may well constitute one of our major needs at the moment. If a good environment is our goal then we may need things other than design methods. As August Hecksher said – 'We are not making models, we are making a world.'[1]

There is another implicit assumption in most of the discussion on methods. This is that the designer is the form giver. In fact, he is that only to a limited extent in most cases since there are many social, cultural, political, economic, and other constraints – written and unwritten – which limit his role. In the past, the constraints on vernacular building were primarily the forces of tradition and also the lack of means while the high style designers had to conform to the whims of patrons or prescriptions of church or court. Today, as in the past, in addition to the forces of tradition there are the effects of prejudice ('I want *that*'). A good example of this is the Belvedere restaurant (by Leonard Manasseh) which was greatly praised in the *Architectural Review* (May 1966). In the September issue (p.159) it was reported that the clientele in North Kensington and the wine and dine correspondents resisted the design, and it was changed to neo-Georgian.

There is also the impact of political and social forces on design standards – the effects of laws, taxes, politics (as in the selection of architects), and the like.[2] It has, in fact, been suggested that these institutional and political problems are the principal ones facing design.[3] There are the effects of mortgage authorities and institutional lenders who frequently will not lend on novel designs.[4] Codes, regulations, and zoning not only limit design possibilities but also have aesthetic biases (e.g. for free standing buildings), thus greatly affecting form.[5] Even insurance may affect form and Pushkarev points out the considerable effects which the American obsession with safety, and the prevalence of absurd liability claims has had on design.[6]

All of these are very real social and cultural constraints and there are others as well. An understanding of their operation is critical for an understanding of the design process. The designer is not an innovator or form giver – he is rather the packager and modifier of form. This distinction affects the universe of discourse through the action of these cultural constraints before the designer gets a chance to act. Things are often designed before the designer ever hears of them; there are also the constraints of the surrounding environment and the designer's personal constraints which lead to the final choice among the remaining possibilities, i.e. style. In other words an understanding of the cultural context and constraints, which forms part of the body of facts, may be the most important one to enable problems to be solved – not least through helping with the political problems of implementing innovation when it *is* needed.

These cultural constraints are a function of the values, images, and meanings which attach to the environment. Aldo van Eyck once said 'what you should try and accomplish is built meaning, so get close to meaning and build.' We do know how to build – perhaps we need to know what meaning is.

For van Eyck, the meaning of a door and a threshold, as the transition between two realms, is important and this needs to be known before any method can deal with it. This is a symbolic aspect of the door, and it has been suggested that man tends to symbolize everything and then react to the symbols as though they were the environmental stimuli.[7] Hence we need to know these symbols and their importance for different groups. These symbols and meanings are the results of people's *images*, [8] which include both logical and non-logical values which affect man's view of, and behaviour in, the world. The environment is not, therefore, something 'out there' which acts on someone. Rather it is in a systemic relation with that someone at a given time, not in any absolute sense – although there is an important component of constancy which prevents a situation of complete relativism. The environment is also part of the images of the various participants in its creation and these images involve knowledge and expectations (schemata). Aspects of these images, symbols, associations, and world view all enter into the make-up of the environment, as well as physical components, although the nature of these latter plays a very important role in the relation to the environment. This relation, and the environment, may change as the image changes. Since the image resists change it changes slowly and there may be a considerable time-lag between any stimulus and its response (if any). The man-environment relation cannot, therefore, be seen as a simple stimulus-response model.

Various techniques have been devised to measure, or rather estimate, images – whether personal or socially shared – as well as their changes. These images, moreover, may be self-fulfilling prophecies as was the case with the division of society by American social science into lower, lower–, and upper–middle, and upper classes. The correlation at first was not too good but as the image became accepted a perfect fit was obtained and more so in the U.S. than elsewhere.[9]

Design models tend to be concerned with the handling and arrangement of information rather than with its content. It may be rather difficult to find out information about this image content, and even more difficult to use it in design, but its importance for

[1] *Journal of Environmental Design*, Berkeley, No.2, page 7.
[2] See ED LOGUE in J. B. Holland (Ed.) *Who Designs America?* Garden City, N.Y. Doubleday paperback (1966).
[3] PUSHKAREV, in Holland (Ed.), *op. cit.*, page 86 ff.
[4] S. BAKER. *Visual Persuasion.* (McGraw Hill, New York 1961); LOGUE in Holland (Ed.), *op. cit.*
[5] See DAVID CRANE. The City Symbolic. *AIP Journal* (November 1960), page 282.
[6] PUSHKAREV *ibid.*, pages 113–15.
[7] RENE DUBOS. *Man Adapting.* Yale University Press (New Haven 1966).
[8] KENNETH BOULDING. *The Image.* University of Michigan Press (Ann Arbor 1961).
[9] This information from Horst Rittel, University of California, Berkeley.

both the way in which space is organized and the question of who really organizes it is great. In view of the almost desperate attempts people make to personalize their environment, the image of the non-designer may be as relevant as that of the designer and the stress on the designer's image alone may be misplaced. Getting at these images can be very important. A friend was once asked to do a colonial house. Needing work he resisted his first impulse to kick the prospective client down the stairs. He began to probe the image behind the concept 'colonial' which, interestingly enough, was the client's main concern. He discovered that it was one of serenity, simplicity, and elegance, reliance on proportions and unobtrusiveness in the setting. This was quite possible with *his* image of the architect's form integrity and the result made both him and the client happy – as well as being a very fine house.

The work of Glowczewski and his team at Aswan is an instructive example. In this case, the sophisticated design methods proposed had to be changed due to the lack of information. After the design was produced, the Governor and others intervened. Their image was of the grand waterfront avenue which is typical of the great cities of the Mediterranean (Alexandria, Nice, Cannes, and others) with which they identified. This image of grandeur, this symbol of being a great city, was essential and had to be provided despite a number of serious disadvantages. In this case, therefore, the image affected the solution and the type of information affected the method of design.

What I am suggesting is that the information used and what you want to do with it may be more significant than the methods of arranging or handling that information. For example, it seems rather important whether we view the house as built 'to keep in a consistent climate and to keep out predators'[10] or as being primarily a sacred space.[11] It is this which will be one of the crucial factors in the form the house will take. Whether socio-cultural or physical factors are considered as primary in the organization of space is very important in relation to the data used and the results that follow.

Sheldon Wollin (Professor of Political Science. Berkeley) describes models as typical of our age. 'What is interesting about the notion of models is that you could create a kind of separate world. Depending on how you construct it, it can be made for feeding-in certain facts and data, and can be made to behave, act, or operate in a certain way.'[12] In other words a model can be unrelated to reality. If the information is unreal we may get logically consistent answers, provided the axioms are accepted but which otherwise make little sense since the end results may be quite unrelated to people. In this connexion the fact that many of the design methods proposed in the early days of the development were not architectural design orientated, and most workers in the field were either not architects or not engaged in architectural design, may be significant since there may be different value systems involved.

One could argue that the consideration of some of the more subtle factors has been resisted not only because they are much more difficult to deal with than the simpler physical factors, but also because they involve areas of human action which are currently unfashionable. They are not 'rational' or 'objective', nor do they lend themselves to simple models, classifications, or manipulations. The selection of data to be used in design and their priorities in the final design are partly arbitrary and reflect the implicit values of the people concerned. This is an aspect of the cultural context of models to which I will now turn.

The cultural context of models

It could be suggested that the interest in conceptual models and design methods is a cultural phenomenon reflecting implicit values such as objectivity. I have already suggested that the types of facts which are used in design and the values which the design objectives represent are, at least partly, related to culture. One could say that any model reflects this cultural context and the implicit value judgements more than it does what it sets out to portray. The changes over time in the types of models used could be an indicator of their cultural context and such a history would be most useful. Demographers have refused to accept the evidence of the impact of cultural values on population change because their values prevent them seeing these facts. Their models reflect their biases more than they do the reasons for the way populations change.[13] An analogous situation is Humphrey Osmond's suggestion that mental hospitals tell more about who builds them and runs them than about who is locked up in them.

The present cultural context of the desire for clarity and certainty in architectural design may reflect a felt need for constraints in design. In the past such constraints were given through the traditional nature of the culture and its prohibitions, the forces of nature and site and the lack of choice. While there are still constraints acting, there is much more choice, and there seems to be a search for new constraints which will not, hopefully, eliminate the very real increase in the choices available. Yet the difficulty of coping with this vast choice, which is more psychological than methodological, because of the rather low criticality of architecture, leads to a fear of uncertainty and ambiguity.

[10] BRUCE ARCHER. Systematic method for designers, reprinted from *Design* (1963–4).
[11] LORD RAGLAN. *The Temple and the House*. Norton (New York 1964).
[12] *Journal of Environmental Design*, Berkeley, No.2, page 9.
[13] W. ZELINSKI. *Prologue to Population Geography*. Prentice Hall (Englewood Cliffs, N.J. 1966), page 65.

This striving for new methods and models seems to reflect a rather romantic view of the successes of the physical sciences. Koestler makes the interesting suggestion that scientists often stress the irrational and intuitive in their work while artists tend to stress the 'scientific' and rational in their creation.[14] In fact, painters, sculptors, and architects have often been obsessed with scientific theories. In the past architectural theories have been based on technology, biology (health), climate, the mathematics of proportion, and many other concepts of the day. Current models may reflect current values rather than the real nature of the design process or the needs of the environment. It would, once again, be very interesting to study the history of architectural design methods and their changes. For example, work on colour was seen as being a problem of aesthetics in the 1900's, then one of function in terms of efficiency, and more recently as one of therapeutics. The colours used and why they were used have probably changed accordingly.[15]

Design methods strive for objectivity but they are not objective – neither are they neutral. Any model represents a theoretical position which colours and affects the whole *weltanschauung* and determines which material is regarded as important, how it is seen, investigated, and used. Consider two aspects of *Atoms of environmental structure* (Alexander/Poyner) where it is denied that the environment is a question of goals, values and the like and asserted that it can be objectively right or wrong. The paper stresses the 'scientific' nature of the attitude adopted which seems to be a value judgement *par excellence*. This assumes that science is the only world view possible and does not even consider the view that there may be a body of information and material to which that particular attitude and mode of discourse is not applicable, that the scientific mode is merely one among many others,[16] and that to arrive at certain facts non-scientific descriptions may be more useful than scientific ones. Kurt Lewin (p.13, *op. cit.*, footnote 31) suggests that a description of behaviour by Dostoyevski may give more insight and be of more value than a more 'scientific' description, and Riesman (*op. cit.*, footnote 27) makes a similar point. As a result of this value judgement we find the attempt to isolate variables and hence a non-systemic approach.[17] Another extreme value judgement is implied by the search for freedom from conflict. Not only has it been suggested that some conflict may be necessary and indeed desirable,[18] but modern architecture has been criticized for being too dedicated to the elimination of conflict.[19] The very decision as to what constitutes conflict and which tendencies in man are innate also involves value judgements. I am not, at this time, concerned with the validity of the proposed method, merely with showing that there are many value judgements implicit in it and that they imply a theoretical position. This position will distort the information and it is important to realize that new methods may not necessarily eliminate distortions – they may merely change the type of distortion. The elimination of some independent variables because they seem unimportant, or cannot be measured, or in order to simplify the model can involve some real losses (as well as being the result of value judgements). If one only considers *misfits* or *conflicts* this greatly affects both the information considered and the results as well as their evaluation before any design work is done.

The main problem is that these values are often represented in the methods implicitly. This bias, whether of a group or the individual, is a function of the image and an image which is believed becomes a self-fulfilling prophecy as I have already mentioned and as is the case with economics.[20] An interesting example of the subjective nature of models in town planning is the fact that in the U.S. such models tend to be aggregated while in England they tend to be more unitary. This reflects real differences in the two cultures. These find expression in the reality of political and other systems which in the U.S. are in aggregate of contending choices and decisions of many individuals and groups to a greater extent than in England. At the same time, however, the cultural *milieu* finds a direct reflection in the types of models used and may colour the way the city is seen to behave. An even more striking difference can be found in the urban literature of France and the U.S. In France there is much more concern with the symbolic, visual, and hierarchic elements of the city which are largely ignored in the American preoccupation with process and information handling.

Models of reality differ greatly depending on one's background. This is even the case with system analysts who, after all, are members of one subculture of considerable rigour and with many attitudes, values, and goals in common.[21] A physicist and a chemist may attach quite different meanings to a concept such as a 'molecule' depending on the intellectual model which they implicitly use.[22] A brief consideration of the history of science shows that the effects of attitude and culture play a major role in the selection of facts and phenomena considered relevant and in the choice of models.[23] A

[14] ARTHUR KOESTLER. *The Act of Creation*. Macmillan (New York 1964), pages 229–30.
[15] This example is from Robert Sommer, University of California, Davis.
[16] BOULDING, *op. cit.*, page 16.
[17] See STAFFORD BEER. The World, the Flesh and the Metal. *Nature*, No.4968 (16 January 1965), page 223.
[18] DUBOS, *op. cit.*, BERLYNE and others.
[19] WILLIAM H. JORDY. Humanism in Contemporary Architecture: Tough & Tender Minded. *Journal of Architectural Education*, Volume 15, No.2 (Summer 1960), pages 3–10.
[20] BOULDING, *op. cit.*, pages 90–92.
[21] See STAFFORD BEER. *op. cit.*, page 224. He discusses the differences based on the differing backgrounds of physics, games theory, biology or what have you.
[22] T. S. KUHN. *The Structure of Scientific Revolutions*. University of Chicago Press (Chicago 1965).
[23] KUHN, *op. cit.*

number of writers have commented on the subjectivity as shown by the tendency of science not to see the evidence which does not fit the system.[24] As an interesting comment a study (Pastore, 1949) showed that the position of scientists on the relative effects of heredity and environment correlated more closely with their politics than with the evidence.

There seems to be a 'scientific taste just as there is a literary or artistic one'.[25] Certain problems tend to become fashionable, work on them is supported and produces results regarded as 'good'. This becomes even clearer in the fields of psychology and human behaviour which are more directly relevant to our field. The different views of reality of behaviourism, *gestalt*, and other schools of psychology are too well known to merit discussion. There is evidence that the experimental results themselves are affected by the procedure adopted, so that in many rat experiments the equipment used has tended to give results expected by the various experimenters. The interpretation of similar results is even more variable; the same observations of cats in boxes are given totally different interpretations by different observers (e.g. Adams and Thorndike). Most recently it has been shown that not only are pupils' results affected by the teachers' expectations, but that the behaviour of rats seems to be similarly affected by the research workers' expectations (Rosenthal, at Harvard).

It is clear that the collection of facts and their interpretation is a discriminating activity which is partly a matter of personal or group choice. As a group choice science has deliberately restricted the classes of data and techniques with which it deals and their universe of discourse.[26] In the field of architectural design it needs to be consciously decided whether these particular restrictions are the most valid. It is possible that in the case of the built environment values, images, emotions, and multiple interpretations are much more important than they are in the physical sciences where the methods adopted have, admittedly, worked brilliantly.

The selection and use of the facts is often made through the use of the model which reflects the goals and preferences of the user. There is thus a clear relation between the nature of the model and the data. All too often, however, the first step in design methods is said to be the arrangement of facts rather than a conscious decision as to which of them are considered to be relevant. Since this selection affects the results to a great degree it needs to be made *explicitly*, by adopting a view which consciously structures the selection of data. Some methods, of course, do this and a discussion about the nature of the choice becomes possible. All this involves the need for some theory or philosophy of the environment since *any* model seems to depend on being part of some broader, more general theory or paradigm.

In view of the cultural controls and constraints described before, and in the absence of any generally accepted theory of the environment which would help select relevant classes of information, the acceptance of any method is an act of faith and a value judgement. Possibly we should adopt a more eclectic position, and use any method that works· As practitioners in the real world we have to use whatever is relevant. Robert Sommer points out that in real life situations psychologists give up their strict theoretical position in order to deal with the problems they face. In the social sciences there have recently been a number of criticisms of the excessive reliance on single methodologies or even sets of them.[27] While we need to be able to design when all the data we consider necessary are not available, there is also a need for data and an awareness of their relevance to design. What we need to know is what are the facts? Which of them are relevant? Where and how can we get them? How can we use them? How can we test them? It is the lack of this information rather than its systematic handling which seems to be the major weakness in our work. Our great need is for more work to be done on obtaining facts and methods for testing their relevance. This depends on the ends desired and, in turn, on a world view, and hence on some theory of the environment. Only such a theory can tell us which facts are relevant to man's relation with the environment, what the important characteristics of this environment are, the right degree of specificity or generality of data and how it can meaningfully be tested.

The role of facts

I have suggested that because the discussion of design methods has tended to concentrate on how to handle information some very important questions as to the nature of this information, its content and the relevant image and value systems have been neglected. These aspects may be equally, or even more, important and the best method will fail if we lack information to use with it.

Let me give some examples of how important this can be. Frequently one finds the figure of 400 metres given as the maximum distance that people will walk.[28] This becomes the input in the design of

[24] See KUHN, *op. cit.*; MICHAEL POLANYI. *Personal Knowledge*. Routledge and Kegan Paul (London 1958); ARDREY. *African Genesis* and *The Territorial Imperative* regarding the rejection of the evidence presented by Dart and Carpenter because it conflicted with the orthodox position and biases of the sub-culture.
[25] KOESTLER, *op. cit.*, pages 146–7; also pages 246–7.
[26] See BOULDING, *op. cit.*, pages 16–17.
[27] See DAVID REISMAN, preface to *Return to Laughter*, Elenore Smith Bowen (1964), page xvi; The work of Oscar Lewis; particularly WEBB, CAMPBELL *et al.*, *Unobtrusive Measures*. Rand McNally (Chicago 1966).
[28] See GABRIEL BELADON. Transport. *Science* (October 1967), page 93; JOHN W. DYCKMAN. Transportation. *Scientific American* (September 1965) (Special issue on cities), and elsewhere.

movement and transportation systems. This design is reduced to a problem to be solved – how walking distances can be kept down to that level, and sophisticated techniques are used. However, if this figure is not correct all that follows becomes invalid. The point is, however, that this figure is not a simple and directly observable fact. Values and complex questions need to be considered. Why won't people walk? Which people and where? Do some people walk more and why? Would people walk if they had a different environment? In my experience they well might and others also suggest that they would.[29] If the environment were changed in certain ways people might not only walk farther, they might want to walk more. There may thus be an alternative way of seeing the problem in terms of environment and 'finding ways to make the paths of encounter more appealing is probably more important than anything that can be done about the origins and destinations . . .'[30] Here we have two ways of looking at the problem, two hypotheses, both possibly valid which will lead to different solutions irrespective of the design method used. We can only decide between the two on the basis of a knowledge of the facts – which partly depend on values, attitudes and changes in them, cultural differences, views on health, and the nature and information content of the environment – and by evaluating the results in the light of these facts.

If we look again at *Atoms of Environmental Structure* (Alexander/Poyner) and accept the argument as it stands we find that its conclusions depend on the facts rather than the method. Given the wrong facts the rest of the argument and conclusions will inevitably be wrong. But the basic premise that buildings are only required to give free reign to tendencies is a question of fact as well as of value. In fact, the example above of walking distance is an instance of this. There is an alternative view that the environment does not merely facilitate the inherent tendencies of man, but that man and environment are part of a total system of great complexity. We are possibly not dealing with the effects of environment on people but with a dynamic system of people and environment parallelling a biological eco-system in which the effects are complex and difficult to predict.[31] In this case the tendencies cannot be separated from the environment and, in turn, from the symbols and images used.

The effect of images and value systems in limiting the solutions and ruling out a particular land use and space organization before any design method is applied, is well shown by considering a tongue-in-cheek advertisement in the *New York Times*.[32] This proposes that Central Park be used for car parking and shows an aerial view of the park in that state. Shown to most architects, students, and others of that type, it elicits an immediate laugh, but there is nothing inherently unreasonable with the proposal on the face of it. The argument in it actually makes a

crazy sort of sense; given certain values it might be eminently reasonable. Objectives, therefore, become very important and for most designers these are the creation of perceptually, emotionally, and socially satisfying environments. We tend to be interested in, and think in terms of, the physical consequences of all these factors, but there are two problems. Firstly, we tend to design for our own peer group rather than the client, both because we want their approval and the material advantages which follow; and because of the natural tendency to assume that others are like ourselves. As a result, we need to know a great deal more than we do about people, their attitudes, cultural settings, and the like. Secondly, we lack the knowledge about the relation of the physical environment to people and are hence unable to specify its important aspects, i.e. we do not know the goals towards which our methods should be aimed.

A great deal of information is, therefore, needed about what is meant by a good environment, good for whom and when; how the public sees the environment and so forth. The insights of disciplines such as ethology (territoriality, personal space, etc.), cultural geography (the different forces in the organisation of space), cross cultural studies, anthropology, sociology and psychology (man and environment, the need for complexity, etc.) among others, seem to be promising. For example, consider the changes in thinking and dealing with urban design which would occur if one accepts the many types of urban space proposed by de Lauwe: social, topographical, biological, anthropological, economic, cultural, total geographic, time space, and others.[33]

Consider the need for complexity and how it can achieve through ambiguity, which I use in Empson's sense of admitting of more than one meaning rather than as doubtfulness, uncertainty, or hesitation. This need seems to me to be undeniable and of great importance, as I have recently tried to show.[34] There is evidence that greater tolerance of these factors is linked with greater experience and creativity (Barron; Kassen and Munsinger and others) as well as mental health (McReynolds; Kantor and others), many models today tend to eliminate complexity not merely because of a conscious goal of simplicity, which we can at least discuss, but by the way they are drawn. If we consider the use of boxes and single lines we cannot but wonder about their

[29] See, for example, A. E. PARR. Environmental Design and Psychology. *Landscape*, Volume 14, No.2 (Winter 1964–5); 'Paths and Dispersal and Encounter in the City' an unpublished manuscript which he has allowed me to quote.
[30] A. E. PARR, unpublished manuscript, *op. cit.*
[31] KURT LEWIN. *Topological Psychology*, pages 11–12; 33.
[32] 11 September 1967, pages 20–1.
[33] P. H. CHOMBERT DE LAUWE. *Paris - essai de Sociologie.* Editions Ouvrières (Paris 1965), page 28.
[34] See RAPOPORT and KANTOR. Complexity and Ambiguity in Environmental Design. *AIP Journal* (July 1967), for an extensive although not exhaustive survey of the literature.

effects on *thinking* in terms of complexity of environment.[35] In some ways intuitive design enables some of its best practitioners to empathise more with the need for complexity and lack of excessive clarity, which may be partly due to their greater concern with the lessons embodied in tradition and partly to their rather more woolly thinking. As well as having many clear and obvious disadvantages, such thinking may be more in accord with the way we really are and behave. For example, when Thor Heyerdahl was designing Kon Tiki he was concerned with visual and textural complexity and allowed for it. He seems to feel rather apologetic and sheepish about it. Could he have justified it in a systematic design? Yet he *felt* it – and after all even planaria show this need[36] and it may well be that if man and animals have been doing something since time immemorial there may be very good reasons for doing it. Methods could be found developed which could cope with this problem – but the need, the facts, need to be known and acknowledged.

Many of the methods and models proposed have had a bias for the measurable and the clearly known. This has had several consequences. One is that such models have tended to emphasize physical factors (and I am not referring to physical *consequences*). The other has been the elimination of ambiguity (in the sense defined above) both through attempting rigorously to give everything one sole meaning forgetting Mechanel Polanyi's point about knowledge which cannot be explicitly stated and, even more importantly, through the tendency to overdesign by aiming for very precise fit.

One could question both whether physical forces are the principal influences on the organization of space and also whether the physical criticality of most architecture isn't rather low. If that is the case (and I have argued at length that this is so in a forthcoming book, Amos Rapoport, *House Form and Culture*, Prentice-Hall (Englewood Cliffs, N.J., in press)) then the effort of so many new methods to achieve *tighter fit* may be misapplied. This can only be determined by knowing the facts about how important these various factors really are. The need *may* be found for looser fit to enable adaptation, to allow ambiguity giving many meanings and hence complexity; and the possibility to personalize and territorialize. There may be a need to relax the high degree of control of the environment by the designer and to allow the consumer to become a *participant* in the design process. This, once again, introduces the question of two image systems.[37] Loose fit and the primacy of the socio-cultural factors are made possible by the low *physical* criticality of much architecture. The degree of criticality, and consequently how much of the environment should be designed – and how completely – needs to be determined. The fact that man adapts *to* the environment and adapts *it* to himself, personalizes and territorializes it is very suggestive.

Many examples of this, as well as the primacy of socio-cultural factors, can be seen in many cultures, which suggests not only the validity of this view but the value of cross cultural studies and studies over time. The time dimension gives the insights of history and tradition as well as allowing for the fact that one cannot rely on immediate responses or lack of them.

The striving towards tight fit has also been criticized by Peter Cowan who argues that the 'more closely a design is tailored to a particular function the more quickly it becomes out of date',[38] while John Weeks speaks of the need for less precise fit between form and function.[39] The contrasts of such thinking with many of the new methods, notably Alexander's, which stress tight fit, is rather clear. The only way the different goals could be resolved is through a knowledge of the facts of the matter.

The elimination of a specific misfit, even if we accept the need for it and the definition of it, may generate another misfit and the context may also change while one designs. This change may occur over time and most methods have rather too little interest in the time dimension, possibly due to their distrust of the past and the value of tradition. The change may also occur immediately as when the French in North Africa introduced running water, only to find great resistance because of the importance of the social function of the well as the only outside activity allowed women in a Moslem society. Even under primitive conditions where the physical constraints are very severe, the primacy of non-physical forces suggests that the real problems may be images, values, symbols, perceptual needs and the like, since it is they which most affect space organization and form. The question which needs to be asked of any new model and method is whether it can deal with these kinds of problems or whether it is, by its very nature, limited to certain classes of information which then define a universe of discourse without reference to the real problems (what I call the Procrustes Bed syndrome). Only a knowledge of the needs of various groups and sub-groups of people and their environments can help determine what information is needed without repeating the mistakes of logical positivism and behaviourism.

[35] See STAFFORD BEER. Below the Twilight Arch – A Mythology of Systems in *Systems: Research and Design* (New York and London 1961), page 14, where he asks about the variety and complexity in each box and the channel capacity of each line; see also T. S. KUHN, *op. cit.*, who describes the process of science as an attempt to force nature into often arbitrary and relatively inflexible boxes.
[36] See BEST AND RUBINSTEIN. Environmental Familiarity and Feeding in the Planarian. *Science*, 135; 916–18 (1962).
[37] See RAPOPORT. *Whose* Meaning in Architecture? *Arena/Interbuild* (October 1967). The Personal Element in Housing: An Argument for open-ended design. *RIBA Journal*, July 1968, pages 300–307.
[38] *Bartlett Transactions* (1962–3).
[39] *Bartlett Transactions 3* and even more clearly in a paper before the Ontario Hospital Conference – 'Design for Growth and Change and the Project Team Concept.'

It could be argued that the types of considerations I have been describing above are less significant in the case of low cost housing, and the developing countries where the minima is low, urgent physical needs must be satisfied, and where many of the serious design problems lie. My experience, however, is different. In the course of a research project on low cost housing prototypes for agricultural workers in California we found that although the houses were climatically and economically successful they were not accepted by their intended occupants because their image was wrong.[40] Those same people when putting up self-help houses in the same area were producing suburban houses of very low functional adequacy but of that middle-class image, which is so important in terms of upward mobility and which became the overriding factor. The houses we designed were too far removed from this image and too close to the architect's image of a house.

Similar forces are at work in the case of primitive and pre-industrial cultures where, in economies of scarcity, the stress is on symbolic, religious, and other similar factors in housing, agriculture, and the domestication of animals rather than on the physical aspects.[41] There are similar examples in the developing countries. In the Barriadas of Peru, for example, the installation of an elaborate and expensive front door, which is the symbol of *home*, may precede the installation of a roof by several years even though the house is inhabited and the climate severe.[42]

In our thinking the stress has been on those aspects which are currently measurable, which lend themselves to systematic handling or for which one can easily optimize. As a result matters such as anthropometrics, proximity, cost and the like have tended to come to the fore. It is interesting to note that the reviews of Kira's recent study of the bathroom which, in my view, shows the overwhelming importance of the cultural and depth-psychological aspects of the bathroom, have tended to stress the anthropometric and practical results of the study. These symbolic aspects can be rather important as shown in John Hazard's analysis of courtrooms where he argues that the furniture arrangement can tell a great deal about the legal system. This shows that an understanding of the subtle symbolism may be as important as, if not more so than, the physical criteria of courtroom design.[43] There is an enlightening letter to the editor of the *New York Times*[44] regarding circulation in new courts which helps make clear the implications of some of these types of information for design. Circulation has become a common topic of concern due, at least in part, to our work methods, since it is easily measurable. As a result the concern has been expressed in a currently held value in the architectural sub-culture that minimum circulation is the desired goal and designs are optimized for it (it is, in fact, a favourite example). The letter points out that many new courts, where circulation has been reduced to a minimum, do not work. The lack of corridors with dim corners where informal conferences and settlements can take place means that many more cases come to trial, the court calendars tend to become overloaded, and this interferes with the administration of justice. In our concern with minimizing circulation we have tended to forget the environmental aspects of circulation, as I have already suggested with regard to urban problems. The Louisiana Museum near Copenhagen provides an instructive example. There is a 300-foot walk down a passage from the entrance to the first pavilion and circulation spaces generally exceed exhibition spaces. In practice, this theoretically excessive circulation is so superb experientially that not only do people walk it gladly but it becomes an essential part of the museum experience.

How, then, can we obtain this type of information? It will involve a concern with specifics as well as generalities, with differences as well as similarities, with the scale at which comparisons are made (often too crude, or gross, in generalizing and too fine, or detailed, in actual design). It is an immensely difficult problem, which is why we have so little information of this type although we need so much. It is much more difficult to obtain such information than on, say, anthropometrics or other physical factors. But we have great need for these facts relating to images, symbols, perceptual needs and many others, and they cannot always be got from laboratory experiments. In these, as Chapanis has recently pointed out, too few variables are used and the many variables of real life ignored or kept constant. As a result the hidden or unsuspected interactions tend to disappear. The variables used are variables of convenience and the methods are often unrealistic and artificial. At the same time they are extremely sophisticated, yet tend to give a very simplified, neat, and tidy view of the world.[45] In experiments people are either a captive audience, volunteers or interested, and experimental data need to be *supplemented* by real-life data. In this connexion the insights of designers may be very useful to behavioural scientists. We may need the development of various sorts of *unobtrusive measures*, the use of the popular press and other sources not used before – the possibilities are endless.

[40] SANOFF, PORTER and RAPOPORT. *Low Cost Housing Demonstration.* University of California (Berkeley 1965); SANOFF and RAPOPORT. *Evaluation of Three Case Study Dwellings.* University of California (Berkeley 1966); and personal observation.

[41] Cf. BRUCE ARCHER, *op. cit.*, 'We grow, gather and eat food to keep our metabolism on an even keel'. Even primitive man does much more than that.

[42] WILLIAM MANGIN. Urbanisation Case History in Peru. *Architectural Design* (August 1963), page 369.

[43] See JOHN N. HAZARD. Furniture Arrangement as a Symbol of Judicial Role. *ETC: A Review of General Semantics,* Volume XIX, No.2 (July 1962), pages 181–8.

[44] 1 August 1966.

[45] A. CHAPANIS. The Relevance of Laboratory Studies to Practical Situations. *Ergonomics,* Volume 10, No.5 (1967), pages 557–77; see also many criticisms of attempts to transfer experimental results on rats to human situations, e.g. KOESTLER, *op. cit.*, BERLYNE and others.

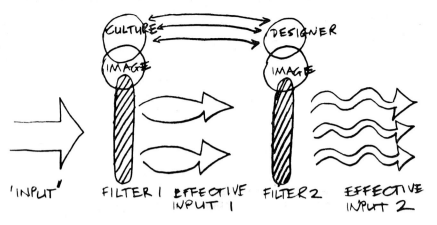

THERE ARE ALSO THE CULTURAL CONSTRAINTS AT THE SPACE ORGANIZATION LEVEL, WHICH ARE ALSO MEDIATED BY IMAGES.

Image component of input

In architecture the effects are subtle, indirect, and often beyond awareness. People are not certain what affects them and find it difficult to say how they feel in different places. The emotional content of the environment makes the influence of the image more influential than in other fields (e.g. the physical sciences). There is much evidence that the cultural context and mental set of the observer greatly affect perception, archetypes, and schemata.[46] Thus even while many methods are becoming more sophisticated in allowing more complex data as well as information from inside oneself, there is still a tendency to overvalue 'hard' data and to consider 'information' from outside the observer as being more 'objective'. In fact, however, this information is filtered by the designer – his experience, expectations, values, images, goals and the culture to which he belongs all filter the information and this filter is of the greatest importance in the total picture since if we want to be able to reduce their effect we need to know of the presence and *what* they are.

For all these reasons obtaining the right information in a *usable form* is a very difficult task which needs much work. The usable form of the information is a crucial point which I can only mention. The form must be such that the information becomes meaningful and usable, otherwise even those facts that are available will not be used and the greater the amount of information available the less it might be used. If the form were wrong the information may not be used at all. This form is related to the goals, the nature of the facts and how they are obtained. To deal with this problem we possibly need to consider the need for new types of specialists – a series of middlemen who can communicate with other specialists and put the information in a form designers can use, and *will* use. It will also involve vast problems of information retrieval. All in all the whole problem is much wider than one of methods for design.

The first creative leap

The question I have been asking is whether the problems of environmental design are due to methodological weaknesses in how information is handled, or whether they are due to a *lack* of information, the *wrong form* of the information available, the difficulties of *obtaining* information and the lack of concern with certain specific *types* of information (pertaining to culture, perception, behaviour, symbolism, images, value systems and the like).

John Weeks has suggested that too much detailed information too early may clog the design process,[47] i.e. that the timing of the input information is important. In his approach – at least as I interpret it – the concept is primary and determines the information needed and when it is needed and in what detail. The implication is that the information needs to be of the right type and not too detailed. What Weeks has done is to generate a hypothesis about the design of hospitals from which the design process and the design *both* follow. This is what good designers have always done although in his case the hypothesis is more explicit than is usual. If one equates architectural design with the generation of hypotheses, and my whole argument which follows hinges on this, then the question of how hypotheses are generated becomes important. This is what I call the first creative leap.

We cannot, therefore, ignore what happens in the box labelled 'designer', but need to consider how hypotheses are generated. This is a very important part of the design process as distinct from the product. How the first creative leap takes place seems to be an important part of any discussion of the design process. It seems to me that there is an insight in Koestler's view of creativity which is worth discussing.

[46] On perception in general see SEGALL, CAMPBELL and HERSKOVITS. *The Influence of Culture on Visual Perception.* Bobbs Merill (Indiannapolis 1966), the work of Whorf and his followers on language and many others; on realistic art see GOMBRICH, *Art and Illusion*; on space organization see the work of E. T. HALL, *The Silent Language* and *The Hidden Dimension*, and many others.
[47] Ontario Conference, *op. cit.*

As most of you know, for Koestler creativity means seeing situations or ideas which are normally seen in two different frames of reference as being in one single frame of reference.[48] He suggests that for this to happen what he calls the 'dream state' is necessary which I tend to regard as a more extreme view of the flexible schemata of Jane Abercrombie. This state helps the 'act of bisociation' where this connexion is set up, and this is an unconscious process.[49] Problems are normally tackled through 'rules of the game' which are codified in models and methods of procedure corresponding, I would suggest, to Kuhn's 'normal science' but which rarely lead to hypotheses. Hypotheses are generated during the dream state when random attacks are made and things tried which logic would never accept. These irrational aspects of creativity are very common in science, with mathematics and mathematical physics as prime examples.[50] The history of these fields, and others, shows a constant thread of the belittling of logic and deductive reasoning; a horror of the one-track mind; a distrust of too much consistency; scepticism of all-too-conscious thinking; trust in intuition and unconscious guidance often on the basis of aesthetic sensibilities.[51] This always after saturating oneself with the problem – i.e. knowing the relevant facts. Polyani also points out that one cannot work by definite rules and that generating hypotheses cannot be a strictly logical performance, while others have suggested that one never seems to work by a process of purely conscious calculations.[52]

A recent description of this creative leap is a discussion of the work of Pierre Weiss on 'domains' and 'molecular fields' in magnetism. 'Even these scientific workers who frequently accept the role of speculative leaps [and, as we have seen, most good ones do] might boggle at Weiss's flight of fancy. There appeared to be not the slightest theoretical justification for the new concepts he introduced . . .[53]

New ideas are thus generated by artistic and intuitive imagination even in science which was well summed up by Kekulé – 'let us learn to dream gentlemen'.[54] It has been suggested by Einstein, among others, that, in a way, one needs to think non-precisely and visually rather than verbally or symbolically since it is then easier to avoid eliminating contradictions on the way to a new synthesis.[55] I would suggest that this way of working is something architects have been very good at due to their visual bias and use of the visual mode – doodling and sketching – which are very much like the process described above. Some of the intuitive design methods may actually be more flexible and more receptive to ambiguous schemata and may also more easily empathise with the aspects of the problem which I have been discussing.

This first creative leap occurs not only in designing but also in the generation of hypotheses about the collection of information. Usually one must look at a situation with a specific model in mind to avoid the dangers of inductivism and help structure perceptions. There are, however, situations where one needs to look at the evidence with an open mind so as to decide on a model or generate a hypothesis.[56] The need for fluidity rather than rigidity is also a factor if one accepts the view that creativity involves seeing connexions between apparently unrelated universes and hence accepting unexpected novelty. In this respect the rigidity of clear cut models may actually be inhibiting. Kuhn points out that much of 'normal science' is concerned with puzzles rather than problems and resists unexpected novelty. There may, therefore, be a conflict between the rigour and systematic nature of many work methods and the manner in which hypotheses seem to be generated.

The generation of hypotheses about the environment may often involve the past as an indicator. Kurt Lewin makes an interesting point about the importance of history in finding out why certain things happen (and, by the way, showing the impact of the model used on the type of information considered). He uses the example of a tree sheltering one from the rain. Answers to the question why it does that can be given both in terms of systematic causality, e.g. physics, involving a consideration of factors such as the trajectory of the rain drops, the path of the wind, the position of the person, the geometry of the leaves and the like; alternatively the answers can be in terms of history, involving the fact that the grandfather planted the tree, why he did so, why his descendants preserved it, and so on. Lewin suggests that in the psychology of both individuals and groups the historical type of answer is very important.[57] I have already suggested several times that a study of the past can be useful for the generation of hypotheses about environmental needs. This can take the form of case studies, cross cultural comparisons over time, the consideration of tradition, and constancy and change, as well as the observation of specifics rather than generalities.

Consider the example of privacy. An examination of traditional housing in many cultures in which this need is particularly important can be most enlightening in terms of some contemporary needs and

[48] KOESTLER, op. cit., page 35.
[49] Examples are the printing press, gravity and evolution (page 121), also page 111 ff. PASTEUR and vaccination, POINCARÉ and Fuchsian functions, JACQUES HADAMARD, AMPÈRE, GAUSS and others.
[50] Ibid, pages 118–19; pages 144–6.
[51] E.g. citing Dirac (page 245) 'it is more important to have beauty in one's equations than to have them fit the experiments'.
[52] BREWSTER GHISELIN. The Creative Process. Mentor Paperbacks (New York 1961).
[53] FREDERICK KEFFER. The Magnetic Properties of Materials. Scientific American (September 1967), page 222.
[54] KOESTLER, op. cit., page 118.
[55] Ibid., page 183.
[56] See, for example, STANLEY H. UDY, JR. Cross Cultural Analysis: A Case Study, in P. E. Hammond (Ed.) Sociologists at work, Basic Books (New York and London 1964).
[57] LEWIN, op. cit., page 30.

proposed solutions. A cross-cultured analysis of this sort will also show that the concept of privacy is much more complex and variable than one anticipates, and that the specificity of observations used in the generation of hypotheses is important. The crux of the work method, therefore – assuming that architectural design is a creative act – is to saturate oneself in the relevant facts and then generate hypotheses in the ways described.[58]

The creative generation of hypotheses never seems to be done in a systematic way. What *is* systematic is the testing of hypotheses. Polya asserts that when we know things to be true we set out to prove them.[59] Popper would say that we should set out to disprove them. In either case the importance of testing one's hypotheses is of the essence. What is needed is the development of rigorous and systematic methods for testing and evaluating hypotheses – i.e. designs. Since all design is prediction – if so and so then such and such – one cannot really work without testing, evaluation, and the appraisal of results. This is of the essence yet we have not yet begun to tackle the problem of how to evaluate and to answer some questions: What is a good environment and is this one? Good for whom and when? How do we find out how good the public thinks it is and why? This need may well be more important than the development of methods which try to systematize the *generation of designs*.

Designs which are unevaluated are just assertions no matter how they are derived. Testing and evaluation are the only way of deciding whether a design is a success and of building up a *body of knowledge*. These evaluations must be done cross culturally so as to gain insight into the range of possibilities and choices, even if our own current culture excludes many of these options. They also need to be done over time – both in terms of past designs and the behaviour of a given design, once constructed, with prolonged use. This rather major gap and weakness in our skills needs to be filled. This will require much study to develop techniques to answer some of these questions, to cross-check the results of laboratory findings, and to obtain data in the right form.

I would argue, pragmatically, that all, or any, design methods should be used to supplement existing ones rather than supplant them. We should design in any way we can and feel most at ease with and then use the relevant knowledge and techniques to evaluate their validity. The selection of any method should be based on its success as revealed by an evaluation of the designs produced. It seems strange that architects seem anxious to give up their traditional models, to which I have already referred, which are uniquely theirs and are a flexible and powerful skill – at least in the estimation of many outside observers.

Rather than an *either–or* attitude we need an *and* attitude and at most we should probably supplement our existing methods rather than give them up.

The second creative leap

There is one final question which needs to be briefly considered. This is the problem of the synthesis of the conclusions, generated by whatever method one has used, into a building – what we could call the second creative leap. The diagrams and relationships are still very far from being a building or a city – it is a long way from a diagram to an environment. In much of the discussion on methods, the quality of the architecture or the physical environment is not discussed at all. The methodology seems to become an end in itself, sometimes almost scholastic in its lack of relation to the real world, its concerns and motivations. The synthesis of the various ideas and conclusions, however derived, is fully as difficult or even more difficult than the traditional synthesis of information. Often *how* a building is done, how the space organization is fleshed out, may be more important than *what* is done since it is more closely related to the image and to what is perceived. One of the influences that comes to bear at this point is that of *style* – the selection from the many possibilities and alternatives still available due to the relatively low criticality of architecture. So far the physical results of new methods do not seem to be any better than those of traditional design methods, although it is as yet probably too early to judge. When I say better, this is, of course, a value judgement but then as I have tried to show, there are implicit values in anything we do.

[58] Following Poincaré in Gheselin, *op. cit.*, pages 33–42.
[59] Cited KOESTLER, *op. cit.*, page 118.

Method and intention in architectural design

by Gordon Best

'*It is only too easy, in a discussion of this kind, to lapse into vague generalities; to use terms like element, entity, relationship, structure, pattern, with which we can write so much and say so little. It is precision, above all, that is desired in social studies; we need to know relationships as mathematical and statistical laws, yet heaven knows how easy it is to say this, and how appallingly difficult and laborious it is to gather the necessary data to formulate social laws! . . .*'
Colin Cherry *On Human Communication*

Introduction

This paper is about variety in design. It is an attempt to show that designing can be usefully interpreted as a variety-reducing process. The argument is this: in practice, architectural and planning design situations are so variable and idiosyncratic that they cannot be understood in a definitive sense; further, a great deal of design methodology is an attempt to explore and explain design definitively. The outcome has been a general inapplicability of these methods in practice.

To put the argument in another way, design problems encountered in practice are different from those that we conceive in our heads. Practical problems are more variable; they arise in space and time; they have no precise boundaries and each one is different from every other. Yet to tackle these problems we have to interpret them and this interpretation is always a simplification that we can comprehend. It is a definitive simplification and it is from this that we develop our methods for designing. Our methods are appropriate to the problem simplifications we hold in our heads while being of little use in solving the problems we face in practice.

To take an example: we all know that a design problem reflects the interests of a client. A client who has personal interests; a client who may like to play golf and therefore feels that building sites near golf courses make the best building sites. A client who may be easily influenced by his sales manager and therefore feels that 'cheap and beautiful' buildings

are the best sorts of buildings. These are characteristics of real clients. They are variable and idiosyncratic characteristics that make design problems variable and idiosyncratic.

By contrast, when we talk about design problems in the abstract we simplify them. We refer to 'the' client. We endow him with certain characteristics: (he thinks he wants an office block); we attribute to him a mental capacity: (he doesn't really understand the problem); and so on. This is typical of the kind of simplifications we find convenient.

A real client rarely cares what we think about his intentions. They are variable and may change irrationally and if our conceptions cannot cope with these changes then our methods for designing will seem restrictive. Not because the methods themselves are faulty in any objective sense, but simply because they are informed by an unrealistic attitude. And by 'unrealistic' I mean not variable enough.

So my intention here is to illustrate that practical design problems are incredibly variable and not describable in a definitive sense. I will try to show that in practice we often adopt designing strategies or attitudes that help us to simplify these problems. Building on this argument, I will then illustrate how 'design methods' often amount to procedures which mechanically lead us to design proposals having little relationship to the underlying problems at hand. And this is perhaps the crux of my argument, for no matter how seductive a designing method is in the abstract, it is of little use if it breaks down when exposed to the variety of practice.

Part I
Coping with variety in practice

There are numerous ways in which we simplify practical design problems. I will consider two fairly common ways. The first is a *professional simplification*, introduced when we 'allocate' problem types to various design professions. The second is a *conceptual simplification* introduced by the design theorist who recognizes the professional simplification to be a distortion of reality. I will try to show that both these simplifications are largely arbitrary when applied to practice.

Variety-restriction in practice

Consider how one decides if any real-world difficulty is an architectural, planning, or any other design problem. The basis upon which such a decision is made must be questionable. 'Design problems' are usually defined according to the potential a given profession has for solving them. This, to an extent, must make a problem arbitrary because real-world difficulties can't possibly arise neatly packaged in little groups that reflect our professional distinctions.

Practical difficulties that arise in the world are different from the conceptions of these same difficulties that we conjure up in our heads: more important, our professional distinctions reinforce our unrealistic conceptions. We have architectural problems that architects solve; economic problems that economists solve; planning problems that planners

solve; and so on. The same point has been made by others before.

In Fig.1 I have attempted to take this argument further. The diagram is a simplified representation of what might be called a 'real-world situation'. The outer circle represents such a situation; the four inner circles represent some of the environments that contribute to the whole. The environments stand for classes of systems or events that we usually refer to generically, calling some 'economic', some 'administrative'; and so on. By examining the diagram one can get an idea of how these account for the concept of a 'real-world' situation. A system of material incentives within a society is typical of a system that contributes to the economic environment. A system of building by-laws is one of a system of rules that contributes to the administrative environment of a society. A real-world situation is an identifiable part of the interactions between these different environments.

The important thing about each of the circles in Fig.1 is that they are meant to represent an environment that contributes to, *and in part, controls,*

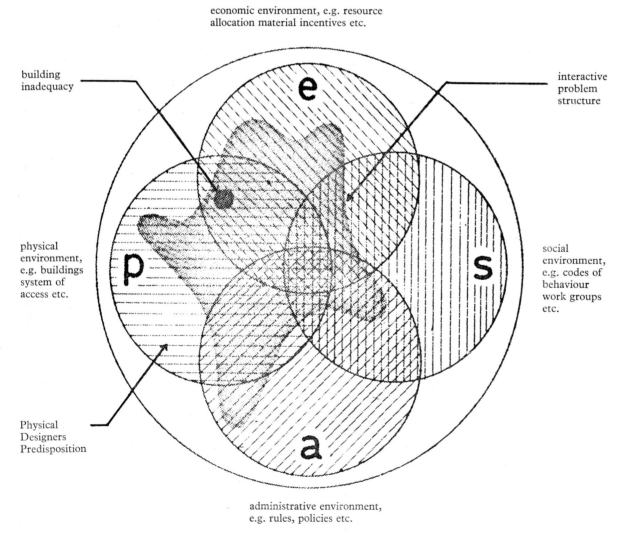

economic environment, e.g. resource allocation material incentives etc.

building inadequacy

interactive problem structure

physical environment, e.g. buildings system of access etc.

social environment, e.g. codes of behaviour work groups etc.

Physical Designers Predisposition

administrative environment, e.g. rules, policies etc.

Fig.1
design situation

behaviour in situations arising in the real world. The four environments shown are only representative; no claim is made for comprehensiveness; the circles symbolize the interactions that create real-world variety.

Figure 1 is useful if we go back to the question of how practical design problems are defined. Say that a building inadequacy is detected within such a situation. This inadequacy would fall within the circle labelled PHYSICAL ENVIRONMENT. Quite naturally one concludes that a *physical* design problem exists. But the building inadequacy will almost always result from the interactions between the different environments. An *economic* policy may be calling for expansion or a change of building function; this will make the existing built environment seem inadequate. A change of function will generate a need for a modified *administrative* organization; this will make the built environment seem inadequate. A changed administrative organization will in turn require a new *social* organization; again, the built environment will seem inadequate. The building inadequacy actually reflects the interactions between many contributing environments and can only arbitrarily be said to fall within the boundaries of one or the other.

Why then do we allocate real-world incompatibilities to different domains calling some physical problems, some social problems, some administrative problems, and so on? A probable answer to this question is that these distinctions are abstract and therefore conceptually clear. They are easier to define than the more confusing distinctions that separate one real-world difficulty from another. It is a very complicated matter to attempt a definitive description of a real-world problem, but as human beings, and as designers, we still try.

Consider a concept such as 'location'. A design problem will vary depending on the location envisaged for the solution. In order definitively to understand design we must be able to understand the implications of designing for a *particular* location. This means understanding the generic concept of location so that we might then apply this understanding to the particular. In terms of Fig.1, one might begin to define the term location by identifying the environments which operate in determining the implications of dealing with a particular building site. We might explain the location of a building site in terms of the allocation of resources related to that site; in terms of the administrative laws which govern land use; in terms of the physical geography of the land; in terms of a sociological or ecological prediction concerning a human demand pattern; or simply in terms of our client's golfing habits. However we define it, there shall be a number of dimensions along which the concept of 'location' might vary. This is only one small factor determining how physical design relates to the situation in which it

occurs. Any one factor could vary along many dimensions. This is real-world variety. The definitive description of such variety is impossible. We restrict it by defining problems according to the way in which we are used to 'solving' them.

The diagram shown in Fig.1 makes clear this difference between the 'interactive structure' of a real-world problem, and the conceptual/professional domains that cut it into convenient pieces. We are unable to describe our problems in detail, in the concrete; so instead we simplify, allocate and impose clear professional boundaries where they may make no sense. Unable to cope with the variety of the real, we resort to the apparent clarity of the artificial.

Variety–restriction in theory

The recent emergence of the 'design methodologist' can partially be attributed to the fact that design methods are supposed to help a designer escape the dilemmas outlined above. The methodologist's strategy for avoiding these pitfalls includes what I referred to earlier as a *conceptual simplification*. His argument usually goes something like this: 'client's opinions, economic restrictions, technical limitations, people's behaviour, by-law, or whatever, are all *decision variables*; (or forces, or tendencies, or design factors, etc., etc.). I, the methodologist, do not care what the empiricist thinks these factors are in the phenomenological sense. I know that they are variables whose behavioural features impinge upon the problem domain of the designer'. (And they inevitably use these unfamiliar words in presenting their argument.) 'I shall call these different factors 'decision-variables'. The advantage in doing this is that I shall then be able to reduce all these considerations to a common language and deal with them symbolically. I shall then employ decision theory, mathematics, or whatever tools I require in order to tackle design problems no matter what their variety or complexity.'

One must admit that this sort of argument has appeal. Why not, if we can, reduce all this apparent variety to a symbolic representation and then use methods which can cope with variety at the symbolic level? But it is not so easy. Here is what often happens when this strategy is adopted.

Recently, a well known design methodologist arose at a conference to explain his method of designing. The first step in his procedure involved 'identifying the decision variables within the problem'. The way to do this was not clearly explained. The fact that all the rest of his method depended on some sort of operational definition of a decision variable must not have bothered him. "After all', he probably thought, 'everyone knows what decisions are, designers are always making them'. But are they? Consider this quote from a recent research report:

'I have been making a study of the urban design process at fairly close quarters. (Within a practice.) I set out at the beginning to look for decisions. I still feel that this was a laudable intention, but the execution proved to be exceedingly difficult. It was like trying to put your finger on a blob of mercury; you can't. It's always somewhere else. In just the same way what one thinks is a decision keeps turning out to be merely the consequence of other decisions taken earlier. Sometimes, of course, the converse happens. One can actually witness a decision being made, a specific course of action being decided upon, perhaps at a special meeting called for that purpose. The snag is a month or two later, say, it becomes apparent that a different course of action is being followed.'

Here a researcher has gone into practice and observed how this practice copes with the problems that arise in the real-world. Yet after two years of searching he decides that it is impossible to identify a decision. Still, we are presented with theories and methods for designing that grow from the theoretical simplifications of the design methodologist. Such general and ill-considered terms as 'decision variable' are symptomatic of the methodologists failure to deal with the variety one encounters in practice.

Real situations are variable and idiosyncratic; professional and conceptual simplifications of these situations seem necessary because their variety cannot be understood in a definitive sense. The resulting simplifications, while apparently clear, are unrealistic; they restrict, destroy and ignore natural variety.

Designing situations

Why, if design problems are so variable and our conceptions so general, was the designer of the past able to design in a way that we now admire? Why has variety not always overcome our attempts to deal with it?

The question is an interesting one and both Christopher Alexander and Christopher Jones have dealt with it previously. The reason I raise it here is that both of these authors have used a slightly different language in dealing with the question and have come to a different conclusion about the lesson for designers.

Both of these authors have pointed out the differences between traditional and modern methods of designing. Alexander has called the designer of the past, 'the unself-conscious' designer. He has shown that historically, designers have responded to their problems in an intimate manner while today we act consciously to design a specific end-product. Alexander argues that traditional designers have responded not only to difficulties arising from 'mis-fitting' forms, but to *any difficulties* that arose within the situations they were concerned with. These designers dealt with more than just physical form. They knew no explicit divisions of their problem and concerned themselves with situational difficulties wherever they emerged.

Similarly, Jones has shown that the craftsman of old not only engaged in physical design, but also in social, economic, and in short, total design. The wheelwright, for instance, in designing farm wagons made incremental changes in their design in response to changing social behavioural and economic demands. In addition, the wheelwright was his own economist, sociologist, administrative consultant and so on. He made changes not only in wagons but in the way wagons could be purchased, the way in which they could be repaired, the way in which they could be used and the ways in which he could design them. In other words, the wheelwright not only designed the wagon, but *he designed the situation in which the wagons were designed*.

This seems to me to be significant. Both Jones and Alexander have pointed out that physical designers *did not exist* in the past in the sense that they do today. They have shown that physical changes in a situation were not seen as an isolated activity. If a situation arose in which design was required then design was carried out. Whether or not it was physical design, was largely irrelevant. An insight into the argument presented earlier can be gained here. The designer of the past responded to variety as it arose. He did not impose classifications and divisions that meant he could only respond in pre-specified ways; he was free to regulate the variety imposed by his situation. No artificial restrictions were required.

Part II
Designing: The reduction of variety

I have presented my argument in the abstract. To talk about the idea of restricting variety one often has to resort to a level of discussion that may appear unrelated to the problems of everyday design. I now want to discuss actual designing and in so doing draw a distinction between *restricting* variety and *regulating* variety through design. To do this, I shall have to divert rather radically from the train of thought I have so far been pursuing. I will return to the original argument in time.

I want to examine three different designing strategies by relating these to a model of the designing process. I hope to be able to show how all three strategies are attempts to restrict and deal with variety in differing ways.

Three designing strategies

The three designing strategies that I have chosen to compare are different in that the first is informed primarily by a *theoretical attitude toward design*, the second primarily by *experience of designing*, and the third by a *formal design methodology*. I think that these three strategies are good examples of prevalent and differing procedures which many designers will recognize and, in part at least, identify with.

The first strategy is outlined in *Notes on the Synthesis of Form*, by Christopher Alexander. I refer to it as a strategy informed by theory for it sets out to attain a particular sort of end result which has validity only if one accepts the theoretical ideas underlying the methodology. Alexander describes the physical world as essentially consisting of 'physical sub-systems' (pp.41–3). Knowing this he is then able to devise a strategy for designing in such a world. The strategy is informed by theory; if one does not believe that the world can be thought of as a series of physical sub-systems then one does not employ this method in design; if one accepts the theoretical basis, then the methodology is worth considering.

Alexander has since modified the views expressed in *Notes on the Synthesis of Form*. He has developed further interpretations of design meant to replace these expressed in his book. Nevertheless, I have chosen his earlier work for this paper, first because it is the most definitive and secondly because most designers are probably familiar with it.

The second designing strategy is that of Alvar Aalto. I have chosen Aalto because he is an example of a designer who operates and is informed by designing experience. He is representative of what many would call a great designer. His strategy, at a descriptive level, is clear and I expect typical of many practising architects today.

My third example is taken from the Bartlett and is representative of the struggles many students have when they are first faced with a formal design methodology. I have closely monitored many such strategies and feel that they differ fundamentally from either of the first two. Although the comparison of a student with Alexander and Aalto may seem odd, in fact, the limitations imposed by the student's lack of experience ensures that the formal methodology prevails in directing his behaviour. This provides one with an opportunity to compare the constraints exerted by a 'design method' with those imposed by experience and theory.

A designing model

The designing model chosen is a distortion of reality. It is not a psychological model; it is a logical picture of the way in which information flows in a designing situation; it is useful in a discussion like this. A diagram of the model is shown in Fig.2.

The diagram characterizes the information-flow patterns in design. Each component part of the diagram stands for a source of information, an operation on information, or both. The box labelled INPUT is meant to stand for the external classes of information that are specifically fed into a design situation. Typical inputs might be a brief, some opinions of people other than the designer, building codes, facts

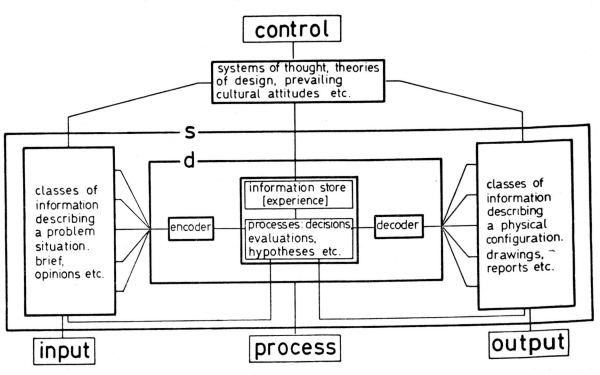

Fig.2
Information in design

describing performance baselines, facts describing the state of labour and technology, and so on. In any project the inputs will vary; they are the classes of external information on which a designer will operate in a given set of circumstances.

The box labelled ENCODER stands for a process that a designer goes through in interpreting the inputs in his situation. It is a process of coding external (and perhaps internal) information so that it makes sense with respect to the problem. Typical encoding procedures are sketching, diagramming or even doodling. These encoding methods are useful in seeing how various requirements or ideas affect the actual design as the designer sees it.

The box labelled PROCESS can be equated with the designer's mind. Here there are two components of interest. First there is the INFORMATION STORE or memory. It is here that internal information from the designer's mind is fed into the problem so that the external inputs match up to experience or common sense. It is the individual designer's own private store of facts opinions and ideas. The second component within the box is labelled PROCESSES. It stands for the operations a designer goes through when responding to the input information and weighing this up against the information supplied by his memory. It is here that he decides, predicts, hypothesises and mentally copes with his problem.

The box labelled DECODER is similar to the encoder. The designer must be able to get ideas out of his head and into some communicable form. Decoding is the transforming of information so that it can be communicated to people outside the specific situation in a manner that they can comprehend.

The box labelled OUTPUTS stands for the information that a designer produces. These are the classes of design information which describe configurations of changes in a real-world situation. Typical outputs from the designing process are drawings, specifications and reports.

The final box is labelled CONTROL. This is an important component within the model for it stands for something outside the specific design situation and outside the designer. It is meant to include systems of thought, current architectural or other design theory, cultural attitudes and so on. It constrains the whole of the process by limiting the way in which information can flow. As an example, one recent output of many design offices has been the Feasibility Study. This output has largely been encouraged by a cultural tendency towards more rational approaches to the planning of environments. In terms of the model, a prevailing attitude (CONTROL), has constrained the way in which designers produce information (OUTPUT).

The model is a simple one. It emphasizes the changing form of information in design. It is convenient to think of the designer as being primarily the internal box (d). The inputs and outputs which complete the outer box (s), refer to information about a specific situation. The control box refers to information that may be related to design in a general way. It is important to think of each box as changing state with time. Information about a problem situation is presented; it is coded, processed, supplemented, constrained, and operated on over and over again. The boxes within the diagram are continually changing state; eventually a design configuration emerges.

Strategy 1

It is now time to see what this model can tell us about the way in which designers design. We can begin by examining Alexander's process in the light of the model. Figure 3 is a representation of four parts of Alexander's process which can be equated with components of the model. The first part shows a list of 'misfit variables' which Alexander uses as a description of the problem a designer faces in creating an Indian Village. With respect to the model, these are Alexander's INPUTS; he has defined and limited these by reference to the top box labelled CONTROL. His theory, *which is a system of thought outside the confines of any specific situation*, explains that only an understanding of misfit variables and physical sub-systems are important to our understanding of the design problem. By thinking carefully about these concepts, says Alexander, we can limit our designing INPUTS to only those which are important to the problem. The behaviours that go on in the box labelled PROCESS, are largely constrained by the box CONTROL. If one believes in this system of thinking about a problem, only misfit variables are relevant; our processes of design are aimed at considering the problem in this light and eventually defining and limiting the INPUTS to the problem.

The next two parts of Figure 3 show how these INPUTS (lists of misfit variables) are ENCODED AND DECODED. First, one transforms the lists of misfits into groups of highly interacting variables; in doing this, the PROCESSES carried out are again constrained by the box CONTROL for the procedure is based on graph theory. One constructs matrices of interacting variables and in so doing manages to ENCODE the INPUTS in the 'correct' way.

Working according to the principles of the graph-theoretic formulation, the ENCODING process merges with the DECODING. The sets of interacting variables, once encoded in the form of a matrix, are separated into 'reasonably independent sub-sets' so that they can be diagrammed as inde-

'complete'. In terms of the model in Fig.2, Alexander has looked to the box CONTROL for guidance; for a system of abstract analysis that extends normal perceptions to the point where they are capable of describing a design problem completely before it is tackled. By contrast, Aalto looks to the innermost box of the model (PROCESSING), and depends on the ENCODING of an incomplete problem description to 'coax' information from his head. For Aalto the problem is never made explicit.

Strategy 3

Finally, we come to the student designer. Figure 5 illustrates certain features of this strategy. The student, in common with Alexander and Aalto, begins with certain INPUTS. He was given a brief, part of which is shown in Fig.5. He explored his situation to see if a building was required. He made observations and collected data in an attempt to structure the problem. The second part of Fig.5 is indicative of the search he made while attempting to explore the problem INPUTS.

After various attempts to ENCODE information about the problem, the student became immersed in a formal coding procedure (a design method). This is illustrated in the third part of Fig.5. Having had little immediate experience with design situations, as Aalto would have had, and having no formal theory such as Alexander's, the student's behaviour could only marginally be affected by the internal INPUTS he might feed into the process. As a result, the coding procedure became significant in directing his behaviour.

The student's only knowledge of formal designing was related to the use of the designing methods often in evidence at the Bartlett. This knowledge soon overcame him. As is obvious from Fig.5, he discovered that a matrix encoding of some of his information would lead to what he thought would be a building. The ENCODING–DECODING procedure (the matrix, the interaction net, the bubble diagram, the plan), not constrained by experience or a external frame of reference, soon prevailed. As one can see, there is no topological difference between the net diagram (the ENCODING), and the plan (the OUTPUT). The step by step 'logic' of the methodology actually led the student to his solution.

The plan shown does not constitute a complete design. In this case it was significant. This was clear from the student's behaviour throughout the rest of the programme. He attempted to service it; he tried to impose a structural logic on it, and so on. The diagram was pushed and pulled, changed and refined, and occasionally violated; but it was always the evolving filter through which the rest of the situation had to pass before it became, 'relevant to the problem'.

The simplicity of this procedure is surprising. After weeks of struggling with the problem the student arrived at a design in a matter of hours. The contrast of this method with those of Aalto and Alexander is striking. All three approaches constitute designing strategies: all three are similar and different in important ways: perhaps most important, all three are representative of existing schools of thought in design.

Part III

The regulation of variety in design

In the first part of the paper I described a dilemma which, it seems to me, designers face in almost all practical situations. Briefly, it is this:

Practical design problems are variable and idiosyncratic. They generate a variety so great that it is nearly impossible to describe such problems let alone understand them. Despite this, practising designers must interpret these problems if they are going to deal with them. Their interpretations can never be definitive; more often than not they are simplifications which lead to a distorted conception of existing difficulties. Yet the interpretations are necessary and the concepts they generate are apparently clear. Thus, we find professional people accepting them and design methodologists re-wording them. The dilemma is this: to act we must interpret; to interpret is often to distort; in design these distortions are made probable by the very variety we are trying to interpret.

The second part of the paper, although a diversion from the initial argument, may be regarded as a collection of loosely formulated empirical observations that support some of the earlier contentions. It is now important to relate these observations to the practical problems posed earlier.

Homomorphic-reductions in design

Figure 6 is an abstracted diagram of some of the recognizable stages present in all three of the designing strategies examined. By re-examining each in the light of Fig.6 it is possible to be more precise about the difference between *variety-restriction* and *variety-regulation* in design.

The first component of the diagram represents the unstructured problem space a designer perceives when first tackling a problem. All three designers had a more or less detailed description of such a problem space. Alexander's list of misfits is a rather elaborate description; it includes factors having to do with marital rituals, something many physical designers might rightly or wrongly have left out. The description Aalto initially worked with was supplied

1. Input

CAMP HOUSE:

FAMILIARISATION CHECK LIST

1. **ESTABLISH**
   1 CONSTANTS
   2 VARIABLES

2. **CRITICISE**
   1 SITE
      - PLANNING ROUTES ; MOVEMENT SYSTEMS
      - TOPOGRAPHY ; ORIENTATION
      - LANDSCAPE ; PICTURESQUE
      - PLANTING ; SOIL CONDITIONS
      - HISTORY ; SYMBOLIC CONTENT
      - SYSTEMIC CONTENT

   2 CATERING
      - WHAT SELLS ; HOW IS IT OBTAINED
      - HOW SOLD ; WHAT DO PEOPLE DO WITH IT
      - HOW MUCH IS SOLD ; HOW IS IT DISPOSED OF

   3 PUBLIC NEEDS
      - WHO USES THE FACILITY ; TOURISTS OFFICE STAFF ; TIME VARIATION
      - WHAT PURPOSES DOES IT SERVE ; LUNCH SNACKS ; ATTRACTION
      - WHAT BEHAVIOURAL SYSTEMS ARE INVOLVED

   4 RESTRICTIONS
      - LOCAL AUTHORITIES ; CROWN ; BYE-LAWS ; BUILDING CODES

   5 OTHER BUILDINGS
   etc

Brief

2. Encoding

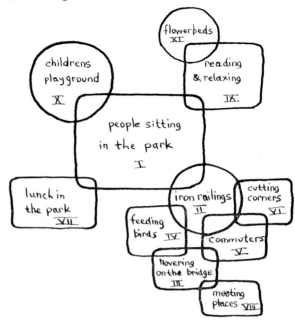

Diagram

3. Decoding

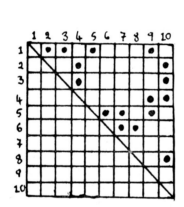

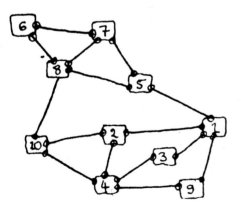

Matrix and interaction net

4. Output

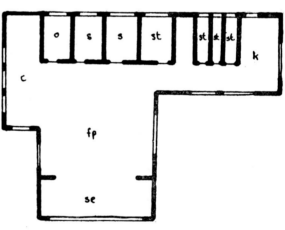

Student building

Fig.5
Student design process

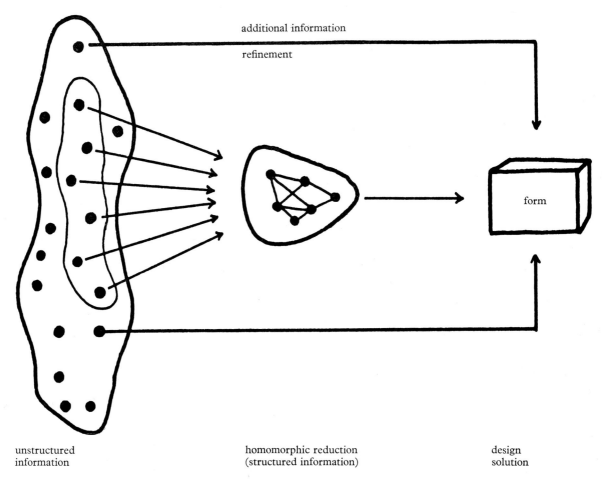

additional information

refinement

form

unstructured
information

homomorphic reduction
(structured information)

design
solution

Fig.6
Design variety restriction

by a number of people all expressing facts, opinions, and ideas in the form of a stadium brief. The student's description of his problem was in the form of a brief which he supplemented by spending a week making observations and collecting data concerned with the design context.

All three attempted to make this information 'meaningful'. Alexander looked for the 'sub-systems present'; his theory would give these a concrete meaning. Aalto sketched, presumably searching for what he might call 'the essence' of the problem;[2] his experience would allow him to recognize this. It is difficult to say what the student was searching for but his earlier diagrams implied that he was seeking some meaningful structure within his problem. It is at this very point, i.e. when a designer begins to *interpret* his problem, that the arguments in this paper are directed.

We cannot understand without interpreting. By definition, an interpretation is a reduction of a situation to some understandable representation or description.[3] The second part of Fig.6 represents this phase of the designing process. I have used the term 'homomorphic-reduction' to describe it. In the broadest sense, a homomorphic-reduction is meant here to mean *an interpretation*. In a more rigorous

sense, *a homomorphic-reduction is a many-to-one mapping* which associates elements in one set (in this case, the items of information in the unstructured problem space), with elements in any other set, (in this case, the concepts implicit in the designer's interpretations of reality), such that *many* elements in the first set may be related to only *one* element in the second. It is the process we, as designers, go through in attempting to make sense out of a complex of information that may have no obvious structure.[4]

[2] The idea of a sketch (such as Aalto's) embodying essential relationships within a problem can be made clear by reference to the following quotation: '*When facts are well expressed in terms of symbolic systems, it becomes clear that certain relations between the participants are necessary. When this symbolic system is imposed upon reality a similar kind of necessity is attached to physical efforts. Where, before, a relation may have seemed arbitrary or accidental it now inherits requiredness from its symbolic representation.*' (Miller, reference 20, page 312). Aalto's sketch is a symbolic system expressing the essential relations which embody 'the essence' of the problem.

[3] While it may be said that an interpretation constitutes a reduction of that situation to certain essential characteristics, it could be argued that this same process is an elaboration in that something is added via the interpretation. This point seems to be valid. In terms of an information-processing analysis it is convenient and useful to think of this step as a reductive one even if something is added to the problem. This point is dealt with in some detail by Simon and Paige; see especially their comments on page 109.

[4] An example of a many-to-one mapping might be the

Figure 6a illustrates this point. A designer examines a set of information intended to describe his problem; he looks for correlations and dependencies within the information that appear to make sense. He tries to see how given requirements or ideas relate to one another. When he discovers relationships within the information he has *interpreted*. He has invented concepts that subsume for many unrelated ideas or facts concerning his problem. His interpretation is *structured* because it relates to his experience and understanding of the problem; it is a reduction because a relatively small number of interwoven concepts represent a vastly larger field of information. Singly, each of many factors may only be peripherally relevant to a particular problem; together, they can be related to (or mapped into), a specific design.

The three designers carried out this step. They would not refer to their interpretations as 'homomorphic reductions', but all three reduced their problems in a way not dissimilar to my description. Alexander called his reduction a 'picture of the physical sub-systems' (Fig.3/3); Aalto would probably refer to his as a sketch of 'the essence of the problem' (Fig.4/2); the student called his a 'relational diagram' (Fig.5/3). It makes little difference what name one gives to such interpretations, for their operational properties remain unchanged. Each

association of the children, living along a given street, denoted by the set $C = (c_1, \ldots c_n)$, with the houses on that street, denoted by the set $H = (h_1, h_2, \ldots h_n)$. If there are fewer houses than children then obviously certain children, say, c_1, and c_2, will be associated with the same house say, h_3. House h_3, might therefore be said to *stand for*, or be the home of, children c_1, and c_2. When one has succeeded in associating each child from the set C, with their corresponding houses in the set H, a many-to-one mapping has been carried out. A more detailed discussion is given by Allen (Chapter 7, pages 171, 181).

serves as a 'filter' through which the rest of the problem must pass before the designer can act upon it.

Earlier I described how the student designer attempted to distort his diagram to make it into a building. His pushing, pulling, and rearranging of the diagram is, in fact, *a literal example* of how the interpretation of the problem was used as a filter through which the remaining information (that not embodied in the diagram) was processed. Information describing site conditions, structure, servicing, vehicular access and other such factors, was introduced into his process *only via* the diagram. The similarity of Aalto's sketch to his final design implies that he too processed information in this way. It seems that all designers (perhaps at varying levels of detail) carry out this filtering process. Indeed, it is difficult to see how one can avoid it for design problems cannot be understood until they are interpreted and the interpretation acts as the information filter. Here we return to the practical problems outlined in Part I: *it is this very reduction-interpretation-filtering process that allows one to operate effectively in the face of real-world variety.*

When a designer reduces a problem in this way he is attempting to restrict the variety generated by a real-world design situation. The need for this restriction can be understood in terms of Fig.7. A design problem is represented as an abstract space containing a number of items of information. Looking at design in this way, it becomes obvious that the complexity, or variety, of a design problem grows not out of its informational description in any objective sense, but out of the *interpretations* we impose upon that description. Such a problem has a *potential* informational variety; *the actual variety we encounter is determined by the interpretations we consider.*

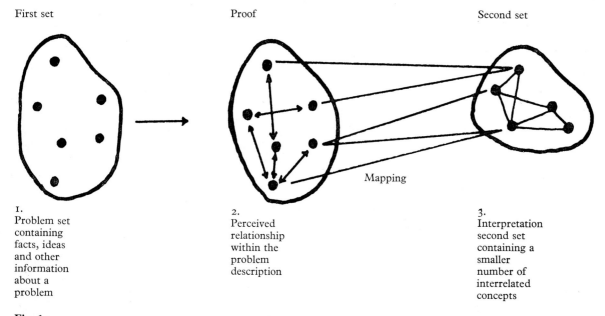

First set   Proof   Second set

Mapping

1.
Problem set containing facts, ideas and other information about a problem

2.
Perceived relationship within the problem description

3.
Interpretation second set containing a smaller number of interrelated concepts

Fig. 6a
Homomorphic reduction of Design information

A simple example which will illustrate this point is a problem space concerned with a town centre design that includes requirements traditionally fulfilled by the design of a 'high street'. At first, the idea of designing a high street in response to a number of requirements may seem a simple one. The actual variety associated with such a concept only becomes obvious when we realize that it has different connotations (and therefore different requirements associated with it) for everyone concerned with the problem.

To a transport engineer, for example, a high street may primarily be seen as a channel requiring certain capacities and conditions sufficient to allow a number of vehicles to get from A to B rapidly and safely.

To a real-estate investor, a high street may primarily be seen as an economic artery providing strips of investment property on either side.

To a social scientist, a high street may be seen as a receptacle for an important social function.

To a building scientist, it may primarily be seen as a potential source of noise and fumes.

To a shop owner, it may be seen as a potential source of customers, and so on.

When a physical designer prepares a model or a drawing of a high street, he is formalizing *his* interpretation of the concept. This is the variety-reduction. The designer has interpreted the problem in physical terms; other people's understanding of the problem must now grow from this representation. This is when much of the *actual* variety of the situation becomes apparent, for these people may 'see' the problem differently.

As one can see from Fig.7 this actual variety is often great. If we deal with a problem in terms of twenty considerations (and the figure twenty is unrealistically low), it is clear that such a problem will rapidly increase in complexity as additional interpretations are introduced: i.e.

one interpretation can result in 20 considerations;

two interpretations can result in 400 considerations;

three interpretations can result in 8,000 considerations;

four interpretations can result in 160,000 considerations; etc.

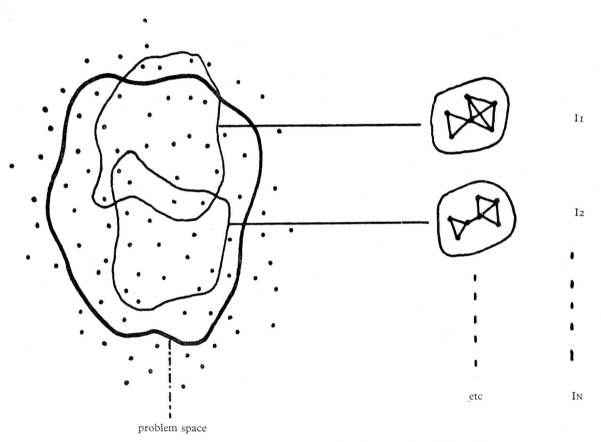

problem space

Abstract problem space inclusive of N bits of information

various interpretations of the problem space

variety $= fN^1$

Where: N = the number of bits of information implicit in the problem space and: I = the number of interpretations of that information considered.

variety increases exponentially as a function of the number of interpretations imposed upon a problem space.

Fig.7
Variety in design

Three or four opinions of the same problem can make a definitive investigation impossible. This is why a designer reduces such problems to one formal interpretation that can be evaluated. It is *only* when the multitude of design considerations are made explicit in terms of a drawing or other formal picture, that different people concerned with the problem can understand how their ideas are different from that of the physical designer.

Referring back to Fig.6, this aspect of the designing process can be equated with the third part of the diagram. A design proposal is transformed from the initial homomorphic-reduction to the form implied by that reduction. In terms of everyday designing, this is the process of submitting sketch designs to a client, an engineer, a local authority and to others whose interpretations may be different from ours. Where these interpretations differ, it is often necessary to modify the formal picture of the form until it responds to the variety generated by the different opinions. The resultant design is then a response to varied interpretations, but an explicit understanding of how the design relates to the 'problem' is never possible.

Elegance in architectural design

The outcome of the procedure I have just described is occasionally a building, or a group of buildings, that may be considered an example of 'elegant' design. More often, the result is a compromise of interpretations. It is worth considering the difference between these two possible resultants.

The idea of *homomorphically* reducing information is an important one for a designer does not just accept *any* mapping of information into concepts. He intends his reduction to embody a subtle but precise *structural similarity* to the whole problem description. Using Aalto's words, we might say that he intends his mapping to 'capture the essence' of the situation. It is here that one of the differences between a successful designer and a lesser one becomes clear.

One attribute of a great designer is his ability to interpret (or homomorphically structure) a situation in such a way that his picture of that situation does capture its important aspects. His interpretation of the problem is so rich that other interpretations are either implicit within his or can be readily accepted without a loss of the *consistency* that leads to the quality we call 'elegance'. His interpretation will be structured in such a way that it can absorb the variety generated by alternatives.[5]

[5] The hospital 'interpretations' of John Weeks are just such consistent interpretations. Development of these *hospital designs* has grown out of an intricate understanding of how *hospital buildings* are seen and used by *different* groups of individuals concerned with the planning and running of hospitals.

A lesser designer does not have this ability. Often, his interpretations, or sketches, will be significantly restructured in the light of other considerations. The process of submitting the designed interpretation to other people is then not one of refinement and realization (Fig.6), but one of dissolution and realization.

This, of course, brings us back to the original arguments of the paper. Few architects or planners have the capabilities or freedoms to evolve design concepts capable of *regulating* variety. More often, designers are forced to rely on generalized theoretical concepts or hard professional divisions that *apparently cope with but actually restrict* variety. But these are unrealistic; they are attempts to replace the variety-responsive concepts of the perceptive designer with concepts that create a practice of non-design.

An alternative in principle

Return for a moment to the designing procedures exemplified by Alexander, Aalto, and the student. It may be useful to ask whether there are any positive characteristics of these strategies that could be useful to a designer in the light of the problems posed.

For a designing strategy to be useful it must be *operational*. One must follow a methodology that will allow hypotheses to be tested.

The operational aspects of Alexander's theory are an extreme example of this. The methodology associated with his ideas is a rigorous one and so limits the types of hypotheses one can actually test. His theory deals with a select class of variables (e.g. misfits, conflicts, etc.), and therefore by definition is only one sort of *mapping* of reality into theory. It ignores other possible mappings (e.g. client's irrational opinions), and so breaks down when submitted to the test of practice.

There is, however, something to be gained from Alexander's ideas. The arguments presented here include theoretical assumptions that define a mapping of reality into theory. I have claimed that design problems can be regarded as *sets of information*; that sets of information have a *variety potential*; that *interpretations* of these sets are sources of variety; that designers are in the position of having to *restrict variety*; and so on. These arguments may seem straightforward but they are not so, for these statements are hypotheses concerned with the nature of reality. They are terms (just as 'misfit' and 'conflict' are) that stand for assumptions about the workings of the world.

The mapping outlined here is only one of an infinite number of reality-to-theory mappings. An alternative might be 'talking in practical terms'. But if there is a drawback to this alternative, it includes the difficulty of organizing one's thoughts in the light of the possible meanings 'practical terms' may have built up through usage. It is difficult, if not impossible, to see past the complexity of the everyday world without some picture, or mapping, of that world that is capable of extending our perceptions beyond the 'practical'.

But one must distinguish between the mapping used to conceptualize reality and the behaviours or operations these imply. There is a tendency to assume that unfamiliar intentions imply novel methods: there seems to be no reason why this must be the case. There is no reason why new problems (that may be revealed through a theoretical mapping) cannot be tackled in familiar ways. An intention simply requires practical methods for implementing it.

In this context, it seems quite natural to turn to Aalto. Two reasons for this are immediately apparent. First, Aalto's designing is *practical*: he designs credible buildings that get built. Second, his designing strategy is *flexible*: there is little doubt that he is able to design in the way that he does because he operates intuitively, dependent upon the *variety-responsive device par excellence* – the human brain.

Aalto's strategy for arriving at a design involves no explicit methodology. The strength of the strategy may reside in its flexibility, for it allows him to respond to different possible mappings of the same problem regulating change by extrapolating from experience. His design results suggest such a process for they are consistent interpretations implying that one *variety-regulating device* (Aalto's brain) has constrained the whole of the process.

There is, however, a drawback to this strategy for although Aalto's structurally rich interpretation of a problem is the source of the *physically* elegant result, it is this same interpretation that 'filters out' other mappings that might be important to the same problem. Who is to say, for instance, that Aalto's interpretation of a design problem is the filter through which a sociologist's mapping of the same problem should pass? Perhaps a more expedient question is to ask if other interpretations of a design problem necessarily 'filter out' the quality of architectural elegance provided by a designer such as Aalto.

A designer such as Aalto expresses his interpretation of a problem in a language (e.g. models and drawings) that is a rather immediate analogue to reality. Consequently, his interpretation may well be the basis upon which others decide if their interpretations are different. *People other than the physical designer often formalize their ideas in terms of the reality implied by the designer's picture of the problem.* This is the 'filtering' process; it is a reflection of the language used to express a problem.[6]

The problem, therefore, is one of linking up a number of brains so that they may effectively operate without creating a variety likely to destroy the consistencies that characterize the operation of one brain. A code or language is required that is capable of expressing a number of different mappings of reality in a communicable and consistent way.

In principle, a designing procedure such as shown in Fig.8 would go some way toward overcoming this difficulty. The difference between this diagram and the one in Fig.6, is that it includes more than one homomorphic-reduction of a design situation. This implies that not only does a physical designer formalize his interpretation of a problem, but other interpretations are also sought out and defined. From these, would grow a more comprehensive (not necessarily physical) design specification *embodying the structural characteristics of many homomorphic-reductions*. This process, in theory, would have the following practical advantages:

(i) a number of interpretations of the problem would be developed in parallel; much information about the problem would be generated and evaluated early on in the process;

(ii) a design would be an outgrowth of these interpretations; it would embody a more relevant homomorphic-relationship to the real-world situation;[7]

(iii) the differing interpretations, being expressed in a common language, would be comparable; a designer would be free to move flexibly between different mappings of the problem evaluating his physical proposals in light of other interpretations.

Many practising design offices already carry out this procedure in some form. Planning teams develop many aspects of a design in parallel. Formal reductive pictures are made of land use, transport networks, demand patterns and other aspects of the whole. Design teams working on hospitals, universities, and other building complexes often develop operational, structural, and formal designs all in parallel. Difficulties centre around the interpretations of the client, the users, the social scientist, and other parties not directly concerned with 'the hardware'. Their languages are so different from those of the designer that it is often difficult to evolve an integrated design. More often, we find ourselves generating informational variety late on in the process when these people first understand the designer's intentions. When this happens, one usually uses the

---

[6] The 'filtering' process is dealt with in differing languages by both Meister and Sullivan and Simon and Paige. A discussion of this same concept in terms of information-theory is in Garner (especially chs. 1 and 5).

[7] In this paper I am discussing how this process would affect the *physical* designer and therefore talk about the homomorphic relationship between reality and the proposed *physical* design. More likely than not, varied interpretations of a problem would reveal that the solution was only partly physical or, perhaps, not physical at all. This, in fact, is always the case but because of our 'allocation' of problems by professions most designers fail to realize this. Both Stafford Beer and J. C. Jones discuss this problem in a different context.

physical proposal as a 'variety filter'. And as I have tried to show, it is this very process that destroys the integrated qualities of a design.

The important feature of Fig.8 therefore, is the inclusion of a common language for expressing varying interpretations of a problem. It does not yet exist. All that I am suggesting is that 'design methods', as they have been dealt with in this paper (as methods for encoding information), present us with an opportunity to express differing conceptions of reality in comparable languages. Indeed, design methods can be used to express design intentions without restricting the flexibility that characterizes the working of the perceptive designer. But this is all speculation: it is time to see how these principles might work in practice.

The principles in practice

I will describe briefly how a limited effort was made to explore, in a practical context, the feasibility of some of the constructs in this paper. The project was the design of a large teaching hospital. When the study was initiated, a design proposal for the hospital already existed (schematic model and plan).

This was regarded as the architect's formal interpretation of the problem. The purpose of this study was to solicit other interpretations of the very same problem before the architect's proposal was taken beyond the schematic stage.

It was hoped that as many as four or five different interpretations of the hospital could be defined. As it turned out, we were forced to accept only two in addition to the architect's, these two, ultimately being combined into one. The information generated by this study, however, has been so great that it is unlikely that further interpretations could have been handled in the time available.

An attempt was made to define the way in which medical, administrative, and nursing staffs envisaged a hospital. Questionnaires, data sheets, and observations were needed in order to get an idea of how these different groups thought a hospital should be organized. The study was arranged so that data were collected in the form of a ranked evaluation where ranks referred to preferred relationships. Data matrices were derived that represented what each group *thought at the time* were optimal relationships linking different functions.

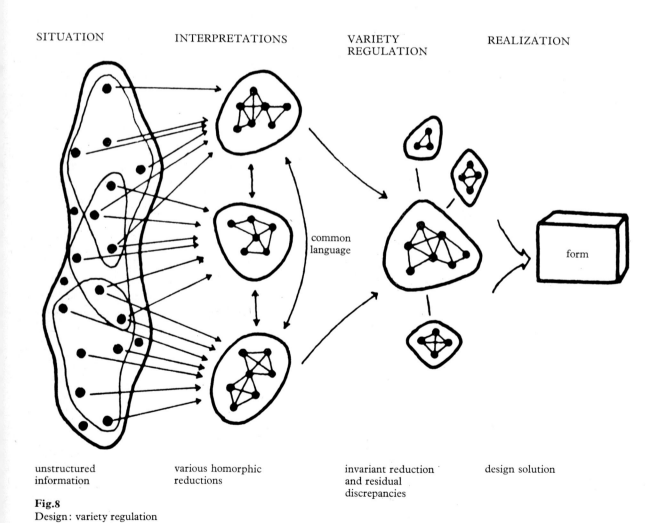

SITUATION   INTERPRETATIONS   VARIETY REGULATION   REALIZATION

common language

form

unstructured information

various homorphic reductions

invariant reduction and residual discrepancies

design solution

Fig.8
Design: variety regulation

By examining the architect's development proposal it was possible to determine how these functions were accommodated within the proposed building. We therefore had two distinct sets of data referring to the same breakdown of a hospital, but each being generated by different interpretations of what a hospital should be. This made it possible to compare the opinions of the client's representatives (the different classes of staff) with the intentions of the architect *at that point in time*.

Figures 9 and 9a are typical of the sort of results that grew from this study. The data matrices were submitted to a clustering programme that was designed to extract significant clusters of relationships implied by such matrices. The lists of numbers at the top of each figure are representative of the computer output. The diagrams at the bottom of each figure can be derived from the numerical patterns within the clusters. The two examples shown are simple ones but almost all the exercises followed this format.[8]

In terms of the earlier arguments, the diagrams in Figs.9 and 9a represent the common language whereby differences in interpretations of the same problem can be clearly identified. The results of these studies have been rewarding and suggest that these encoding methods have practical potential. It is interesting to consider some specific examples of how these studies have proved useful to the architect.

When information was first collected for the analysis, recipients were asked to consider the relationships between such things as, 'The Accident Department'; 'The Neurosurgical Bed Areas'; 'The Central Laboratories'; and so on. Each of these terms was meant to refer to physical/functional concepts making up a hospital. Each term had a clear meaning to the architect and was embedded in his design conception. When the analysis was complete, it became apparent that these same terms meant something quite different to others concerned with the project. Indeed, many of these conceptual divisions were modified or completely done away with. For example, the architect initially worked with a 'Central Medical Records Department' as one design element. When it became apparent what the hospital staff thought a 'Central Medical Records Department' was, however, we soon came to the conclusion that this concept had little operational reality and that an alternative would have to be found. Examination of the different bed areas led to similar conclusions and it is now clear how the idea of 'medical records' and 'patient accommodation' relate within this design context. The designers began designing with rather generalized hospital concepts that 'would do', to get started. By encoding these concepts via the cluster

level of cluster	elements clustered
1	2, 8
2	4, 8
3	2, 5
4	3, 5
5	3, 8
6	3, 5, 8
7	2, 3, 5, 8
8	1, 8
9	4, 5, 8
10	1, 2, 8
11	5, 6
12	1, 2, 5, 8
etc	1, 2, 3, 4, 5, 6, 7, 8

Table II
Cluster analysis of eight hospital departments whose traffic characteristics were ranked theoretically.

[8] A more detailed discussion of this work is given by Best (1968). The computer programmes are described by Reynolds and Best (1968).

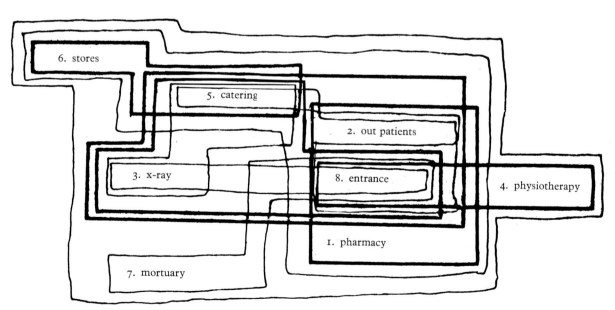

Diagram generated by the clusters in Table II.

Fig.9
Clients interpretation

(Diagram of the pattern of relationships between departments as these were built up theoretically.)

analysis, their design consequences have emerged. No doubt, they would have emerged at some later date, but the whole purpose of this study was to expose their meanings early on. The discovery of what these general terms meant to different people within the project has clarified the architect's task; the design team is now freer to move between these different meanings trying to find a physical accommodation that is responsive to other mappings of the problem.

I have lightly passed over the work that has been carried out and this is because I am not interested in presenting a 'method', but in the relationship between method and intention. The principles underlying this work have been applied to an on-going town centre design programme with varying degrees

level of cluster	elements clustered		
1	5, 6		
2	1, 7		
3	2, 8		
4	1, 8		
5	5, 7		
6	3, 4		
7	1, 6		
8	1, 2, 8		
9	3, 6		
10	5, 6, 7	1, 6, 7	
11	1, 5, 6, 7	1, 7, 8	3, 5, 6
etc.	1, 2, 3, 4, 5, 6, 7, 8		

Table I
Cluster analysis of eight departments in a proposed hospital design.

of success. What *is* emerging from these studies are results that are useful. The hospital work shows that this way of conceptualizing design exposes issues that have a design consequence. The computer analysis is a rapid and economical way to formalize different interpretations of a design and make explicit the requirements and needs associated with these interpretations. Recent activities suggest that the designers are now freer to explore different patterns of form that may be parts of more integrated and relevant designs.

Conclusion

The diagram shown in Fig.8 may now seem a more realistic representation for it is a picture of the procedure followed in the hospital work just described. The 'clustering' language employed is a limited one only capable of describing a very small part of a design problem. The principle involved, however, is evident and it is clear that differing interpretations of a problem lead to a wider understanding of its nature. It will be a long time before a language is evolved for expressing all the important interpretations one can think of: but it is worth looking for.

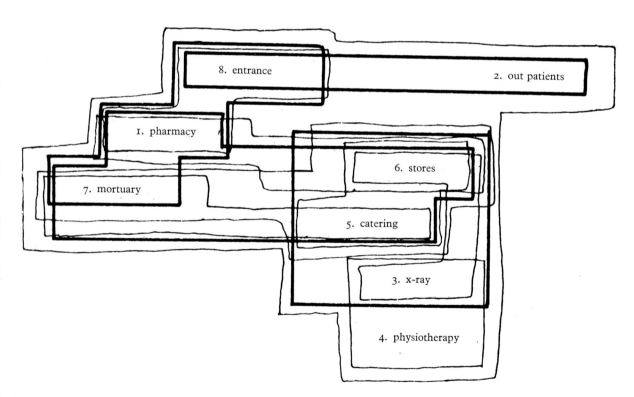

Diagram generated by the clusters in Table I

(Diagram of the pattern of relationships between departments in a design proposal)

Fig. 9a
Architects interpretation

REFERENCES

A. AALTO. *Complete Works*. Girsberger (Zurich 1963).

C. A. ALEXANDER. *Notes on the Synthesis of Form*. Harvard University Press (1964).

C. A. ALEXANDER. *The Atoms of Environmental Structure* (W. Poyner) M.P.B.W. (London 1966).

C. A. ALEXANDER. *The Co-ordination of the Urban Rule System*. Center for Planning Research and Development, Berkeley (1967).

C. A. ALEXANDER. The City as a Mechanism for Sustaining Human Contact. *Transactions of the Bartlett Society*, Volume 4, University College London (1966).

R. G. D. ALLEN. *Basic Mathematics*. Macmillan (London 1962).

W. R. ASHBY. *Design for a Brain*. Science Paperback, Chapman & Hall. (London 1960).

S. BEER. *Decision and Control*. John Wiley & Sons (London 1966).

G. A. BEST. *Patterns for Form*. Information Paper, RIBA Symposium on Computer-Aided Design (London 1968).

C. CHERRY. *On Human Communication*. Science Paperback, John Wiley (London 1961).

C. M. EASTMAN. *The Design Process*. Mimeograph, Department of Architecture and Computer Science, Carnegie Institute of Technology (1967).

W. R. GARNER. *Uncertainty and Structure as Psychological Concepts*. John Wiley, London (1962).

S. GUTHEIM. *Alvar Aalto*. Mayflower Press (London 1960).

K. R. HAMMOND and J. N. CASTELLAN. *Analysing Information-Seeking Strategies*. Behaviour Research Report 59. Institute of Behavioural Science, University of Colorado (1966).

J. C. JONES. *Systematic Design Methods*. Mimeograph, Department of Industrial Design Technology, University of Manchester, Institute of Science and Technology (1962).

J. C. JONES. Design Methods Reviewed in: S. GREGORY: *The Design Method*. Butterworth (London 1966).

J. C. JONES. *The Designing of Man-Machine Systems*. Proceedings of the Conference on the Human Operator in Complex Systems, University of Aston, Birmingham (1966).

P. H. LEVIN. *Decision Making in Urban Design*. Building Research Station, Current Paper, Design Series 49. Ministry of Technology (1966).

D. MEISTER and D. J. SULLIVAN. *A Further Study of the Use of Human Factors Information by Designers*. System Effectiveness Lab., The Bunker-Ramo Corp., Canoga Park, California (1967).

G. A. MILLER. *Language and Communication*. McGraw-Hill (New York 1951).

C. NORBERG-SCHULZ. *Intentions in Architecture*. Allen & Unwin Ltd. (London 1966).

R. A. REYNOLDS and G. A. BEST. *R. A .Reynolds/Prog DA*. Experimental Data Analysis Programmes, Bartlett School of Architecture, University College London (1968).

H. A. SIMON and J. PAIGE. Cognitive Processes in Solving Algebra Word Problems. *Problem solving: Research Method, and Theory*, Kleinmuntz, B. (Ed.), John Wiley (London 1966).

G. STURT. *The Wheelwright's Shop*. Cambridge University Press (1955).

J. WEEKS. Indeterminate Architecture. *Transactions of the Bartlett Society*, Volume 2, University College London (1963).

Rightness and wrongness in the physical environment

by Anthony Ward

*'Human existence identifies and defines itself by
the ends it pursues'*
J. P. Sartre
*'We are going forward at twice the speed of sound
and half the speed of sense'*
Thomas Griffiths

Introduction

One can never be sure of using terms and references
which have the same meaning for the reader, so I will
begin by trying to establish a context for my later
comments about 'rightness' and 'wrongness'.

It seems to me that there is a current tendency to
'rationalize' the design process, without considering
the possible consequences. We hope that the end
product will in some way be 'better', but we have
hardly ever stopped to consider the role of ethics in
design – better for whom and in what way?

The problem of 'rightness' and 'wrongness' con-
fronting every designer of physical environment
seems to fall into two separate classes.
(1) *There is a class of decisions about what the environment should do.* Should it make people dependent or
independent, social or antisocial, creative or accept-
ant, active or passive, etc. This is a question of *ethics*.
(2) *There is another class of decision, about whether the
environment I have specified actually fulfils all the
things I say it should.* This class of decision corres-
ponds to what Alexander calls fit/misfit and is a
question of *mechanics*.

Most people who criticize the fit/misfit concept tend
to confuse these two classes, but this paper will deal
mostly with the first. It is necessary to specify what
the environment should do before we can decide
whether it actually does it.

Ethics

Unfortunately, design method techniques culled from
operational research and systems analysis do not
make ethical judgements for us. Yet the role of value
judgements in design method has become obscured
behind the numerous techniques and mechanisms
which the architects have so readily accepted. The
classic design method cycle: analysis, synthesis,
evaluation, which seems to include all other subdivis-

ions that various designers attribute to their activities
(Asimow, Archer, RIBA Handbook, etc.), is permeated with value judgement. Sometimes the sequence
changes, sometimes the stages merge into each other,
and sometimes complex combinations are used. One
such variation places its emphasis upon the *evolution*
of design forms from an analysis or appraisal of
existing situations.

Design evolution

In the evolutionary approach to design, formal
qualities in existing situations are evaluated and
abstracted, and used as the basic geometry of new
solutions. The choice of qualities for abstraction is
determined by observing the behaviour of people in
existing situations, abstracting the physical quality of
the situations, and using the abstractions to produce
new solutions to new problems. It differs from current practice, in that it attempts to be scientifically
'objective'. The 'evolutionists' maintain that there are
ways of objectively evaluating what already exists,
and that any value judgements can be safely relegated
to the synthesis stage in the design process. But this is
a tautology. These values are applied at the very
beginning of the process, and the subjective choice of
evaluative criteria implicitly predetermines the formal
context of the solution. Any 'objective' analysis is
built upon a framework of criteria or standards against
which achieved changes can be measured, and these
criteria are often derived from social and cultural
pressures and traditions. The *choice* of an objective
method, with all its *chosen* criteria and standards of

evaluation, is itself based upon personal value constructs, so that a person will often choose mechanisms which seem appropriate to his view of the world. It sometimes happens that, as at present, inadequate mechanisms are chosen because of inadequate and unhealthy personal values.

There is ample evidence, for instance, that when objective analysis techniques are applied to the human condition, they create difficulties. This is not to say that they are not relevant to certain *aspects* of the design problem, but that those aspects do not include the analysis of human needs except in a very abstract way.

Mechanistic limitations

Systems analysis, information theory, statistics, and other similar mechanisms create difficulties by their very structural nature. It is characteristic of all these techniques that they break their problems down into simple 'atoms'. The 'input' and 'output' concepts in systems analysis are very typical. What goes on within the system can be gauged by varying the input and observing the change in output. The output is often a diagram in which varying thicknesses of line become physical widths of a system 'Channel', as in the 'Clover-leaf'.

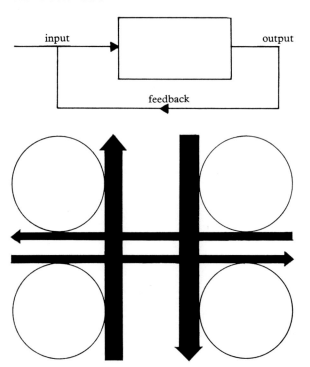

Thus, a problem of traffic congestion would be approached by changing the 'channel width' and observing the changed speed (and hence density per unit time of flow). From this, an abstract model can be developed which generalizes this relationship, and which can be applied to new situations. Even in more complicated examples, where the output from one system becomes the input to another, etc., the fundamentally *linear* quality of the organization is not even remotely comparable to the dynamics of

human experience, and no number of iterations can ever overcome this basic structural limitation. Experience seems to work in Gestalt. We respond to pattern, rather than to a simple causal line. For instance, the traffic density found in the first example could be changed to find its relationship to the form of flow. However, we are left with no concept of *meaning* about the traffic situations for the people involved, unless we begin to interject our own experience. The abstracted relationships will otherwise always remain abstractions which result in a paucity of user experience.

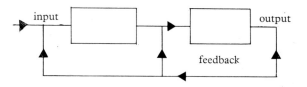

'Atoms' processed within these systems must be of a very uniform nature, otherwise they must be rendered consistent by the application of statistical method. This is often done with behavioural and physiological data. For example, the wide range of human dimensions taken into account in designing chairs is averaged out by the application of standard deviation techniques. Any giants or midgets are automatically eliminated from the analysis in order to facilitate data manipulation.

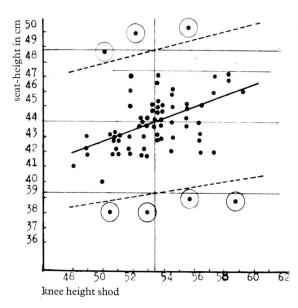

Most tall or tiny people will have had direct experience of this kind of discrimination, but there are many examples which concern us all. Take the location of pedestrian crossings: a survey is made to establish the location of existing crossing points. The standard deviation is found, and, taken together with data (from past situations) about the effect of crossings on behaviour, this produces a solution. Yet people still ignore a crossing (see photos overleaf), and so the authorities have to erect barriers to make people behave consistently.

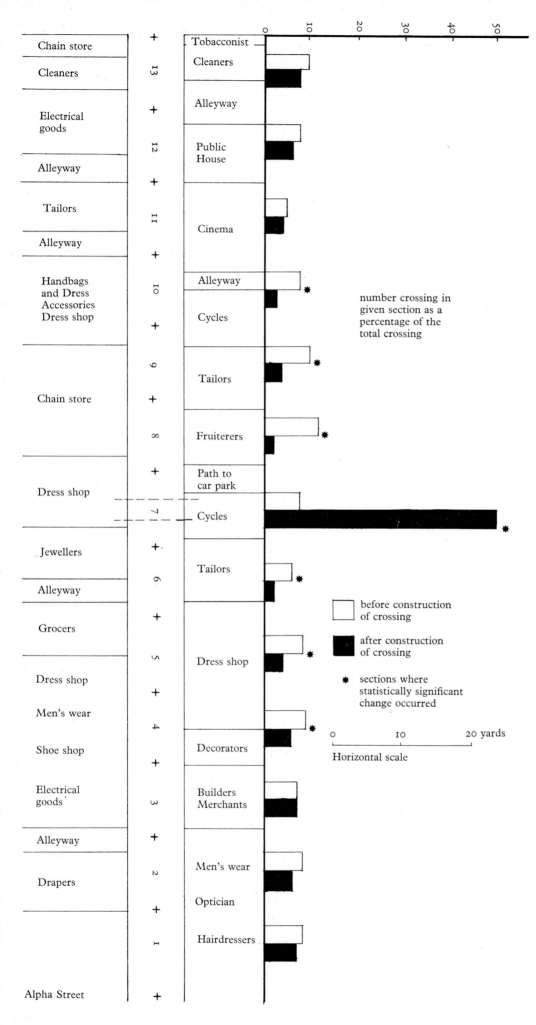

number crossing in
given section as a
percentage of the
total crossing

before construction
of crossing

after construction
of crossing

sections where
statistically significant
change occurred

Horizontal scale

0   10   20 yards

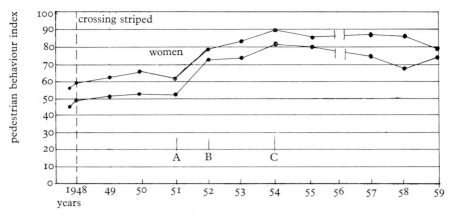

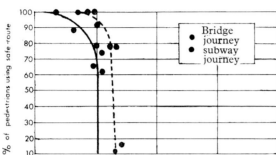

a. crossing stripes in poor condition

b. new regulations in force and crossing restriped

c. beacons flashing

This kind of behaviour is not so surprising when we consider how the techniques described constrain the individual and limit his freedom to choose experiences for himself. When we try to explain the human being as the 'intersection of universal schemata', or as bundles of 'tendencies' or atomized drives, we automatically lose the one to whom the drives or tendencies have happened – who stands at their source. An extreme example in which I was involved was the design of a university electrical engineering faculty, where Cost, Movement, Structural and Services criteria were optimized by computer into the most efficient possible free form which was then transformed into a 'building' form, in which capital and running costs for all criteria were at a minimum.

The final product, in retrospect, constrained not only the high degree of efficiency intended, but also the potential for user choice. The user was allocated a structure, where movement *and choice* were minimized. The observed behaviour of the person cannot be seen as a manipulable abstraction – a meaningless 'bit', but only as an expression of the total person, which must be interpreted further if meaning is to be found. It is this totality of experience which can never be captured by the linear mechanisms used at the moment. As Koestler says, 'If learning and knowing (experiencing) consist of making oneself a private model of the universe it follows that the model can never include a complete model of itself because it must always lag one step behind the process it is supposed to represent'. This is precisely the problem which current 'objective' attitudes towards the human condition in architecture ignore. They are the cause (together with similar mechanisms used in almost every other discipline) of the current social situation. The three illustrations on page 170 show optimum model, formal evolution and final form.[1]

[1] Note that the optimum model represents the minimum total journey distance/salary expenditure. The lift block is located in the final plan form at the centroid of the movement density.

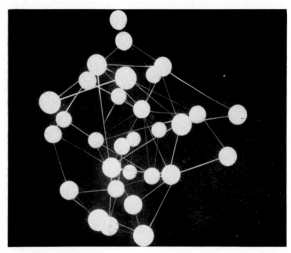

(a) Optimum model

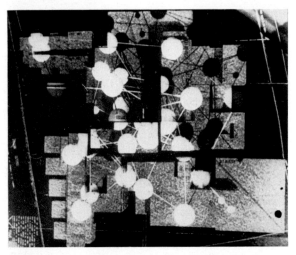

(b) Formal evolution

(c) Final form

Experience

By far the largest proportion of recent psychiatric patients complain of 'lack of identity', of 'feeling not to exist', or 'thing-less' or 'alienation', and so on. It is now becoming more accepted that a substantial majority of society feels alienated and that the treatments suggested by Freud, and later by the aversion therapists of the Behaviourist school, are totally unable to cope with the problem. *In fact, they make the problem worse.* Carl Rogers, a well-known American

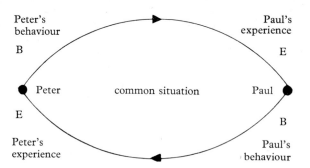

psychiatrist, has said explicitly that when he tries to interpret the patient's problem on the basis of an objective abstraction (such as Stimulus-Response) it actually gets in the way. He finds that *an objective attitude towards the patients ills actually increases his feeling of alienation.* This happens in a very peculiar way, which has been brilliantly analysed by Laing, whose model of human relationships is based upon a notion of *process.* Taking two people in a common situation, each behaves towards the other on the basis of his interpretation of the other's behaviour towards himself and so on. Since this interpretation is based upon each person's unique experiences, a supposedly gentle act by one may be construed as harsh by the other. When one classifies the other as an object or social unit (who will behave consistently with all objects of that class) he automatically categorizes himself as an object in a class of objects which is 'not other'. The other reciprocates, and a spiral is established which can only be broken down with great difficulty, and through an attempt to see the other not as an object, but as free subjectivity. But this is difficult for architects, who have to cope with large numbers of people. Alan Lipman, in his studies of old peoples' homes in Cardiff, found himself being referred to by the old people as 'the meter-man', or 'the gas-man' or 'the kitchen help'. We often feel the need to adopt an objective and cumulative attitude to design because of the sheer size of the problem, but when we do this our need to categorize *increases* the problem we are trying to solve. The people we are designing for *become* objects in solution – who in defence of their identity reduce everyone else to the same object-status, for whom they need carry no responsibility.

We see this happening, for instance, in the Federal Street Development in Chicago, where a very personal and self-oriented environment has been replaced by anonymous human batteries (see photo). Even in Britain the situation is no better. At Llanishen, Cardiff, in 1955, a group of owner-occupiers requested, and got, a six foot wall between their homes and a local authority housing development, even though the wall had to be built across a main road. It need hardly be said that in their enforced conformity the 'Estaters' were not recognized as human beings by either the designers or the owner-occupiers, nor can we confidently expect that they will not reinforce this classification themselves. It is hardly surprising that in most local authority housing estates in this country the degree of vandalism and lack of concern is increasing in direct proportion to the degree of

Chicago slum was photographed in 1944 from a building on Federal Street. In the 1950's this neighbourhood was demolished and rebuilt under the auspices of the U.S. Urban Renewal Authority, the Chicago Housing Authority and several other agencies.

Renewed neighbourhood was photographed from same perspective in 1965. Federal Street has been rerouted and is now adjacent to the railroad tracks. The development at centre and right consists of eight units housing mostly middle-income families.

generalization we make about human needs in design. Muzafer Sherif has found, for instance, that when goals are shared, a 'we-ness' develops which not only distinguishes one group from another with different and sometimes opposed goals, but that the group has no existence apart from the people who compose it, and that the group's concensus *becomes* the individual's perception, rendering him less free to develop his own goals and personality. Thus, the formation of a house-owner group at Llanishen renders the individual within that group less capable of distinguishing sub-classes of estate tenants. The erection of a wall then creates further solidarity between local authority tenants, who lose their capacity to distinguish any individuality amongst the house-owners and so on.

I am becoming more and more confirmed in my opinion that these attempts to be objective, particu-larly in the human sphere, are nothing but very clever covers for attempts to evade moral responsibility for *design* decisions. *My own view is that I must eventually decide what kind of people I would like my clients to become.* I believe that it is impossible to avoid this decision, although we sometimes try, when we attempt to find out what people want to do, and to design an environment which will allow them to do it. We have to decide whether to encourage or change the attitudes of the owner-occupiers at Llanishen.

Responsibility

The decision process itself hinges around a point of personal responsibility. When we decide upon a particular action, we automatically decide that 'to decide' is right, and 'not to decide' is wrong. We have choice and the choice 'not to decide' is still a positive action determined by a personal value construct. To decide 'not to decide' is as much a positive expression of ourselves as the decision 'to decide'. No matter how far back we take this decision process – 'to decide to decide to decide, etc.', the result is always the same – personal choice on the basis of personal values, for which we cannot abdicate responsibility. The responsibility for deciding to let people do what they want to do (even if it is detrimental to themselves) is unavoidably ours in any design situation.

Eliot's prophecy

'*We shall die,*
of the absolute paternal care,
that will not leave us, but prevents us everywhere'

has never seemed more appropriate. Current social science theories consider any form of deviance as a social or statistical problem. A small minority of people are judged to be deviant *because they are a minority*. This concept of madness or deviance is administrative and ignores the relevance of such constructs as 'personality' or 'motivation' – the person as such does not exist. Yet we have no way of being absolutely certain that the deviant is not sane, and society mad. Laing quotes an experiment in which a patient who said he was Napoleon was given a lie detector test. When he answered that he was not Napoleon, the machine registered a lie. To 'condition' this patient to what is euphemistically called 'social therapy' would be to subject him to patently destructive tensions. A sensible approach to the problem of deviance must stem from the understanding that a person is *abnormal within himself*, and no amount of recourse to consensus values can otherwise justify the label. This administrative notion of normality seems at present to be applied in design situations, beyond the examples already quoted.

Often, if unconsciously, we accept the *values* of society (or the majority of it) as a starting point. At no time do we actually treat the user as our equal, as a designer in his own right. We never, for instance, ask the user what kinds of questions he would like to answer. We always give him questions which *we* want *him* to answer. Yet this causes a spiralling conflict which can be seen in our social security offices where we produce 'thrifty' solutions. We must not be seen to be spending public money upon our second class citizenry. The impersonal quality of the environmental solution only reinforces a social stigma upon the person himself, producing a self-fulfilling social prophecy where the person reacts to the staff *as a second class citizen*. Little wonder, then, that the Ministry of Social Security had to work 2,000,000 hours in overtime in 1967, caused by an acute staff recruitment problem. Yet the money spent in overtime would go far towards a complete solution to the problem were it spent instead upon the physical environment of Ministry of Social Security establishments.

We see only our capacity to give society the forms it wants, and reject our ability to actually create a new social order through physical organization. This results in what Laing has called 'ontological insecurity' – an overdependence upon others for one's own existence, an almost pathological tendency to be dependent upon others for one's sense of one's self.

In my own experience of designing for prisoners, for instance, I have found that a tendency to objectify or classify 'the prisoner' (that is, to treat him as an object in a class of objects called 'prisoners'), actually makes him into an object in solution. The grouping temporarily assumed for analysis is actualized, and the inmate sub-culture becomes more cohesive, because each prisoner is forced to greater dependency upon it. He can only find any concept of 'self' in the company of his fellow prisoners. This sets up a very much 'us and them' situation with the staff which is not only unhealthy but financially stupid. I think we would be surprised if we knew how many prisoners would refuse to leave were we to throw open all the prison gates. Yet the Home Office expenditure on prison care per annum runs into many millions of pounds – not surprisingly when I recall one prisoner in a joinery vocational training course whom I saw having to smash a chair he had just made because there was no space to store it.

A similar situation exists in the choice of a site for our public facilities. We find that prisons, blind workshops, general hospitals and mental hospitals are allocated to the cheapest land available. This is usually on the peripheral areas of a conurbation, or in the open country. Hence we are left with the mental hospital situation in London, where almost all establishments are far removed from the boroughs they serve. The inmates can never be visited because of inadequate transport facilities, they become estranged from their 'normal' contacts, and become institutionalized on the basis of a financially expedient

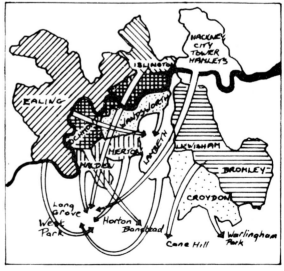

Map of London showing location of mental institutions relative to the areas they serve. The choice of cheap land makes visiting almost impossible.

planning decision, which in any case costs more in the long term. Indeed, this schism results from a dualistic approach at present applied to design problems. The city is seen either as a group of people, or as a class of physical objects, either of which can be spatially manipulated. The difference is that in the first case the people are seen as subject and the physical fabric as object, whilst in the second case the converse is true. The location of a factory is seen either as the problem of locating a facility where people can work, or alternatively as a facility, incorporating localized production factors (labour supply).

User participation

Much has recently been said about solving this problem by 'User Participation' in the design solution. This participation can be of two kinds:

(1) *Participation before the design solution is reached.*

(2) *Physical participation after it has been built.*

It is hoped that by using these two forms of participation, the person is helped to express his freedom, to recognize his independence. I would like to talk about the second kind of participation.

We find that there is a growing awareness of the need for 'open-ended' design solutions. We are increasingly advised to 'leave more' for the user to do, but even where choice for the user is provided, it is often not accepted nor even recognized. This is not surprising because before a person can perceive the environment's capacity for change he has first to conceive his capacity to change it and this requires a sense of self (which can only be acquired by active participation with the environment), which is completely negated by our insistence upon seeing the human being as a social organism. *It is self-evident that any open-ended design must therefore stem from a concept of misfit which is as specific as any concept of fit proposed by Alexander. It is not enough simply to produce large, open, flexible, spaces, because one has first to be able to produce enough stress in the person to overcome his basic inertia.* Yet any attempt to define the limit of acceptable environmental stress finds itself inexorably entrenched in a further search into the meaning and substance of the stressing phenomenon for the person himself – and this is unique to him. We need to question not only his behaviour, but the meaning of the motivation behind it for him, for as we found earlier he cannot be seen simultaneously as the sum of diverse behaviours, and as a person.

Motivation

Two basic kinds of motivation are recognized in psychology:

(1) Motivation to achieve success.
(2) Motivation to avoid failure.

and both of these have been found to be connected with a third concept – the person's past experience of conflict.[2] The Gestaltists Lewin, Rosenweig and Amsel and Hancock have all conducted revealing experiments in this field. They have found that a constant series of conflict experiences actually increases the probability that future experiences will be conflicting: the 'frustration threshold' of the person is reduced. On the other hand Atkinson and Litwin have discovered that when a person never experiences conflict situations, his motivation to achieve success begins to outweigh his motivation to avoid failure. In simple terms this means that he becomes more adventurous, curious and willing to put himself in testing situations, from which he can begin to develop a more cogent concept of 'self'. In contrast, the frequently conflicted person 'plays safe'. Heckhausen's experiments with children indicate that those who have a backlog of many conflict experiences in problem-solving situations choose problems which are either very easy (which they have done several times before) or too difficult. Either way, their 'self' is never in danger of negation. They risk nothing. He also found that non-conflicted children choose 'middling' ranges of difficulty which will 'stretch' their capabilities, but from which they can develop a satisfactory notion of 'self', which further leads to increasingly wise choice.

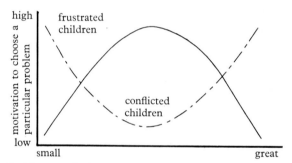

Problem complexity
(Perceived difference between known and unknown factors)

If we wish to help the person to develop some notion of himself as a unique individual, creative in his every act, then quite literally it becomes a question of ensuring that (a) we do not objectify him, and (b) he never experiences conflict. Yet this is immeasurably difficult, since he himself is the source of his experiences and hence of his conflicts, for it is not the *abstract* but the *perceived* complexity of a situation

[2] Conflict is here used in its special psychological sense, and then as a subdivision of this definition. If a person is blocked in a drive towards a goal, he experiences frustration, which increases and fragments his drive. He becomes more determined. However, if this blocking is continued, he begins to adopt a reticence towards the goal which is manifest in avoidance. Conflict refers to the experience beyond this point, where ongoing and avoidant attitudes towards the goal co-exist within the person simultaneously. This leads to aggression, regression and other non-goal-directed side effects. The point at which frustration becomes conflict is called the frustration threshold, which can be altered according to past experiences. It is the point at which stress becomes distress.

which lies at the root of his motivation. It is the *psychic* distance between known and unknown levels of complexity which counts. Festinger, for instance, has shown that a chosen goal becomes more attractive in the event of failure whilst an enforced goal becomes less attractive. We are thus involved in a spiral in which not only can the person's motivation affect his choice, but can itself be affected, given choice.

Yet choice is the very thing that we eliminate by using such linear analysis techniques as those described. In their use we implicitly discourage individuation and encourage the development of group-identification – the subculture phenomenon. An example will make this clear. In Neville Longbone's study, an experiment was uncovered which was concerned with the mobility and orientation of blind people. Cratty and Williams conducted a series of experiments with blindfolded sighted people, to determine their amount of 'veer' in trying to walk a straight line. Taking a very broad classification, a wide range of differences was found between trained and untrained subjects.

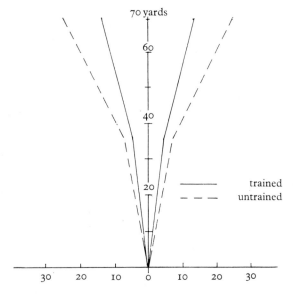

Some (trained) people veered as little as two or three yards over a distance of 20 yards, whilst other (untrained) people often veered as much as five or six yards. Taking this information from a design viewpoint, the implications are fairly obvious. We can say, for instance, that (assuming blind people have similar deviations) physical objects must be placed closer together for 'untrained' than for 'trained' blind people, otherwise they will become disoriented and lost. Conversely if the physical objects in the environment are too close together for 'trained' blind people their 'superior' faculties for self-orientation will atrophy. Either way, in a uniformly complex environment which caters for both classes dependency is increased. The 'untrained' come to rely upon the 'trained' to get around, whilst the 'trained' begin to rely upon the 'untrained' in an attempt to identify themselves in an unsatisfying situation. The subculture becomes very strong, at the expense of the individuality of its members.

What happens, in practice, is that these situations become stagnant and incestuous.

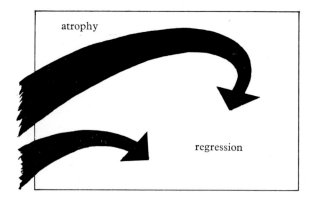

My experience of prisons, blind workshops, mental hospitals, and old people's homes seems to indicate that this stagnation is the dominant problem in all 'closed' environmental complexes. The blind workshops and prisons in this country are slowly becoming filled with a *residual* population who have no notion of their own value as human beings, but can only find solace in an alienating 'us and them' relationship with the staff.

One example comes to mind immediately. I was being guided, with a group of students, through a mental hospital by a senior male nurse. One of the (MSN) patients, with a horribly disfigured head, and an almost inhuman voice, called inarticulately to him as we passed, and asked a series of questions about a previous promise that the nurse had made but not kept. Turning to the group, he withdrew the bedcovers, and, completely ignoring the patient, waggled his lifeless transparent legs, saying 'He's quite content you know – no intelligence or feeling whatever! Have you Joe?' despite the preceding conversation. He never even asked permission, because a moronic vegetable would be incapable of refusing!

This is the present normality to which we have no answer, and are unlikely to find one using our present techniques.

174

Solutions

I would like to make it plain that I do not have any 'cut and dried' solution to this problem. Accepting the need for new techniques, it is clear that they must hinge around the individual, and not the group, since what is a conflict for me may not be for you, and what is a conflict for me today may not be tomorrow.

Further, the existence of conflict must, as stated, be seen in terms of situational meaning for the person himself. As yet, we have no language for helping the user to communicate his meaning to the designer. An 'objective' analysis of a conflict situation with all its contingent regressive and aggressive behaviours can still only be interpreted on the basis of an abstraction. We have no indication, for instance, of the *qualities* of a situation which have attractive and repulsive meaning for the person. One can only surmise, that a blind person trying to be orientationally independent has at least two tendencies towards the environmental situation within which he finds himself:

(a) He is trying to move about
(b) He is trying to avoid reliance upon a colleague

If these are his aims, it will be readily apparent that for different individuals only different kinds of geometry will allow their resolution. In certain (changing) situations the aims will be brought to a state of mutual incompatibility. Yet watching a blind person in such a conflict situation would never reveal the dynamic structure of his intentions. His relationship to the environment is ambivalent in that any relationship inherently contains positive and negative attributes. It

Note: The introduction of the 'long cane' into mobility training courses goes some way towards helping the blind person to become independent.

is impossible to decide whether an action is predominantly avoidant or attractive since it could be either, or even both. It may even be that the blind person himself has aims which are totally different to those which I have allocated him on an 'objective' observation.

Meaning can only be sketchily derived from this situation by encouraging the person himself to explicitly describe his feelings. Yet even when this is done, we cannot trace the meaning of his communication *without including ourselves* in the experiment too. We need to know not only what he feels about the situation, but also

(a) What we feel about it
(b) What we think he feels about it
(c) What we think he thinks we feel about it
(d) What he feels about it
(e) What he thinks we feel about it
(f) What he thinks we think he feels about it, and so on

We may find, for instance, that the blind person believes that we think he has the attitudes described, whilst in reality we may believe that he thinks our interpretation of his situation is quite different. This kind of discrepancy will undoubtedly affect his behaviour and unless we understand the communication structure there is every possibility that his *real* intentions will remain hidden.

Often, very valuable sources of information about how the person perceives his environment are ignored by the designer. Newspaper clippings, prohibition notices, and symbolic references in his existing environment are all important expressions of user motivation and perception, and can all be very explicit.

175

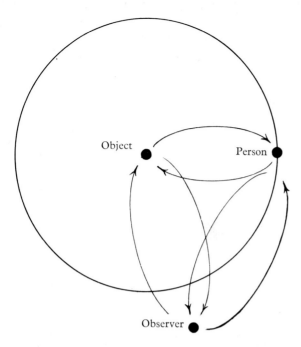

Object

Person

Observer

Disillusioned

We ignore them all. Yet even if we know how to use them, we are still left with the fundamental choice-motivation dilemma which determines physical participation. I have no solution for this problem save the very direct contact between the designer and the user which I try to encourage in my own studies. Yet this is not a very easy thing to develop. We assume that emotional contact will in some way warp our objectivity and confuse our research reasoning. Yet it *can* be used to actually help one's reasoning. (Lipman actually found himself cleaning kitchen tables in his old person's home.) To involve oneself on an emotional

plane, to 'zone into' major problems in this way is the most rewarding guide I know to the other person's perceptions. As Carl Rogers says, 'I have found that my total organsinic sensing is more trustworthy than my intellect'. But all this is of no consequence without some medium for structuring ones findings, whilst maintaining the individuality necessary. This problem is so extensive that I will limit myself to a discussion of my experiences of very small extreme situations.

We find, for instance, that five different people in the same overall complex experience difficulty with different ranges of forms. Some forms may be common to all users, some may be common to only a small proportion and some may be unique to everybody. The problem is thus to produce a fit/misfit solution for each person with a minimum of deviation from this (changing) pattern. This can only be done by combining the person's own capacity to modify his environment with the designer's capacity to indicate a point of origin, a basic framework which will prompt the person to action.

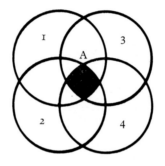 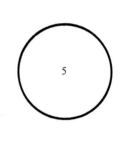

Any solution must be dynamic (by definition), and must be developed equally by the person himself. We can say, for instance, that there is some consistency in the 'kinds' of form causing trouble to one particular person, but these 'kinds' of forms will change as he progresses or regresses. His own choices are indicative of his experiences, and hence, can be exhaustively incorporated into a dynamic library of data derived from comparative studies.

In our own studies, the outcome has been a range of different complexes ranging from easy (helpful) at one end to difficult (unhelpful) at the other. Sometimes these have been small and relatively self-contained (workplace), whilst often they have been large (workshop), depending upon the degree of congruence of the perspectives of the people involved.

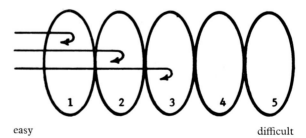

easy   difficult

There may be varying 'zones' of identification for the person, which determine his own personal range of

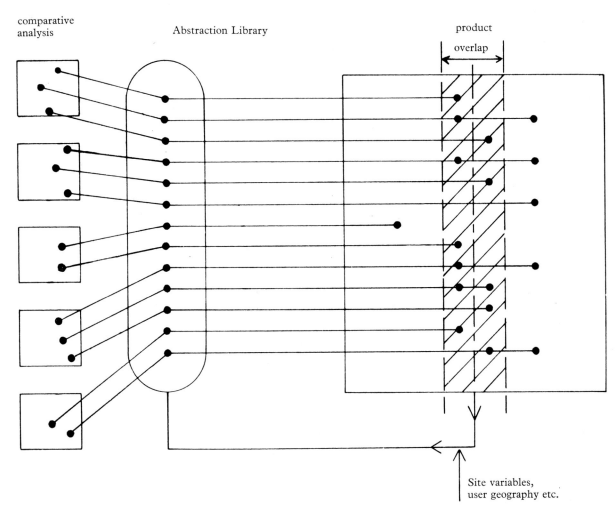

comparative analysis Abstraction Library product

overlap

Site variables,
user geography etc.

valuable experiences. One person may want to be completely self-contained, another may wish to work and live communally. Indeed, these 'zones' themselves will change and overlap. So that the person who was last year afraid to venture further than the end of his workbench unaccompanied may this year tour the factory alone.

For this reason, it is never possible to produce abrupt delineation between elements as shown above, nor is it desirable. The essence of a good solution is that it should form a continuum, since any abrupt change in complexity (1:2, 2:3 and so on) creates an insurmountable barrier for the user's choice. Areas of overlap are therefore used to bridge this obstacle. They are usually made up of both familiar and unfamiliar formal patterns in much the same way that Dembar and Earl conceptualize their 'pacer'.[3]

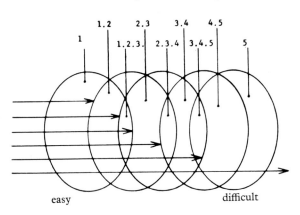

In this way, the working area of the individual is always extending his capacity to a point which is uncritical. He begins to monitor his own development, and to develop a capacity to modify his own environment. *In a successful solution it is therefore possible for the person to progress from a state of complete dependency to a state of being totally independent.* In prisons and blind workshops, for instance, he would eventually emerge into the 'open environment' with complete self-confidence, never to return. At the moment the vast majority of prison cells in this country are occupied by recidivists – people who have a lifetime of petty convictions behind them. They are totally unable to maintain an autonomous existence in society, and the present physical systems used in prison reforms only increase the problem.

Of course this whole thesis implies a continuing relationship between the designer and the users after the form has achieved concrete reality. This is hardly ever done at the moment. The architect is usually all too ready to disappear with his glossy photographs of the unoccupied solution. Certainly, such continuation is not encouraged by the present fee structure, any more than the initial research. Yet the cumulative development of data now evolving through development and research organizations only leads, as I said earlier, to the creation of the problem it tries to solve.

[3] I am indebted to Amos Rapoport for bringing this concept to my notice.

Three plates showing blind people achieving individual mobility in a physical context.

Indeed, this problem is accentuated in the present situation, where research within a context of actual buildings, rather than experimental laboratories, is not called research, but 'development'. Design is a problem of assisting individuation and the designer can only be successful when he becomes superfluous. Present facilities prevent this kind of success. We desperately need a (phenomenological) method perhaps of a similar kind to the one which Laing has found necessary to create in the field of psychiatry, for we are basically concerned about the same problem.

Conclusions

To return to the title of this paper, I have tried to show how 'rightness' and 'wrongness' in the physical environment are very personal issues. I hope that it will be clear that any analysis techniques which originate in the context of 'absolute', 'atomistic' or 'deterministic' notions lead to difficulty and dishonesty for the designer and alienation for the user. This alienation is of prime concern in a situation where National Housing Standards, like Parker Morris, are seen as limits rather than baselines, where Building Societies will not lend money on unconventional house forms, where building regulations inhibit experimentation, where planning regulations limit the choice of site, where rate assessments discourage improvement, where tenants' associations even dictate the colour of doors and curtains, where pre-finished industrialized building components limit the range of internal finishes, and where the large furnishing monopolies have reduced the choice of furniture to that of 'the best buy', where only the wrapping is different but the soap-flakes are the same.

In my own work I have tried to make people independent, but this is operationally difficult, because as yet we have no phenomenological method which we can apply to design problems. We need to develop ways of including the user into the total process in an active role. Unless we do this, we can expect only an increasing feeling of impotence to result, from the present use of insensitively averaging models. I was recently very much impressed by the insight of a 12 year old girl in a magazine survey of childrens attitudes:

'I'm told that I'm a member of the younger generation, that ours is the task to put the world right and to sort out the mistakes that you have made. How can you expect me to do this if you try and make me like yourself?'

I believe that John Stuart Mill was right when he said that 'a state which dwarfs its men, in order that they may be more docile instruments in its hands, even for beneficial purposes, will find that with small men no great thing can really be accomplished.'

The physical organization of sheltered workshops for the blind

by Neville Longbone

The nature of the subject: Introduction

This paper is based upon 'The Physical Organization of Sheltered Workshops for the Blind', a study undertaken by the author and a fellow student – Stephen Mendes – as a final thesis subject, at Kingston School of Architecture, in the spring and summer of 1967. It is a case history about the procedure and problems of a Relational Analysis.

The subject of 'Workshops for the Blind' was one about which there existed little knowledge. The subject of actual 'Blindness' has been well documented, yet little information was available as to how blind people operate within an environment and how it can and does affect them. Even less was known about the effects and problems in a blind workshop. We ourselves knew nothing about the problem and in this respect we hoped to extend our personal knowledge and our experience of people in general through the medium of the blind.

One of our immediate realizations lay in the fact that we had no preconceptions whatsoever as to what a blind workshop should consist of. This realization naturally altered our concept of the way in which we attacked the problem and resulted in our using a Relational Analysis Mechanism.[1]

[1] See paper *The evolution of environmental structures.* BARRY POYNER; *The atoms of environmental structure.* ALEXANDER and POYNER, (MPBW), 1967; Also paper *Rightness and wrongness in the physical environment* by ANTHONY WARD.

In view of the time factor involved, much of the information produced in the study was in no way to be considered as being final. The data have subsequently been found useful where none before existed in such a form. Each Relation could be regarded in its own right as an area for further research; a hypothesis which would hold good, only until such time that it was proven otherwise. I am now undertaking further research in order to test our hypotheses.

As I indicated earlier, there is a vast body of knowledge on the subject of 'Blindness', but for the greater part this knowledge was not consistent with, nor was it related to, the exact requirements of blind people and how they operate within or are affected by the environment.

One needs to be able to answer some very basic questions. What is it that blind people really need and are these needs symptomatic of the environment that they operate within or are they more basic? How do blind people attempt to acquire what it is they need? In a way the blind are a privileged class among those with physical disabilities and *are* well 'provided for', yet is this consistent with what they need? What are the physical arrangements that deter or stop the blind from acquiring their own predetermined goals? Is their goal-orientation conditioned by their environment? What constitutes 'architectural barriers' for the blind, are they architect designed or are they self-made?

These are some of the questions that we were faced with at the beginning of the study and to which we hoped we might provide some answers. Though they are not central to the theme of this paper, I hope that what I will say will show their relevance to the way in which the study was conducted and some of the results achieved.

We were faced with finding out what, if anything, was wrong with the existing arrangements provided for blind people before we could deal with them effectively.

The final question that evolved from our initial thinking on the subject was, 'Is the problem a purely physical problem anyway?'.

Where to begin

At the inception of the study, because we knew so little, we decided to find out what other people thought the problem was. This meant hours of listening to others, comparing what was said, advocating, in some cases, what we knew to be an opposite point of view in order to obtain the maximum reaction. This would, we hoped, lead us into asking and looking for more meaningful information.

Basically the attitudes of other people to the problem of workshops fell into three broad categories, *viz:*

(i) Those who thought that little was required in the form of radical change in the environmental conditions prevailing in workshops. That the real problem was one of inefficiency organizationally and economically.[2]

(ii) Those that acknowledged a physical problem yet could not realize its nature or its solution.

(iii) Finally the attitude of the blind themselves, one of frustration, in knowing the problem yet being unable to effect or communicate a solution.

To continue our study on the basis of any of these attitudes would, we felt, be to start from a false assumption and result in a value judgement, with little prior knowledge, of their relative appropriateness. As a consequence of this diversity we had to attempt to assimilate the information upon which these views were constructed. We had to start by investigating the current fields of knowledge relative to blind people before we could propose a structure to the problem. The essential basis for any problem structure is the development of cumulative data, which can only be achieved by a Hypothesis and Test method.

Expansion and relational work

From the original problem of the requirements of a workshop for the blind, we now had to look at the whole field, concepts and attitudes towards the blind. This involved a shift in emphasis from an apparently small isolated problem to one which questioned the whole structure of provisions for the blind, within which the validity of the workshop's role was seriously in doubt. The basis of our doubt lay in the recognition that there were some blind people apparently well adapted to open employment, while others who seemed equally capable remained in sheltered employment. This seemed strange.

The expansion of the problem to this level of thinking is, it appears, a characteristic of a Relational study. Of the other studies that have been carried out on an apparently well-defined problem type, namely the Prison Workshop discussed by Tony Ward,[3] it was necessary to investigate the whole range and field of treatment and care of users and their problems prior to any reorganization of the environment. In practice it is rarely possible to expand the problem to this level, in part because of the inadequacy of present briefing techniques. In some respects the brief limits the scope for further research by the designer, and is not really conducive to change.

The process begins

As far as our program of work was concerned, we attempted to develop field and background researches simultaneously (see Fig.1).

We started out by analysing the systems of training, education, and treatment that are afforded to both the congenitally and the adventitiously blind. It was necessary to identify the stages that these people

[2] See *Report of the Working Party on Workshops for the Blind*, Ministry of Labour. H.M.S.O. 1962.

[3] ANTHONY WARD, *The Organization of Prison Workshops*, a Report for the Penal Establishments Group (MPBW), 1967.

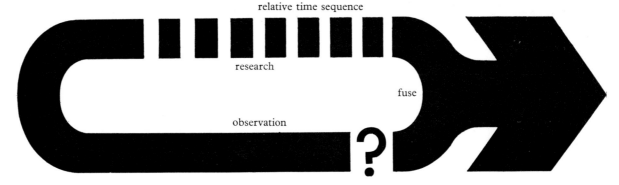

relative time sequence

research

observation

fuse

?

Fig.1

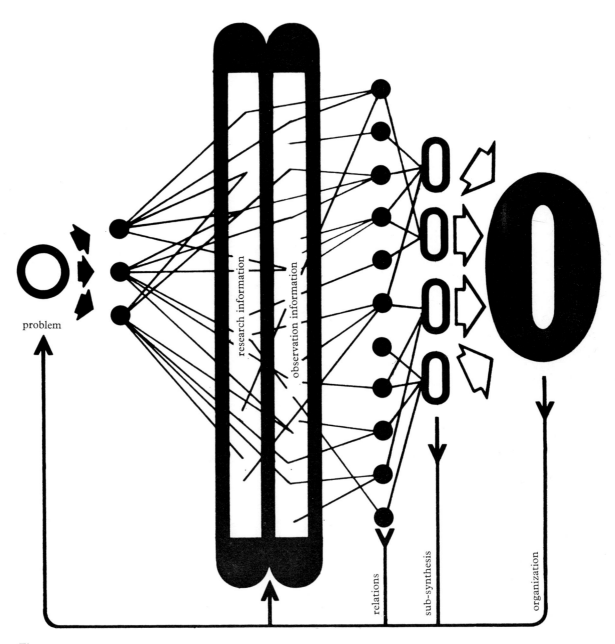

problem

research information

observation information

relations

sub-synthesis

organization

Fig.2

Note: The overall development of the project was *actually* a 'to-ing' and 'fro-ing' between abstract research and direct observation. The attempted *fusion* of relations resulted in further development of relations, both qualitively and quantitively.

went through at various times of their life and how these affected them. Did this treatment appear to work well and how deeply was it affected by the environment?

Trying to find out about blind people's 'perception' was an important factor of the study, for it is through their perception that they understand their environment. It was therefore necessary for us to try to understand the type of information that they picked up from the environment, how it was picked up, and interpreted. Already we had noted that the blind have a greater dependence upon their environment, which can be seen through their behaviour as a result of perceptual needs. Purely because the incoming sensory data are limited, this in turn limits the patterns of behavioural activity and shows the types of physical forms and physical stimulation that the blind use in different environmental situations.

One very interesting piece of research which we came across during our investigations that has direct relevance to what I have just outlined was the work done by Cratty and Williams on the 'Perceptual Thresholds of Non-Visual Locomotion'.[4] This paper laid down some limits of physical forms beyond which the blind would not readily be able to differentiate between geometric properties, i.e. radii of curves, angles of slope, etc. (see Figs.2 and 3). Such information can be of direct use to the designer because of the conclusion drawn between geometric properties and human behaviours, which makes it possible to predict the consequences of design actions with greater accuracy. Also, the degree of abstraction of the data renders it 'information rich' from a design point of view.

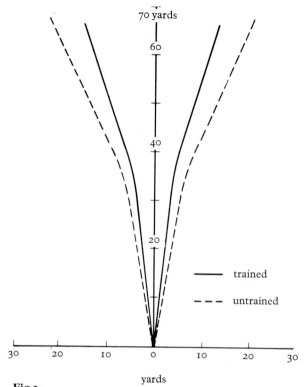

Fig.3
Comparison of the mean veer of 'trained' (experimental) subjects and untrained subjects (control).

In order partially to compensate for their lack of sight, the blind make use of a heightened auditory perception through a process of echolocation. Unfortunately this method has its drawbacks. Firstly, the human ear is limited in its detection of two closely timed sounds. Secondly, it only suffices for the purpose of *ascertaining* the existence of an object without, however, imparting further information as to its shape.[5]

From the work that we did, it would appear that for most activities the blind person organizes his sensory perceptions within a spatial framework of auditory-tactile interactions.

This obviously has implications on the types of form that one can produce for use in building-design for the blind. As an example, simplicity of shape allows for ease of identification and simple sound reflections.

After perception we became involved, to some extent, in studying how the blind man fits into society and some of the difficulties that he encounters. One of his main problems probably stems from his social learning. Some people learn very little as a result of leading an isolated or an over-protected life when young. Over-protection or isolation can probably cause wrong or inadequate social responses for the blind person. His relations with sighted people may produce reciprocal misunderstandings. This in turn

[4] CRATTY and WILLIAMS, *Perceptual Thresholds of Non-Visual Locomotion*, University of California, (1966).
[5] D. R. GRIFFIN, *Listening in the Dark*.

may lead the blind person to seek out social situations in which his behaviour is considered 'normal', i.e. with other blind people. This inevitably restricts his range of interactions, thus furthering the growth of a 'sub-culture'.[6, 7]

In a way this type of thinking is perpetuated, perhaps unwittingly, by the authorities who deal with blind people. It has always been an agreed aim that the blind should be integrated into society, but how is this to be achieved? The integration of the handicapped invididual implies his assimilation by the community at large. Workshops employing blind people along with those who have a different type of handicap are frequently designated 'integrated' on the strength of the argument that in such a workshop the blind are integrated with workers who are not blind and thus avoid the conditions commonly attributed to segregation. But we felt that this was not so. It was our experience that this kind of 'integration' created an even sharper definition of the sub-culture.

Lastly, we studied the 'mobility' of blind people. We looked at the techniques used to train blind people and the techniques used by blind people to become more mobile. Yet the more we looked, the more it became evident to us that mobility was intrinsically tied up with blind persons' knowledge and operational use of the environment. Mobility in a human being enables him to interact with his surroundings to influence his environment as well as be influenced by it. Orientation and mobility for the blind involves, as it does for the sighted, the establishment of meaningful relations with his surroundings. It means awareness of, and effective interaction with the physical, psychological, and social factors in the environment. Mobility is perhaps the most researched subject to do with blindness; all of it not of very direct use to us as designers, although some bore an implicit relationship to our hypotheses, and this was useful.[8-10]

While we were conducting our enquiries into other (abstract) research, we were also involved in a considerable amount of fieldwork. Without conducting this fieldwork, none of the other investigations that we conducted would, I feel, have had much point to them. The field work gave us the terms of refer-

ence that we needed in which to analyse the results of all the data which we had collected. It helped in the posing of hypotheses (i.e. in the construction of relations) and it also provided points for discussion about the actuality of the situation to which we could apply the findings or deductions of other research.

Above all it indicated what was going wrong in blind workshops and the types of problem that face the blind workers.

Observation

The basic component of a Relational Study is that of the 'observation' of people and their behaviour in a specific situation or context. Observation depends entirely upon the *inference* based upon experience, and it is often difficult to develop an appropriate level of observation to a required level of inference. For instance, as a general rule, it is dangerous to infer motive forces of a social level from observations of individual behaviours. In spite of all the work done to integrate blind people into society, they still tend to form themselves into 'sub-cultures'. Each sub-culture has its own laws and own ways of operating. These are defined by unique behaviour patterns which are manifest in greater dependence upon interaction with the environment. This dependence upon physical form and the stimulation that it offers increases as soon as any activity is initiated.

[6] M. ARGYLE, *Psychology of Interpersonal Behaviour*.
[7] J. KLEIN, *The Study of Groups*.
[8] *Proceedings of the Mobility Research Conference*, (1961).
[9] *Proceedings of the Rotterdam Mobility Research Conference*, (1961).
[10] The work of Dr Leonard, of Nottingham University, on Mobility and the many papers that he has produced.

The exaggeration of this interdependence upon the environment makes the observation of behaviour much simpler and the derivation of patterns easier.

Having inferred the nature of the behaviour being manifest and having *related this to the environment in which it was taking place* it was possible to determine which forms were conducive to which behaviours and which were not. This then became our aim, 'That we would look for and observe arrangements of physical environment that were causing conflicting stresses within the blind and preventing them from achieving their self-determined goals'.

Although I said that literal investigation was being attempted at the same time as the fieldwork studies, the two did not keep pace and the former lagged behind the latter. Not only did this happen, but it became increasingly more difficult to do the necessary field work. We did not know what to look for,

or to be more precise what we were looking at did not hold any significance for us at this point in time. We were not at all proficient about making observations nor did we sufficiently understand the behaviour that we were looking at. The crudity of the initial relations and their scarcity led us to believe that there was much more involved and that we had as yet only scratched the surface. In a review of the information that we did have we found that a pattern was beginning to emerge yet within this pattern there were great gaps of knowledge. This again is a favourable aspect of relational work in that it highlights any inadequacy in the information.

The next stage was to fragment the studies that we were engaged upon into smaller components of a more diverse nature. This fragmentation and diversification was helped by allowing our technical researches to catch up to the same standard as our fieldwork (see Fig.1). Also evidence of a pattern or structure to the problem that we were dealing with made it possible for a constant feedback and reappraisal of the stages in our investigations. We could see that parts needed filling in or needed more detail to complete the component under consideration. It gave indications as to the areas in which it would be most useful to concentrate (see Fig.4).

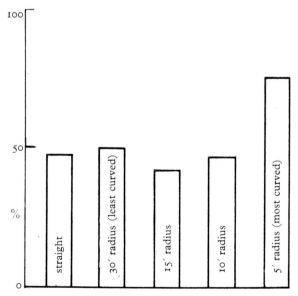

Fig.4
% of correct responses to various amounts of curvature in the curbs.

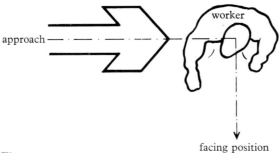

Fig.5

Workspace approach

Tendencies:
1) The blind workers seek to be aware of approaching people.
2) They try to avoid disorientation.

Conflict:
Where the blind person can be approached from more than one direction, binaural differences may make it difficult for him to be aware of their approach and thus orientate properly.

Relation:
The provision of only one approach and that to be at approx. 90° to the facing position of worker.

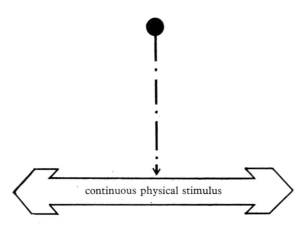

Fig.6

Location

Tendencies:
1) Blind people try to walk reasonably quickly (2–3 m.p.h.).
2) They try and avoid disorientation.

Conflict:

A large open space will cause disorientation, unless the blind take a lot of time moving through or within it.

Relation:
No point in a workshop to be more than 15′ 0″ from some physical continuous stimulus.

The more detailed we became in our fragmentation process the more we became aware of the correlations that existed between the behaviour in specific arrangements of form and the perceptual limits of the blind person. This was where the research work became important in the construction of some of the relations. We could now relate the observation of conflicts with the physical and perceptual limits of blindness and our fieldwork investigations took on

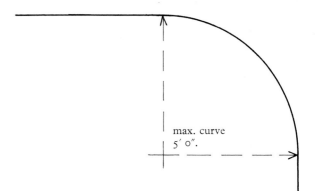

Fig.7

Curvature judgement

Tendencies:
1) Try to locate themselves easily.
2) Try to walk as quickly as possible

Conflict:
Large radius curves confuse location discrimination so that they cannot walk quickly.

Relation:
Curves to be of a radius of not greater than 5′ 0″.

a more meaningful role. We found fusions of observational and research information, and where these fusions occurred it became apparent that this was an important piece of data to record and use.

The Relations shown in Figs.5, 6, and 7 show the correlations between form and perceptual limits as outlined above.

Summary

The information we now had led to a re-definition of the role of the blind workshop. In defining this role it was also possible to define a general organizational pattern for the workshop within which arrangements of the relations would fit (see Fig.4). It now became a matter of putting all the little pieces of information together in a coherent and consistent form. This was easily accomplished because of the nature of the decomposition process that we employed (Fig.4). The relations formed fields or sub-groups which were synthesized into larger components and finally these sub-syntheses were fused into a final organization diagram (see Fig.4 and examples at end of paper).

Finally, we decided to apply the hypothetical organization to an actual site. All that we needed to know about the proposed workshop, in this case was the number of people it was intended to house, and where the site was. As far as our relations went we would not have advocated the site which we were called upon to use; still, we carried on with the exercise. For all the restrictions imposed by the site we eventually managed to apply the organizational principles to this site and to satisfy all relations without compromise (except the ones related to siting) within a very short period of time – about two days.

For the practising architect the procedure adopted in our study would be difficult to follow because of the present day-to-day running of jobs and the necessity to remain solvent. Very few could afford the six months to a year that it requires to sort out the problems from the non-problems. Probably even fewer practising architects have the opportunity of having a useful design 'brief' which illustrates the *consequences* of design decisions. They work in ignorance of the effects of their formal solutions.

Although such research information is not generally feasible in practice, it is possible, under the auspices of a research and development organization to make available *to the individual designer*, information about the *consequences* of his design decisions. Even so, it is requisite upon the architect to understand how such information has been derived so that the research data may be up-dated and extended in the light of practical application. Only within such a framework is it possible to extend the experience of the individual and to develop a cohesive programme of environmental change.

The series of diagrams which follow on pages 187–192 were produced as a *formal* brief for blind workshops. They contain altogether some 112 relations, comparable to those on page 185.
The diagrams illustrated are, in sequence:
Facing page 186: Master diagram
Page 187: Vehicular access (7 relations)
         Approach access (12 relations)
Page 188: Entry and reception (9 relations)
Page 189: Work areas (4 relations)
Page 190: Workshop (9 relations)
Page 191: Loading bay/stores (6 relations)
         Workspace (10 relations)
Page 192: Eating space (15 relations)
         Personal hygiene (12 relations)
The diagrams are *not* plans of the building solution, but 'formal' extensions of the written brief, which specify the field in which particular solutions may be found for a specific site.

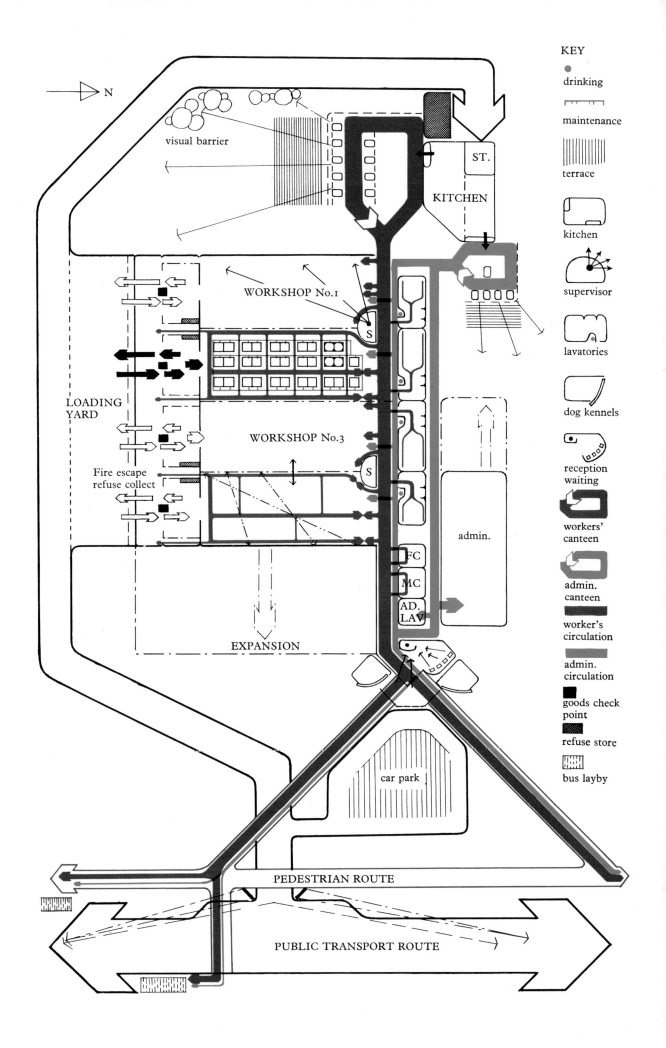

KEY

- drinking
- maintenance
- terrace
- kitchen
- supervisor
- lavatories
- dog kennels
- reception waiting
- workers' canteen
- admin. canteen
- worker's circulation
- admin. circulation
- goods check point
- refuse store
- bus layby

N

visual barrier

ST.

KITCHEN

WORKSHOP No.1

S

LOADING YARD

WORKSHOP No.3

S

Fire escape refuse collect

admin.

FC

MC

AD. LAV

EXPANSION

car park

PEDESTRIAN ROUTE

PUBLIC TRANSPORT ROUTE

Vehicular access sub-synthesis

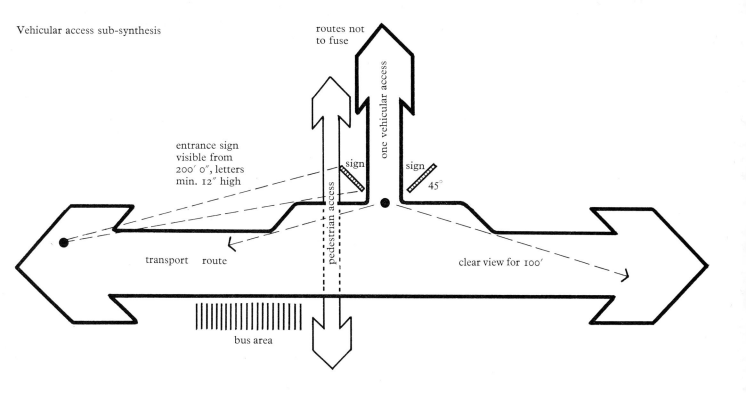

routes not
to fuse

one vehicular access

entrance sign
visible from
200′ 0″, letters
min. 12″ high

sign

sign

45°

pedestrian access

transport route

clear view for 100′

bus area

Approach/access sub-synthesis

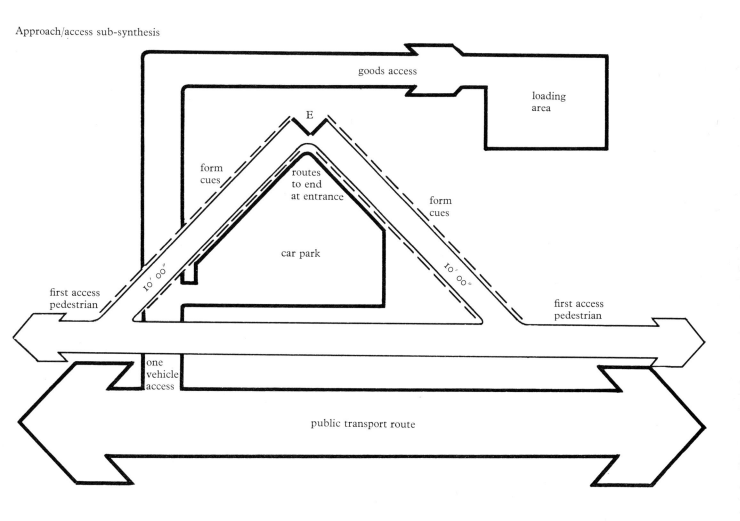

goods access

loading
area

E

form
cues

routes
to end
at entrance

form
cues

car park

10′ 00″

10′ 00″

first access
pedestrian

first access
pedestrian

one
vehicle
access

public transport route

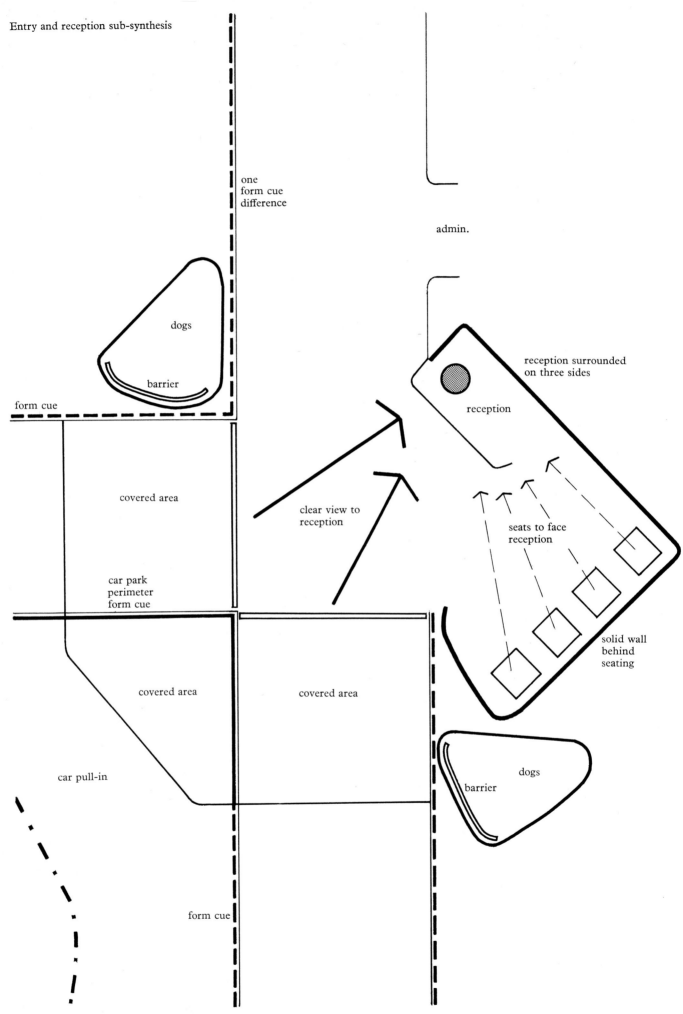

Entry and reception sub-synthesis

one
form cue
difference

admin.

form cue

dogs

barrier

covered area

car park
perimeter
form cue

covered area

car pull-in

covered area

form cue

reception surrounded
on three sides

reception

clear view to
reception

seats to face
reception

solid wall
behind
seating

dogs

barrier

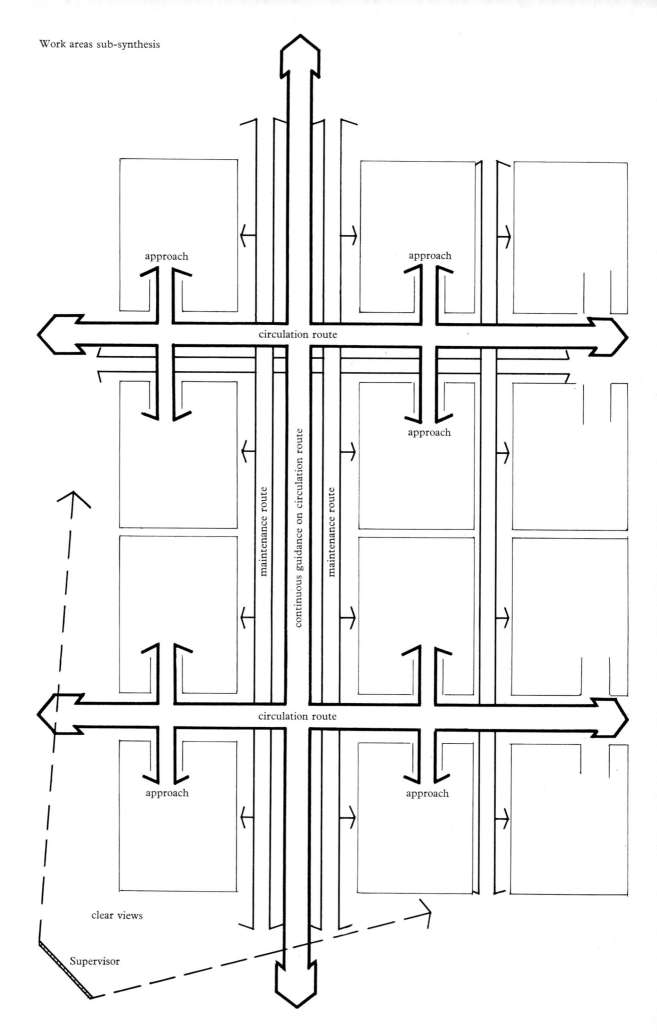

Workshop sub-synthesis

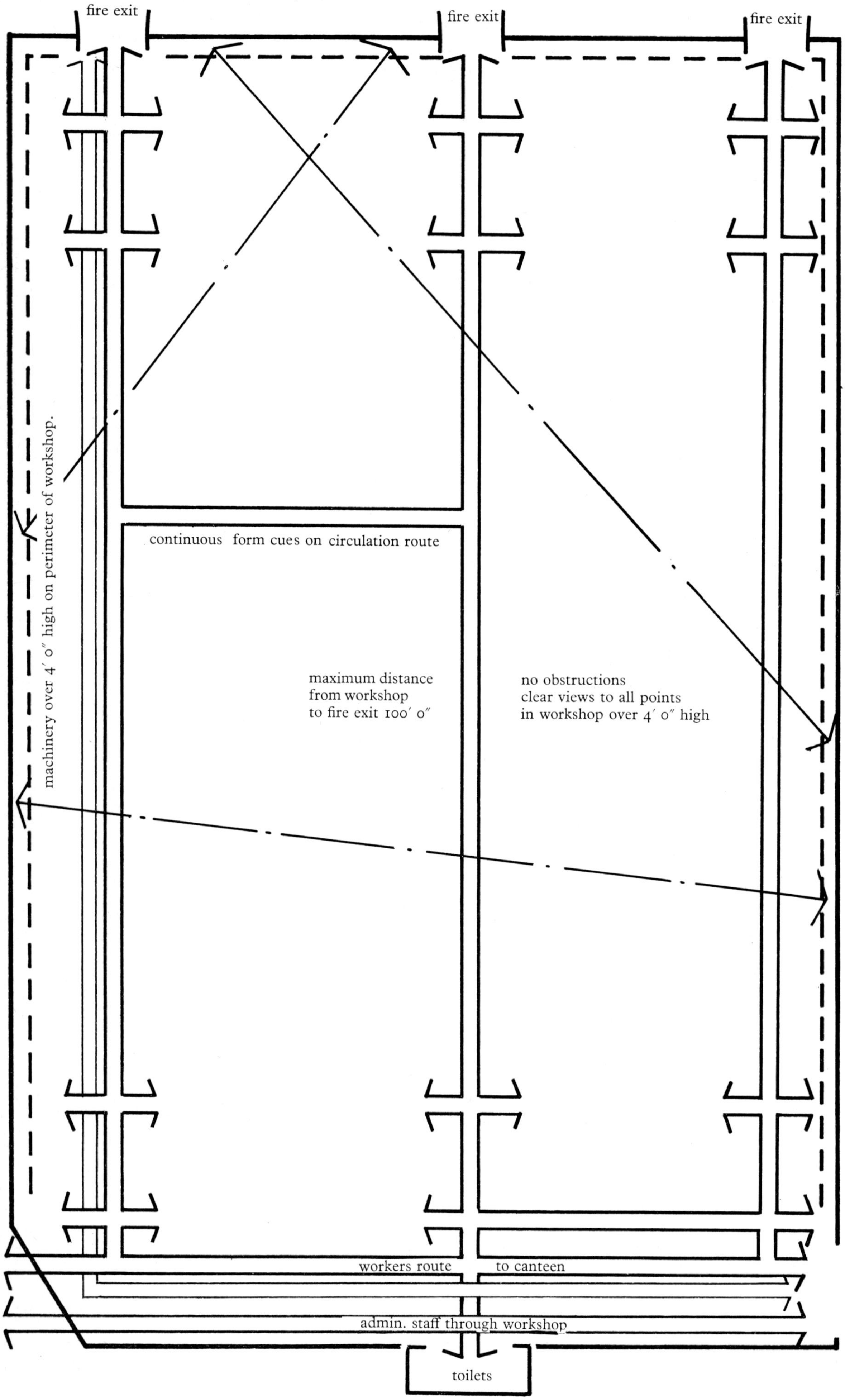

fire exit

fire exit

fire exit

machinery over 4′ 0″ high on perimeter of workshop.

continuous form cues on circulation route

maximum distance
from workshop
to fire exit 100′ 0″

no obstructions
clear views to all points
in workshop over 4′ 0″ high

workers route   to canteen

admin. staff through workshop

toilets

190

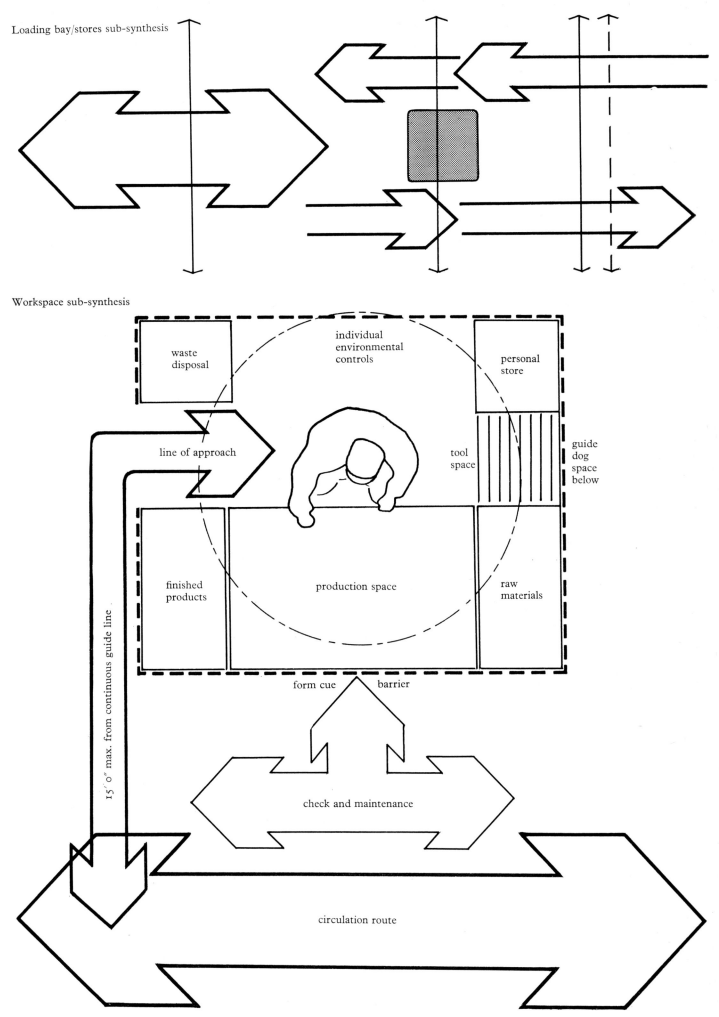

Loading bay/stores sub-synthesis

Workspace sub-synthesis

waste disposal

individual environmental controls

personal store

line of approach

tool space

guide dog space below

finished products

production space

raw materials

15´ 0˝ max. from continuous guide line

form cue   barrier

check and maintenance

circulation route

191

Eating space sub synthesis

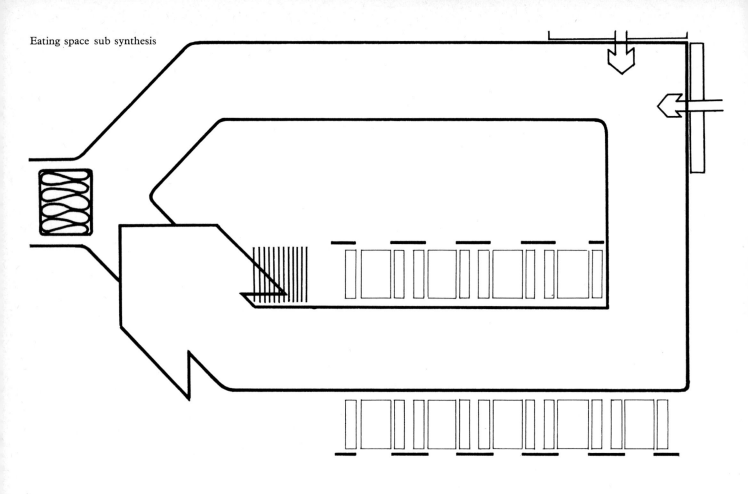

Personal hygiene sub-synthesis

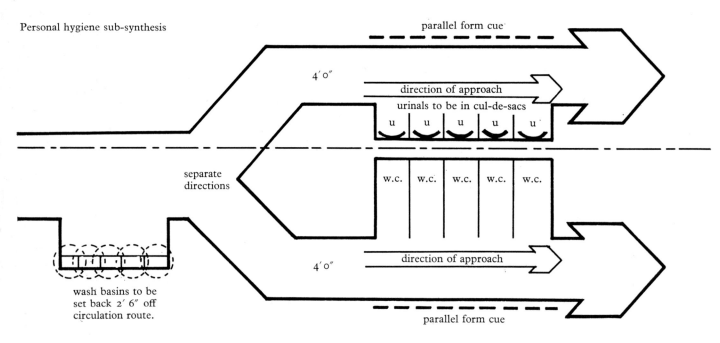

parallel form cue

4′ 0″

direction of approach

urinals to be in cul-de-sacs

u   u   u   u   u

separate
directions

w.c.   w.c.   w.c.   w.c.   w.c.

direction of approach

4′ 0″

wash basins to be
set back 2′ 6″ off
circulation route.

parallel form cue

The state-of-the-art in design methods

by J. Christopher Jones

It is not easy to see what the new methods of designing have in common with each other and with the traditional methods that they are intended to replace. The great variety of techniques, ranging from brainstorming and synectics to decision theory and systems engineering, may appear at first sight to be both contradictory and impractical. A second impression is that the apparent diversity may conceal a few new principles of designing that would be of more use to designers than are the methods themselves. Yet a third impression is that the new methods are not concerned with designing as we know it but with the thinking that *precedes* the making of drawings and designs. It is the aim of this paper to explore such doubts and questions and to provide explanations that may be helpful to students of design and to practising designers.

The first question to be answered is 'What do the new methods have in common?' The most obvious answer is that all the methods are attempts to make public the hitherto private thinking of designers; to *externalize* the design process. In some cases this is done in words, sometimes in mathematical symbols, and nearly always with a diagram representing parts of the design problem and the relationships between them. Clearly, the underlying aim is to bring designing into the open so that other people can see what is going on and contribute to it information and insights that are outside the designer's knowledge and experience.

Having seen that the common aim of the new methods is to externalize design thinking we can ask ourselves why, at this period in history, so many people have tried to achieve it. Surely the answer is that there is a world-wide dissatisfaction with traditional methods of designing. The high cost of design errors, particularly in the case of complex systems, is a strong incentive to the externalizing of design thought because only in this way can that thinking be subjected to criticism and testing before expensive mistakes are made. The sudden appearance, in many parts of the world, of methods of doing this, is, in itself, striking evidence that design problems have grown too big and too complicated to

be left to the private judgements of even the most experienced designers. The problem, recognized but not solved, is that of devising languages of design in which the complexity and speed of the designer's artistic modes of thought can be combined with scientific doubt and rational explanation.

It is doubtful if any of the design languages that have appeared so far provides an adequate answer to this great problem. Nevertheless, it is likely that these first attempts at bridging the gap between applied art and applied science contain the ingredients out of which effective languages for corporate designing will be constructed. Certainly this business of language construction is the essential step between piecemeal evolution of man-made things up to the present and the intelligent control that many people now wish to apply to the whole process of technological change. If the intelligence with which we hope to choose the future is itself to be artificial, i.e. composed of computers and computer languages, it becomes even more evident that the invention of languages for designing is an essential step towards gaining control over technological evolution.

Having looked briefly at the common aim of the very mixed set of design methods that have appeared so far, we can now discuss the differences between them and their usefulness in practice. A simple way of doing this is to review the new methods from three points of view: that of creativity, that of rationality and that of control over the design process. Each of these three views of designing can be symbolized in a cybernetic picture of the designer. From the creative viewpoint the designer is a *black box* out of which comes the mysterious creative leap; from the rational viewpoint the designer is a *glass box* inside which can be discerned a completely explicable rational process; from the control viewpoint the designer is a *self-organizing system* capable of finding short cuts across unknown territory. This last, and least familiar, viewpoint is the one that leads us back most directly to the practical value of design theory and towards the next step in the evolution of usable design methods.

Designers as black boxes

An important minority of design theorists, notably Osborn, Gordon, Matchett and Broadbent, imply that the most valuable part of the design process is that which goes on inside the designer's head and partly out of reach of his conscious control. In making this point the 'creativity' theorists place themselves in opposition to the rationalists of designing and find that many practising designers agree with them. Despite its 'irrational' assumption, the black box view of designing can be quite clearly expressed in cybernetics or physiological terms: we can say that the human designer, like other animals, is capable of producing outputs in which he has confidence, and which often succeed, without his being able to say how these outputs were obtained. Expressed in this way we can see that the mysteries of creativity are only a special case of the equally mysterious way in which we produce *most* of our outputs, or actions, without being able to explain them. The apparently simple action of writing, and the even simpler action of reaching for a pencil, are just as inexplicable as is the composing of a symphony, perhaps more so. (Nobody has yet programmed a computer to produce outputs that are anywhere near as complex as is bodily movement but we seem to be in sight of composing symphonies automatically.) Most human actions can be explained only if one assumes that they are largely governed by the skilled nervous system without the intervention of conscious thought. The creative view of designing, the view of designer as magician, is a poetic description of that which underlies the action of every human or other animal that has a nervous system (Fig.1).

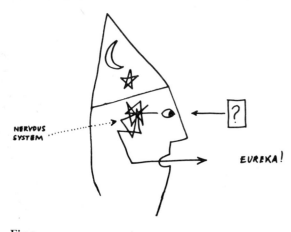

Fig.1
Designer as a magician

It is therefore *rational* to believe that skilled actions are unconsciously controlled and *irrational* to expect designing to be wholly capable of a rational explanation.

Newman (1966) is one of many researchers who have attempted to explain how the nervous system produces its enormously variable output. He suggests that the brain is a variable network that continuously changes its pattern according to the inputs it receives from the outside world. According to this theory, for which there is little physiological evidence, the 'leap of insight', which many creative people report, is the result of the network suddenly adopting, after many fruitless attempts, a pattern that is compatible with the inputs that it has recently received. Experimental studies of memory (Bartlett, 1961), suggest that past experiences are re-patterned every time one tries to remember them. These two findings together lead to the picture of the brain as a semi-automatic device that is capable of resolving incompatibilities between inputs (i.e. solving problems) by assuming a pattern that is compatible not only with the current inputs but also with many previous inputs of which the memory is composed. If we are to believe the clinical psychologists, this can be both hindered and helped by the persistence of unresolved conflicts from as long ago as early childhood. Certainly there is no doubt that the output from the brain is conditioned not only by the current situation but also by situations encountered in the past. This is, of course, a long-winded way of stating the obvious practical fact that nobody can be a good designer without the right experience.

The main conclusions that we can draw about black box design methods are as follows:
1. The output of a designer is governed by inputs received recently from the problem and also by other inputs received from previous problems and experiences.
2. His output can be speeded up, but made more random, by the agreement to relax social inhibitions for a period.
3. His capacity to produce outputs relevant to the problem is dependent upon his being given time to assimilate and to manipulate within himself images representing the structure of the problem as a whole. During a long and seemingly fruitless search for a solution he may suddenly perceive a new way of structuring the problem so that conflicts are resolved. This pleasant experience is sometimes called the 'leap of insight'.
4. Intelligent control over the forms in which the problem structure is fed into the human black box is likely to increase the chances of obtaining outputs that are relevant to the design problem.

Designers as glass boxes

The majority of design methods are concerned with externalized thought and are therefore based on rational rather than mystical assumptions. The design process is assumed to be entirely explicable, even though practising designers may be unable to give convincing reasons for all the decisions that they take. The inventors of most of the *systematic* design methods do not question the idea that a human designer is able to operate with full knowledge of what he is doing and why he is doing it (Fig.2).

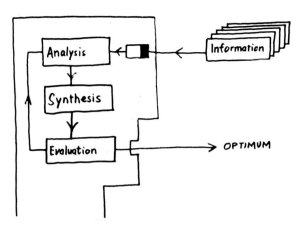

Fig.2
Designer as a computer

The picture of the rational, or systematic, designer is very much that of a human computer, a person who operates only on the information that is fed to him and who follows through a planned sequence of analytical, synthetic and evaluative steps and cycles until he recognizes the best of all possible solutions. This assumption is, of course, valid in the case of computer optimization of the variables within a familiar design situation but it also underlies such design methods as morphology, systems engineering and the decision theory approach which are intended by their inventors for the human 'computer' and for unfamiliar design problems. The common characteristics of the glass box method are as follows:

1. Objectives, variables and criteria are fixed in advance.
2. Analysis is completed, or at least attempted, before solutions are sought.
3. Evaluation is largely linguistic and logical (as opposed to experimental).
4. Strategies are fixed in advance. These are predominantly linear but often include parallel operations, conditional operations and recycling.

The results of applying these seemingly crippling limitations to human designers are not uniformly bad or uniformly good. For some kinds of design problem, glass box methods are found to work better than the black box approach, whereas in other cases they end in confusion from which the designers revert to their accustomed black box behaviour.

Splittable design problems

The crucial question in the case of glass-box methods is whether the design problem can be split up into separate pieces that can be solved in series or in parallel. If a problem *can* be split, more intelligence can be applied to the solution of each sub-problem and the design time can be drastically cut.

Big design problems are, of course, always split up at some point, in order to put many designers to work together, but the stage at which splitting can be done varies very much from one kind of product to an-

other. Chemical plant, electrical supply networks, telephone systems and the like can be split from the start into functional sub-problems each of which can be solved in parallel. This is because they are all *flow systems* in which each function is allocated to a separate physical component that is linked to the others only at predetermined inlets and outlets. There is a one-to-one relationship between functions and physical components. The whole assembly of inputs and outputs can be specified at the start and each of the components can be designed afterwards on the assumption that if it fits the inputs and outputs it fits the system. Minor departures from the original input and output specifications, and trade-offs between components, do not unduly disrupt the planned design sequence. In design situations of this sort, glass-box design methods of a rudimentary kind are essential, if project control is to be maintained, and many of the more complicated design methods would seem to have promising applications provided that the main decisions are independent of the physical details of the components.

Unsplittable design problems

Many design problems, both large and small, are difficult or impossible to split up in this way without prejudice to performance, cost, weight, appearance, or to other objectives that require many trade-offs between components. This occurs in such products as buildings, cars, machine-tools and the like in which functions are not allocated to distinct parts but spread, in a complicated and unpredictable way, over a tightly integrated assembly. The traditional answer in such cases is to give to one experienced man, the leading designer, complete responsibility for all the important decisions whether they concern the general layout or small details of component design which may be critical. A good example is the responsibility of an architect for both the layout of a building and for details of window design that may be critical to the appearance that he aims to achieve. Another example is the chief engineer's responsibility, not only for the performance of a new machine, but also for the choice of its critical components. In all such cases the responsible designer uses experience gained from similar design problems to solve the critical sub-problems before he fixes the general layout and splits the remaining work among his subordinates. This is, of course, the traditional black box method.

In problems that are very repetitive, such as the design of beams, rotors, circuits, electric motors and the like, it is sometimes possible to externalize all the designers' experience and wholly to automate designing. This is the glass-box method in its pure form. In most cases, and certainly in the ones where the risk of expensive design errors is high, this cannot be done because the necessary experience does not exist but has to be generated artificially by testing and research as part of the design process. It is in cases like this that neither glass-box methods nor black-box methods suffice and where we seem to be most in need of new design methods and design aids that combine the best of both approaches.

Designers as self-organizing systems

Both black-box and glass-box methods have the effect of widening the area of search for the solution to a design problem. In the case of black-box methods this is done by removing constraints upon the output from the designer's nervous system or by stimulating it to produce a more varied output. In the case of glass-box methods, the output of the nervous system is generalized, in external symbols, to include all the alternatives of which the designer's ideas are a special case. The main weakness of both of these approaches is that the designer generates a universe of unfamiliar alternatives that is too large to explore by the slow process of conscious thought. He cannot make an intuitive, or black box, choice (for that would re-impose the restrictions of previous experience from which he is trying to escape): neither can he use a high-speed computer to search automatically (for the computer program requires foreknowledge of objectives and criteria of choice that are themselves dependent upon the alternatives that are available). Faced with this dilemma the designer is forced (a) to abandon the new methods, or (b) to make an arbitrary or 'black box' choice of objectives for computer search, or (c) to plod away at the impossible task of consciously evaluating every alternative individually.

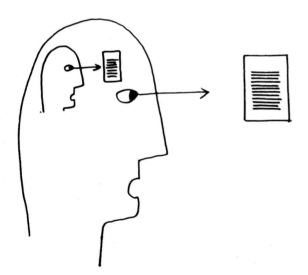

Fig.3
Designer as a self organizing system

The way out of the dilemma of having too much novelty to evaluate all at once is to divide the available design effort into two parts:
(1) that which *carries out* the search for a suitable design
(2) that which *controls* and *evaluates* the pattern of search (strategy control).

If this is done it is possible to replace blind searching of alternatives by an intelligent search that uses both external criteria, and the results of partial search, to find short cuts across the unknown territory. This procedure is possible if the portion of design effort that is reserved for strategy control provides an accurate model of two things: the strategy itself and the external situation that the design is intended to fit (Fig.3).

The purpose of this model of self-plus-situation (or strategy-plus-objective) is to enable each member of the design team to see for himself the degree to which the search actions decided upon do, or do not, produce an acceptable balance between the new design, the situations influenced by the design, and the cost of designing. This is done in two ways. Firstly, through the creation of a *meta-language* which is sufficiently general to describe relationships between a strategy and the design situation. Secondly, through the evaluation in this meta-language of a model which will predict the likely results of alternative strategies yet to be undertaken so that the most promising can be selected.

A good example of such a meta-language is provided by Matchett's Fundamental Design Method (Matchett, 1968). In this case the common language in which external objectives and proposed strategies can be described is a tree of primary, secondary, and tertiary objectives coupled with general purpose checklists describing such things as the product life cycle that are common to all engineering designs. The model for predicting the effect of any proposed design action upon the objectives is initially the teacher's judgement and later that of the pupil, when he has learnt to use the method, i.e. when he is able to foresee the external consequences of his intentions and, as a result, to alter his strategy.

The most useful feature of a strategy control method is that it should relate the results of small pieces of search to the ultimate objectives, even if, as is likely, the objectives are in a state of flux. The essential condition for this detailed evaluation to be achieved is that the outcome of each sub-action of a design strategy can be compared with the desired consequences of the strategy as a whole. One way of doing this is to estimate the size of the penalty for wrongly guessing the outcome of a given sub-action and to compare this with the cost of carrying it out. This trick is embodied in the slogan 'The cost of not knowing must exceed the cost of finding out.' Estimating the cost of not knowing requires a model in which the sensitivity of the ultimate objectives to non-attainment of sub-objectives can be predicted, at least roughly. It can be logically proved that an organism that is capable of making such a prediction must make a model of itself and is incapable of describing how this model has been constructed (Fogel *et al.*, 1966).

It is now clear that the major weakness of all design methods, and particularly of the new methods discussed here, is the difficulty of controlling strategy in novel design situations and when many people are engaged upon a single design project. This being the case, we can see that the next step in design methodology is to evolve some reliable methods for generating and controlling the strategies of design teams.

REFERENCES

F. BARTLETT. *Remembering*. Cambridge University Press (London 1961).

L. J. FOGEL, A. J. OWENS, and M. J. WALSH. *Artificial Intelligence Through Simulated Evolution*. John Wiley and Sons (New York, London, Sydney 1966).

E. MATCHETT. Control of Thought in Creative Work. *The Chartered Mechanical Engineer* (April 1968).

A. D. NEWMAN. Patterns. *The Design Method* (edited by S. A. Gregory). Butterworth (London 1966).

Notes on design method

by Geoffrey Broadbent

Reply to a question at the Portsmouth Symposium on Design Methods in Architecture, 4–6 December, 1967.

Systematic design methods, so far, have tended to complexity and abstraction to such an extent that few practising architects believe that they have much validity in the 'real' situation. These notes are intended to show how design method could be applied in the office or, for that matter, in the school of architecture, so as to result, finally, in the actual design of real buildings. They are open to grave misinterpretation from those:

(a) who think it is what they do already, and

(b) who think it is too simple, and therefore has nothing to do with systematic design.

The premises behind these are as follows:

(1) That up to now, there has been a tendency in developing 'systematic' design methods, to take techniques which happen to be available, and to force these onto design, without questioning their actual relevance. These include Graph Theory, Set Theory, Systems Analysis, Critical Path Method, Theory of Games. This is not to say that such techniques may not be useful, merely that the selection of techniques should be determined by the nature of the problem.

(2) That the process should be 'solution orientated' – in other words, architecture has certain characteristics which distinguish it from industrial design, chemical engineering and so on; therefore an architectural design process should encourage the development of these characteristics.

(3) That to avoid the 'information explosion' which a massive 'briefing' stage encourages at the beginning of a process, the process itself should define the order in which information is to be obtained, and limit the collection of it to the absolute minimum which will be required at each stage.

(4) That this will be determined, partly, by the resources available in terms of design staff and design time. Using this process one can decide how much cash to invest in design.

(5) That before he starts designing, the architect must recognise that the 'real world' will impose certain constraints on what he does. The site is 'there', solid; it is a piece of ground, and its characteristics may be distorted by converting it into an abstract 'model' of some kind.

(6) That the common words of 'ordinary' language are quite sufficient to describe a design process, except where jargon terms have already been coined for ancillary sources of information, e.g. 'ecology' as the relationship of an organism (man, in our case) to its environment.

An environmental design process

There is one simple fact about any building. It has a site, which is 'real' and physically measurable. That is one of the things which the architect 'knows' before he starts to design. The other things he 'knows' are concerned with what the building is for, who is going to use it and what they hope to do inside it. In many ways, he is less sure about these. But suppose, for a moment, that the users were trying to do those things on the site, before the building was built. Let us take the case of a typist, sitting at her desk, typing. On a June afternoon, she will be very comfortable. She will feel warm, and the air will be moving gently around her. She will have plenty of light, too much, perhaps, if she is facing straight into the sun. She may be enjoying the sounds of nature – bird songs or flowing water, but it is more likely, on an urban site, that she will be disturbed by traffic noise – and smell.

So her comfort is not complete, and when it starts to rain, she will have to stop work altogether. On balance, therefore, it will be better to place a building around her. If we do that, then her 'environment' can be controlled – she will not be subjected to the vagaries of climate and will be able to work, in comfort, whenever she wants to. In a very real sense, then, the building will be a device for reconciling the 'natural' external environment with the needs of human activity. It can be called, in the fashionable jargon, an 'interface' between them.

But it is more than that as well. The 'environment' means so many things. At one level, of course, it comprises the physical surroundings of the building –

roads, spaces, other buildings, trees. But there is a social environment too, and a cultural one, an economic one and a political one. The designer cannot afford to ignore any of these and a knowledge of them will form part of his stock-in-trade as a designer. But they will apply to all his jobs, and at the moment, we are concerned with tracing the design process for a particular project.

Let us suppose, therefore, that we have an instruction to build from a client. The instruction, probably, will be vague, but for our purposes, at the moment, the name of a building type will suffice. Let us say 'office'. Our first, and desperate need, is to find something real and tangible to hold onto. Well, we probably have one such thing – the site. That will be real enough, and what is more, we can measure it. It is no coincidence that some of our greatest architects, from Le Corbusier to Aalto, have started their projects by walking over the site. But our investigation can be as thorough as we wish. We can investigate its shape, humps and hollows, the position of the main services; we might even put down bore-holes to test the structure of the ground.

But there is much more to be learned about the site than that; we can obtain records of the climate from the meteorological office; we can also observe, and measure where necessary, surrounding buildings, open spaces, trees. We can obtain information on traffic patterns, town planning and other restrictions – a good architect would do all this anyway, but we can

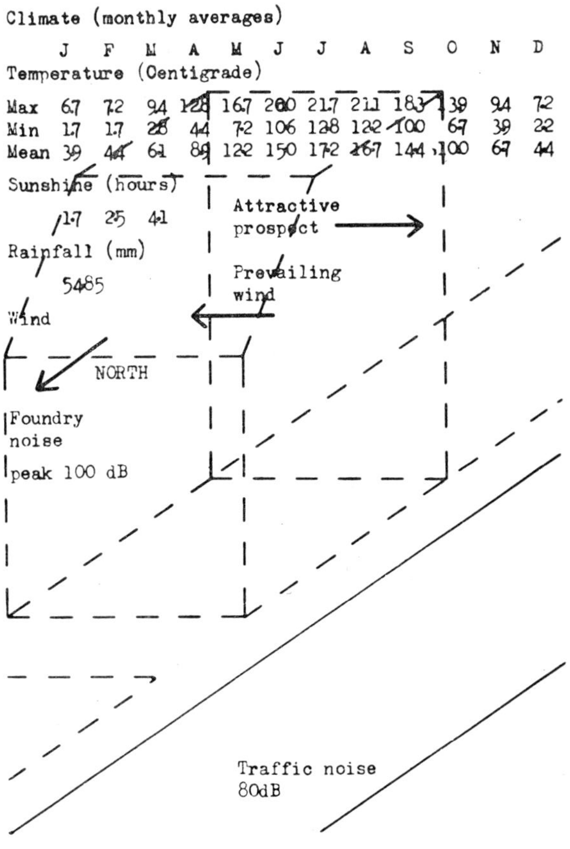

offer him new ways of sorting out this information, and plotting it for later use. The key to this – and I want to introduce two pieces of jargon here – is the 'environmental matrix' – a three dimensional 'model' of the site. 'Environmental', by now, I hope will be self-explanatory, and 'matrix' is 'a place where something is moulded'. 'Model', is rather more difficult. In design method terms, it means almost anything which *represents* the building. A *model*, of course, is a 'model', but so is a drawing, or a diagram, or a computer programme. So the environmental matrix can be built in any of these ways – as a three-dimensional model, perhaps, of the site – onto which, using wire, or perspex, a shape can be built, representing the *space* available for building into, the 'mould' into which the building can be designed (Fig.1).

Or, it can be any of the other things I have just mentioned – a three-dimensional drawing or, most certainly, a computer programme. What is essential is that the 'matrix' has plotted around it *all* the information about the surrounding environment which, in any way, will affect the way in which the building is designed – climate, sources of noise in the neighbourhood and smell, pleasant views, and views which should be hidden. So far, therefore, all the information we have collected is based on 'real' facts and we have recorded it as accurately as possible. Some things may be uncertain, of course – the projected line of a road, the future of an adjacent building, but as far as possible, everything we have considered so far is fact.

The other half of our information, at this early stage, will be concerned with what people are going to do in the building. That will be more difficult to obtain. Often, they will not know, in detail – they may not even decide until the building is complete. But that need not deter us much for even here, certain things are definite. It is highly likely, for instance, that our building will be occupied by human beings. They have certain shapes and sizes, and certain general needs. Not only that, but the pattern of things they do is not all that varied. Many of them, when they are working, sit at desks typing, reading papers, speaking on the 'phone, or maybe just thinking. The needs of one are very like the needs of another. They all want to be warm enough, to be able to see what they are doing, to be free of unpleasant noises or smells. Once we have investigated in detail what one such person needs, we shall have a fair idea of what they all need (Fig.2).

That is one kind of 'activity'. Other people, in the course of their work, may talk to each other, in pairs, in small groups, in large meetings; they may even be talked-at by a speaker of some kind. Others again will sit, or stand, at drawing boards, laboratory benches, lathes, but the number of kinds of activity will not be all that great. So we would do well to look in some detail at the 'needs' of the most common types; that will stand us in good stead, not just for this building, but for many others.

Fig.1
site survey (environmental)

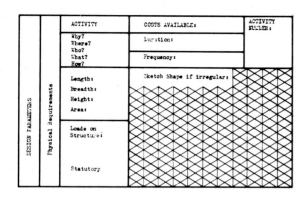

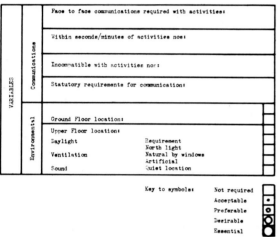

Fig. 2

So we will take the 'activity' of typing as typical, and see how we might investigate the typist's needs. We could approach this from a highly theoretical point of view, speculating about her drives and urges, her tendency to behave in certain ways. But in the long run, she is going to 'experience' our building through her senses – she is going to see, hear, feel and smell it, and on that basis, she is going to criticise it, whatever we think she *should* do. We could, of course, consider all her senses – the usual five, and several more known to psychology, – and form an enormous list of the ways in which they might be affected by the building. We might think of minute graduations in temperature, air movement, humidity, and equivalent subtleties in terms of light and sound control.

But let us take stock for a moment, and ask what this information is *for*. We have our environmental matrix, and our primary aim now is to place individual activities within it, so that those which have particular environmental needs will take up positions in the matrix which suit their requirements best. So we need some information on environmental needs, but in very broad terms, such as whether the activity needs daylight or not, artificial ventilation or sound control. We shall find that perhaps six questions will determine all we need to know at this stage. There is other information, however, which we ought to collect about each activity, such as how it relates to other activities. Will people actually need to talk, face to face, or will they move from one place to another? If they have to move, we can express that movement in

terms of time; the boss, for instance, may ring for his secretary, and expect to see her in front of his desk within, say, 30 seconds. Other activities may be much further apart than that, but the *time* expression of movement allows for all modes of travel between them – walking along corridors, up or down staircases, in and out of lifts. Some activities, also, will be quite incompatible with each other. The activity, for instance, of chairing a board meeting is very remote in terms of environmental needs from the activity of working a lathe.

There is a third class of information we might collect, concerned with the size of the space which an activity needs. At first sight, it is a question of 'form follows function' but that is rarely true in architectural matters. There is, in fact, a 'scale of precision' in this. The typist's fingers ought, if possible, to be within $\frac{1}{8}$th inch of the keyboard, but it matters less if her chair is 1″ high, or 1″ low. And if one considers the route she takes across the office to her desk, that may vary several feet, from day to day. Not only that, but if we were feeling particulalry brutal we could enclose the typist, and her desk, in something like a 4′ 6″ cube. But she wouldn't like it. For quite profound psychological reasons, she must have more space around her than she actually 'needs'. So between the 'space' required for her 'function', and the room in which it is contained, we must build in an 'environmental tolerance' – in many ways, the architect's prime task is to design this 'tolerance', and that requires a massive exercise of judgement on his part – to balance what the secretary 'wants' with what can be allowed for the money available.

His judgement, in fact, will have to be very complex. If we take our activity of typing, and consider only one of the secretary's senses, we find some curious things. It is obvious, for instance, that she will need light at the typewriter which is adequate for her to see what she is doing. So far so good. We can consult the appropriate standards, specifying window sizes and lighting fittings which seem to satisfy them. But there is more to it than that. If, by some mischance, we illuminated only the working surface, it would be difficult for the typist to *see*. Every time she looked up from her work, her eyes would have to accommodate to the surrounding gloom, and she would be dazzled when she looked down at the paper again. So we provide 'amenity' lighting, light in the room which provides a pleasant background. But that means she can see the room, and people in it. If she talks to one of them, part of the *communication* between them will depend on their being able to see each other's faces, 'modelled' by light which allows subtle changes of expression to be seen. Our task is rather like the photographer's, illuminating a face with spotlights, adjusting each one with precise judgement so that the face is 'modelled' to best advantage. The photographer has a general idea of how the lights should go, but he cannot position them finally by calculation and measurement because each face is different. We can hardly design buildings around individual faces, but the example shows that in matters such as lighting, there is no firm distinction between what can be calculated and what must be judged; they shade subtly into each other and neither will be adequate without the other.

In many ways, vision is the most complex of senses, but the others too will demand an equivalent combination of measurement and judgement. The critical ones will include hearing, smell, the senses of heat and cold, and others which we tend to forget, such as the sense of equilibrium and the kinaesthetic senses, concerned with the position and motion of muscles and joints. Serious things can happen if we forget any one of these senses. A school has been built in Wallasey which has no separate heating plant; the exterior walls are insulated to a very high standard and, internally, heat is generated by lighting fittings and human bodies. But the sense which receives the greatest stimulus, on entering the building, is the sense of smell, so perhaps it was unwise to save money on heating, when, for real comfort, a massive ventilation plant would be needed to compensate this other sense.

Our aim, then, is to record for each activity, or group of activities, the absolute minimum of information which will enable us to place it sensibly within the environmental matrix. And this information will be of three kinds – the physical characteristics of the activity – size, shape, the load it imposes on the structure; the relationship of this activity to others, in terms of time; and a number of environmental requirements – those which actually affect its position in three-dimensional space.

The next step, and probably the most complex, is to place the activities within the environmental matrix. That can be done in many ways. We might make a model of the environmental matrix in perspex, and place model figures within it. Or we might support a wire mesh horizontally over a model of the site, and suspend model figures from that. We might do the whole thing on an axonometric drawing, using overlays where it begins to get complicated. Or we might do it mathematically, using co-ordinates to express the positions of activities. This could form the basis of a computer programme, and possibly not a very difficult one. The essential principle here is to start with the activities which have particularly critical environmental needs. The managing director probably will want a quiet office, and if we are being rather old-fashioned, we might put a drawing office where it will be exposed to north light. It may be difficult to allocate priorities to the various activities, in environmental terms, but there are certain techniques from operational research which might be helpful.

Decision theory for instance will allow us to allocate priorities for activities on the basis of 'expected utility', using a simple equation:

$$\text{Expected utility} = \frac{\text{Probability of success} \times \text{Value of success}}{\text{Probability of failure} \times \text{Cost of failure}}$$

In other words, priority is reduced to a matter of cash value, and on this basis the managing director's comfort *will* be more valuable than anyone else's. But inevitably there will be conflicts, where two or more activities compete for the same space in the environmental matrix. In this case, we might use games theory in which one plots on a chart, or 'matrix', the 'outcome' when each of them is favoured in turn. It is possible then to choose the combination of placings which offers the best possible compromise.

Let us suppose, therefore, that using any of these available techniques, including our own judgement, we have allocated the important activities to their appropriate place in the environmental matrix. It will now be possible to plot the less critical activities around them – using the information which is available to us. Some of them will be related to the critical group because they share certain environmental requirements with them. We can place them accordingly. Others will form parts of circulation patterns between critical activities – we shall have available information on their relationships in terms of the time allowed to move from one activity to another, and again using mathematical techniques, it will be possible to plot these relationships onto charts. There are, for instance, the various kinds of flow chart in which each activity may be represented by, say, a circle, and the connections between them by lines.

Graph theory is extraordinarily rich in ways for manipulating such information. One can plot the connections to a particular activity in such a way that it is *bound* to become a centre of social interaction. A great many planning problems can be solved very quickly by its aid, or proved impossible of solution. 'Map colouring' for instance shows that on a flat surface, it will never be possible to connect more than four rooms, in such a way that they open into each other. So graph theory alone can tell us almost everything we need to know about the connections between activities and, if it fails, we can always draw on such operational research techniques as network analysis. There have been several attempts to plot the design process itself by critical path method, but these seem to me misguided. The essence of this, and similar techniques, is that at the beginning of a project one plots all the jobs that have to be done, and places an estimated time against each. Some jobs, of necessity, follow on from others, others can run in parallel. But through the whole network, there will be a 'thread' of the jobs which tend to hold others up, and this is called the 'critical path'. But the purpose of making the diagram is that one shall realise this, and take steps to minimise the difficulty. So if one *acts* on a network analysis, it quickly becomes redundant; the critical path changes, and one has to draw a new diagram. For this reason, then, there is little point in drawing a generalised critical path network of the design process; it will, in fact, be misleading.

So using the three types of information available to us, on the various activities, we have now placed them all within the environmental matrix. The critical ones have been placed according to their environmental requirements, the less critical ones have been plotted around these according to the circulation pattern, and all the time, we have been conscious of the *space* needs of the various activities. But we have not been concerned with *rooms* or corridors, or other kinds of space designated for special purposes. Our activities have been taking place in space, with no building there to house them. We can now think in these terms. We put a dozen directors together, for instance, for the activity of attending a Board Meeting; it would be reasonable to surround them with a Board Room. We put twenty draughtsmen together, all engaged in the activity of drawing. It would be reasonable to build a drawing office around them; and so on (Fig. 3).

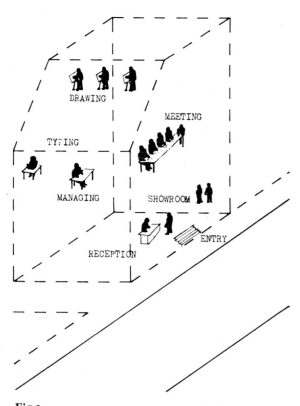

Fig.3
environmental matrix: activities planned

Again, there will be some adjustment, as the spatial demands of one set of activities impinge on the spatial demands of another. But we shall finish up with a pattern of rooms, and other specialised spaces, which is the nearest we have come yet to an actual building. We shall know also, from the nature of the activities what *loads* they will transmit to the structure. In some cases, we may have *weighed* an activity, with all its attendant equipment, but usually there will be some statutory requirement that we design for a particular floor loading. So at this stage, we have a

pattern of floor loading, spread throughout the building, and we can begin to think in terms of *structure*. We have several clues which will help us decide the kind of structure to adopt. These will be:
(a) The pattern of activities and the distribution of loads from them.
(b) The nature of the ground and what it will support.
(c) The current availability, basic properties and constructability of materials suitable for building.
(d) The need for environmental control within the building, in relation to the outside, uncontrolled environment.
(c) The required or expected life of the building, related to the need for flexibility and change within that life.
(f) The amount of money available.
(g) The controls on siting and construction imposed by statutory bodies.
(h) The nature of the surrounding buildings (where there is some requirement to 'blend in').

And given these clues, we can consider the structural types available to us, which depend on the characteristics of the available materials. These may be solid, consisting of rods, blocks or sheets, or formless masses and fluids. With 'rod' forms, the main loadbearing structure is composed of the smallest possible elements of strong, and possibly expensive, materials, in tension or compression. Additional cladding or space-dividing elements may be needed, and the structural loading may be discontinuous. Blocks and sheet materials may be built into 'surface' forms in which the loadbearing structure may itself also act as space-divider, both within the building and from inside to outside. Structural loadings should be continuous, and for the sake of stiffness, geometrically determined shapes may have to be used.

Using materials in these ways, we find that four fundamentally different ways of building are possible. Few buildings will use one of them exclusively, although there may be structural and aesthetic advantages from allowing one to dominate. They are:

1. *Mass Construction*
Consisting of solid masonry – blocks of stone, brickwork and concrete, or poured concrete, into which spaces *appear* to have been hollowed to accommodate the various activities. The Pyramids are good examples of mass construction in this sense and so, in spite of appearances, are the early Classical temples, Romanesque churches, many of Gaudí's buildings and of Frank Lloyd Wright's. Wright spoke of 'tenuity' in defining the 'all of a piece' character of mass construction. Mass construction is unsuitable for bad ground, it is uneconomical where activities are distributed in a regular pattern, excellent for environmental control, particularly insulation from *airborne* sound, and the mass of the building also acts as a heat reservoir. Totally inflexible, possibly cheap, and appropriate for building into many kinds of historical context.

2. Frame Construction

Using steel, steel and concrete or timber 'rods' to form a 'cage' which only forms a supporting structure, and needs cladding panels, partitions, floors and roofs (usually as planar surfaces) to make it habitable. Lever House in New York, the Seagram Building and much else of Mies van der Rohe's work are typical of frame construction. 'Modern' architecture as defined by Le Corbusier, Gropius and others was essentially frame construction, and so is a great deal of systems building. Possible, on piles, for bad ground, excellent where rooms are disposed in a regular pattern and for irregular room-shapes where partitions need not meet the frame. Environmental control may be difficult, especially sound insulation, and many early framed systems were extraordinarily poor in this respect until SCSD. Often very flexible, rather expensive and unsuitable for building into some historical contexts.

3. Planar Construction

In which solid masonry (using similar materials to mass construction) is built in *relatively* thin, planar walls which support the building and, supplemented by glazed or other screens, separate the internal spaces from each other, and the inside from the outside. In Mies van der Rohe's Barcelona Pavilion, the horizontal roof plane was supported on two rows of columns (forming an open 'screen'), but otherwise the entire spatial division was planar in this sense. His brick house plan (1923) was a very pure example of planar design; most traditional house building is also planar but compromises the principle to give the appearance of mass construction. Unsuitable for bad ground; excellent, in the form of cross-wall construction, for repetitive room patterns. Good for environmental control, when structural planes predominate for spatial division, not inherently flexible, cheap, and good for building into some historical contexts.

4. Skin Construction

Self-supporting, timber, concrete, steel or reinforced plastic shells, are one form of skin construction; others are inflated or suspended plastic enclosures. Inflated versions are inherently consistent, but suspended versions need a steel, concrete or timber frame for support; the plastic then becomes infill. Shells may be used wherever large spaces have to be enclosed – often they take the form of circular domes, but apart from exhibition buildings, circuses and Cinerama, no real use has been found for inflatable and suspended structures. They may be possible on bad ground, internal space division will be quite separate from the enclosure and flexible within it; little environmental control (or mechanical security – the skin can be cut with a knife). Often surprisingly expensive, only suitable for temporary purposes.

Given these possibilities, it is highly likely that the pattern of activities, their spatial and environmental needs, will help determine the appropriate structural type. But it may be that no one type of structural shell offers overwhelming advantages over the others.

In that case, a range of structural types, as applied to the building in question, can be tested in terms of stability, cost of materials and construction, feasibility of construction, environmental control and so on, using decision theory or other comparable techniques. At this stage, we need not be concerned with absolute values, we simply need to know that for the qualities we have chosen to test, one type of structure is better than the others.

And once we have committed ourselves to a structural type, we can test it more thoroughly, using all the prediction techniques available to us. The structure itself can be examined, using models and mathematical tests. We can check the ways in which the building shell itself will *modify* the external environment, using models or, better still, by looking at existing buildings constructed in the same way. An existing building is the best possible 'model' for checking the environmental characteristics of a new one. We can see what kind of internal climate it offers its inhabitants and actually measure it physically. We shall then be in a position to decide how well our proposed building shell is likely to satisfy the environmental needs of the various activities it is to contain. Having placed each activity in space, we have a much clearer idea as to how its particular needs will be satisfied; we can describe to the client what he is likely to get, and to discuss with him, in considerable detail, whether this will be adequate or not.

In many respects, of course, it won't be. Our typist, it is true, will have gained freedom from the wind and rain, from traffic noises and smells, but we shall have cut out a great deal of daylight; we shall have given her a 'box' which may well be warmer than the external environment in winter but is likely also to suffer from solar heat gain in summer. So we shall have to *modify* the internal climate, by using services – heating and ventilating plant, lighting and sound control. We can, in fact, be quite brutal about this. We can say to the client 'For x pounds, we can give you precisely the standards of lighting, heating and sound control which you want for your various activities, but if you are not prepared to spend so much, then the environmental standards will suffer.' We can also tell him how much they will suffer by.

So, like the structure, the provision of services will be determined by three things – the stated need, the means available for satisfying that need, and – to determine the *quality* of the provision – the amount of money available. The same principle can be extended through the rest of the building, including the choice of finishes and equipment. It so happens that, up to now, it will have been possible, although not necessarily economical in terms of design time, to make every decision on the basis of objective fact and analysis. But that will not be true of internal or external finishes, or certain kinds of equipment or even of landscaping. There is no objective means whatsoever of determining that a wall should be painted blue. That will depend on the taste and judgement of the designer, functions of the social, historical, and cultural environments in which he finds himself.

His choice will be based on experience, the things he has seen in the past, and admired. Nor can it be based on a consensus of what he, his colleagues and clients admire. For inevitably a consensus, on, say matters of colour will lead to impotent neutrality, expressed in shades of grey. To be systematic about this phase in design, therefore, he will inform himself about what is going on in the world. He will observe the colours around him, in posters, magazines and colour supplements. Above all, he will be aware of the world of art, of painting – op., pop and kinetic – of textiles and materials, of stage decor. He will form his own consensus, a synthesis of all these things he has seen, ordered and sifted by his own predilections, which will enable him to make judgements as secure and 'absolute' as any of those which he can support by physical measurement and calculation, because they will be *culturally* right. By this means, he will avoid the vagaries of fashion. In particular, of course, he will be able to draw analogies from other fields – personal, concrete or abstract, in the manner of synectics, which *ensure* the cultural 'rightness' of what he is doing.

All this, then, leads to a *feasibility* study for the design. It can be tested very rigorously, against the user's requirements, as stated, the conditions imposed by the site, environmental and ergonomic standards, circulation, construction, appearance, cost. And obviously, before it is built, the design must be represented by something else which can be tested – drawings, models, mathematical data. Nor should we forget the immense power of other, completed buildings as 'analogues' for the one we are designing. They allow the most potent tests of all.

Finally, of course, the design must be translated into terms which other people understand – again we shall use drawings and models, supported by descriptions, specification, schedules, a Bill of Quantities; as in all communications exercises, we should express our ideas in a 'language' that the 'receiver' can understand. So a drawing for the client will, and should be different from one for the engineer. Their needs are different, and so is their understanding. So communications theory, particularly in its psychological manifestations, has a great deal to offer us at this stage in design.

I have, therefore, attempted to describe a design process in architecture which does *not* impose alien techniques on the architect, but looks at the nature of his problem, the things he is stuck with, the things which he *has* to do, and I have used these as the basis for my scheme. Many people will object that this is what a good architect does already; it may be, and I hope it is, but few would claim to apply it with consistency which a 'design process' implies. Others will object that it throws overboard the advantages to design which have been gained by the study of design process, that it is too simple and therefore naive. I am delighted to have thrown overboard a great deal of what design process seems to offer, in the way of jargon and unnecessary complexity. They seem to me to have very little to do with real design, and once you have penetrated the intellectual fog which surrounds them, there is very little substance, in many cases, and certainly no logic. Lastly, it will be said that my process is so closely related to what the architect does already, that it can only encourage repetition, there is no place within it for innovation, for looking at the problem in a new light.

I have indicated elsewhere my delight in creativity (*in* Gregory 1966) and that delight is in no way diminished. But it is important to know where and when to be creative. It is assumed in most design processes that one takes a full and factual brief, analyses it systematically and then, maybe, allows oneself a 'creative leap'. But such a brief is bound to be based on the client's present knowledge, based on his experience of that past. He is expecting, at best, from the designer, a new combination of old ideas, so if, on the basis of a conventional brief, the architect is wilfully 'creative', he must expect resistance to his new form of solution. The time to be creative, therefore, is in taking the brief. 'Have you ever thought' we might say to the client 'what would happen if you did this thing quite differently?' right at the start. We assume, for instance, that a typist will sit at a desk, on a chair with maybe a telephone, a couple of filing trays and a drawer for odds and ends. If we build on this assumption, we shall find that this activity can be accommodated in quite an ordinary room. But, we might have a hunch that a completely different suite of furniture would serve her better, based on our observations of what she actually does. Very well, then, let's make a mock-up of this new arrangement, and let her try it for a while. Then we shall *know* if it suits her better. In other words, the feasibility of innovation will depend very largely on how the brief is taken.

REFERENCE

S. GREGORY (Ed.). *The Design Method*. Butterworth (London 1966).